MILITARY INTERFERENCE
WITH THE ELECTION IN DELAWARE
NOVEMBER 4, 1862

Report

of the

Committee of the General Assembly of the State of Delaware

together with the

Journal of the Committee,

and the testimony taken before them,

in regard to the

Interference by United States Troops

with the

General Election

Held in the State on the Fourth Day
of November, 1862.

Published by Order of the General Assembly.

Dover, Del.
Printed by James Kirk.
1863.

Bald Cypress Books
Laurel, Delaware

baldcypressbooks.com

This book is a new edition of an out-of-print work which is in the public domain, with a new introduction and index.

Introduction copyright © 2020 Christopher Slavens.

ISBN: 978-1-7361370-0-0 (hardcover)

ISBN: 978-1-7361370-1-7 (paperback)

Library of Congress Control Number: 2020923167

Revised February 2021.

Publisher's Cataloging-in-Publication Data

Names: Slavens, Christopher, editor.
Title: Military interference with the election in Delaware, November 4, 1862 / Delaware General Assembly.
Description: Reprint edition 2020.
Identifiers: LCCN: 2020923167 | ISBN: 978-1-7361370-0-0 (hardcover) | ISBN: 978-1-7361370-1-7 (paperback).
Subjects: LCSH: Delaware—History—Civil War, 1861-1865. | Delaware—Politics and government—1861-1865. | Border States (U.S. Civil War)—Delaware. | Elections—Delaware.

Front cover images, left to right:
1. Major-General John E. Wool.
2. Gov. William Cannon, courtesy of the Delaware Public Archives.
3. Sen. Gove Saulsbury, courtesy of the Delaware Public Archives.

Back cover images, left to right:
1. Congressman George P. Fisher.
2. Colonel James Wallace.

Introduction.

Military Interference With the Election in Delaware, published by order of the state legislature and printed by Dover printer James Kirk in 1863, is one of the most important books ever published in the First State. Inexplicably, it is also one of the rarest books. The scarcity of the original edition is not surprising, despite the fact that three thousand copies were printed; a lot can happen to a book in a century and half. It is less easy to explain why there has never been a second edition until now. Brief selections relating to particular towns were inserted into community histories during the 20th century, but these isolated excerpts could not begin to tell the whole story. In recent years, there have been reprintings of a sort—low-quality, print-on-demand copies of the original, created by scanning the well-worn pages of a volume in a university library—but nobody bothered to transcribe the text and publish a new edition, despite the fact that the book has been in the public domain for decades.

Consequently, the astonishing events of 1861 and 1862, and the investigation that followed in 1863, have not received the attention they deserve. It is my hope that the long overdue publication of a new edition will provoke renewed interest in this dramatic episode of Delaware's history.

In transcribing the original text, I have corrected many typographical errors, while undoubtedly introducing new ones of my own, for which I apologize in advance. The page numbers in the index have been updated, of course. I have also made minor editorial changes which are simply a matter of taste; for example, 1st, 2^d, and 3^d instead of 1st, 2d, and 3d. Additionally, I have retained a number of alternative spellings—e.g., "partizan" for partisan, and "sabre" for saber—which appear throughout the text.

The one hundred and twenty-some testimonies preserved in this extraordinary book, taken at face value, are eyewitness accounts of politically motivated gun seizures, illegal arrests and imprisonments, harassment, assaults, and election tampering, up and down the state, orchestrated by Republican or Union politicians and enforced by federal troops. There are also dissenting voices which maintain that Southern-sympathizing Democrats planned to suppress Republican voters, and had to be restrained by force.

I leave it to the reader to read the testimonies and form an opinion about what happened, and why.

CHRISTOPHER SLAVENS
Laurel, Delaware
November 3, 2020

Report.

The Joint Committee of the two houses of the General Assembly of the State of Delaware, to whom was referred so much of the Governor's Message as relates to military interference by troops in the service of the United States with the election in this State on the 4th day of November, 1862, beg leave to submit their report:

On the 8th of January, 1863, the following joint resolution was passed by both branches of the Legislature, to wit:

"*Resolved by the Senate and House of Representatives of the State of Delaware in General Assembly met*, That so much of the Governor's Message as refers to the interference by troops in the service of the United States with the elections in this State on the 4th day of November last, be referred to a Committee of three members on the part of the Senate, and five members on the part of House of Representatives, and that said Committee have power to send for persons and papers, and leave to report by bill or otherwise."

The importance of the subject submitted to the Committee for investigation, involving the grave fact of actual interference by the Federal Government with the most sacred right of the people of the State, the right to the free expression of their opinion at the ballot-box, in the choice of State and local officers, induced your Committee to summon before them one hundred and twenty-four witnesses, residents in different parts of the State, and representing both the political parties. The testimony of these witnesses will be found in the Journal of the Committee accompanying this Report.

The subject of inquiry to which the attention of the Committee was specially directed, are,

First. The invasion of the State during the years 1861 and 1862 by a part of General Lockwood's command, and subsequently by the Maryland Home Guard, under command of Colonel James Wallace, and the disarming of all the volunteer companies of the State which were commanded by Democrats, while all the volunteer companies which were commanded by Republicans were permitted to retain possession of their arms. Also, the presence of a company of cavalry in the two lower counties of this State immediately preceding the election, and their attendance upon the political meetings of the Republican party in said counties—the effect of their presence upon the public mind, and the means adopted by the opposite party to allay the apprehensions naturally resulting from their presence in those counties at such time and under such circumstances. And whether troops in the service of the United States were present at the election in this State on the fourth day of November, one thousand eight hundred and sixty-two; what number of troops were present; when they arrived in the State; under whose command at the time of arrival; by what conveyance they were brought to the State; when and how they were distributed and conveyed to the different voting places; and under whose command they were placed at the polls.

Second. Whether his Excellency, the then Governor of the State, under authority conferred upon him by Section 4, Article 4 of the Constitution of the United States, which reads as follows, to wit: "The

United States shall guarantee to every State in this Union a Republican form of government, and shall protect each of them against invasion, and on application of the Legislature, or of the Executive (when the Legislature cannot be convened) against domestic violence," made application for troops to be sent into this State on the fourth day of November, one thousand eight hundred and sixty-two, or whether he was applied to to make such application.

Third. Upon whose application troops were brought into the State, and under what circumstances, and for what reason such application was made, and for what purpose they were sent.

Fourth. Whether they acted under the command of the Provost Marshals for the purposes and objects for which they were professedly asked for and professedly sent; or whether they acted in concert with, and for the benefit of one political party, to the prejudice and injury of the other, and to prevent, instead of insure, a fair and impartial election.

Fifth. Whether their presence was necessary to preserve the public peace, and insure a fair and impartial election, and whether they conduced to that effect.

Sixth. The Committee, in accordance with their own sense of duty, inquired generally as to the character and conduct of the Provost Marshals, through the agency of the troops that were under and subject to their command at the polls, and also generally into the conduct of the troops sent into the State.

The Committee do not propose in this Report following strictly the course of the examination, but to allude to the facts proved, without regard to the time at which they were elicited in the order of examination. This course has been rendered necessary from considerations of convenience to witnesses, as well as to the Committee. With a view to discharge witnesses, and allow them to return to their homes, and thereby save trouble to them and expense to the State, each witness was, as a general rule, examined at the time he was called, upon all the facts known to be in his possession relating to the subject under consideration. It will, therefore, be perceived that much of the testimony, alluded to in the commencement of the Report, was elicited towards the close of the examination. In order to show a deliberate and settled purpose on the part of evil-disposed persons in this State to carry out their own evil designs, and promote their own selfish partizan ends by intimidating the Democratic voters of the State, the Committee examined witnesses to prove, and did prove beyond question, that some time previous to the last general election in this State, all the volunteer companies in the State, which were commanded by Democrats, had been deprived of the arms which had been furnished them by the order of the Governor of the State, and that all the volunteer companies, which were commanded by Republicans, were permitted to retain possession of their arms until and subsequent to the election. For the proof of this fact, the Committee refer to the testimony of Hon. Edward Wootten, Judge in the Superior Court in this State, John B. Penington, Esq., Shepard P. Houston, Esq., Alfred P. Robinson, Esq., Edward L. Martin, Esq., and others. William Cannon, the present Governor of the State, was also examined upon this subject, and attempted by his testimony to make the impression that all the volunteer companies in the State, without regard to party, had been deprived of their arms previous to the last election; but in a subsequent part of his examination, admitted that he knew nothing about any company commanded by Republican officers, except the one in his own town, and that the arms of that company had not been delivered to the authorities of the General Government, but were stacked up in his own store at the very time he was delivering his testimony. His testimony upon the subject is as follows, to wit:

"Question. Do you not know, or was it not your understanding, that the volunteer companies, commanded by Union men or Republicans, retained possession of their arms?

"Answer. Not at the time the others were taken away, so far as I understand.

"Question. Do you not know, or was it not your understanding, that the volunteer companies, commanded by Union men or

Republicans, had possession of their arms on the day of the little election, and between that time and the general election?

"I do not know of any; there may have been some in the County, but I do not recollect them."

The above testimony was delivered on Wednesday evening, the 4th day of February. On the following morning, the examination of Governor Cannon was resumed, after the Committee had had time to inquire and learn what was the fact in reference to the subject. In this latter examination Mr. Cannon's memory became refreshed in regard to important facts, which had escaped it the evening before. His testimony, as delivered, is as follows:

"Question. Do you not know that William O. Redden, previous to the time of his appointment as Colonel, was Captain of a volunteer company at Bridgeville, and whether that company did not retain possession of their arms?

"Answer. I did not recollect last night any company in the Hundred, but since then I recollect William O. Redden was Captain of a volunteer company, called the "Governor's Guard," which was voluntarily disbanded by giving up their arms soon after his appointment as colonel of the Third Delaware Regiment.

"Question. To whom did they give up their arms?

"Answer. I do not recollect. There was some one appointed, I am not sure whether it was Richard Cannon or some other person. It was my impression it was he. Richard Cannon is a half brother of mine, and a clerk in my store. The arms were stacked up in my store, to be delivered up to the proper authorities. I believe those arms are in my store now."

The testimony of Mr. Cannon, in this respect, will speak for itself. An intelligent people will draw their own conclusions in reference to its fairness and impartiality. The Committee, however, cannot refrain from the expression of their opinion that this part of the testimony of Mr.

Cannon, when considered in connection with other portions of his testimony relating to other subjects of inquiry, furnishes abundant evidence of his complicity with unscrupulous partizans in a conspiracy to deprive citizens of this State of their constitutional right to the free and undisturbed exercise of the elective franchise.

The raid of a part of the command of General Lockwood into this State, to deprive Democratic companies of the arms which had been furnished them from the State Arsenal by order of the Governor, commenced in the lower part of this State, by depriving the companies of Captain Paynter, at Georgetown, Captain Martin, at Seaford, and other Democratic companies of their arms, and was followed by the foray of Colonel James Wallace, of unenviable notoriety in this State, with his celebrated "Maryland Home Guards." Colonel Wallace visited the town of Dover, after night, in the month of March, eighteen hundred and sixty-two, took possession of the Court House, and proceeded to arrest a number of our most respectable, law-abiding citizens—among whom were Captain Penington and Lieutenant Atkinson of the "Hazlet Guard," and John L. Pratt, and others, who were members of the same company—and took them to Salisbury, in the State of Maryland, and kept them in close confinement, in uncomfortable quarters, for several days, and then discharged them without trial or accusation, other than that they were in possession of arms furnished by the Governor under existing laws in this State. Colonel Wallace subsequently returned to the State, took possession of the arms of the "Hazlet Guard," proceeded to Smyrna, took the arms from Captain Carr's company, and then continued his visit to New Castle County, depriving all the Democratic companies in that County of their arms, spending some two or three weeks in the State, and then returned to his headquarters at Salisbury; and during all this time did not ask or receive the arms of any volunteer company which was commanded by Republicans. The Committee have thought it important to consider this branch of the investigation somewhat minutely, as they consider it the first step taken by the United States authorities, in connection with evil-disposed persons in this State, to deprive the people of this State of their constitutional rights as freemen.

The second step in the conspiracy, to prevent, by intimidation, a free election on the fourth of November last, was the parade of a company of mounted and armed cavalry through this State, to attend political meetings of the Republican party, at the expense of the United States Government. The testimony on this subject proves conclusively that a company of cavalry, amounting to from one hundred to one hundred and twenty, visited Kent County about the sixteenth of October last, and remained in Kent and Sussex Counties from two to three weeks, and until within a very short time of the general election; that they were commanded by Republican officers; that they passed through the town of Smyrna, *en route* for Dover, and there, by manifestations of approval of the Republican party, indicated by demonstrations of applause at the residences of its leading members, and by unprovoked and uncalled-for manifestations of opposition to the Democratic party indicated by indignities and insulting conduct towards the Democratic candidate for Congress, and other leading members of that party, they left no reason to doubt that their mission through the State was for political effect. Upon their arrival at Dover, they proceeded to the Fair Grounds of the Agricultural Society of Kent County, and, notwithstanding it was at the time of the Annual Exhibition of the Society, took possession of the ground without permission of the Society or any person acting for it, and held and made said ground their headquarters, or place of rendezvous, during their stay in the County. They occupied the time they were in the County in attending political meetings of the Republican party, and from their general bearing and conduct, created the impression that they were brought into the lower counties for the purpose of spreading alarm and producing intimidation among the Democrats.

It was proved before the Committee, that in order to remove the impression, and counteract the intimidation created by the presence of the cavalry, the Democratic speakers, at all their meetings subsequent to the cavalry raid, took especial pains to persuade the people not to be deterred from going to the election, and advised them to be unusually prudent, to avoid all excitement and controversy, so as to leave no excuse for interference with the election. The testimony of all the witnesses who were before the Committee, concurs in proving that the cavalry raid above referred to, was followed by what was previously threatened by persons belonging to the Republican party, and feared by many Democrats—the introduction into the State, and distribution to all the voting places in Kent and Sussex Counties, except two, and to the city of Wilmington, Christiana Hundred, and Mill Creek Hundred, in New Castle County, of troops in the service of the United States, amounting, in the two lower counties, to one thousand or twelve hundred; that they remained in the State about eight days, were distributed in squads of from forty to sixty, and placed under the command of Provost Marshals at the different voting places above alluded to. All the Provost Marshals were, according to the proof before the Committee, violent and prejudiced partizans of the Republican party, and several of them men of the lowest order, utterly destitute of character or respectability in their neighborhoods, and capable of any act which would promote their own political fortunes, or contribute to the success of the party to which they were attached. The testimony further proves to the entire satisfaction of the Committee, that the commissions, under which the Provost Marshals acted, were sent to this State in blank, and filled up by George P. Fisher and James R. Lofland, on the Sabbath previous to the election. For the proof of this fact, we refer to the testimony of Hon. Edward Wootten, John L. Bacon, and Samuel W. Lacy. The Committee invite attention to the testimony of the Provost Marshals, and especially of those from Duck Creek, Mispillion, and other hundreds in Kent County, and of those from Baltimore, Broad Creek, and other hundreds in Sussex County, as corroborative of the proof of other witnesses in reference to their characters. The Committee would also ask a careful perusal of the testimony in relation to the characters of the Provost Marshals of North Murderkill, and East and West Dover Hundreds, who were out of reach of process by the Committee.

Upon the second general subject of inquiry, the Committee caused to be summoned before them His Excellency, William Burton, who was, at the date of the last general election, the Governor of this State, and who, by the provisions of Section 4, Article 4 of the Constitution of the United States, hereinbefore recited, had the undoubted right to ask protection for the State against domestic violence, if such domestic violence existed as, in his judgment, to render protection from the General Government necessary.

Governor Burton, in his testimony before the Committee, stated that he never applied to the General Government for troops to be sent into this State at any time; that he never was requested to make such application, and that he never received information that troops would be sent into the State. The Committee, therefore, felt it their duty to ascertain, if possible, whether any other citizens of this State, in violation of the obligation of citizenship, and in violation of the spirit of the Constitution of the United States, had so far disregarded their obligation to their own State Government, as secretly to ask military interference for the mere purpose of party success, to the injury of the State and the humiliation and degradation of the people thereof. The Committee felt this duty to be the more imperative from the fact, that no intimation had been given to the Executive of the State that troops were needed or desired, and no notice had been given him by the Executive of the Federal Government, that they would be sent, facts, in the judgment of the Committee, significant of a deliberate purpose, on the part of those making the request, clandestinely to introduce troops to prevent, instead of insure, a fair, free, and peaceable election. This view of the Committee was strengthened by the fact, that the troops were placed, after they reached the State, under the entire and absolute control of Provost Marshals, selected from the ranks of the Republican party at whatever sacrifice of honor or fidelity to the State. The fact that no notice had been given by the Federal authorities that troops would be sent to the State, justified the suspicion that had before existed of complicity by the authorities at Washington with the conspirators in this State, to prevent a fair expression of public sentiment through the peaceable and constitutional agency of the ballot-box. With this conviction the Committee caused to be summoned to appear before them a number of persons from different parts of the State, to discover, if possible, the *animus* with which troops had been solicited and sent. The pertinacity with which every prominent Republican denied any knowledge of the cause of the presence of troops, the solemnity of their protestations of innocence of either having requested or desired them, and the profound secrecy on the part of the leading Republicans here, and the authorities at Washington, in regard to the subject, embarrassed the Committee as to the best manner of proceeding in order to ascertain who were the parties guilty of so grave an offence against the sovereignty of the State and the rights of the people, as to encourage, solicit, or induce the invasion of the State on election day by armed soldiery, to prevent a free, full, and fair expression of public sentiment at the polls, and the untrammeled exercise of the right of suffrage in selecting their agents or public servants—a crime against the State, in the judgment of the Committee, little, if at all, less than treason. Under these circumstances, the Committee determined to cause to be summoned before them such persons as circumstances justified them in believing to be either cognizant of or connected with the conspiracy. Having learned that an engine, with a single passenger car, had passed over the Delaware railroad from Wilmington to Milford, on the Sabbath preceding the last general election, and having also learned that John D. Rodney, Esq., had left Georgetown on Saturday night before the election at about eleven o'clock, and of his being at Milford the next day on some secret political mission, they determined to cause him (Mr. Rodney) to be summoned before them. The testimony of Mr. Rodney, in connection with the testimony of Mr. Cannon, the present Governor of the State, which followed it, gave the Committee the key to the whole of the subsequent examination. Mr. Rodney's testimony fully establishes the facts that he left Georgetown on Saturday night previous to the election at about eleven o'clock, that he arrived in Milford at about two o'clock on Sunday morning, that be conversed with a number of prominent Republicans in Milford on the Sabbath day, in reference to bringing soldiers into this State, that among them was George P. Fisher, who was then a candidate for Congress, James R. Lofland, who was Provost Marshal for the State, N. B. Smithers, who is now Secretary of State under Governor Cannon, and Hiram W. McColley, a brother-in-law of Mr. George P. Fisher, and several others. Mr. Rodney says, in his testimony, that it "was deemed advisable to ask the General Government to send us troops to preserve the peace on election day, some two weeks after the little election." In reply to the question, "By whom was it deemed advisable?" Mr. Rodney answered: "I believe by all the Union men in the County with whom I conversed; I don't remember whether William Cannon was one of them, he may have been. Jacob Moore was one, William Ellegood another, and men of that party generally."

"Question. What individuals in this County, with whom you conversed, desired it?

"Answer. I would not like to say.

"Question. Was George P. Fisher one of them?

"Answer. He was. Nathaniel B. Smithers was one. I do not remember conversing with James R. Lofland. I remember, on reflecting, that he was. Hiram W. McColley was another. I do not remember any other in Dover. There may have been, as I was in Dover about that time. I do not remember that I conversed with Judge Harrington and Dr. Jump."

Mr. Rodney's testimony also proves that he received, a little after dark, on Sunday evening, from James R. Lofland, commissions for Provost Marshals for Broadkiln, Lewes and Rehoboth, Georgetown, Dagsborough, Broad Creek and Baltimore Hundreds, which he either delivered in person or sent by special messengers. His testimony also established the fact that James R. Lofland, George P. Fisher and Nathaniel B. Smithers passed up the railroad on that Sabbath, and that all the Provost Marshals for the hundreds he named belonged to what he called the "Union party."

Having established these preliminary facts, the Committee felt justified in causing to be summoned before them William Cannon, the present Governor. Mr. Cannon's testimony establishes the fact, beyond cavil or controversy, that himself and George P. Fisher were the guilty agents of the Republican party, through whose instrumentality troops in the service of the United States were brought into this State to interfere with and control the election. Mr. Cannon's testimony, which was elicited by the most searching examination and cross-examination of which the Committee were capable, proves that he (Mr. Cannon) requested Colonel James Wallace, of the Maryland Home Guards, to bring his forces, or so many of them as were necessary, into certain hundreds of Sussex County, to be present on the day of the election. He alleged that he made the request "from facts and reasonable grounds of which I (he) knew from responsible men in Baltimore and other hundreds that the Secessionists of Maryland and Democrats of Delaware had threatened to take the polls in Baltimore and other hundreds in Sussex County," &c., &c. Especial attention is hereby invited to the whole testimony of Mr. Cannon upon this subject. The first question propounded to him, was:

"Question. Do you know at whose solicitation troops were brought into this State to be here on the day of the last general election?

"Answer. From facts and reasonable grounds, of which I know from responsible men in Baltimore and other hundreds, that the Secessionists of Maryland and Democrats in Delaware had threatened to take the polls in Baltimore and other hundreds of Sussex County, and from the threatening of a man, with an unlawful weapon, at the little election in Broad Creek Hundred, that the Union men should not vote, induced me to write to Colonel Wallace, requesting him, if compatible with his official duty, to see that there was a fair election in Little Creek, Broad Creek, Dagsborough, and Baltimore Hundreds. I feared there would be a conflict between the Union men and those who intended to prevent them from voting.

"Question. Will you state who were the responsible men in Baltimore and other Hundreds to whom you alluded, and from whom you received the information upon which you acted?

"Answer. Their names are not on my mind now. I do not recollect their names. I had satisfactory information that Curtis W. Jacobs had threatened to come over from Maryland, and I believe he did come over on the 4th of November to deter the Union men from voting on that day. I was informed that there were fifteen or twenty who did come over from Maryland on horseback for that purpose.

"Question. When did you receive the information that Curtis W. Jacobs intended to come, and did come over from Maryland for the purpose of preventing a fair election?

"Answer. I think I was informed about the fifteenth of October, and also about a week before the election, of his threatening to come over.

"Question. Will you state from whom you received that information?

"Answer. The citizens of Baltimore Hundred.

"Question. Can you name any of them?

"Answer. I do not like to answer certainly, as I might make a mistake.

"Question. Do you say that you do not recollect a single individual who gave you that information?

"Answer. Not to name him. I am certain I was told by several.

"Question. Do you say that you cannot recollect any single individual who gave you that information with sufficient accuracy to name him?

"Answer. I cannot remember any one with sufficient accuracy to name him."

It will be perceived that the Governor's memory was exceeding acute in regard to the fact that he had information sufficient to warrant him in the act of bringing troops into this State to control the elective franchise—an act, in the judgment of your Committee, graver in its character, and more serious in its consequences than any act of any public man that has heretofore lived in this State—but when he was interrogated as to the sources of his information and the names of his informers, his memory was unaccountably oblivious, so much so as to prevent him from remembering the names of a single one of the reliable citizens upon the representations of whom he made the request. How strange that upon a question involving the most sacred rights of his fellow-citizens, the Governor should have acted upon information too trifling to impress upon his mind the sources from which he received it. The Committee will be pardoned for the avowal of their want of sufficient credulity to credit this part of the Governor's testimony.

The Governor was asked:

"Question.   What man was it in Broad Creek Hundred, of whom you have spoken as having acted badly, and having threatened to prevent Union men from voting on the day of the little election?

"Answer.   I have forgotten the name."

This is another one of the circumstances upon which he was induced to violate the laws of the State, and outrage the rights of her citizens, and yet the circumstance was too trifling in its character to impress upon his mind the name of his informer. But the Committee invite especial attention to the following testimony of the Governor, from page [seventy-five] of the printed journal:

"Question.   Do you know whether any person in this State ever went to Washington with the view of soliciting soldiers to be brought into this State on the day of the last general election?

"Answer   I do not know.

"Question.   Do you know whether any citizen of this State, being in

Washington, did solicit soldiers in the service of the United States to be brought into this State, and to be present on the day of the last general election?

"Answer.   I solicited the Secretary of War to send troops to the places I have named in Sussex County, to see that there was a fair election, and to keep the peace, while I was on other business at Washington."

Mark the phraseology of this answer. The Governor distinctly says that his request of the Secretary of War was to send troops "to the places I (he) have named in Sussex County." In a subsequent part of his testimony, which will be hereafter quoted, he contradicts his own statement.

"Question.   How long was this previous to the day of the last general election?

"Answer.   About two or three weeks.

"Question.   Do you know whether any person other than yourself made the same request?

"Answer.   It is my impression that Mr. George P. Fisher made the same request. I do not remember any other person who made the request.

"Question.   Was George P. Fisher a candidate on the ticket with you for election last fall?

"Answer.   He was.

"Question.   Was the instance you have named the only time that you or any other person solicited the Secretary of War to send troops to be here on the day of the last general election?

"Answer.   I think I solicited him once before. Soon after the Inspector's election, I was informed of a man being injured at Georgetown, and at Milford, and was fearful that there would be trouble at the general election, if there was not a police force.

"Question.   Were the two instances which you have named the only times when you or any other person, so far as you know, solicited United States forces to be sent into this State, and to be here on the day of the last general election?

"Answer. I may have asked the Secretary of War more than twice. I do not recollect."

The Governor further said, in reply to another question: "I was informed by various individuals of the necessity of troops being present to see that all sides should have a fair vote."

"Question. Will you state who those individuals were?

"Answer. I think I recollect William H. Taylor; I think Samuel Lacy, of Baltimore Hundred, and John L. Bacon, in Little Creek Hundred, were others. There is no other individual on my mind."

His testimony also proves that he understood William H. Taylor was Provost Marshal for Mispillion Hundred; Samuel W. Lacy for Baltimore Hundred, and John L. Bacon for Little Creek Hundred, and that they were all members of the Republican, or as he chooses to term it, the "Union party."

Mr. Cannon further testified as follows, in reply to the

"Question. Do you say that you solicited Colonel Wallace, by letter, to bring the troops under his command, or a part of them, into this State, to be present on the day of the last general election, and that you twice, and probably more frequently, solicited the Secretary of War to send troops into this State to be present on the same day; and that Mr. George P. Fisher made a similar request of the Secretary of War?

"Answer. I wrote to Colonel Wallace on Saturday previous to the election, after I supposed that the Secretary of War would not send any. I had previously solicited the Secretary of War to send troops, and supposed they would be here before that time; but as they failed to come, I wrote to Wallace to send troops for the four hundreds I have mentioned. I think Mr. George P. Fisher made a similar request of the Secretary of War.

"Question. Did you understand, at the time you wrote to Colonel Wallace, that the Secretary of War had refused or declined to send troops into this State?

"Answer. I had received no recent information from him by letter or otherwise."

Here is an express and emphatic avowal by the Governor that, disregarding not only the rights, interests and dignity of his State, but the decision of the Secretary of War—for it was at a time when he thought the Federal authorities would not send troops—upon his own responsibility, and in violation of what he supposed had been decided on at Washington, he did solicit Colonel Wallace (a subordinate in the military service of the country) to come with his forces into this State. Such a declaration is, to the minds of your Committee, too grossly inconsistent with his professions of obedience to the Federal authority to admit of any other interpretation than that his only purpose was to secure his own election, at whatever sacrifice of principle, even by insubordination to law.

In a subsequent part of the Governor's examination, he was asked:

"Question. In the request you made of the Secretary of War to send troops, did you confine that request to the four hundreds you have just named?

"Answer. I did not designate the hundreds. I left it to his own judgment, according to the best of my recollection."

The Governor further said (page [eighty] of printed report) to the question, viz:

"Question. Do you know at whose expense the troops were sent into this State to be present on the day of the last general election?

"Answer. I suppose they were employed and paid by the General Government."

The Committee do not wish to be censorious or even severe in their criticisms of the Governor's testimony. They would have been gratified if his answers to their questions had been fair, frank, or candid. Such, however, was not the character of his testimony. Your Committee refrain from characterizing it as it deserves.

That troops under the command of Major-General Wool, amounting to two hundred cavalry and two hundred infantry, arrived at Seaford on Monday, the third day of November last, is a fact established by too many witnesses to admit of doubt or require comment; and that an additional force of from six to seven hundred and fifty Maryland Home Guards, also arrived at Seaford, under the command of Colonel Wallace, by railroad, is also established by the testimony of Thomas H. Hawkins, and corroborated by the testimony of other witnesses. That the forces which arrived under the command of Colonel Wallace, were immediately transferred to the command of General Wool, will be apparent from reference to the testimony.

It was also proved conclusively to the minds of your Committee, that a large number of persons of the Republican party were present to witness the arrival of troops under the command of General Wool; that immediately upon his arrival, he was taken possession of by a band of political Provost Marshals, selected from the ranks of the Republican party; that a reception or complimentary address was delivered, welcoming the troops to this State, by a boy of about eighteen years, a non-resident of this State and resident of one of the New England States. It is also proved that General Wool was conducted by the Provost Marshals, above referred to, to the hotel of Mr. Coulborn, in Seaford; that he was there occupied making arrangements with the partizan Provost Marshals, from the time of his arrival in the afternoon until ten or eleven o'clock at night; and it is further proved by the testimony of Ex-Governor Ross, Charles Wright, Esq., Dr. Shipley, Dr. McFerran and others, that efforts were made by Governor Ross and others, from the time of his arrival at Seaford, until near eleven o'clock at night, to obtain an interview with General Wool, to ascertain the object of his visit to this State with a military force under his command; that they were denied an interview, by the Provost Marshals, until the hour named, and then only obtained it by contriving to get a letter from Governor Ross into the hands of General Wool, reminding the General of a former acquaintance, &c. After obtaining the long-sought interview, which lasted less than twenty minutes altogether, the only satisfaction they could get was that the Democrats would be allowed a fair election, and this opinion was given only after consultation with the Provost Marshals, under the command of whom, General Wool subsequently acknowledged to Governor Ross, that he (General Wool) was for the time being.

The fact that troops were in this State on the day of the election aforesaid; that they were not asked for by the Executive of this State, and that he had no knowledge they would be sent by the General Government; that they were placed under charge of partizan Provost Marshals, and distributed, and placed at the voting places in the hundreds before named; and, further, that they were sent to the State upon the solicitation of William Cannon, who was at that time the candidate of the Republican party for Governor, and George P. Fisher, who was also a candidate upon the Republican ticket for Representative in Congress, and that the application was indorsed and approved by leading Republican partizans, are facts that have been, in the judgment of your Committee, too fully proved to require further comment.

In regard to the third general subject of inquiry, viz.: Whether they (the troops) acted under the command of the Provost Marshals for the purposes and objects for which they were professedly asked for and professedly sent, or whether they acted in concert with and for the benefit of one political party to the prejudice and injury of the other, and to prevent, instead of insuring, a fair and impartial election, the Committee will remark that an examination of the whole current of testimony cannot fail to convince any fair or honest man, however prejudiced in his partizan views, that the whole object of bringing troops into this State on the day of election was to coerce, by military power, a concurrence of public sentiment with the views and wishes of the Administration of the Federal Government, and to insure by force, what the guilty agents of despotic power knew could not be effected through the peaceful and constitutional agency of the ballot-box, the election of the Republican ticket in this State, and especially the election of George P. Fisher as Representative in Congress, and William Cannon as Governor of the State.

And in this connection the Committee refer to the testimony of Mr. Minos Conoway, who deposed that on the day succeeding the little election, Caleb S. Layton, Esq., a prominent Republican, said in substance, that the Democrats had beaten the Republicans badly at the little election, and that they (the Republicans) must have a force to prevent it, or they would do the same thing at the general election. The testimony of the same witness also proves that Mr. Layton afterwards drew a petition, asking troops to be sent into the State, to be present at the voting places on the day of the general election, which petition was signed by himself, Jacob Moore, John D. Rodney, and other Republicans. This statement corroborates the testimony of Governor Cannon, that he made the request for troops a short time after the little election.

The failure of these wicked conspirators against the rights of the people and the sovereignty of the State to accomplish their principal purpose—the returning George P. Fisher to Congress, is regarded by your Committee as little less than miraculous, in view of the unscrupulous and corrupt means resorted to by them for the accomplishment of their design. Your Committee confidently refer to the concurrent testimony of at least a hundred out of one hundred and twenty-four witnesses examined, to prove that the whole power of the military who were brought to this State was, under the command of the Provost Marshals, used to promote the success of the Republican ticket, and to trample upon the rights of Democrats by requiring the taking of unconstitutional test-oaths; the preventing of them from going to the polls to vote, except at such time and in such way as the Republican partizan Provost Marshals might determine; by the arrest and incarceration of some, the frightening and driving from the polls of others, and the general effort to intimidate and humiliate all who did not avow themselves the willing slaves of despotic or irresponsible power. For the establishing of the foregoing facts, the Committee confidently refer to the testimony of Ex-Governor Ross, Hon. Edward Wootten, Charles Wright, Esq., Doctors Shipley and McFerran, Isaac Giles, Esq., Dr. Stephen Green, Curtis W. Jacobs, Esq., Louder N. Hearn, Esq., Captain John James, Henry W. Long, John Sorden, Esq., Alfred P. Robinson, Esq., Cornelius Colter Hart, Esq., James Ponder, Esq., William V. Coulter, Esq., and many others of Sussex County; and to the testimony of Hon. Charles Brown, Hon. Joseph P. Comegys, Jacob M. Hill, Esq., Eli Saulsbury, Esq., John B. Penington, Esq., Colonel George Davis, Robert Hill, Esq., Ex-Governor Tharp, Ex-Governor Burton, Andrew J. Wright, Esq., Charles Williamson, Esq., Alexander Johnson, Esq., Dr. Henry Ridgely, and many others from Kent County; and from New Castle County, to the testimony of Hon. G. R. Riddle, James W. Watson, Esq., Dr. J. A. Brown, Aquilla Derrickson, Milton Steel, James Springer, and others. To the testimony of all the persons above named, and to the above current of testimony of one hundred and twenty-four witnesses, the Committee refer with confidence, but desire to invite especiall attention to the testimony of Isaac Giles, Esq., from Little Creek Hundred, in Sussex County. Mr. Giles' testimony conclusively shows, that for some time previous to the election, difficulties had been courted, by members of the Republican party, with the view, as the witness believed, of affording an excuse for bringing troops into this State, to be present on the day of the election; that great forbearance was exercised by Democrats under the insults and goadings of those unprincipled emissaries of designing Republicans, with a view of preventing any excuse for military interference with the elections. His testimony shows, that the polls at Little Creek Hundred, in Sussex County, were, by the Provost Marshals, placed at the absolute control of Captain Watkins, of the Maryland Home Guards; that said Captain forced the Inspector to receive illegal votes, threatening, if he did not, to destroy the ballot-box; that he compelled several Democrats to leave the polls, arrested and kept others in confinement, and, in short, used the whole power of the military under his command to prevent a fair election, and to promote the success of the Republican ticket by any and every means in his power. It is fully proved by the testimony of Dr. Stephen Green, Louder N. Hearn, and others, that in Broad Creek Hundred, Provost Marshal Betts, by means of the troops under his command, prevented a fair expression of public sentiment by drawing a line around the widow, and placing armed soldiers outside the line to prevent Democrats from going to the window to vote in any other than the way directed by the Provost Marshal, and then not until all or most of the Republicans had voted. The testimony further proves that Republicans were permitted to cross the line aforesaid at any time to go the polls; that certain Republicans were marked by a badge of ribbon tied in the button-hole of the vest or coat as a mark by which they were known, and were permitted to cross the line at any place and go to the polls at any time, alone, or with other voters—a privilege which was accorded no Democrat; that said Betts remained most of the day within the ring formed by the soldiers; that he was seen to take Democratic tickets from voters after they had started to the polls, and place Republican tickets in their hands; that he prevented, through the agency of the military, old and respectable citizens, residents in that Hundred (Democrats) from voting for many hours, aiding the Republicans through the same agency all the while, and that he caused unconstitutional test-oaths to be administered to a number of the most respectable residents of the Hundred; that the said Betts (Provost Marshal) is a man distinguished only for vindictiveness and want of principle, and capable of prostituting any position he might occupy to the purpose of party success, and that the military interference did make a difference in the vote of that Hundred of from fifty to one hundred votes. Without quoting it, the Committee refer to the testimony of the witnesses from that Hundred, including the testimony of the Provost Marshal himself. For proof of similar outrages committed by Samuel W. Lacy, of Baltimore Hundred, through the agency of the troops under his command, the Committee refer to the evidence of Captain James, Henry W. Long, Curtis W. Jacobs, and others, including the testimony of the

Provost Marshal, Samuel W. Lacy himself. For proof of the outrage committed in Dagsborough Hundred, the Committee refer to the testimony of Joseph Marvel, Aaron V. Marvel, and other witnesses from that Hundred. For the evidence of the outrage in Georgetown Hundred, they refer to the testimony of the Hon. Edward Wootten, and others from that Hundred. For the outrage committed in Broadkiln Hundred, to the testimony of James Ponder, William V. Coulter, and other witnesses from that Hundred.

Without further reference to the testimony of the witnesses in relation to this subject, the Committee invite the consideration of the General Assembly to the fourth general subject of inquiry, to wit: Whether the presence of troops was necessary to preserve the public peace and insure a fair and impartial election, and whether their presence conduced to that result?

The Committee do not deem it necessary to refer in detail to the testimony of Governor Cannon on this subject. The substance of his testimony is incorporated into a former part of this report, from which the General Assembly will draw their own conclusion. Without reviewing the testimony of the witnesses, the Committee refer with confidence to the whole current of testimony on this subject. It is true, that a few of the witnesses, amounting to not more than about six or eight in all, ventured the opinion that troops were necessary; but it will be perceived, by reference to their testimony, that most of these were interested from having advised the bringing of the troops into this State, from having acted as Provost Marshals, or having been candidates on the Republican ticket. The reasons generally given by these witnesses for the opinion that troops were necessary were, that there had been disorder at previous elections. There was no attempt, by any witness, to deny that there has always been more or less disorder necessarily incident to popular elections, but the testimony fully proves that the civil authorities in this State have always been sufficient for, and adequate to the preservation of the public peace, and that there never was less necessity for military interference in this State than at the last election. In the judgment of the

Committee, to advocate the presence of the military for the reason assigned, is to advocate the placing the free voters of the State, in the exercise of the elective franchise, in absolute servility to military power, which would in effect destroy the great principle underlying the whole system of American liberty, the untrammelled exercise of the right of suffrage in selecting public officers.

Other reasons were given for this outrage, but too trifling in their nature to admit of serious consideration. The Committee refer with entire confidence to the testimony of from eighty to one hundred witnesses from every part of the State, selected from the most intelligent, respectable and responsible classes of our citizens, as proving conclusively that troops were not necessary on the day of the election, either to preserve the public peace or insure a fair election; and this testimony was concurred in by some of the persons who acted as Provost Marshals, among whom were the Provost Marshals from Broadkiln, and Lewes and Rehoboth Hundreds in Sussex County. The attempt on the part of some of the Provost Marshals and other Republicans, summoned before the Committee, to justify the outrage upon the elective franchise of the people of the State by insinuating that it was necessary to insure a fair election, had ever come to their knowledge, but that from their position in the party, no such purpose could have existed without their knowledge; that the Democrats were very sanguine and perfectly confident of electing, by large majorities, the county tickets in Kent and Sussex, and also the State ticket; that they therefore not only desired but considered it their interest that the election should be a fair, free and peaceable one, and that, in view of these facts, the Democratic speakers at all their meetings counseled unusual prudence, advising the people to avoid excitement or controversy in order that no excuse might exist for the introduction into this State of troops to prevent a fair election. The Committee refer with great confidence to the testimony and invite a critical examination of the whole subject. In this connection, we think it proper to say that we should have been gratified if the Senate of the United States, when requested by our representatives in that body to do so, would have examined into this subject. The people of this State will ever regard their refusal to do so as an act of gross injustice, and as evidence of complicity by the Federal administration with designing and unscrupulous partizans here to override the provisions of the Constitution, and subject the free and law-abiding people of a small but gallant State to a humiliation that would not have been practiced towards those of a larger and more powerful State, for no other purpose than to prevent the fair expression of what was known to be the sentiment of the State in regard to the dominant party of the country. The testimony proves that the Provost Marshals acted, through the agency of the troops under their command, in concert with the Republican party, to insure the success of the Republican ticket, and to prevent instead of insure a fair election.

Your Committee particularly invite a careful perusal and consideration of the testimony of the Honorable Vincent W. Gilpin, Mayor of the city of Wilmington, which will be found in the journal of evidence accompanying this report. Mayor Gilpin's testimony conclusively proves that George P. Fisher, Nathaniel B. Smithers, and James R. Lofland, visited Wilmington on the Sabbath preceding the last general election in this State; that he (the Mayor) was summoned by a note, sent to him while in church, to meet these persons at the house of Henry McCoombs; that he did meet them in compliance with the request; that their business with him was to know how many troops he wanted stationed at the polls in the city of Wilmington on election day; that his reply to them was that he did not need or desire any troops in the city of Wilmington; that his police force was adequate to preserve the peace in that city, and that he remonstrated against the sending of troops, and did not know they would be present until he found them at the polls. His testimony further proves that the presence of the military did not conduce to the preservation of the peace, and that there would have been much better order without the troops than there was with them. The testimony of Honorable George R. Riddle and of James M. Watson, corroborates the statement of the Major in regard to the disturbances created at the polls by the military.

Here was not only a wanton disregard of the advice of the Major of Wilmington, but an uncalled-for and unjustified interference with the police regulations of that city, and an outrage upon the rights of the citizens, producing, according to the sworn testimony of Hon. George R. Riddle, a difference, according to his estimate, in the vote of the city in favor of the Republican ticket, of about four hundred and fifty votes. The testimony of Mr. Riddle is, in substance, that without the frauds which the Republican party was enabled to commit through the agency of the military, their majority in that city would not have exceeded one hundred and fifty votes. The testimony of Major Gilpin establishes the further fact that the whole subject of appointing Provost Marshals was discussed on that Sabbath day; that the fact that Henry McCoombs had previously visited Washington in regard to those troops was also talked of, and that a general conversation and consultation ensued in regard to the military invasion of this State.

Here is undeniable evidence of the violation of the sanctity of the holy Sabbath in the completion of one of the most damning conspiracies that ever entered into the conception of wicked and corrupt men against free government or human liberty, evidencing to the minds of your Committee, on the part of its perpetrators, a depth of infamy and corruption greater than which it is difficult for the human intellect to conceive, and should consign the guilty actors to everlasting contempt and disgrace.

The Committee do not propose to consider at length the last general subject of inquiry, viz: the character of the Provost Marshals, and their conduct through the agency of the troops under and subject to their command at the polls, and also generally into the conduct of the troops which were sent into the State. Upon this subject, the testimony of the witnesses will speak for itself. No extended comment from your Committee is necessary. A careful review of the testimony sufficiently proves that in all the hundreds in Kent and Sussex Counties, to which troops were sent by the General Government, they were placed under and made subject to the absolute control of partizan Provost Marshals, many of them entirely destitute of character, and capable of being influenced by designing partizans to the commission of any act of outrage or violence which might become necessary to the accomplishment of their object—the carrying the election in favor of the Republican ticket. That the Provost Marshals did, in violation of the constitutional and legal rights of the citizens of the State, use the military force under their command, to intimidate and deter Democratic voters from the expression of their opinions and the fair exercise of the elective franchise; that in some hundreds they arrested unoffending citizens and kept them in confinement for hours, and in others they frightened the voters from the polls, and caused them to flee to the woods to avoid arrest; in Baltimore and Broad Creek Hundreds, they required most respectable citizens and large property-holders to take test-oaths as a condition of voting, and in Dover and some other hundreds, they caused the troops to charge bayonets upon quiet and peaceable citizens, knocking down and trampling under foot old and feeble men, crippling some, piercing the garments and in some instances the persons of others, and in every hundred in the State, where troops were present, their effort seemed to be to intimidate and alarm Democrats and encourage Republicans. In some hundreds Inspectors were compelled by the military to take illegal votes and refuse legal votes. This was particularly the case in Little Creek Hundred, Sussex County, as will appear from a review of the testimony of Isaac Giles, Esq., who was a Judge of the Election. The testimony fully proves that in a number of instances citizens were compelled to vote contrary to their known and expressed sentiments. In Milford Hundred, according to the testimony of a number of witnesses, the Provost Marshal caused a citizen to be arrested after he had got within a few yards of the polls, with his ticket in hand, declaring his purpose to vote the Democratic ticket, and to be kept in confinement for several hours and brought out just before the polls closed to vote a Republican ticket. In the town of Dover, a young Lieutenant, scarcely of age, is proved to have taken a Democratic ticket from the hands of a voter, who protested that he was a Democrat, and had never voted any other ticket, and compelled him, in the presence of some of the most respectable citizens of this State, to vote a Republican ticket against his known and expressed sentiments.

The Committee, within proper limits for this report, cannot refer more in detail to the many instances of violence and outrage committed by the military at the polls. An impartial consideration of the testimony, in the judgment of your Committee, cannot fail to convince any impartial and unbiassed mind that the troops, which were at the polls on the fourth of November, one thousand eight hundred and sixty-two, were there for the purpose of producing intimidation and alarm; that they were there for the benefit of one of the political parties and the injury of the other; that they were there to prevent a free and fair expression of public sentiment; that they were there to produce by intimidation and coercion an apparent concurrence of public sentiment in this State with the views and wishes of the Federal administration at Washington; that they were there against law, against right, against the requirements of common justice; that they were there in disregard of the honor, interest and dignity of the State; that they were there at the request of George P. Fisher and William Cannon—a request made at the sacrifice of every principle of honor, integrity and common decency—and that they were there to secure the election by force and fraud of the persons making the request and their associates on the Republican ticket.

The Committee will further submit that the testimony of the witnesses prove that the presence of military at the polls did produce great intimidation and alarm; did result in favor of the Republican party and the injury of the Democratic party; did prevent a free and fair expression of public sentiment; and did secure the election of William Cannon as Governor of this State, against the known wishes of a large majority of the legal voters of the State; but that their presence did not, as was designed, secure the election of George P. Fisher, to Congress, or the election of his comrades on the Republican ticket in two of the three counties of the State; nor did their presence coerce a concurrence of public sentiment with the views of the Federal administration.

Your Committee have looked in vain to the history of all the States in this Union, previous to the installation of the present Federal

Executive, for a precedent for these outrages. It may be true that popular excitements in large cities have sometimes rendered the presence of a police force necessary on the day of election, but not oftener than on other occasions.

No instance, however, in the history of any other Administration of the Federal Government is known to your Committee, where an armed military force has been by Federal authority sent, under command of Federal officers, into a sovereign State not in rebellion against the authority of the Federal Government, where no insurrection or domestic violence existed, and where no application had been made by the State authorities for such force, and no apprehension was felt by said authorities that such force would be necessary.

It has been a subject of astonishment to the Committee that, in a country like ours, where the "blessings of government, like the dews of heaven, have been dispensed alike upon the rich and the poor," and where the experience of a sense of security under the protection of a government of laws has been enjoyed alike by every class and condition in society, there should still be found a class of men laboring under the delusion that any good can be effected by lawlessness and disregard of the rights of their fellow citizens. But that such is the case, the evidence elicited by this examination abundantly proves.

The love of power, desire for position, the spirit of avarice, and hope of gain, have so infatuated a large body of men in this country as to render them not only unmindful of their obligations to their fellow men and callous to the claims of humanity, but imbued them with the demoniac spirit which seeks to elevate self by libelous slander of their fellow citizens. This spirit, in the commencement of our Federal difficulties, induced men of low and groveling intellects and tastes to seek their own elevation at the cost of the reputation of others. Unmindful alike of the lessons of philosophy, the teachings of history, and the injunctions of Christianity, wicked men in our own State sought their own promotion at the cost and reputation of their neighbors, and by redundant professions of loyalty to administrations, succeeded in gaining favor with the powers that be. The history of mankind proves this to be nothing new or wonderful. In all great civil commotions the chaff of society rises to the surface, and true merit seeks retirement amid the ostentation and superciliousness of ignorance and power. It has been thus in the history of our own State. At the inception of our Federal difficulties, we were all of one mind; conciliation and compromise, and not coercion, was the watchword of our people. We believed, with the lamented Douglas, that "war was disunion." Soon the spirit of empiricism was manifested by those conscious of their own want of merit in our midst, and an effort was made by the ignorant and vicious to displace real merit, and elevate themselves by detraction and slander of others. All who did not yield a willing and slavish obedience and subserviency to irresponsible despotic power, were charged with infidelity to the Government, and loyalty to the Federal Administration was attempted to be made the standard by which every man was to be judged; and all who had the temerity to think for themselves, and the independence to act in obedience to their convictions of right, were charged with disloyalty to the Government. Happily for the State, these charges met a prompt rebuke in the action of the State authorities. The Legislature of the State promptly rebuked the suggestion of secession as a remedy for our national troubles, and the Executive of the State responded without hesitation to every requisition made upon it by the General Government. The Federal authorities were compelled to acknowledge, as a reason for suspending the draft in this State, that the State had furnished her full quota of men to the General Government. Your Committee deny that the people of this State have ever been wanting in fidelity to their constitutional obligation to the General Government, established by the fathers of the country, and denounce, as slanderous and libelous, all such charges, let them emanate from whatever source they may. The people of the State "ardently desire a restoration of the Federal Union upon its original basis, and will labor for the accomplishment of that result by proper and constitutional means, and with a sacred regard to the rights of all the States and the people of all the States," but will never willingly consent to the violation of the Federal compact, or tacitly submit to be made the slaves of despotic power. The people of this State will continue to be faithful to their constitutional obligations, but claim the right "to manage their own domestic institutions in their own way," without interference or molestation from the General Government.

It will be observed that all the witnesses examined by your Committee, who attempted to justify the invasion of the State by Federal soldiery, and their presence at the polls on the day of the last general election, place that justification on the ground of their individual apprehension of a disturbance of the public peace and a denial of free suffrage on that occasion. Your Committee do not credit the sincerity of the witnesses who have thus testified; their own testimony furnishes full and complete evidence that they wilfully trifled with the solemnity of their oaths in making such an allegation. None of them have stated any fact or circumstance to warrant the belief that any disturbance of the public peace was reasonably to be apprehended, or that any attempt would be made to deprive any legal voter of the right of free suffrage. The little election, immediately preceding the invasion, had been one of unusual quiet and order. No outbreak of popular violence had occurred within the State. The political campaign had been, so far as the Democratic party was concerned, conducted in a quiet and orderly manner. The only attempt at intimidation or outrage that had been made was by the Republican party, by their military parades at political meetings, and their denunciations of those who were opposed to them as secessionists and traitors, and their arrests and threatened arrests of Democrats for no other reason than that they would not vote the Republican ticket. The insults and slanders of the members of that party had, for the sake of peace, been quietly submitted to by their opponents, and even the wrongful arrests of unoffending citizens were not resisted. It was apparent to all that the sentiment of the people of this State was opposed to the principles and policy of the Republican party, and that, through the peaceful and constitutional method of the ballot-box, that sentiment would be unmistakably manifested. To prevent the free expression of the popular will, the introduction of Federal soldiers into the state was sought and procured. For the first time in the history of the State of Delaware, the sovereignty of the State was set at defiance, and our republican institutions attempted to be subverted by the union of traitorous citizens at home with the usurpers of undelegated authority at Washington. Such an outrage upon the rights and liberties of the people of the State had no nobler object for accomplishment than the obtaining of the possession of the local offices of the State. The names of the base co-conspirators in this outrage upon the people and principles of free government will, and ought to be, forever infamous. The present will loathe and shun them, and history, if the names of such political insects are allowed a place in history, will embalm their memories in everlasting infamy.

Had there been any apprehension of popular disorder on the day of the last general election, what was the proper authority to prevent its occurrence? To whom is confided and to whom belongs the regulation of the internal police of the State, and the preservation of the public peace within a State to the State or Federal authorities? This seems to be a question which had entirely escaped the attention of the traitorous political conspirators. The line dividing State and Federal jurisdiction in such case is broad, clear, and ineffaceable. The State, and the State alone, has authority to preserve the public peace within its limits. It is nowhere, and by no one contended, that the power of the State was not adequate for the preservation of the public order. No disturbance had occurred, and no threat of disturbance had been made, and no intimation had ever been given to the Governor, or any other civil officer within this State, that any was apprehended.

In one case only can the Federal authority constitutionally act for the preservation of public order in a State. By Section 4, Article 4 of the Constitution of the United States, it is provided, that "the United States shall guarantee to every State in this Union a republican form of government, and shall protect each of them against invasion; and on application of the Legislature, or of the Executive (when the Legislature cannot be convened) against domestic violence." This is the only authority for Federal interference, even for the preservation of public order in a State. No one not basely dishonest will pretend that the invasion of this State, on the day of the last general election, was authorized by this provision of the Federal Constitution. No domestic violence existed in the State. Neither the Legislature nor the Governor made application for Federal aid to protect the people against domestic violence. The evidence submitted by your Committee establishes the fact that William Cannon, George P. Fisher, and their co-conspirators made application to the Secretary of War, and to a Colonel of the Maryland Home Guards, to invade this State with armed soldiery on the day of the last general election, and notwithstanding the pretence that the object of the application was to preserve the public peace and secure a fair election, no honest man can possibly doubt that the real object was to prevent the free electors of the State from selecting the public agents of their will.

By the Constitution of this State, Section 3, Article 1, it is provided, that "all elections shall be free and equal;" and the Legislature of this State, to guard against any infraction of this provision, has solemnly enacted, Section 22, Chapter 16 of the Revised Code, as follows: "If any officer or other person shall call out, or order any of the militia of this State to appear, exercise, or muster, on the day of any election, or within ten days before any general election, or three days before any special election or election for Assessor or Inspector, or within three days after either of such elections, except in case of invasion or insurrection, every such officer or other person shall, for every such offence, forfeit and pay to the State a fine of one thousand dollars."

Your Committee might, perhaps, with propriety here close their report, submitting the facts elicited without further comment, to the General Assembly and people of the State, as conclusive of a deliberate design and purpose on the part of the leading Republican politicians of the State, and an unscrupulous and despotic administration at Washington to invade the sovereignty of Delaware, and trample under foot the most sacred right of her citizens. The great indignity however offered to the State by the Federal authorities in the invasion of her soil by Federal soldiery for the purpose of influencing the result of an election, will justify the Committee in expressing in conclusion their un-qualified condemnation, both of the action of the Federal administration and the traitorous conspirators among our own citizens who, for partizan purposes alone, sought to defeat the fair expression of the popular will at the polls by the potent influence of Federal bayonets.

The relations of State and Federal authority are too plainly defined by the written Constitution, that gives to the General Government every power which it can rightfully exercise, and are too well understood by the people of the whole country to permit your Committee, even in the exercise of the most liberal charity, to ascribe this great outrage to the ignorance and imbecility of the novices at Washington. Influenced by party considerations alone, the Federal administration, disregarding the limitations upon Federal power plainly written in the Constitution of the country, has been guilty before the whole country of invading one of the smallest States of the Union, not at the instance and request of the constituted authorities of the State, but at the solicitation of corrupt and unscrupulous neighborhood politicians. If this administration had done no previous wrongful act; if its history had been marked by a strict regard for constitutional obligations; if it had not unnecessarily plunged the whole country in ruinous civil war; if it had built no bastiles; deprived no man of his liberty; suspended no writs of *habeas corpus*; muzzled no presses, nor invaded the right of free thought and free speech, this single act of invading one of the feeblest States of the Union, for no other purpose than to determine the result of her local election, is and ought to be sufficient to brand it with infamy and everlasting disgrace. Reprehensible, however, as has been the action of the powers at Washington, its criminality finds a parallel in the disgraceful, wicked, damning treachery of the ingrate conspirators in our own midst, who, with malign hearts and lying lips, assured the administration of the necessity for its interference with the domestic concerns of Delaware, and by deception and falsehood gave the excuse to irresponsible power for the outrage and wrong of which your Committee complain. No language could betray their baseness. No time can efface their guilt, or remove the stigma from their memory. Your Committee will therefore turn from objects so loathing, and leave them to the judgment of their fellow-men, objects of contempt and scorn.

GOVE SAULSBURY
THOMAS CAHALL,   *Of the Senate.*
WILLIAM HITCH,

JAMES WILLIAMS,
JOHN SLAY,
WM. B. STUBBS,   *Of the House of Representatives.*
WM. D. WAPLES,
G. W. HORSEY,

Journal and Testimony.

THURSDAY, January 8, 1863—8 o'clock, P.M.

The Joint Committee, appointed in pursuance of the following joint resolution of the General Assembly of the State of Delaware, adopted on the 8th inst., viz:

"*Resolved, by the Senate and House of Representatives of the State of Delaware in General Assembly met,* That so much of the Governor's Message as refers to the interference by troops in the service of the United States with the elections in this State on the 4th day of November last be referred to a Committee of three members on the part of the Senate and five members on the part of the House of Representatives, and that said committee have power to send for persons and papers, and leave to report by bill or otherwise."

Met this day.

Present—All the members, viz: Messrs. Saulsbury, Cahall, Hitch, Slay, Stubbs, Williams, Waples, and Horsey.

The Committee organized by appointing Mr. Saulsbury Chairman and Mr. Williams Secretary, *pro tem.*

In pursuance of the following joint resolution of the General Assembly of the State of Delaware, adopted on the 8th inst., viz:

"*Be it Resolved, by the Senate and House of Representatives of the State of Delaware in General Assembly met,* That the Joint Committee to whom was referred that part of the Governor's Message in relation to the military interference with the election held on the 4th of November, 1862, be authorized to employ a Clerk, and to report to the General Assembly a reasonable compensation for his services,"

Mr. Williams proposed the appointment of John O. Slay as Clerk to the Committee, which was agreed to.

On motion of Mr. Horsey,

The Committee adjourned to meet on Tuesday evening next, the 13th inst., at 8 o'clock.

TUESDAY, January 13, 1863—8 o'clock, P.M.

The Committee met pursuant to adjournment.

Present—Messrs. Saulsbury, Cahall, Hitch, Slay, Stubbs, Williams, Waples, and Horsey.

John O. Slay appeared, was duly qualified, and took his seat as Clerk of the Committee.

On motion of Mr. Williams, John S. Jester was appointed to serve subpoenas on witnesses.

On motion of Mr. Williams,

The Committee adjourned to meet to-morrow evening at 7 o'clock.

WEDNESDAY, January 14, 1863—7 o'clock, P.M.

The Committee met pursuant to adjournment.

Present—Messrs. Saulsbury, Cahall, Hitch, Slay, Stubbs, Williams, Waples, and Horsey.

A list of witnesses, from Sussex County, was presented by Mr. Horsey, and filed by the Clerk.

John S. Jester appeared, was duly qualified, and entered upon his duties as Sergeant-at-Arms of the Committee.

On motion,

The Committee adjourned until to-morrow evening at 7 o'clock.

THURSDAY, January 15, 1863—7 o'clock, P.M.

The Committee met pursuant to adjournment.

Present—Messrs. Saulsbury, Cahall, Hitch, Slay, Stubbs, Williams, Waples, and Horsey.

No business appearing,

On motion,

The Committee adjourned to meet on Tuesday, the 20th inst., at 7 ½ o'clock, P.M.

TUESDAY, January 20, 1863—7 ½ o'clock, P.M.

The Committee met pursuant to adjournment.

Present—Messrs. Saulsbury, Hitch, Slay, Stubbs, Williams, and Waples.

No business appearing.

On motion,

The Committee adjourned until Friday evening at 7 o'clock.

FRIDAY, January 23, 1863—7 o'clock, P.M.

The Committee met pursuant to adjournment.

Present—Messrs. Saulsbury, Hitch, Slay, Waples, and Horsey.

The two Houses of the General Assembly, on the 23[d] inst., having adopted the following joint resolutions, viz:

"*Resolved, by the Senate and House of Representatives of the State of Delaware in General Assembly met*, That the Speaker of the Senate and

Speaker of the House of Representatives jointly be, and they are hereby authorized to issue subpoenas for witnesses to appear before the Joint Committee of the two Houses on so much of the Governor's Message as relates to the interference by troops in the service of the United States with the late elections, and that said subpoenas be directed to John S. Jester, who has been appointed by said Joint Committee to be Sergeant-at-Arms thereof;

"*And be it further Resolved, by the authority aforesaid*, That the Chairman of the Joint Committee aforesaid be, and he is hereby authorized to administer the proper oath or affirmation to all witnesses who may appear before said Committee;"

The Clerk of the Committee was directed to draw a form of subpoena, with due reference to the foregoing resolutions, and to have copies thereof printed.

The Chairman was authorized to have the following persons summoned to attend as witnesses before the Committee on Wednesday, the 28th day of January, viz:

Gov. William Cannon, Ex-Gov. William Burton, Ex-Gov. William H. Ross, Charles Wright, Joseph McFerran, James Stuart, Catesby F. Rust, Major W. Allen, Rhodes Hazzard, John L. Coulborn, John E. Martin, Garrett Layton.

On motion,

The Committee adjourned until Wednesday next, at 8 o'clock, P.M.

WEDNESDAY, January 28, 1863—8 o'clock, P.M.

The Committee met pursuant to adjournment.

Present—Messrs. Cahall, Slay, Stubbs, Williams, Waples, and Horsey. The Chairman being absent,

On motion of Mr. Williams,

Mr. Cahall was appointed Chairman *pro tem.*

WILLIAM BURTON sworn and examined.

By Mr. Williams:

Question. Were you Governor of the State of Delaware on the 4th day of November, A.D. 1862?

Answer. I was.

Question. When did you enter upon the duties of that office, and when did your term of office expire?

Answer. I entered upon the duties on the 18th day of January, A.D. 1859, and my term of office expired on the 20th day of January, A.D. 1863.

Question. Did you, at any time, during your term of office, apply to any Department of the General Government for military forces to be sent into this State for any purpose?

Answer. No, sir; I did not.

Question. Were you applied to by any citizen of this State to make application to the General Government for military forces to be sent into this State?

Answer. No sir; not that I recollect.

Question. Had you any official information from the General Government that troops would be sent into this State on or about the 3d day of November, A.D. 1862?

Answer. I had not.

Question. Did you vote at the General Election in this State, held November 4th, 1862?

Answer. I did, sir.

Question. In what Hundred did you vote?

Answer. In Milford Hundred.

Question. Were there any armed soldiers at the polls at the time you voted?

Answer. There were.

On motion of Mr. Williams,

The Committee adjourned until Thursday, at 9 o'clock, A.M.

THURSDAY, January 28—9 o'clock, A.M.

Committee met pursuant to adjournment.

Present—Messrs. Saulsbury, Cahall, Hitch, Horsey, Slay, Stubbs, Waples, and Williams.

The examination of WILLIAM BURTON was resumed, he being recalled.

By the Chairman:

Question. You have stated that there were armed soldiers at the polls, on the day of the last General Election in this State. Who appeared to be in command of these soldiers at the polls?

Answer. James R. Lofland.

Question. Who is James R. Lofland?

Answer. James R. Lofland is a citizen of Milford and holds a commission of Provost Marshal from the General Government.

Question. Why do you say that James R. Lofland was in command of the soldiers at the polls?

Answer. He did command, and they obeyed.

Question. Is James R. Lofland an active and violent politician?

Answer. He is.

Question. Is he a member of the party that elected the present President of the United States; and is he a supporter of that party?

Answer. He is.

WILLIAM BURTON.

JOHN L. COULBOURN, sworn and examined.

By the Chairman:

Question. Mr. Coulborn, where do you reside?
Answer. I reside in Seaford.
Question. What is your occupation?
Answer. I am a hotel-keeper.
Question. Were you at home on the 3^d day of November last?
Answer. I was.
Question. Have you any knowledge of the arrival, at Seaford, of any soldiers or military forces in the service of the United States, on that day?
Answer. Yes, sir.
Question. At what time did they arrive at Seaford?
Answer. About 2 o'clock, P.M.
Question. Under whose command did they seem to be?
Answer. General Wool's.
Question. How did they come to Seaford?
Answer. They were brought by two steamboats and a gunboat.
Question. Were there any other soldiers present? If so, who were they?
Answer. Some of the Maryland Home Guards were there.
Question. How long did the soldiers remain at Seaford?
Answer. They were distributed to different parts of the State that night.
Question. Have you any knowledge by what means they were conveyed to different parts of Sussex County?
Answer. The Cavalry went away on their own horses. There were wagons from different parts of the County.
Question. Do you know from what Hundreds those wagons came?
Answer. I cannot say certainly that those wagons conveyed the soldiers; they *did* convey their baggage.
Question. Do you recollect the owners of any of the wagons which conveyed the baggage belonging to the soldiers?
Answer. I remember that Mr. Cannon's from Bridgeville, Mr. Sudler's, and Martin Morgan's were there at Seaford.

Question.   Who is Mr. Cannon?
Answer.   The present Governor of the State.
Question.   Was he a candidate at that time?
Answer.   He was.
Question.   Of what political party was he a candidate?
Answer.   The Republican party.
Question.   Who is Mr. Sudler?
Answer.   Dr. John Sudler.
Question.   Do you know to what party Mr. Sudler belongs?
Answer.   The Republican party.
Question.   Do you know any other wagons that were present on that occasion?
Answer.   There were others, but I cannot now recollect them.
Question.   At what time did those wagons leave Seaford?
Answer.   After night.
Question.   Were there many persons at Seaford that day to witness the arrival of troops?
Answer.   There were.
Question.   Do you remember any person who was there?
Answer.   I do.
Question.   Will you give us their names?
Answer.   Labal Lyons, from Lewes; William Ellegood, from Georgetown; J. C. Hazzard, from Milton; Garrett Layton, from Bridgeville; and Jacob Knowles, from Broad Creek Hundred; also, John L. Bacon, from Laurel; and Jesse P. Conoway.
Question.   Do you remember any person from Baltimore Hundred?
Answer.   I do not.
Question.   Do you know to what political party those gentlemen belong?
Answer.   To the Republican party.

By Mr. Williams:

Question. Do you know whether there were any persons at Seaford, from Kent County, to witness the arrival of soldiers?

Answer. I do not.

By the Chairman:

Question. When did you first learn that troops were expected to be at Seaford?

Answer. When the boats came in sight.

Question. Did you see Samuel Lacey leave Seaford that day?

Answer. I saw a man, who, I have since learned, was Samuel Lacey, leave, followed by a number of troops.

JOHN L. COULBORN.

GEORGE T. KAY, sworn and examined.

By the Chairman:

Question. Mr. Kay, where do you reside?

Answer. At Seaford.

Question. How long have you resided there?

Answer. My family have lived there four years; I have lived there two years and a half.

Question. What is your business?

Answer. I am agent for the Railroad Company, also telegraphic operator.

Question. Were you at home on the 3^d day of November last, the day before the General Election?

Answer. I was.

Question. Do you know anything about the arrival at Seaford, on that day, of military forces in the service of the United States?

Answer. Some came there.

Question. By what conveyances were they brought?

Answer. Part came in boats; others by railroad.

Question. What portion came in boats?

Answer. That I do not know.

Question. Under whose command were those soldiers, who came in boats?

Answer. I do not know.

Question. Who commanded those who came by railroad?

Answer. I do not know.

Question. How many troops were there on that day, according to the best of your judgment?

Answer. I do not know exactly. About three hundred came by railroad.

Question. Can you not form an opinion as to the whole number?

Answer. Cannot, because two boats ran aground below Seaford, and the soldiers went ashore.

Question. When did you first learn that troops were expected at Seaford?

Answer. I cannot form any idea. There was outside talk from all parties two or three months before.

Question. Did you receive, from no source, an intimation, a short time before their arrival, that troops were expected to be there that day?

Answer. No information was sent to me. I was of the impression that troops would be there.

Question. What gave you that impression?

(No answer.)

Question. Did you, as telegraphic operator, receive the impression that troops would be there, from any telegrams that passed along the line?

Answer. On my oath, I say that as telegraphic operator, I am not allowed to divulge any messages that pass over the road, and for that reason I decline answering the question for the present.

Question. Do you know what became of the troops after leaving Seaford?

Answer. I understand they were sent to the different Hundreds.

Question. Have you any knowledge by what conveyances the

soldiers were carried to any of the Hundreds of the County?

    Answer.   Part were carried by railroad to different points along the road.

    Question.   Do you know how their baggage was conveyed?

    Answer.   I do not.

    Question.   Did any troops leave for the North by railroad?

    Answer.   They did.

    Question.   How many?

    Answer.   I do not know.

By Mr. Williams:

    Question.   Were they conveyed by regular or special trains?

    Answer.   By a special train.

By the Chairman:

    Question.   When were you first informed that a special train would be sent for them?

    Answer.   Not until its arrival. I knew a special train would come, but I did not know for what purpose.

    Question.   Do you know whether any troops left Seaford, on horses, for the eastern part of Sussex County?

    Answer.   There were; but where they went I am not able to say.

    Question.   How did you learn that a special train of cars would be at Seaford that day?

    Answer.   By telegraph.

    Question.   Are you at liberty to say by whom the telegram was sent?

    Answer.   I received my information from the operators above.

    Question.   Were you at the polls, and did you vote on the fourth day of November last?

    Answer.   I did.

    Question.   At what place?

    Answer.   Seaford.

    Question.   Were there troops stationed near the polls?

Answer. There were.
Question. Under whose command were they?
Answer. Lieutenant O'Riley's.
Question. Was there a Provost Marshal?
Answer. There was.
Question. Who was he?
Answer. Rhodes Hazzard.
Question. Who is Rhodes Hazzard?
Answer. A citizen of Seaford.
Question. To what party does he belong?
Answer. The Union party.
Question. Do you know whether Mr. Hazzard is an active and violent partizan?
Answer. I do not.

GEORGE T. KAY.

MAJOR W. ALLEN sworn and examined.

By the Chairman:
Question. Mr. Allen, where do you reside?
Answer. About five miles from Seaford?
Question. Were you at or about Seaford on the third day of November last?
Answer. Yes, sir.
Question. Do you know whether any troops in the service of the United States arrived at Seaford that day?
Answer. Yes, sir.
Question. By what conveyances were they brought?
Answer. By steamboats and the railroad. Some were Maryland Home Guards, and the balance came from Baltimore.
Question. How many came on steamboats?
Answer. There were four boats and a great many soldiers.

Question. Are you confident there were four boats?

Answer. Three were in sight, and I understood there was one below.

Question. Have you any knowledge of how many Maryland Home Guards were there?

Answer. Colonel Wallace's regiment was there.

Question. Was Colonel Wallace in command?

Answer. He was.

Question. Do you know who was in command of the troops on the boats?

Answer. Major-General Wool.

Question. Where did they encamp?

Answer. At Nanticoke City, in tents.

Question. How long did they remain?

Answer. I do not know; during the night they were dispersed, I think.

Question. Do you say that Provost Marshals from different parts of the State were at Seaford to receive the soldiers and take them in charge?

Answer. Yes, sir.

Question. Do you know who the Provost Marshals were, or any of them?

Answer. Rhodes Hazzard was Provost Marshal at Seaford; Garrett Layton was Provost Marshal at Bridgeville; William Ellegood, Provost Marshal at Georgetown; a man by the name of Betts, for Broad Creek Hundred; and John L. Bacon, at Laurel, I understand.

Question. Was J. C. Hazzard, from Milton, there?

Answer. I did not see him.

Question. Are you acquainted with Rhodes Hazzard?

Answer. Yes, sir.

Question. What is his business?

Answer. He owns a farm which he rents out.

Question. Do you know whether Rhodes Hazzard is an active and violent partizan?

Answer. I do, sir.

Question. Is he, or is he not?

Answer. He was at the last election more so than I ever knew him to be.

Question. To what political party does he belong?

Answer. The Republican party.

Question. Do you know who had charge of the soldiers at Seaford?

Answer. I do not recollect.

Question. Had the Provost Marshal command over the soldiers?

Answer. He had.

Question. Do you say that Rhodes Hazzard was Provost Marshal for Seaford, and that you learned from General Wool that the Provost Marshals of the county had command of the soldiers?

Answer. Mr. Hazzard had complete charge of the franchise of the people who were legal voters. He ordered my son, J. W. Allen, from the polls, and said if he didn't leave he would have him arrested.

Question. Did Mr. Hazzard interfere in other areas?

Answer. Yes, sir, he did. I took an old gentleman, of about 80 years of age, up to the polls; he offered his vote and it was disputed by Mr. Hazzard and others on the ground that his tax receipt was forged, in their opinion. I had him there a second time, and was refused again, on the same ground.

Question. Was the refusal made by the Inspector and Judges of the election, or by Mr. Hazzard?

Answer. By Mr. Hazzard and his friends outside, I think. Our Collector, Wm. Allen, then came forward and said that the tax receipt was genuine, and that he himself had given it to the old gentleman, over his own signature. He then voted.

Question. How many soldiers were near the polls at Seaford that day?

Answer. One of the cavalry officers told me he had sixty.

Question. How far from the polls were they stationed?

Answer. Some thirty yards. There were some twelve of fifteen, on horses, on each side of the window where we were voting.

Question. Was there much intimidation among the people that day?

Answer. Very much, and had in my opinion a powerful effect on the election.

Question. You state that the presence of the soldiers had a powerful effect on the election. What do you mean by this?

Answer. I mean that the effect was to intimidate Democrats from voting, and it had its desired effect to the amount of twenty-five or thirty votes, in my judgment.

Question. Have you lived long in and near Seaford?

Answer. For twenty-five or twenty-eight years.

Question. Are you well acquainted with the voters of Seaford?

Answer. I think I know as many voters as any man in our hundred.

Question. From your knowledge of the voters of the hundred, and from knowledge derived from your presence at the polls on the day of the election, do you say upon your oath that you believe the presence of the soldiers made a difference of twenty-five votes in the election?

Answer. I do, on the Democratic ticket.

Question. Do you mean that you believe the Democratic vote was twenty-five less than it would have been if no soldiers had been there?

Answer. I do. There was a soldier, a resident of the hundred, who had his tax receipt, and wanted to vote the Democratic ticket. He was told by Louis Wallace, belonging to the Delaware Cavalry, under Colonel Fisher, that if he did not leave the polls he would have him arrested, for he was a deserter. The soldier went off and did not get to vote.

Question. You have stated that you applied to General Wool for protection that day. Did you do so under the impression that there was danger without such protection?

Answer. I did.

Question.   What answer did you receive?

Answer.   He said his object was to give fair play, but he was under the control of the Provost Marshals, at least so I understood him. He thought my son was entitled to a vote, but he would see the Provost Marshal.

Question.   Did you ask General Wool who appointed the Provost Marshals?

Answer.   I think he said he did not know. I asked him why the soldiers were sent. He said he had been informed that the Democrats of the State intended to take charge of the polls.

Question.   Were you a candidate on the Democratic ticket at the time?

Answer.   Yes, sir.

Question.   Were you not in the perfect confidence of the Democratic party?

Answer.   Yes, sir.

Question.   Were you not cognizant of all the plans and purposes of the Democratic party during the last campaign?

Answer.   I was, sir.

Question.   If there had been any intention on the part of the Democratic party to interfere with the election on that day, would you not have known it?

Answer.   I think I would.

Question.   Are you not confident that you did know all the material plans and purposes of the party?

Answer.   I think I did.

Question.   Was there any purpose, or desire, or intention, or intimation of such purpose on the part of the Democratic party to interfere with the election?

Answer.   There was not, and we were well able to beat them without any interference.

Question.   Do you not believe, and is it not the prevailing opinion in your county, that the soldiers were brought there for the purpose of preventing a fair election?

    Answer.   I do, with all my heart.

    Question.   Was any portion of the Democratic party permitted to know or understand anything in relation to the bringing of soldiers to the polls, previous to their arrival at Seaford?

    Answer.   No, sir; not at all.

M. W. ALLEN.

On motion of Mr. Cahall,
The Committee adjourned until 1 ½ o'clock, P.M.

SAME DAY, 1 ½ o'clock, P.M.

Committee met pursuant to adjournment.

    Present—Messrs. Saulsbury, Cahall, Hitch, Slay, Stubbs, Williams, Waples, and Horsey.

JAMES STUART, sworn and examined.

By the Chairman.

    Question.   Mr. Stuart, where do you reside?
    Answer.   In Seaford.
    Question.   How long have you resided there?
    Answer.   A year last September.
    Question.   Where did you live on the 4th day of November last?
    Answer.   In Seaford.
    Question.   Do you know any thing about the arrival at Seaford of forces in the United States service, on the 4th day of November last?
    Answer.   Yes, sir.
    Question.   By what conveyances were they brought?
    Answer.   Some in steamboats and some in cars.
    Question.   When and what was the first intimation you had that soldiers were expected to be there?

Answer.	On Sunday I received positive information.

Question.	How did you get that information?

Answer.	I heard it from somebody; I do not remember whom; it was general rumor.

Question.	How many soldiers do you suppose there were?

Answer.	There were some cavalry and some infantry. There were two or three hundred infantry.

Question.	How long did they remain at Seaford?

Answer.	A week, I presume.

Question.	Did they all remain?

Answer.	No, sir.

Question.	What became of those who left?

Answer.	They were dispersed; I do not know where.

Question.	How long did those who left Seaford remain away before they returned?

Answer.	Some returned on Thursday or Friday.

Question.	Did you say a portion remained until they left for Baltimore?

Answer.	Yes, sir.

Question.	How many?

Answer.	A company.

Question.	What were they doing, especially on the 4th day of November?

Answer.	They were at the polls.

Question.	Were they infantry or cavalry?

Answer.	Cavalry.

Question.	How far were they from the polls?

Answer.	Right near the window.

Question.	Were you at the polls that day?

Answer.	I was Judge of the election.

Question.	Who were the Judges?

Answer.	Dr. Jones was the other Judge. Jesse W. Robinson was the Inspector.

Question. Were any of the soldiers at the polls that day on horseback?
Answer. They were.
Question. Under whose command were the soldiers at the polls?
Answer. It was understood that they were under the command of the Provost Marshal?
Question. Do you know the Provost Marshal?
Answer. I do.
Question. Who was he?
Answer. Rhodes Hazzard.
Question. Is Mr. Hazzard regarded as an active partizan?
Answer. He is.
Question. To what political party does he belong?
Answer. The Republican party.
Question. Did Mr. Hazzard, as Provost Marshal, interfere with the election that day?
Answer. He stood at the window to challenge votes.
Question. Did he make much objection to votes that day?
Answer. He did not more than usual.
Question. Did there seem to be much intimidation by reason of the presence of the soldiers?
Answer. I was not in a situation to judge. Mr. Hazzard would bring his own friends up by a private way. Members of the other party were not permitted to come up that way.
Question. Do you know when the soldiers took their final departure?
Answer. They were there a week, I know.
Question. Did you vote at the last election?
Answer. I did.
Question. To what political party do you belong?
Answer. The Democratic party.
Question. Are you not in the confidence of the party, in reference to its plans and purposes?

Answer.   I am.

Question.   Are you not confident that even in the last campaign, you knew all the principal plans and purposes of the party?

Answer.   I am.

Question.   Did you ever hear an intimation of a desire or purpose, on the part of the Democratic party to interfere with the polls at the last election, so as to prevent a fair election?

Answer.   I never did.

Question.   Do you not feel confident that there was no such purpose?

Answer.   I do.

Question.   From being a Judge of the election, and observing the voters there that day, do you believe there was any necessity for the presence of soldiers?

Answer.   I do not.

Question.   Do you know anything about how they were conveyed away?

Answer.   I saw wagons which, I was informed, were intended to carry baggage.

Question.   From what direction did the wagons come?

Answer.   From Georgetown and Bridgeville; one belonged to Mr. Cannon, the present Governor.

Question.   Was there any proclamation, announcing any one as Provost Marshal?

Answer.   I did not see nor hear of any. I heard Mr. Hazzard was Provost Marshal.

JAMES STUART.

On motion of Mr. Williams,

The Committee adjourned to 8 o'clock, P.M.

SAME DAY, 8 o'clock, P.M.

The Committee met pursuant to adjournment.

Present—Messrs. Saulsbury, Hitch, Cahall, Slay, Stubbs, Williams, Waples, and Horsey.

RHODES HAZZARD, sworn and examined.

By the Chairman:
Question. Mr. Hazzard, where do you reside?
Answer. At Seaford.
Question. Were you there on the day of the last General Election?
Answer. Yes, sir.
Question. Were you Provost Marshal for that place?
Answer. I was.
Question. When did you receive your commission as Provost Marshal?
Answer. On Sunday evening.
Question. From whom?
Answer. I do not remember his name.
Question. Had you, as Provost Marshal, charge of the troops stationed at the polls that day?
Answer. I had, under the direction of Gen. Wool.
Question. From whom did you receive your commission?
Answer. From the War Department.
Question. Over whose signature was the commission?
Answer. Edward M. Stanton's.

RHODES HAZZARD.

GARRETT S. LAYTON, sworn and examined.

By the Chairman:
Question. Where do you reside?
Answer. I am Clerk in Mr. Cannon's store.
Question. Is Mr. Cannon the present Governor?

Answer. He is.

Question. Were you Provost Marshal at the polls on that day at Bridgeville?

Answer. I was.

Question. When did you receive your commission?

Answer. On Sunday night.

Question. Do you know by what means it was conveyed to you?

Answer. I was told, a gentleman on the railroad brought it.

Question. From whom did you receive your commission?

Answer. From Secretary of War, E. M. Stanton.

Question. Had you charge of troops, as Provost Marshal?

Answer. I had.

G. S. LAYTON.

CHARLES WRIGHT, sworn and examined.

By the Chairman:

Question. Mr. Wright, where do you reside?

Answer. In Seaford.

Question. Were you at home on the 3^d day of November last, the day preceding the General Election?

Answer. Yes, sir; a part of the day.

Question. Have you any knowledge of the arrival of troops there?

Answer. Yes, sir.

Question. You say you were at home on the 3^d day of November last, soon after the arrival of Col. Wallace. Was there a regiment under Col. Wallace which came there?

Answer. The men that kept guard told me there were four hundred.

Question. At what time did they arrive?

Answer. About 12 o'clock.

Question. Do you know how they were brought?

Answer. They came by railroad.
Question. Are you a Director of the Delaware Railroad?
Answer. Yes, sir.
Question. Was the train a regular or special train?
Answer. A special train, I believe.
Question. Did you call on the sentinel and ask who had charge of the troops?
Answer. I did. He said, Col. Wallace. Gov. Ross and myself saw him. We asked him what all this meant. He said, Gen. Wool was coming, who could tell us. He told us that Gen. Wool would be there, at 2 o'clock, to meet him.
Question. Were there other troops there that day?
Answer. There were.
Question. Where did they come from?
Answer. Fort McHenry. They left Fort McHenry on Sunday.
Question. By what conveyance?
Answer. They came in three steamboats.
Question. How many came on the steamboats?
Answer. The soldiers told us, 200 cavalry, 200 infantry, and 200 horses.
Question. What disposition was made of them after their arrival?
Answer. Col. Wallace promised to give us an introduction to Gen. Wool. We went down to the boat for that purpose. We could not get on board. Mr. Hazzard, Laban Lyons, Wm. Ellegood, Col. Wallace, and others, did get on the boat.
Question. How long after the arrival of the boats was it before the troops landed?
Answer. I suppose an hour.
Question. How many boats were there in all?
Answer. Three.
Question. When they did land, where did they go?
Answer. To Seaford.
Question. Did they encamp?

Answer. No, sir.

Question. Do you know by what means they left Seaford?

Answer. Some on horseback and some in wagons. The wagons carried baggage.

Question. Do you know who owned them?

Answer. I do not know who owned them. They said one was William Cannon's and another Benjamin Burton's.

Question. Do you know where the troops went?

Answer. I do not. They afterwards told me they had been at Cedar Creek, Georgetown and Nanticoke.

Question. Do you say that you tried to get an introduction to General Wool?

Answer. Yes, sir. After a while we succeeded. Finally Governor Ross addressed him a note. General Wool came out immediately and said he would see us in a few minutes. This was about 5 o'clock. About 10 o'clock we had an interview of about five minutes. We asked what this meant? If they would allow us to have an election? He said he came to see that we should have a fair election. He remained only a few minutes. He soon returned. Troops were gone when we left, except about 100. This was 11 o'clock.

Question. Did you learn any arrangements?

Answer. We did not.

Question. Were there many persons at Seaford at or about the time the troops arrived?

Answer. A good many.

Question. You are at Seaford every day?

Answer. Yes, sir.

Question. Were more people there than usually?

Answer. Yes, sir.

Question. How many?

Answer. From five hundred to one thousand, from Seaford and other places.

Question. You had no introduction to General Wool that night?

Answer. No, sir. I saw him the next day.

Question. Where were the troops stationed in Seaford on election day?

Answer. They were in double files, coming out from the window, and running like a funnel. They had their swords drawn.

Question. Did they remain during the whole time of the election?

Answer. They did.

Question. Did you vote at Seaford?

Answer. Yes, sir.

Question. Did you walk between the files of soldiers?

Answer. I did.

Question. You are well acquainted with the voters of that hundred, are you not?

Answer. I am. I have lived there a long time.

Question. Did there seem to be much intimidation among the voters there, on account of the presence of the soldiers?

Answer. There did in the forenoon, but not so much in the afternoon.

Question. Do you know whether the presence of the soldiers had any effect on the vote that day?

Answer. I think it had.

Question. Do you know of any instance?

Answer. I do not. I have heard others say.

Question. Who was Provost Marshal at Seaford?

Answer. I understood that Mr. Rhodes Hazzard was.

Question. Did he seem to take an active part?

Answer. I did not see him. I was too far from the window.

Question. Who is Mr. Rhodes Hazzard?

Answer. He has lived at Seaford thirty or forty years.

Question. Is he an active and violent partizan?

Answer. Not very. He is positive. He was not as active as I have seen him.

Question. To what political party does he belong?

Answer. The Republican party.

Question. You have spoken of Labal Lyons, of Lewes, and William Ellegood, of Georgetown, as being present at Seaford, on the 3^d day of November. Were there others whom you remember?

Answer. I cannot now call them to mind.

Question. Did you see John L. Bacon?

Answer. I did.

Question. Was he Provost Marshal at Laurel?

Answer. I do not know, personally.

CHAS. WRIGHT.

JOHN E. MARTIN, sworn and examined,

By the Chairman:

Question. Where do you reside?

Answer. At Seaford.

Question. How long have you lived at Seaford?

Answer. I was born and raised there.

Question. Was you at home on the 3^d day of November last, the day preceding the general election?

Answer. I was.

Question. Do you know anything about the arrival of troops at Seaford?

Answer. I know troops arrived there that day.

Question. By what conveyance were they brought to Seaford?

Answer. They came on the railroad and steamboats.

Question. Under whose command were those that came on the railroad?

Answer. Colonel Wallace's.

Question. Were they known as Maryland Home Guards?

Answer. I think they were.

Question. Under whose command were the soldiers that came in boats?

Answer.   General Wool's.

Question.   Do you know how many were under General Wool's command?

Answer.   I suppose 400, probably more.

Question.   Do you know how many were under the command of Colonel Wallace?

Answer.   I think there were from 200 to 300.

Question.   What disposition was made of them after their arrival at Seaford?

Answer.   At first General Wool and Staff had their headquarters at Mr. Coulborn's Hotel. In the evening, they drew off in line, and received orders and proceeded by companies.

Question.   Did you hear orders given?

Answer.   I did not.

Question.   Did you see them when they left?

Answer.   Yes, sir.

Question.   Were any persons from different parts of the county at Seaford to receive the soldiers and guide them to their place of destination?

Answer.   I think there were.

Question.   Who were they, according to your recollection?

Answer.   I saw William Ellegood, Dr. Jacob Knowles, John L. Bacon, from Laurel, and others.

Question.   Do you know whether Dr. Jacob Knowles' wagon was present to convey the soldiers or their baggage?

Answer.   I think not.

Question.   Did you vote at Seaford on the 4th day of November last?

Answer.   I did.

Question.   Were you about the window, among the people?

Answer.   Yes, sir.

Question.   How were the troops distributed?—in what position?

Answer. They were drawn up in files on each side of the windows, with drawn sabres.

Question. Who was commanding them?

Answer. Rhodes Hazzard.

Question. Was there much intimidation among the voters on account of the presence of the soldiers?

Answer. There was, in the morning, considerable.

Question. Did that intimidation influence the vote of the election?

Answer. I think it did, in the morning.

Question. Do you know of any failure to vote on account of the presence of soldiers?

Answer. I know several who did not get to vote, and who claimed a right to vote.

Question. Did there seem to be any difference of feeling between the voters of the different parties?—the one seeming dispirited and the other confident and enthusiastic?

Answer. I think there was. In the morning the Lieutenant had occasion to go to the Provost Marshal and told him something had occurred, and he would have to take his men from the polls. He took his men away, and after they left, the Republican party took possession of the window, and voted the men pell-mell, and before they were only allowed to go up one at a time.

Question. From the disposition manifested on the part of the Democratic party, did you think there was a necessity of soldiers to preserve order?

Answer. No, sir.

Question. You are a Democrat?

Answer. Yes, sir.

Question. Are you not in the confidence of the Democratic party, and acquainted with all its material plans and purposes in regard to elections?

Answer. I think I am.

Question. Did you ever hear any intimation of desire or purpose on the part of the Democratic party to interfere with the polls at the last election, so as to prevent a fair election?

Answer.   Never.

Question.   Do you not think you would certainly have known it if there had been any such purpose?

Answer.   I think I should.

Question.   Is Rhodes Hazzard a warm supporter of the present administration?

Answer.   I have never heard him express himself very freely.

JOHN E. MARTIN.

The examination of CHARLES WRIGHT was resumed, he being recalled.

By the Chairman:

Question.   Have you not been during the greater part of your life an active Democrat, and as such have you not been in the confidence of the party with reference to all its material plans and purposes?

Answer.   Yes, sir.

Question.   Had you any knowledge of any intention or purpose on the part of the Democratic party to interfere with the polls at the last election so as to prevent a fair election?

Answer.   Not at all. I do not think any such thing was ever thought of.

Question.   Are you not confident from your position in the party, that if such a thing had been in contemplation, you would have known it?

Answer.   I am sure I should.

CHAS. WRIGHT.

On motion of Mr. Williams,

The Committee adjourned till nine o'clock to-morrow morning.

FRIDAY, January 30, 1863—9 o'clock, A.M.

The Committee met pursuant to adjournment.

Present—Messrs. Saulsbury, Hitch, Slay, Williams, Waples, and Horsey.

The examination of GEORGE T. KAY continued, he being recalled.

Question.   Do you know whether a car or train of cars passed to Seaford, on the Delaware Railroad, on the Sabbath previous to our last General Election?

Answer.   There was a hand-car which came down; there was no train of cars.

Question.   Do you know who had charge of that hand-car?

Answer.   Thomas F. Hawkins, conductor of freight.

Question.   Had you any intimation that a car of any kind would pass to Seaford before it arrived there that day?

Answer.   Half-an-hour previous I received a dispatch to have a car ready to convey Mr. Hawkins to Salisbury.

Question.   Did you procure two men to work the car to Salisbury?

Answer.   I went and told the men having charge of the section to send down men for that purpose.

Question.   Had you any knowledge of the purpose for which the car was to go down the road that day?

Answer.   I had not.

GEO. T. KAY.

The examination of JOHN L. COULBORN continued, he being recalled.

Question.   Do you know whether a hand-car passed by Seaford and stopped at Seaford on the Sabbath previous to the last General Election?

Answer. Mr. Thomas F. Hawkins came down on the road and stopped at Seaford that day. He came up to my house and called for supper, saying he was in extreme haste. I think he said he would have to stop at Laurel, and also go to Salisbury.

Question. Do you know whether he went to any other place in Seaford previous to his coming to your house, or after leaving it?

Answer. No, sir; I do not.

Question. Did you observe the Inspector, Jesse W. Robinson, that day?

Answer. I did.

Question. Did he seem to be intimidated by the presence of the troops?

Answer. He seemed to be, having been arrested some time previous.

Question. Did he seem to be much intimidated?

Answer. He did, very much, in my opinion.

J. L. COULBORN.

THOMAS JACOBS sworn and examined.

By the Chairman:
Question. Mr. Jacobs, where do you reside?
Answer. In North West Fork Hundred, in Sussex County.
Question. What is your age?
Answer. I am seventy-three years of age.
Question. Were you at the election on the fourth day of November last?
Answer. Yes, sir.
Question. Did you vote on that day?
Answer. Yes, sir.
Question. Where?
Answer. At Bridgeville.

Question.   Were there soldiers about the polls that day?

Answer.   There were. I did not observe them much, being unwell. They were stationed near the polls.

Question.   Did you ever before in a life of seventy years see armed soldiers stationed near the polls on election day?

Answer.   I never did.

Question.   Have you not been for the most of your life an active and prominent Democrat in your county?

Answer.   Yes, sir; for the most of my life I have.

Question.   You have frequently served in the Legislature, have you not?

Answer.   Yes, sir.

Question.   Have you not been, and are you not now, in the confidence of the Democratic party, knowing all its plans and purposes?

Answer.   Yes, sir.

Question.   Did you ever hear of any purpose or intention or desire on the part of the Democratic party to interfere with the polls, so as to prevent a fair election on the fourth day of November last?

Answer.   I never heard anything of the kind at all.

Question.   Are you not confident, from your position in the party, that if there had been any such intention or desire on the part of the Democratic party, that you would have known it?

Answer.   I think I would.

Question.   Do you know who acted as Provost Marshal at the polls at Bridgeville, on the day of the last election?

Answer.   It was said to be Garrett S. Layton.

Question.   Did you see him around the polls when you voted?

Answer.   I saw him near the polls.

Question.   Do you know who Garrett S. Layton is, and what is his occupation?

Answer.   I know him when I see him. He is in the store of Mr. Cannon, the present Governor, whether as clerk or partner I do not know.

Question. Do you know whether he is a brother-in-law of Mr. Cannon?

Answer. He married a sister to Mr. Cannon's wife, I think.

THOS. JACOBS.

CATESBY F. RUST, sworn and examined.

By the Chairman:

Question. Where do you reside?

Answer. In North West Fork Hundred, in Sussex County.

Question. Did you vote on the day of the last General Election?

Answer. I did.

Question. Where?

Answer. At Bridgeville.

Question. At what time did you arrive at Bridgeville that day?

Answer. About 11 o'clock, A.M.

Question. Have you not been in the habit of going to the elections earlier than 11 o'clock?

Answer. I have generally been there at the opening of the polls.

Question. What induced you to defer going to the election until so late an hour, on the day of the last General Election?

Answer. On Saturday night previous to the day of the election, I saw a letter directed to Dr. Shipley, of Seaford, postmarked Dover, stating that if he (Dr. Shipley), Jeremiah McNealy, Nathaniel Horsey, or myself, went to the election on Tuesday, we would be arrested—that there was a Cavalry company coming down for that purpose, and that when we saw them we might look out. I observed to Dr. Shipley that I should go and vote on Tuesday, but thought it best not to go until the polls were open, so that I could vote immediately after arriving and before they could have a chance to arrest me.

Question. When you arrived at Bridgeville and went to the polls to vote, what did you observe there unusual?

Answer. I saw men dressed in uniform. Those at the window were not armed, to my knowledge, but there were armed soldiers present. Those who were armed were near the window.

Question. Did there seem to be any interference with the election, on the part of the men in uniform near the window?

Answer. There did. When I went to vote, I think there were five or six surrounding the windows. I had great difficulty in getting to the window to vote. Some person spoke of having Esquire Davis to clear the window. One of the men dressed in uniform, by the name of Johnson, as I was told, observed that Esquire Davis had nothing to do with it; that "Uncle Sam" had charge there.

Question. Was there any other disturbance sufficient to induce you to go to the officer in command of the armed soldiers present?

Answer. I saw that the Democrats were kept from the window by these men. I went to the hotel and inquired for the Captain of Gen Wool's Cavalry company. A man sitting in the parlor got up and said he was the captain. I told him that I was a Democrat and we wanted a fair chance that day—that I was informed he was sent there for that purpose. He said he was. I then stated to him, that there were men dressed in cavalry uniform, who, I thought, lived in North West Fork Hundred, who were in possession of the window and Democrats could not get up to vote. He replied, that the Provost Marshal ought to attend to that. I asked him who the Provost Marshal was. He said, Garrett Layton. I then told him if that were the case no Democrat would get to vote there that day, and requested him to go to the window and see for himself. He did so, and after looking at them, I suppose two minutes, took the men in uniform from the window and sent them off.

Question. Do you know to what company the men in uniform, near the window, belonged?

Answer. They were said to belong to the Delaware Cavalry company.

Question. Do you know who were the officers of that company?

Answer. I think that William L. Cannon was Captain of the

company.

Question. Who is William L. Cannon?
Answer. A son of Governor William Cannon.
Question. Do you say that you learned that Garrett S. Layton was Provost Marshal there that day?
Answer. Yes, sir.
Question. Do you know Garrett S. Layton?
Answer. Yes, sir.
Question. Was he about the polls?
Answer. He was.
Question. Who is he and what is his occupation?
Answer. He lives in Bridgeville, and with Mr. Cannon.
Question. Is he an active and violent politician?
Answer. He is generally so considered in the neighborhood.
Question. To what political party does he belong?
Answer. To the Republican party.
Question. Were you favored, after the election was over, with a visit from the military, or any portion of them?
Answer. A Lieutenant and eleven men came to my house about night, on Wednesday night after the election.
Question. For what purpose did they come?
Answer. To arrest me.
Question. Did they show you any authority, or leave any authority at your house for your arrest?
Answer. No, sir.
Question. Did you learn from them, or do you now know the charge upon which they proposed to arrest you?
Answer. Not of my own knowledge.
Question. Were you at home when they came to your house?
Answer. No, sir.
Question. When did you come home?
Answer. On the Saturday following.
Question. How did you learn the visit of the military?

Answer.   My wife told me.

Question.   What did you then do?

Answer.   I immediately went to Seaford, called on the Major left in command, and stated to him that he had sent a number of cavalry to my house; that I was not at home when they came, and as soon as I learned it, I had come down to see what it was for. He replied that he had nothing to do with it; that the matter was in the hands of the Provost Marshal at Seaford. I asked who the Provost Marshal was. He replied, Mr. Rhodes Hazzard was Provost Marshal. I told him I should go home, and if Mr. Hazzard wanted me, he knew where to find me.

Question.   By whom was the letter to which you have referred, signed?

Answer.   I think the letter was signed "Justice;" it was anonymous. I think Dr. Shipley has the letter.

Question.   Had you any conversation with Garrett S. Layton that day?

Answer.   I had.

Question.   Will you relate that conversation as nearly as you can?

Answer.   Mr. Layton came to me and said he wished I would get that man (pointing to a person) to go home. I asked why he wanted him to go home. He said if he did not he would be arrested. I told him that was what he (Layton) was trying to do. He said he did not want to arrest him. I told him he did. I heard him tell the Captain of the Cavalry company that was the man, with a light coat on. He (Layton) said he could have him arrested. I told him I doubted it very much. He said he could convince me, pulled out his pocketbook, took out a paper which he said was his commission. I did not wish to see it; I was willing to take his word, so far as that.

Question.   Did he say anything else to you in reference to men's talk that day?

Answer.   He told me he would have any of us arrested who called them Black Republicans or Abolitionists. I told him he must arrest Black Republicans for calling Democrats Secessionists. He said they would not do it. I told him I heard Dr. Cahall tell a man at the window not to call them Democrats, but Secessionists.

Question.   Who is Dr. Cahall?

Answer.   A physician at Bridgeville and a son-in-law of Governor Cannon.

CATESBY F. RUST.

On motion of Mr. Hitch,
The Committee adjourned to 7 ½ o'clock, P.M.

FRIDAY, January 30—7 ½ o'clock, P.M.

The Committee met pursuant to adjournment.

Present—Messrs. Saulsbury, Cahall, Slay, Williams, Waples, and Horsey.

THOMAS F. HAWKINS, sworn and examined.

By the Chairman:

Question.   Where do you reside?
Answer.   In Wilmington.
Question.   What is your occupation?
Answer.   Freight conductor on the Delaware Railroad.
Question.   How long have you occupied the position of freight conductor on the Delaware Railroad?
Answer.   Three years.
Question.   Where were you on the Sabbath previous to the last General Election?
Answer.   In Wilmington a part of the time.
Question.   Where, during the remaining part of the day?
Answer.   On the railroad.

Question. Did a car or train of cars pass over the road that day?

Answer. An engine and one car passed over the road that day.

Question. In what capacity were you on the train?

Answer. As a passenger.

Question. Who else were on the train that day?

Answer. Mr. Bacon, the Conductor, Colonel George P. Fisher, a man by the name of Lofland, and Nathaniel B. Smithers, as I understood.

Question. Do you know the purpose for which the car passed over the road that day?

Answer. No, sir.

Question. Where did you get on the car?

Answer. At Wilmington.

Question. How far down the road did you go?

Answer. To Farmington.

Question. Did Mr. Fisher, Mr. Lofland and Mr. Smithers get off the train at Farmington?

Answer. They did not, but backed up to Harrington, and went into Milford, as I understood.

Question. Did you get off the train at Farmington?

Answer. Yes, sir.

Question. Where did you go after leaving the car at Farmington?

Answer. To Salisbury in a hand-car.

Question. For what purpose did you go down the road in a hand-car?

Answer. I went down to take the place of Conductor on the freight train.

Question. Was that the only reason for which you went down on the Sabbath?

Answer. Yes, sir; the only reason I know.

Question. Did you on Saturday expect to go down the road on Sunday?

Answer. No, sir.

Question. Did you or did you not convey to certain persons at different points on the road that day letters or papers of some description?

Answer. Yes, sir.

Question. To whom did you convey those letters or papers?

Answer. One letter was for Governor Cannon and one for Mr. Hazzard.

Question. Do you know or were you told by any person what those papers were?

Answer. No, sir.

Question. Did you leave one letter in Seaford?

Answer. I left one for Mr. Rhodes Hazzard.

Question. Did you leave any communication of any kind at Laurel?

Answer. I left a letter for John L. Bacon.

Question. Had you any letter or paper for any person at Salisbury?

Answer. I had one for Colonel Wallace.

Question. From whom did you receive the several communications of which you have spoken?

Answer. I think I received them from Mr. Smithers or Colonel Fisher from one or the other I know.

Question. Did he give you any directions as to the delivery of those papers?

Answer. He told me to be sure to deliver them.

Question. Did you take down any other packages of any kind in the form of papers or otherwise?

Answer. No, sir.

Question. Did you convey any verbal message to any person from any of the gentlemen in the car that day?

Answer. No, sir.

Question. Did you then know, or do you now know, for what purpose the letter was conveyed to Colonel Wallace that day?

Answer. No, sir; I do not.

Question. Had you any knowledge or did you receive any

intimation on that day that Colonel Wallace was expected to come up to Seaford with his regiment on the next day?

    Answer.   I did not. I had no idea of it.

    Question.   How long did you remain at Salisbury?

    Answer.   About nine hours.

    Question.   How did you come up the next day?

    Answer.   I brought the regular train up from Salisbury.

    Question.   Did Colonel Wallace and his regiment come up on that train?

    Answer.   Yes, sir; a part of his regiment.

    Question.   Where did they get off the train?

    Answer.   At different stations.

    Question.   Had you any conversation with Colonel Wallace at the time you delivered the letter of which you have spoken?

    Answer.   No, sir.

    Question.   Did he ask you who sent those letters, or any question of that kind?

    Answer.   No, sir.

    Question.   Will you please to name the points at which Colonel Wallace's regiment got off the train?

    Answer.   Laurel, Bridgeville, Harrington, Milford, Felton, and some at Dover, I think; also some at Smyrna.

    Question.   Was Colonel Wallace on the train that day?

    Answer.   Yes, sir.

    Question.   Where did he get off?

    Answer.   At Smyrna.

    Question.   Are you certain that Colonel Wallace himself got off at Smyrna?

    Answer.   I am not certain about that; but I took no soldiers above Smyrna.

    Question.   Can you form any correct judgment as to the number of soldiers you left at each of those points?

    Answer.   I can form no idea.

Question. Do you know with how many car loads you started from Salisbury that night?

Answer. Five car loads.

Question. How many persons will each of those cars accommodate?

Answer. Sixty or sixty-five.

Question. Were they full when you started from Salisbury?

Answer. Very full.

Question. Would you suppose each one of those cars had sixty-five soldiers in it?

Answer. I should think so.

Question. With how many cars did you leave Salisbury, on the special train in the morning?

Answer. With the same number—five.

Question. Were those five cars loaded full in the morning when you left?

Answer. Yes, sir.

Question. Do you know whether any portion of Colonel Wallace's regiment came up on any other train that day?

Answer. I brought up a part of his regiment to Seaford, backed the train to Salisbury and brought the remainder on the regular train.

Question. How many did you bring on the first train to Seaford?

Answer. One or two companies. I am not certain which.

Question. Are you certain there were not four companies?

Answer. I could not say.

Question. Was not Colonel Wallace himself on the first train?

Answer. I could not say.

Question. Are you certain whether you came up the last time on a special or regular train?

Answer. I came on the regular train.

Question. You say that you left some soldiers at Laurel, some at Bridgeville, some at Harrington, some at Milford, some at Felton, some at Smyrna, and think, but are not positive, that you left some at Seaford and some at Dover?

Answer.   Yes, sir.

Question.   Are you certain whether you left some at Camden?

Answer.   I did.

Question.   Do you suppose each one of the cars had sixty-five persons in it?

Answer.   I should suppose so.

Question.   At what time in the day, on the Sabbath previous to the election, were you notified to come down the road?

Answer.   About 12 o'clock. I had orders to come down the road.

Question.   Who give you the orders to come down the road?

Answer.   Mr. Brown, the General Freight Agent.

Question.   Did he tell you for what purpose he wished you to go down on Sunday?

Answer.   No, sir; they never tell us.

Question.   How long before you left Salisbury did you learn that you were to bring soldiers up?

Answer.   The Colonel sent me word to be ready about 9 o'clock, but did not get ready to start before 11 o'clock.

Question.   At what time did he send you that word?

Answer.   Between 7 and 8 o'clock.

Question.   Was that the first knowledge you had that you were to bring up a load of soldiers that morning?

Answer.   No, sir; I think the captain of the guard told me he expected he was going up the road somewhere.

Question.   At what time did the captain of the guard tell you this?

Answer.   About half-past five o'clock, A.M.

Question.   By whom were you directed to take a load of soldiers up the road the next morning?

Answer.   William Waller, the agent, told me they would be there.

Question.   About what time did Mr. Waller tell you this?

Answer.   About 8 o'clock on Monday morning.

Question.   You went to Wilmington after leaving the soldiers at different points, did you?

Answer. I did, but did not get there till the next morning.

Question. At what time did you leave Salisbury on Monday evening?

Answer. About 2 ¼ o'clock.

Question. About what time did you arrive at Dover?

Answer. I cannot tell.

By Mr. Cahall:

Question. What was the cause of your being so late the next morning in getting to Wilmington?

Answer. We did not leave Seaford until between 5 o'clock and 6 o'clock.

Question. What was the cause of your detention at Seaford until that time?

Answer. The soldiers were not ready to go.

Question. Was the train a regular passenger train?

Answer. No, sir.

Question. Was it a special train?

Answer. Yes, sir; I believe it was.

By the Chairman:

Question. Were the soldiers armed when they got on the train at Salisbury?

Answer. Yes, sir.

Question. Were they armed when they left the train at the different points on the road?

Answer. Yes, sir.

By Mr. Cahall:

Question. How did you first obtain the knowledge that you would have to act as conductor on the train from Salisbury on Monday?

Answer. The conductors are in the habit of assisting each other.

Alexander Gearl, a conductor on the road, left Salisbury, went up to Wilmington on Saturday, evening, and did not wish to go down on Sunday and requested me to go down in his place. Mr. Brown told me to go down, and I went.

T. F. HAWKINS.

On motion of Mr. Cahall,
The Committee adjourned to Monday evening at nine o'clock.

MONDAY, February 2, 1863—9 o'clock, P.M.

The Committee met pursuant to adjournment.
Present—Messrs. Saulsbury, Cahall, Hitch, Slay, Stubbs, Williams, Waples, and Horsey.

JOHN DALE affirmed and examined.

By the Chairman:
Question.   Where do you reside?
Answer.   Near Bridgeville, in Sussex County.
Question.   How long have you been a citizen of this State?
Answer.   All my life; since I arrived at the age of manhood.
Question.   Do you recollect whether at any period of your life you have witnessed the presence of soldiers at the polls on election day?
Answer.   Never, until the last election.
Question.   Where did you vote on the last election day?
Answer.   At Bridgeville, in Sussex County.
Question.   Were there soldiers at or near the polls that day?
Answer.   There were.
Question.   Have you any knowledge, derived from any source, at whose solicitation soldiers were brought into this State and stationed at

the polls on that day?

Answer.   I have.

Question.   Please state your information and the sources of it?

Answer.   On the morning of the election day I met Mr. William Cannon at our polls at Bridgeville, and asked him if he had anything to do with bringing soldiers into this State. He said he had; that he had written to Col. Wallace for them and had his answer in the house at that time, but did not wish to have any brought to the polls at Bridgeville; and that he had requested Col. Wallace to have troops sent to Baltimore Hundred, to Dagsborough Hundred, and Broad and Little Creek Hundreds. I am not positive in reference to the names of the two Hundreds last mentioned. I am confident there were four Hundreds. He said his object was to secure a fair election; that a party in Maryland had threatened to take possession of the polls in Baltimore Hundred; and that in Broad Creek, at the little election, a man had stood at the window with a loaded revolver, hurrahing for Jeff. Davis, and threatening to shoot any one of the opposite party who came up to vote; that if he were defeated he wanted to be defeated fairly, and that if he could not be elected fairly he did not wish the office.

Question.   Did you tell you what man it was who stood at the polls in Broad Creek Hundred, threatening to shoot persons who came up to vote?

Answer.   He did not. I understood, from other sources, that there was no such person there.

Question.   Did he tell you what persons they were in Maryland, who had threatened to take possession of the polls in Baltimore Hundred?

Answer.   He did not. He merely said a party threatened to come.

Question.   Have you not been an active and prominent Democrat during the most of your life?

Answer.   I have been, when at home I have been absent during one or two campaigns during the last twenty years.

Question.   Have you not always been, and are you not now, in the confidence of the Democratic party, knowing all its principal plans and operations?

Answer. I have been generally so, during the last eighteen or twenty years.

Question. Did you ever hear an intimation of a desire or purpose on the part of the Democratic party to interfere with the polls on the last election day, so as to prevent a fair election?

Answer. No, sir, not the slightest.

Question. From your position in the party and your association with its leading members, if there had been any such purpose, would you not have known it?

Answer. I think I certainly should.

Question. Do you know anything else bearing upon this subject?

Answer. I was told by a friend of George Nebeker, that he (Nebeker) had carried seven thousand dollars into Sussex County.

Question. For what purpose did he carry that money?

Answer. To influence the election; so he stated.

Question. Was this the same election at which the soldiers were present?

Answer. Yes, sir; the same election.

Question. Do you know whether that money was carried there to defray the expenses of the soldiers?

Answer. I do not.

Question. Do you know whether the soldiers brought their rations with them or not?

Answer. I do not.

Question. Who is this Mr. William Cannon?

Answer. The present Governor of the State of Delaware.

Question. Was he a candidate on the ticket at the last General Election?

Answer. He was.

JOHN DALE.

JOSEPH P. H. SHIPLEY, sworn and examined.

By the Chairman:

Question. Where do you reside?
Answer. At Seaford.
Question. How long have you lived at Seaford?
Answer. Fifteen years.
Question. Were you at home on the 3^d day of November last?
Answer. I was, a part of the day.
Question. Do you know anything about the arrival of armed soldiers at or near Seaford that day?
Answer. I do not know anything in regard to their arrival. I saw them when they were disembarking. I had intimations some two weeks previous that soldiers would be there on the day of the election.
Question. From whom did you receive those intimations?
Answer. I received information through an anonymous letter.
Question. Please state the contents of the letter?
Answer. The letter was post-marked Dover, and was written from Dover. The letter commenced thus: "I am a friend of yours, and seeing you in danger, I think it proper to advise you in regard to it. There will be troops sent to your place some time between the present and the election, and when you see them you may know they are there for the purpose of arresting you and a man by the name of Edward Martin, and one by the name of Jeremiah McNealy, and one by the name of Rust and Nathaniel Horsey, and probably some others. These damned Black Republicans intended to carry the election and free all the negroes." The letter was signed "Justice."
Question. Was that letter written in a natural or disguised hand?
Answer. In a disguised hand, I suppose.
Question. What impression did it make upon your mind?
Answer. The first impression was that it might be real, afterwards I thought it was probably intended to scare me and I took no account of it.

Question.   Did you show that letter to any other person?

Answer.   I showed it to all whose names were mentioned in the letter. I was not in town when the soldiers arrived. As I was returning home I met a person who told me the soldiers were there, and I had better not go home, as I might be arrested. I went home immediately and went to the wharf where the soldiers were landing. I met Gov. Ross, Charles Wright, Dr. McFerran, and several others. We proposed to go aboard of the boat and have an interview with Gen. Wool. The boat was not near enough the wharf to get aboard; at the other end they were landing the horses. We were obliged to wait, and so soon as the boat got near enough there was a party went aboard in advance of us, consisting of Mr. Rhodes Hazzard, Mr. William Ellegood, and, I think, Mr. Labal Lyons, and a number of others whose names I do not remember. They came out immediately in company with Gen. Wool. There was quite a crowd around him on the wharf, which made it impossible for us to see him. There was a reception address delivered by Mr. James Platt, after which they proceeded to the hotel in Seaford. We met in the back room. I was appointed to call on General Wool, to request of him an interview. I was met at the door by Mr. William Ellegood and a Mr. Lacey, who told me I and none of my party had any business with General Wool, and refused to admit me. I returned to the room and reported my services. Dr. McFerran was appointed to assist me. We were requested to return. We did so and met with the same success. We then concluded to address a note to General Wool, requesting an interview with him and succeeded in getting the note conveyed. General Wool immediately came out and informed us that he would meet us in the course of an hour. After waiting probably two hours, the General came out, and we asked him his object in coming to Delaware. He declined giving it. I think he remarked, he was acting under authority and would have to consult them. He returned to their room and soon came back again and reported that he was not here for the purpose of interfering with any legal voting, but for what other purpose he did not know.

Question.   Did you say that he returned to the room to get an answer for you?

Answer. Yes, sir; I suppose that his object was to get an answer from the Provost Marshals in his room.

Question. Who were the Provost Marshals in his room?

Answer. I could not see into his room. William Ellegood, of Georgetown; Mr. Lacey, from Baltimore Hundred, I think; Rhodes Hazzard, from Seaford; Garrett Layton, from Bridgeville; Labal Lyons, John L. Bacon, I think, from Laurel, were the Provost Marshals.

Question. Have you since understood those men to be the Provost Marshals for their several Hundreds?

Answer. I have.

Question. Were all the persons in the room with Major General Wool, at the time you solicited the interview with him, members of one political party?

Answer. Yes, sir.

Question. Of what political party were they members?

Answer. They call themselves the Union party.

Question. Do you say that you and Dr. McFerran, as a committee of the Democratic party, desired permission to enter that room to see General Wool?

Answer. I do, sir.

Question. Were you admitted, or were you refused admission?

Answer. We were refused admission.

Question. By whom were you refused?

Answer. By William Ellegood and Mr. Lacey, who were standing at the door.

Question. What was the answer given at the time of your refusal, as nearly as you can recollect?

Answer. That we had no business with General Wool, or any of our party.

Question. Whom did you understand them to mean by "any of your party?"

Answer. The Democratic party.

Question. When you did obtain an interview, how much time did General Wool devote to you as the representatives of the Democratic party?

Answer. The first interview was not more than two minutes, I suppose; the second, after he returned from the room, I do not think exceeded fifteen minutes.

Question. How long was General Wool in private conference with the Provost Marshals, of whom you have spoken?

Answer. I think, about three hours.

Question. Did you say that during all that time no persons other than members of the Republican party were admitted to his presence?

Answer. Yes, sir; a guard of soldiers were placed at the door after we made the second attempt; Mr. Coulborn, a member of the Democratic party, who was attending to the lights, went in and out of the room, but was not permitted to remain.

Question. Was Mr. Coulborn the landlord of the house?

Answer. Yes, sir.

Question. Do you say that you had a conference that evening with the leading men of the Democratic party in that neighborhood?

Answer. Yes, sir.

Question. What seemed to be the effect of the presence of the soldiers?

Answer. There appeared to be a general timidity almost everywhere.

Question. Was the intimidation so great as to induce any members of the Democratic party seriously to propose to withdraw their ticket, and let the election go by default?

Answer. Yes, sir; there was such a proposition.

Question. Did the same intimidation seem to prevail among residents of that hundred on election day?

Answer. I think it did; more particularly in the morning.

Question. Did you vote on the 4th of November?

Answer. I did.

Question. Were there armed soldiers stationed at the polls?

Answer. Yes, sir; they were stationed on each side of the window, extending for some distance. They were mounted.

Question. Were their arms at their side or in their hands?

Answer. They had both carbines at their sides and sabres in their hands.

Question. Were they stationed in a position and were their arms in a position to produce greater intimidation than could have been produced in any other way?

Answer. Their swords were drawn ready for execution, in such a manner as to produce great intimidation; greater, I think, than they would have produced in any other way.

On motion of Mr. Williams,

The Committee adjourned until 9 o'clock to-morrow morning.

TUESDAY, Feb. 3, 1863, 9 o'clock, A.M.

Present Messrs. Saulsbury, Hitch, Slay, Stubbs, Williams, Waples, Horsey, and Cahall.

The examination of JOSEPH P. W. SHIPLEY was resumed, he being recalled.

By the Chairman:

Question. Who was acting as Provost Marshal that day in Seaford?

Answer. Rhodes Hazzard.

Question. What was his position in reference to the polls?

Answer. In front of the window, and near to it a greater part of the time.

Question. Did he appear to be, and was it generally understood that he was in command of the soldiers there that day?

Answer.   Yes, sir.

Question.   Who is Rhodes Hazzard?

Answer.   He is a resident of Seaford, and has been for a number of years. He is a member of the Republican party.

Question.   Are you well acquainted with Rhodes Hazzard?

Answer.   Yes, sir.

Question.   Is he an active and violent partizan?

Answer.   He is naturally not a very boisterous man, but so far as he has ability he uses it to his utmost for the success of his party.

Question.   You say he is a member of the Republican party?

Answer.   He is.

Question.   Do you know whether he had a private way by which members of his own party were brought up to vote?

Answer.   There was an opening on the side on which the man was stationed by the Republican party to challenge votes, through which I saw several during the day enter and vote.

Question.   Were those who entered through this opening understood to be Republicans?

Answer.   The class that I saw were what we term doubtful voters.

Question.   What do you mean by doubtful voters?

Answer.   Such as can be influenced.

Question.   Was it generally understood by the Democrats that day, that this opening of which you speak was for the accommodation of that class of voters?

Answer.   That was the impression.

Question.   Was it also understood that that way was kept open for the benefit of the Republican party?

Answer.   Yes, sir; it was generally crowded by leading Republicans, when there was any question as to voters' politics.

Question.   Was Mr. Rhodes Hazzard stationed on the same side of the window on which this opening was, of which you speak?

Answer.   I think he was more in front of the window.

Question.   Was there a similar opening on the opposite side of the window for the accommodation of doubtful voters?

Answer. No, sir; the cavalry were stationed close to the house. At one time, I remember, a gentleman was attempting to vote and a question was raised in regard to his age, of which I had some knowledge. I made an effort to get to the window between the cavalry and the house; one of the cavalry thrust his sabre into the house so as to prevent any one from passing on that side. The gentleman did not vote that day.

Question. Was he entitled to a vote?

Answer. He was entitled to a vote.

Question. Did you closely observe the voting that day?

Answer. I did, when I was at the polls; sometimes I was absent.

Question. Do you believe, from your observation and presence at the polls, that the Democrats had an equal chance with the Republicans in the election?

Answer. I think they had not.

Question. Are you not sure they had not?

Answer. Yes, sir.

Question. You have spoken of General Wool. Do you mean Major General Wool in the service of the United States?

Answer. Yes, sir.

Question. Were there any other soldiers present that day except those who came under his command on Monday?

Answer. Col. Wallace's regiment was there.

Question. You are a practising physician in that neighborhood, I believe. Are you not well acquainted and well known to the people of that section?

Answer. I am, sir.

Question. Can you say, from your knowledge of the people, whether there was or was not great intimidation on the part of the Democratic voters, especially in the morning of that day?

Answer. There was.

Question. Was the intimidation, in your judgment, so great as materially to change the result of the vote in that Hundred, that day?

Answer.   I am inclined to think that it was.

Question.   Are you not a Democrat?

Answer.   I am, sir.

Question.   Are you not in the confidence of the Democratic party, knowing all its principal plans and purposes?

Answer.   I am.

Question.   Did you ever hear an intimation of a desire or purpose on the part of the Democratic party to interfere with the polls on the 4th day of November last so as to prevent a fair election?

Answer.   I never did. The opposition had less cause to fear, more particularly in Seaford, from the Democrats, than the Democrats had from them, for we had been deprived of our arms belonging to the United States some time previous to the election, whilst they were permitted to retain theirs.

Question.   If there had been any intention or purpose on the part of the Democratic party to interfere with the polls on the last election day, would you not, from your position in the party, certainly have known it?

Answer.   I should.

Question.   Do you know any other fact bearing on this subject, which you have not related?

Answer.   Not that I remember.

Question.   You have spoken of a reception address delivered by Mr. Platt, on the occasion of the arrival of General Wool with his troops at Seaford. I ask you, who is Mr. Platt?

Answer.   A young man, about eighteen years of age; not a resident of this State.

Question.   Do you say that he is not a native of the State, and not a voter in the State?

Answer.   He is not a native of the State, and not a voter in the State.

Question.   Do you know of what section of the country, or of what State, he is a native?

Answer. He is a native of one of the New England States.
Question. Is he in business at Seaford?
Answer. His father is in business at Seaford. He is assisting his father.
Question. In what business is his father engaged?
Answer. In canning oysters.
Question. Is he understood to be there only temporarily?
Answer. He and his father are there only temporarily, coming in September to can oysters during the winter, and returning in the spring.

JOS. P. W. SHIPLEY.

On motion,
The Committee adjourned until 7 ½ o'clock this evening.

SAME DAY, 7 ½ o'clock, P.M.

Committee met pursuant to adjournment.
Present—Messrs. Saulsbury, Cahall, Hitch, Slay, Stubbs, Williams, Waples, and Horsey.

JOHN SORDEN, sworn and examined.

By the Chairman:
Question. Where do you reside?
Answer. I reside in Georgetown, in Sussex County.
Question. Were you a candidate on the Democratic ticket last fall?
Answer. Yes, sir.
Question. Where did you vote?
Answer. I voted at Georgetown.
Question. Were you about the polls during most of that day?
Answer. Yes, sir; nearly all day.
Question. Did you observe anything unusual and different from what you have heretofore seen, on the day of the election?

Answer.   Yes, sir.

The Chairman.   Please state what it was.

Answer.   Very soon after the polls were opened there were soldiers stationed at the window, with drawn swords, there being five or six on each side, leaving an alley for persons to walk up and vote. The two farthest from the window kept their swords across each other, unless it was when a person went in to vote; they then raised them sufficiently for persons to pass to the window, and again crossed them until the person had voted and wished to return out the alley. They then held up their swords and let him out. There was also a soldier on horseback, who rode up and down the ground, inside of the enclosure of the Court House, with sword in hand, during most, if not all the time of voting.

Question.   Did you ever before see soldiers at the polls?

Answer.   No, sir.

Question.   How old a man are you?

Answer.   I am a little over sixty.

Question.   You have been a voter over forty years?

Answer.   I cast my first vote in 1823.

Question.   You never, before last fall, witnessed the presence of soldiers at the polls on election day?

Answer.   I have seen men in the service at the polls, but not as soldiers.

Question.   What effect had the presence of the soldiers at the polls that day, upon the voters of that Hundred?

Answer.   I think it had the effect to intimidate a great many persons. They arrested at least three, put two of them in jail and kept them there until Friday. There were others that left the election for fear of being arrested; I think, about six of as active working-men as the Democrats had in that Hundred.

Question.   Did those persons who left the ground, leave before voting?

Answer.   No, sir; they left after they had voted.

Question.   Who were the persons arrested of whom you have

spoken?

Answer. One was named Alfred Hart, another, Oliver Greenly, and another, Peter Hart. Peter Hart was soon released.

Question. Were they Democrats, or Republicans?

Answer. They were Democrats.

Question. For what were they arrested?

Answer. I am not able to answer that question.

Question. Had they voted before their arrest?

Answer. Two of them had voted. Alfred Hart attempted to vote on age; his vote was disputed and he was sent or went home for the family record; and before he could get back to the polls he was arrested and did not get to vote.

Question. Did the persons of whom you have spoken as having gone into the woods, go through intimidation?

Answer. That is what they told me.

Question. How long did they remain from their homes?

Answer. About three days.

Question. Did the presence of the soldiers in Georgetown, on the day of the election, produce great disturbance and annoyance in the community there generally?

Answer. Yes sir; among the private portion of the citizens, the soldiers having been straggling about over the town.

Question. Was there better order observed on the election day than you have generally seen heretofore?

Answer. It was pretty much the same during the time of voting.

Question. You were a candidate on the Democratic ticket?

Answer. Yes, sir.

Question. I ask you whether you ever heard an intimation of a desire on the part of the Democratic party to interfere with the polls at the last election, so as to prevent a fair election?

Answer. No, sir.

Question. Have you stated all that you know in reference to the interference of the military, on the 4th day of November last, with the election?

Answer. I think I have.

Question. Who was in command of the soldiers around the polls at Georgetown that day?

Answer. I did not know until some time after the voting had gone on. I heard Judge Layton call William Ellegood, who did not seem to hear him at the first call; he then called him "Marshal;" Mr. Ellegood then heard him. They had some private conversation. This was the first of my knowing who the Provost Marshal was.

Question. Did you understand that Mr. William Ellegood was in command of the soldiers there?

Answer. No, sir; I did not understand so; I, of course, presumed it.

JOHN SORDEN.

JOHN B. WINGATE, sworn and examined.

By the Chairman:

Question. Mr. Wingate, were you ever the bearer of a message to Col. Wallace, or any other person, requesting him to come, or send the soldiers of his command, or any portion of them, into this State, on the 4th day of November last, or about that time?

Answer. I carried a letter to Col. Wallace. After he read the letter, he intimated to me what the purport of it was.

Question. Who gave you the letter?

Answer. I could not say. It was given to me at Laurel. Some other person came to me and asked me if I had the letter. I said I had. He then said it was all right.

Question. Who was this other person of whom you speak?

Answer. I think it was John L. Bacon.

Question. Who is John L. Bacon?

Answer. He is a man living at Laurel, or near there.

Question. Do you know whether he was the Provost Marshal at Laurel on election day?

Answer. I do not, of my own knowledge.

Question. Will you please to state what Col. Wallace told you of the purport of the letter which you carried to him?

Answer. He remarked to me that it seemed, from the purport of the letter, that we were about to have trouble up in Delaware on the election day, and that he was requested to come up into Delaware with what force he could, to protect the polls on election day.

Question. Did you learn from him who was the author of that letter which you conveyed to him?

Answer. I do not think I did.

Question. Have you no idea who was the author of the letter?

Answer. I have an idea.

Question. Who do you suppose, from all you know in regard to the letter, was the author?

Answer. I think it was Jacob Moore.

Question. Why do you believe that Jacob Moore was the author of the letter?

Answer. My impression is that I was told so by John L. Bacon.

Question. Are you acquainted with the hand-writing of Jacob Moore?

Answer. I am not.

Question. Do you know Jacob Moore personally?

Answer. I do, sir.

Question. Was it not he who gave you that letter?

Answer. I could not say.

Question. Were you charged particularly in relation to the delivery of that letter?

Answer. Whoever gave it to me wished me to deliver it in person.

Question. Are you sure that you never conveyed a verbal message from Bridgeville to Col. Wallace, in relation to bringing soldiers into this State?

Answer.   I never did.

Question.   Were you ever the bearer of a message, written or verbal, from Col. Wallace, to any person in this State, in reference to bringing soldiers into this State?

Answer.   Never, sir.

Question.   Do you know anything other than what you have stated, in relation to the visit of soldiers in the service of the United States to this State, on the 4th day of November last?

Answer.   Yes, sir; Colonel Wallace and a portion of his command came up to Seaford from Salisbury on Monday, the 3^{d} of November. I came up in the train as they came, to Seaford, and I returned with the train. They got out there, and the train returned to Salisbury.

Question.   Do you know at whose solicitation soldiers in the service of the United States were brought into this State on the last election day?

Answer.   Nothing more than what I have stated in reference to the letter.

Question.   Did no individuals in this State ever say to you that they had solicited soldiers to come into this State, and that they had done it on their own responsibility?

Answer.   No, sir.

J. B. WINGATE.

PETER MARTIN, sworn and examined.

By the Chairman:

Question.   Where do you reside?
Answer.   In Sussex County, about two miles below Georgetown.
Question.   Did you vote on the last election day?
Answer.   Yes, sir.
Question.   Where?
Answer.   At Georgetown.

Question.   Did you observe anything unusual and different from what you had ever seen before, around the polls that day?

Answer.   Yes, sir. As I went into Georgetown I saw six or eight soldiers stationed at the window.

Question.   How were they stationed?

Answer.   They formed a line on each side, with a small alley between them. Their swords were drawn.

Question.   Had their presence there, with drawn swords, as you have described, the effect to intimidate the voters there, or any portion of them?

Answer.   Yes, sir.

Question.   How many soldiers were in Georgetown that day, according to your best judgment?

Answer.   I think, from the horses I saw, there must have been thirty or forty.

Question.   You state that there were persons in Georgetown intimidated by the presence of the soldiers. Do you know any of them?

Answer.   Yes, sir.

Question.   Were any persons there so much intimidated as to be induced to leave the election ground?

Answer.   Yes, sir.

Question.   Please state who they were?

Answer.   Kendall Wingate, James Wingate, George Pepper, Alfred Kollock, myself, Coulter Hart, Dutton Hart, and Peter Pepper, who are all I remember.

Question.   Do you say that all these persons were induced by intimidation, on account of the presence of the soldiers, to leave the election ground sooner than they would otherwise have done?

Answer.   Yes, sir.

Question.   Where did they go?

Answer.   To the swamp.

Question.   Did they all go together, or in different directions?

Answer.   I believe they all did not start together, but we all, except two, got together that afternoon.

Question. Do you know what became of those two?

Answer. I saw them running into the swamp.

Question. Was it through fear of personal violence or injury from the soldiers, in the way of being deprived of their liberties or any other way, that those persons were induced to leave the polls and go to the swamp?

Answer. It was through fear of being arrested, I believe.

Question. Had any persons been arrested there that day?

Answer. Yes, sir.

Question. Who had been arrested?

Answer. Alfred Hart, Oliver Greenly, and Peter Hart.

Question. Do you know by whose order these arrests were made?

Answer. No, sir.

Question. Do you know the politics of those persons you have named as having been arrested, and also of those persons who were induced to leave the election grounds and go into the woods?

Answer. Yes, sir; they were sound Democrats—all of them.

Question. Had they, or any of them, been guilty of a breach of the peace, or any other act which would have justified their arrest?

Answer. No sir; not that I heard of.

Question. Were they influential and working-men of their party?

Answer. Yes, sir; we considered them the best working-men we had.

Question. Do you know who was the Provost Marshal at the polls in Georgetown that day?

Answer. Yes, sir. William Ellegood.

Question. Is Mr. Ellegood an active and violent partizan?

Answer. Yes, sir; he is so considered, I believe.

Question. To what party does he belong?

Answer. To what they call the Republican party, I believe.

Question. Did you notice him at or near the polls during the time you stayed that day?

Answer. I do not think I did; I recollect having seen him there, but I did not take much notice of him.

Question. Did you leave the election ground that day, from any intimation you had received that you would be likely to be arrested if you remained there?

Answer. Yes, sir.

Question. From whom did you receive that intimation?

Answer. From my brother and my son.

Question. Was there any attempt subsequently made to arrest you?

Answer. Yes, sir.

Question. When, and by whom?

Answer. On the day of the election. I started home as soon as I heard the news that they were going to arrest me. I got about three hundred yards of home and looked back and saw seven or eight soldiers, with Adolphus Ewing ahead of them, running their horses. I jumped into the ditch and remained there until I saw where they were going. I did not know whether they were going to my house or down into Dagsborough Hundred, until I saw them turn into our gate. I then started for the swamp. I looked around and saw two of them ride up through the yard; one of them stopped at the bed room door and the other at the cookhouse door. I could not see the others, as they were on the front side of the house.

Question. Have you since learned what they said or did while there that morning?

Answer. Yes, sir. Those who went up in front jumped off their horses, started into the house, Adolphus Ewing being ahead of them. My wife met them at the door and told them that Adolphus Ewing could not come in, that they were welcome to come in. They inquired if Mr. Martin was at home; she told them, no, sir. They said they were ordered by the commander to come out there to arrest him, and to do whatever Adolphus Ewing told them to do. My wife told them that they were welcome to search the house; they did so, went up stairs and searched every room above, she said, and below, went to the smoke-house, went to the insane apartments, and through the rooms of the poor, back to the house. My wife invited them in and asked them if they would take something to drink; they said they would; she then asked them to take some dinner; they said they would; she told them to take seats; they said no; they would stand up and eat. They ate their dinners and went into the sitting-room. The Lieutenant told my wife that he did not want to arrest me; that they had nothing against me; that she must not think hard of them; it was that damned rascal that stands at the gate who was the cause of their coming. Adolphus Ewing let my wife know he would have her arrested. The soldiers told him no; that they did not come out there to arrest ladies.

Question.   You are the keeper of the alms-house in Sussex County, are you?

Answer.   Yes, sir.

Question.   How did you manage to elude the soldiers after you saw them pass you and ride up to your house?

Answer.   I crawled down the ditch until I got to the swamp, about a quarter of a mile. I went into the swamp and remained there three days and nights.

Question.   Did you meet any other person out there?

Answer.   Yes, sir; I met Kendall Wingate, James Wingate, George Pepper, Alfred Kollock, Peter Pepper, and a man by the name of James Murphey, I believe. Charles Dickerson and Russell Dickerson, from Dagsborough Hundred, came to us. There were a dozen altogether.

Question.   I suppose you established for yourselves a temporary place of abode, did you not?

Answer.   Yes, sir; after it came dark.

Question.   What did you call your new home?

Answer.   Camp Martin.

Question.   Who is Adolphus Ewing, of whom you have spoken?

Answer.   He keeps the hotel at Georgetown.

Question.   Do you know to what political party he belongs?

Answer.   He belongs to the Republican party.

Question.   Was he in any way related to any candidate or candidates on the Republican ticket in Sussex County?

Answer.   Yes, sir; he was son-in-law of the candidate for Sheriff on that ticket.

Question.   Were all you gentlemen at "Camp Martin," who had run away from the polls, through fear of being arrested, Democrats?

Answer.   Yes, sir; we were all Democrats, and good ones, too.

PETER MARTIN.

On motion,

The Committee adjourned to 8 ½ o'clock to-morrow morning.

WEDNESDAY, February 4—8 ½ o'clock, A.M.

The Committee met pursuant to adjournment.

Present—Messrs. Saulsbury, Cahall, Hitch, Slay, Waples, and Horsey.

THOMAS PEPPER, sworn and examined.

By the Chairman:

Question.   Where do you reside?

Answer.   Near Georgetown, in Sussex County.

Question.   Did you vote on the last election day, and if so, where?

Answer.   Yes, sir; at Georgetown.

Question.   Did you observe anything unusual and different from what you had ever seen before, around the polls that day?

Answer.   Yes, sir. Soldiers were stationed on each side of the window, with drawn swords.

Question.   Did their presence, in that position, produce great intimidation among any class of the voters at that place?

Answer.   Yes, sir.

Question. Was any person arrested, or attempted to be arrested, there that day?

Answer. Yes, sir; Alfred Hart, Oliver Greenly, and Peter Hart; Peter Hart was soon released.

Question. Do you know whether any person was induced through intimidation to leave the election ground that day, earlier than usual?

Answer. Yes, sir; Kendall Wingate, James Wingate, James Murphy, Peter Pepper, George Pepper, Edward Smith, Alfred Kollock, Coulter Hart, and Dutton Hart. These are all I remember.

Question. Were all of those persons of whom you have spoken as having been arrested, and all those who, you say, were induced through intimidation to leave the election ground, members of one political party?

Answer. Yes, sir; they belonged to the Democratic party.

Question. Were they active, working men in the party?

Answer. The greater part of them were, I believe.

Question. Was their absence from the polls regarded by the members of the party generally, as a serious loss to them on that day?

Answer. Yes, sir.

Question. Do you know who was the Provost Marshal at Georgetown on that day?

Answer. William Ellegood.

Question. Is William Ellegood an active and violent partizan?

Answer. He is so considered, I believe.

Question. To what political party does he belong?

Answer. To the Republican party.

Question. Is George Pepper any relation of yours?

Answer. Yes, sir; he is my son.

Question. Do you know why he left the election ground that day?

Answer. He left through fear of being arrested.

Question. What caused that fear?

Answer. Some person, I do not now remember whom, came to me and told me that they were going to arrest him, I sent a man to him to tell him to leave.

Question. Had he been guilty of a breach of the peace or any other act which ought to have justified his arrest?

Answer. No, sir.

Question. Where were you on Saturday previous to the election?

Answer. In the afternoon I think I was at a political meeting about two miles below Georgetown. I was in Georgetown also.

Question. It has been said that there was a disturbance in Georgetown, and it has been used as a pretext for bringing soldiers into the State on election day. Do you know anything about that disturbance?

Answer. I did not see much of it. I was standing leaning against the fence on the square with Jonathan Tonohay; people were driving around the square with their wagons; one man had a flag in the wagon, which he dropped, brushing it over our heads; two men then began to fight—Alfred Kollock and Joseph Tucker. Kollock was a Democrat, Tucker a Republican. I stood by them until they quit fighting. I believe this was about all I saw.

Question. Do you recollect whether in lowering the flag, they knocked anybody's hat off?

Answer. I believe they did not. They came very near knocking mine off.

Question. Was or was not the lowering of the flag upon the heads of people as they passed along, the cause of the disturbance that day?

Answer. I think it was.

Question. Was there any disposition or desire on the part of the persons there assembled to insult the flag of the country?

Answer. I do not think there was.

Question. Do you say that, according to your best judgment, the whole of the disturbance was owing to the imprudent conduct of the persons in the wagon in lowering the flag upon the heads of persons as they passed around?

Answer. I think it was.

Question. Do you know any person who was in that wagon?

Answer.   I cannot say that I do, as it was dark.

Question.   You do not know, then, who held that flag-staff?

Answer.   I do not.

Question.   Was it understood then that persons in that wagon were all of one political party?

Answer.   Yes, sir; it was understood that they belonged to the Republican party.

THOMAS PEPPER.

JOHN D. RODNEY, sworn and examined.

By the Chairman:

Question.   Where do you reside?

Answer.   At Georgetown, in Sussex County.

Question.   Where were you on Saturday previous to the last general election?

Answer.   I was at Laurel, and also at Georgetown. I left Georgetown about 11 ½ o'clock that night, and went to Milford.

Question.   For what purpose did you go to Milford?

Answer.   I went to have a consultation with some of our friends in regard to the election.

Question.   Did you go to Milford to have a consultation in reference to bringing soldiers into this State?

Answer.   No, sir; I did not.

Question.   Had you no conference in reference to that subject while in Milford?

Answer.   Yes, sir; I talked with several persons in reference to that subject.

Question.   Please give their names?

Answer.   Joseph Truitt, James R. Lofland, Hiram W. McColley, William Lofland, of Georgetown, the late Sheriff; Nathaniel B. Smithers, George P. Fisher, and several others.

Question. Was it determined, so far as you gentlemen could effect it, that soldiers should be brought into the State on election day?

Answer. It was not on that day.

Question. Was this conference on Saturday or Sunday?

Answer. A part of it was on the Sabbath day. All the conversation I had with Mr. Smithers and Mr. Fisher was on Sunday.

Question. Could you have reached Milford before midnight after leaving Georgetown on Saturday night?

Answer. I reached there in about two hours, leaving Georgetown about 11 o'clock on Saturday night, which made my arrival at Milford after midnight.

Question. In view of these facts, was not the entire conference of which you have spoken on the Sabbath day?

Answer. I have stated that it was.

Question. Did you not understand definitely before you left Milford that day, that soldiers were to be brought into the State on election day?

Answer. I understood it then and before.

Question. When and from whom did you first receive information that soldiers were to be brought here?

Answer. I cannot state positively in relation to that matter. The first idea I had of troops being brought into this State on election day, was some two weeks after the little election. In consequence of the disturbance at the polls on the day after little election at Georgetown Hundred and at Broad Creek Hundred, and in consequence of other violent conduct as reported, it was deemed advisable to ask the General Government to send us troops to preserve the peace on election day.

Question. By whom was it deemed advisable?

Answer. I believe all the Union men of the county with whom I consulted. I don't remember whether William Cannon was one of the men—he may have been. Jacob Moore was one, William Ellegood another, and men of that party generally.

Question. What individuals in this county with whom you

conversed, desired it?

Answer. I would not like to say.

Question. Was George P. Fisher one of them?

Answer. He was. Nathaniel B. Smithers was one. I do not remember conversing with James R. Lofland. I remember, on reflecting, that he was. Hiram W. McColley was another. I don't remember any other from Dover. There may have been, as I was in Dover about that time. I do not remember that I conversed with Judge Harrington or Dr. Jump.

Question. Did you consult and determine as to who should be the Provost Marshals of Sussex County?

Answer. I did not. I received a part of their commissions the night I left Milford.

Question. Who gave you those commissions?

Answer. James R. Lofland.

Question. Name the persons for whom you received commissions?

Answer. For Broadkill Hundred, John C. Hazzard; for Lewes and Rehoboth Hundred, Label L. Lyons; Georgetown Hundred, William Ellegood; Dagsborough Hundred, Nathaniel H. Philips; Broad Creek Hundred, William H. Betts; Baltimore Hundred, Samuel W. Lacey.

Question. Were those commissions filled up at that time by persons in Milford, or were they filled up previously?

Answer. They were filled up when they came into my possession; I know not by whom.

Question. What time in the day on Sunday did you receive those commissions?

Answer. A little after dark.

Question. Do you know whether Mr. Lofland, with other gentlemen, had passed up and down the railroad on that day?

Answer. I understood that he did.

Question. Did you understand who passed up and down with him?

Answer. Mr. Smithers and Mr. Fisher left Milford with him.

Question. Do I understand you to say that it had been determined to bring soldiers into the State on election day?

Answer. It had been determined to ask the General Government to send them.

Question. Through what agency had it been determined to ask the General Government to send them?

Answer. I do not know that.

Question. Do you know, or have you ever heard, who it was that did solicit the General Government to send soldiers into this State?

Answer. I do not know that I have ever heard, other than what I have already stated.

Question. Was there no person appointed, to your knowledge, to make the request?

Answer. None, to my knowledge.

Question. Did you deliver, in person, the commissions to the Provost Marshals you have named?

Answer. I delivered one to John L. Hazzard and one to William Ellegood; the others I sent by special messengers.

Question. Do you know the politics of the Provost Marshals you have named, and if so, what are they?

Answer. They are all men belonging to the Union party.

J. D. RODNEY.

On motion of Mr. Williams,

The Committee adjourned until 7 ½ o'clock this evening.

SAME DAY, 7 ½ o'clock, P.M.

The Committee met pursuant to adjournment.

Present—Messrs. Saulsbury, Hitch, Cahall, Slay, Williams, Waples, and Horsey.

WILLIAM CANNON, sworn and examined.

By the Chairman:
Question. Mr. Cannon, where do you reside?
Answer. At Bridgeville.
Question. Are you the present Governor of this State?
Answer. I am.
Question. Were you a candidate for the office you now hold previous to the last election, and elected on that day?
Answer. I was.
Question. Where did you vote?
Answer. At Bridgeville.
Question. Were there soldiers in the service of the United States in Bridgeville on that day?
Answer. There were cavalry there, but I did not ask them whether they were in the service or not.
Question. Was it understood that they were in the service of the United States, or not?
Answer. It was so understood.
Question. Was there a Provost Marshal at Bridgeville that day?
Answer. I believe there was.
Question. Who was he?
Answer. Garrett S. Layton.
Question. Is Mr. Layton in your employ?
Answer. He is a clerk in my store, but not employed by me on election day.
Question. Do you know from whom he received his commission as Provost Marshal?
Answer. I do. From Edwin M. Stanton, Secretary of War.
Question. Do you know how that commission was conveyed to him?
Answer. I do not know that I do.
Question. Do you know on what day it was conveyed to him?

Answer. I first saw it on Sunday night, I think. I do not know when it was conveyed.

Question. Was it not, according to the best of your information, conveyed to him by Thomas F. Hawkins, who came down the railroad, on a hand car, on Sunday previous to the election?

Answer. Hawkins brought him a letter, as I was informed. I do not know more than that.

Question. Did not Mr. Hawkins, on the same day, convey and deliver to you, or leave at your house, a letter for you?

Answer. I do not recollect of his leaving any letter for me, or his having any for me.

Question. Do you know at whose solicitation troops were brought into the State, to be here on the day of the last General Election?

Answer. From facts and reasonable grounds of which I knew from responsible men in Baltimore and other Hundreds, that the secessionists in Maryland and Democrats in Delaware had threatened to take the polls in Baltimore and other Hundreds of Sussex County, and from the threatening of a man with an unlawful weapon at the little election in Broad Creek Hundred, that the Union men should not vote, induced me to write to Colonel Wallace, requesting him, if compatible with his official duty, to see that there was a fair election in Little Creek, Broad Creek, Dagsborough, and Baltimore Hundreds, for I feared that there would be a conflict between the Union men and those who intended to prevent them from voting.

Question. Will you state who were the responsible men in Baltimore and other Hundreds to whom you allude, and from whom you received the information, upon which you acted?

Answer. Their names are not on my mind now. I do not recollect their names. I had satisfactory information that Curtis W. Jacobs had threatened to come over from Maryland, and I believe he did come over on the 4th of November, to deter the Union men from voting on that day. I was informed that there were fifteen or twenty who did come over from Maryland on horseback for that purpose.

Question. When did you receive the information that Curtis W. Jacobs intended to come, and did come over from Maryland for the purpose of preventing a fair election?

Answer. I think I was informed about the fifteenth of October, and also about a week before the election, of his threatening to come over.

Question. Will you state from whom you received that information?

Answer. The citizens of Baltimore Hundred.

Question. Can you name any of them?

Answer. I do not like to answer certainly, as I might make a mistake.

Question. Do you say that you do not recollect any single individual who gave you that information?

Answer. Not to name him. I am certain I was told by several.

Question. Do you say that you cannot recollect any single individual who gave you that information, with sufficient accuracy to name him?

Answer. I cannot remember any one, with sufficient accuracy to name him.

Question. Do you recollect what your majority was in Baltimore Hundred at the last election?

Answer. Not exactly. I think it was about 230.

Question. Was that about the average majority for the Union or Republican Ticket?

Answer. I think it was about that. It might have been a few votes over.

Question. Do you know which party had a majority of election officers in that hundred at the last general election?

Answer. I was informed that the Union party had, but I could not tell who told me.

Question. Do you know at whose solicitation General Wool, with his forces, or a portion of them, came into this State on the day previous to the last election, and were present at the polls on election day?

Answer.   I do not.

Question.   What man was it, in Broad Creek Hundred, of whom you have spoken, as having acted badly and having threatened to prevent Union men from voting on the day of the little election?

Answer.   I have forgotten the name.

Question.   Do you recollect about the number of votes polled in Baltimore Hundred on the day of the last general election?

Answer.   I think it was between 400 and 500.

Question.   Do you know whether any person from this State ever went to Washington with the view of soliciting soldiers to be brought into this State on the day of the last general election?

Answer.   I do not know.

Question.   Do you know whether any citizen of this State, being in Washington, did solicit soldiers in the service of the United States to be brought into this State, and to be present on the day of the last general election?

Answer.   I solicited the Secretary of War to send troops to the places I have named in Sussex County, to see that there was a fair election, and to keep the peace, while I was on other business at Washington.

Question.   How long was this previous to the day of the last general election?

Answer.   About two or three weeks.

Question.   Do you know whether any person other than yourself made the same request?

Answer.   It is my impression that Mr. George P. Fisher made the same request. I do not remember any other person who made the request.

Question.   Was George P. Fisher a candidate on the ticket with you for election last fall?

Answer.   He was.

Question.   Was the instance which you have named the only time that you or any other person solicited the Secretary of War to send troops to be here on the day of the last general election?

Answer.   I think I solicited him once before. Soon after the Inspectors election I was informed of a man being injured at Georgetown and at Milford, and was fearful that there would be trouble at the general election, if there was not a police force.

Question.   Were the two instances which you have named the only times when you or any other person, so far as you know, solicited United States forces to be sent into the State, and to be here on the day of the last general election?

Answer.   I may have asked the Secretary of War more than twice. I do not now recollect.

Question.   Do you say that you do not know any person but George P. Fisher and yourself who ever made the request that troops should be in this State on the day of the last general election?

Answer.   I do not now recollect any other person.

Question.   Did you at any time, or any other person, so far as you know, ever write to the Secretary of War requesting him to send troops to be here on the day of the last general election?

Answer.   I do not recollect of myself or any other person writing for that purpose.

Question.   Were you at any time, between the day of the last little election and the day of the last general election, present at a meeting in Dover, at which the subject of bringing troops into this State was discussed?

Answer.   I do not recollect being at any meeting in Dover for that purpose.

Question.   Were you ever present, during the last campaign, at any meeting—I mean, not a meeting which convened upon call, but a meeting of several gentlemen together—in this State, or elsewhere, at which the subject of bringing troops into this State was discussed?

Answer.   I do not recollect any meeting. I was informed by various individuals of the necessity of troops being present to see that all sides should have a fair vote.

Question.   Will you state who those individuals were?

Answer. I think I recollect William H. Taylor. I think Samuel Lacey, of Baltimore Hundred, and John L. Bacon, in Little Creek, were others. There is no other individual on my mind.

Question. Do you know where William H. Taylor lives?

Answer. I think in Mispillion Hundred.

Question. Do you know whether he was the Provost Marshal in that Hundred, on the day of the last General Election?

Answer. I think I have been informed of that fact since the election

Question. Do you know where John L. Bacon resides?

Answer. I think he resides in Little Creek Hundred, in Sussex County.

Question. Do you know whether he was the Provost Marshal in that Hundred on the day of the last General Election?

Answer. I have been so informed since the election. I did not know previous to the election.

Question. Do you know where Samuel Lacey resides?

Answer. In Baltimore Hundred.

Question. Do you know whether he was the Provost Marshal for Baltimore Hundred on the day of the last General Election?

Answer. I have been so informed.

Question. Do you know of what political party William H. Taylor, John L. Bacon, and Samuel Lacey were members?

Answer. I think they are members of the Union party.

Question. Do you say that you solicited Colonel Wallace, by letter, to bring the troops under his command, or a part of them into this State, to be present on the day of the last General Election, and that you twice, and probably more frequently, solicited the Secretary of War to send troops into this State to be present on the same day, and that Mr. George P. Fisher made a similar request of the Secretary of War?

Answer. I wrote to Colonel Wallace on Saturday previous to the election, after I supposed that the Secretary of War would not send any. I had previously solicited the Secretary of War to send troops, and supposed they would be here before that time; but as they failed to come, I wrote to Wallace to send troops for the four hundreds I have mentioned. I think Mr. George P. Fisher made a similar request of the Secretary of War.

Question. Did you understand, at the time you wrote to Colonel Wallace, that the Secretary of War had refused or declined to send troops into this State?

Answer. I had received no recent information from him by letter or otherwise.

Question. When did you first receive definite information that the Secretary of War would, in compliance with your and Mr. Fisher's request, send troops into this State?

Answer. Not until I heard they were at Seaford.

Question. Had you no intimation that they would be there until you heard of their arrival?

Answer. I did not know whether they would come, for we expected they would be there before.

Question. Why did you expect they would have been there before?

Answer. We had assurances that the polls should be protected, so that every man could vote, when I was at Washington the Secretary of War said he would send a police force to see that there was no riot.

Question. Did this police force consist of infantry, cavalry, or artillery?

Answer. He did not say, and I did not ask him that I recollect.

Question. Do you know what was the object of appointing Provost Marshals for all the Hundreds of the two lower Counties of this State, where the soldiers were present?

Answer. I do not know.

Question. Do you know whether Provost Marshals are the proper officers for the command of a police force?

Answer. I have not made myself familiar with their duties.

Question. Do you know whether, previous to the last little election, all or most of the volunteer companies of the two lower

Counties of this State, who were commanded by Democrats, had been deprived of their arms?

Answer. I never saw any of them muster. It was reported that all the volunteer companies had their arms taken from them without regard to party.

Question. Do you not know, or was it not your understanding, that the volunteer companies commanded by Union men or Republicans, retained possession of their arms?

Answer. Not at the time the others were taken away, so far as I understood.

Question. Do you not know, or was it not your understanding, that the volunteer companies commanded by Union men, or Republicans, had possession of their arms on the day of the little election and between that time and the General Election?

Answer. I do not know of any. There may have been some in the County, but I do not recollect them.

The Chairman. You have stated that you requested Colonel Wallace to send troops into four Hundreds of Sussex County, viz: Broad Creek Hundred, Baltimore Hundred, Dagsborough Hundred, and Little Creek Hundred.

The Witness. Yes, sir; that is what I wrote to him on Saturday previous to the election.

Question. In the request you made to the Secretary of War to send troops, did you confine that request to the four Hundreds you have just named?

Answer. I did not designate the Hundreds. I left it to his own judgment, according to the best of my recollection.

By Mr. Cahall:

Question. Do you know at whose solicitation, or by whose direction, troops were sent into every Hundred of the two lower Counties, except Little Creek Hundred, in Kent; and Indian River

Hundred, in Sussex County?

Answer. I do not know.

Question. Do you know why troops were not sent to Indian River Hundred, in Sussex County; to Little Creek Hundred, in Kent County, or to any of the Hundreds in New Castle County?

Answer. I do not know.

Question. Do you know by what means the troops were conveyed from Seaford to the different Hundreds in Sussex and Kent Counties?

Answer. I do not know, but I might say it was reported that a part went on the railroad, and twenty cavalry came to Bridgeville and other parts of the County on their horses.

By the Chairman:

Question. Do you know by what means the baggage of the troops was conveyed from Seaford to Bridgeville, or to any other place in the County?

Answer. I believe I do not know.

Question. Did you send your wagon to Seaford to convey either the troops or their baggage to Bridgeville?

Answer. I sent my wagon to Seaford and it was placed at their disposal. It went empty and returned empty.

Question. Do you know who proposed or recommended to the Secretary of War the persons to be appointed Provost Marshals for the different Hundreds, in the two lower Counties of the State?

Answer. I do not.

Question. Do you know at whose expense the troops were sent to this State, to be present on the day of the last general election?

Answer. I suppose they were employed and paid by the General Government.

WILLIAM CANNON.

On motion of Mr. Waples,

The Committee adjourned until to-morrow morning at 8 ½ o'clock.

THURSDAY, February 5, 1863—8 ½ o'clock, A.M.

Committee met pursuant to adjournment.
Present—Messrs. Saulsbury, Hitch, Williams, Waples, and Horsey.

The examination of WILLIAM CANNON was resumed, he being recalled.

By the Chairman:
Question.   You have stated that you sent your wagon to Seaford, to be at the service of the soldiers; that it went empty and returned empty. On what day did your wagon return?
Answer.   I sent it on Monday, the 3^d of November, to Seaford, at the request of Colonel Wallace, to convey his troops or baggage to such points as he might direct; and it returned empty, to the best of my knowledge, on Monday evening.
Question.   Did you, or did you not, at the time or times you solicited the Secretary of War to send soldiers into this State, give him assurances, or say to him, that by the aid of the military the election in this State could be carried for the Union or Republican ticket?
Answer.   I gave him the information that persons in various parts of the State, Democrats and Secessionists, had threatened to take the polls in various Hundreds in said State and prevent the Union men from voting that day; that I was informed by Mr. N. B. Smithers, at the Union meeting at Laurel, that numbers of persons hurrahed for Jeff. Davis, Stonewall Jackson, and Beauregard, and there were several fights by the parties present during his speech there; that I believed there could not be a fair vote of the people without protection at the polls, and that all I desired was a fair, honorable election, and that every man who should vote who had a right to vote, and that nobody should prevent them; and that I was aware that several Democrats and Secessionists at Bridgeville were armed and had been practising shooting with revolvers; one told me that he could hit a dollar; and that I had reason to believe they were

armed in other parts of the State, and that without a police force there would be very likely a collision between the excited parties. I did not say to the Secretary of War that the election could be carried for the Union party by the aid of military.

Question.   Who are they at Bridgeville that you call Secessionists and say were armed?

Answer.   James W. Hessey was one; I believe that James B. Adams was armed, and that Hessey had bought various lots of revolvers, as I was credibly informed.

Question.   Will you please to name the persons for whom Hessey purchased the revolvers of which you have spoken?

Answer.   I am not able to designate the persons. I think that Asa Dawson, at Bridgeville, could tell.

Question.   Do you not know that other persons, Union men and Republicans, in and around Bridgeville, had pistols and other arms in their possession; also, whether your son, William L. Cannon, had not arms in his possession?

Answer.   If any Union man or Republican was armed I do not know it; neither had my son, William L. Cannon, arms in his possession, on that day, to my knowledge.

Question.   Do you not know that William O. Redden, previous to the time of his appointment as Colonel, was captain of a volunteer company at Bridgeville, and whether that company did not retain possession of their arms?

Answer.   I did not recollect, last night, any company in the Hundred, but since then, I recollect William O. Redden was captain of a volunteer company called the Governor's Guards, which was voluntarily disbanded, by giving up their arms soon after he was appointed Colonel of the Third Delaware Regiment.

Question.   To whom did they give up their arms?

Answer.   I do not recollect. There was some one appointed. I am not sure whether it was Richard Cannon or some other person. It was my impression it was he. Richard Cannon is a half-brother of mine and a clerk in my store. The arms were stacked up in my store, to be delivered over to the proper authorities. I believe those arms are in my store now.

Question. Of what political party is Richard Cannon a member?

Answer. He called himself a Douglas Democrat. I believe he voted a Union ticket last fall.

Question. Do you not know that Henry L. Hopkins, at Seaford, was a captain of a volunteer company at that place, and that his company retained possession of their arms until after the day of the last general election?

Answer. I understood he was a captain of a company at Seaford nearly two years ago, and have not heard of their drilling for over a year, and supposed that they had disbanded also.

Question. Do you not know that they held a celebration on the 4th day of July last at Brown's woods, and paraded with their arms on that occasion?

Answer. I do not; and if I have been so informed, it is entirely off my mind.

Question. You have stated that you applied to the Secretary of War and to Colonel Wallace for soldiers to be sent into this State on the day of the last general election. I ask you if you do not know, if soldiers were necessary to be present in this State to preserve the public peace at a time when the Legislature was not in session and could not be convened, that the Executive of the State was the proper channel through which to apply to the General Government for military protection?

Answer. I do not; and if I had, I would have applied to him, and failing there, I would have applied as I did.

Question. Do you know, directly or indirectly, at whose instance the arms in the arsenal of the State were removed from the arsenal?

Answer. I do not know, by report or otherwise. I have no knowledge who gave the order.

Question. Do you not know that Mr. Hessey, of whom you have spoken as having purchased revolvers for persons in and around Bridgeville, had left the State before the little election, and did not return until just before the general election?

Answer. My impression was that he was at the little election and left, and it was reported that he had taken three different carriage-loads of men for the Southern army, and that he returned to Bridgeville and the neighborhood at different times between the little and general election.

Question. Did you understand that he went over to the Southern army in his carriage?

Answer. I understood that he went at night over into Maryland with men for the Southern army.

Question. Who informed you that he went over into Maryland, in the night, with men for the Southern army?

Answer. It was the common report.

Question. Can you not recollect any individual who gave you that information?

Answer. I cannot name the individual, but I believe that Henry Hitch and John D. Dilworth could name them.

Question. Do you mean to say that either Henry Hitch or John D. Dilworth ever gave you such information?

Answer. I believe they know the facts. They did not tell me.

Question. Do you not know, or have you not understood, that Mr. Hessey left that neighborhood, and kept out of the way, through fear of being arrested?

Answer. Such was the report.

Question. I ask you whether your belief that Mr. Hitch and Mr. Dilworth knew of Hessey's going over into Maryland with men for the Southern army is founded upon any definite information or upon mere rumor?

Answer. I believe it is founded upon facts.

Question. Will you state the facts?

Answer. I am not in possession of the facts. I believe that Mr. Dilworth said that his son, Robert G. Dilworth, went to the Southern army without his consent.

Question. Did he say that Hessey carried his son?

Answer. He did not say who took him.

Question. You have stated that one reason for your application to the Secretary of War for troops to be sent into this State, was founded upon representations made to you by Nathaniel B. Smithers, of disturbances which occurred at a public meeting at Laurel. I desire to know when it was that Mr. Smithers told you this?

Answer. Soon after the first meeting we held at Laurel on Saturday.

Question. How long after that meeting was it that Mr. Smithers gave you this information?

Answer. A few days.

Question. Had you not applied to the War Department for troops to be sent into this State previous to receiving that information from Mr. Smithers?

Answer. It is likely I had, previously and afterwards.

WILLIAM CANNON.

WILLIAM ELLEGOOD, sworn and examined.

By the Chairman:

Question. Were you the Provost Marshal in Georgetown Hundred on the day of the last general election?

Answer. Yes, sir.

Question. From whom and when did you receive your commission as Provost Marshal?

Answer. Edwin M. Stanton, Secretary of War. My commission was dated the 1st day of November; it was received on the 2^{d} day of November.

Question. When did you receive the first information that you were to be appointed Provost Marshal?

Answer. When I received the commission.

Question. Do you know now at whose instance Provost Marshals were appointed in the different hundreds in the two lower counties in this State?

Answer. I do not, sir.

Question. Are you familiar with the handwriting in which your commission was filled up?

Answer. I am not.

Question. As Provost Marshal had you command of the troops or soldiers that were stationed at Georgetown?

Answer. Under the instructions issued from General Wool to Captain Sneed to proceed to Georgetown with a squad of forty men in his command under the charge of the Provost Marshal, to perform such duties as he might require, using no coercion or intimidation, taking nothing from the citizens unless voluntarily given or paid for.

Question. Had you charge of the troops under those instructions?

Answer. I had. At the time they arrived at Georgetown, I was in bed. I had nothing to do with the troops and gave no command until an hour after the election had opened.

Question. Did you, at any time that day, place any portion of the troops under your command in charge of the window at which the votes were taken?

Answer. I found two soldiers at the window before I gave any command at all. At that time the voting had commenced and continued, I suppose, half an hour. The window was very much crowded—every prospect of disturbance. I was asked by some of the Democrats to clear the window, to put soldiers on each side, so as to leave an open space for the voters to pass through. Then I ordered it to be done, and more soldiers to be brought, leaving a space in front of the window, on each side, for the two opposite parties to place a man of their own choice to challenge votes at the window, assuring them several times during the day, and at all times when called upon, that every man should vote his sentiments without regard to party so far as was in my power, and that promise was carried out to a letter.

Question. Did the soldiers placed at the window stand in position with drawn swords or sabres?

Answer. Their swords were unsheathed, I believe, with points down by their sides, except two who were at the entrance of the passage with crossed swords. When a voter came to vote, the swords were raised for him to pass through.

Question. As Provost Marshal that day, did you order the arrest of any citizens in that hundred?

Answer. I did not.

Question. As Provost Marshal did you order a squad of soldiers, headed by Adolphus Ewing, to proceed to the Almshouse and arrest Mr. Peter Martin, the keeper thereof?

Answer. No, sir; and no squad went for such purpose.

Question. For what purpose did they go?

Answer. It was reported that Aaron Dodd, who had always voted against the Democrats, and was a strong Union man, and is yet, was kidnapped or cooped, and debarred of his privilege of coming to the election, and he was then believed to be at the Almshouse. This squad of soldiers were sent to the Almshouse to bring him, if found, to Georgetown; turn him out on the square; let him come to the polls and vote as he pleased. Mr. Ewing was requested to show these men, being strangers, and not knowing where the Almshouse was, with positive instructions not to arrest Mr. Martin, or to interfere with him in any way.

Question. Did they find Mr. Dodd at the Almshouse?

Answer. They did not.

Question. Who was the person that had represented that Mr. Dodd was in the Almshouse?

Answer. Peter Dodd, the brother of this Mr. Dodd, believed it. He had no positive proof.

Question. Who were admitted into the room which General Wool made his headquarters at the hotel of John Coulborn, at Seaford, on Monday preceding the election?

Answer. None that I know except the officers under his

command, John L. Coulborn, the proprietor of the house and a Democrat, and the Provost Marshals: Jesse P. Conoway, from Nanticoke Hundred; North West Fork Hundred, Garrett S. Layton; Broad Creek Hundred, William H. Betts; Little Creek Hundred, John L. Bacon; Dagsborough Hundred, Nathaniel H. Phillips; Baltimore Hundred, Samuel W. Lacey; Lewes and Rehoboth Hundred, Labal L. Lyons; Broadkiln Hundred, John C. Hazzard; Georgetown Hundred, myself; from Seaford, Rhodes Hazzard, and, as I hear, Alfred R. Hall, from Cedar Creek Hundred.

 Question. Do you know to what political party these men belong?
 Answer. I believe they all belonged to the Union party.
WILLIAM ELLEGOOD.

The examination of JOSEPH P. H. SHIPLEY was resumed, he having been recalled.

 Question. Do you know of the existence of a volunteer company at Seaford?
 Answer. Yes, sir.
 Question. Who was its commander?
 Answer. Henry L. Hopkins.
 Question. Do you know whether Henry L. Hopkins' company had possession of their arms at the time of the last general election, and still retain possession of them?
 Answer. They had at that time, and still retain possession.
 Question. Do you know to what political party Henry L. Hopkins belonged?
 Answer. He belonged to the Union party; to what I term the Republican party.
 Question. Do you know whether the members of his company generally belonged to the same party?
 Answer. They do, sir.

Question. Do you know of the existence of another volunteer company at Seaford, previous to the last general election?

Answer. There was one some time previous.

Question. By whom was that company commanded?

Answer. By Captain E. L. Martin.

Question. To what political party did Captain E. L. Martin belong?

Answer. He belonged to the Democratic party.

Question. Had Captain E. L. Martin's company possession of their arms at the time of the last general election, and do they still retain possession of them?

Answer. No, sir; they were deprived of them some time, at least six months, before the election.

Question. By whom, and under whose authority, were they deprived of their arms?

Answer. By a company of United States soldiers, acting under the authority of General Lockwood.

Jos. P. H. Shipley.

On motion,
The Committee adjourned until 7 o'clock this evening.

Same Day, 7 o'clock, P.M.

The Committee met pursuant to adjournment.

Present—Messrs. Saulsbury, Hitch, Slay, Williams, Waples, and Horsey.

William F. Jones, sworn and examined.

By the Chairman:

Question. Were you the late Sheriff of Sussex County?

Answer. Yes, sir.

Question. Where do you reside?

Answer. I reside in Georgetown, Sussex County.

Question. Did you vote on the day of the last general election, and if so, where?

Answer. I did, at the Sheriff's office, in Georgetown.

Question. Did you observe anything unusual and different from what you have ever seen before, about the polls that day?

Answer. Nothing, except that soldiers were there—something which I never saw before that day.

Question. How were the soldiers stationed in reference to the polls?

Answer. In the morning, I believe, there were two stationed there at first on each side of the window; in a short time afterwards there were some ten or fifteen more placed in front of the window, and divided so as to make an entrance to the window, the outermost ones with drawn swords; there was one on horseback with a drawn sword, passing backward and forward near the entrance.

Question. Was the position of the soldiers with drawn swords calculated to produce great intimidation among the voters there that day?

Answer. I think their presence, with their swords, did.

Question. Was the intimidation produced so great as to induce a number of the active and influential Democrats to leave the election ground earlier than usual?

Answer. Yes, sir; I think so; I may say I know it.

Question. Were any arrests made there that day by the soldiers?

Answer. Yes, sir; three that I know of.

Question. Do you know whether they had all voted before they were arrested?

Answer. I think one of them had; I think the others did not vote at all.

Question. Are you not an active and prominent Democrat in your county, knowing all the principal plans and purposes of the party?

Answer. I believe I generally know what is going on.

Question. Have you ever heard an intimation of any plan or purpose on the part of the Democratic party to interfere with the polls so as to prevent a fair election on the day of the last general election?

Answer. No, sir.

Question. If there had been any such desire or purpose, from your position in the party, would you not have certainly known it?

Answer. I think I should.

Question. To what political party did the persons you have named as having been arrested, and also the persons who were induced to leave the election ground, belong?

Answer. To the Democratic party.

Question. Were they active working-men of the party?

Answer. I think they were.

Question. Do you know upon whose order the arrests were made there that day?

Answer. I do not.

Question. Do you know who made the arrests?

Answer. I saw them in charge of the soldiers.

Question. Do you know where they were confined after they were arrested?

Answer. They were first carried to Mr. Ewings' hotel, I think. Then the Captain came to me to know if I would not receive them in jail. I was the keeper of the jail, and lived in it. I told him that I did not believe we had room for them without changing some of the prisoners who were there. He told me that I must go with him to the prison, that he might see whether there was not room for them, and did so. I changed some of the prisoners so as to let them have the room; two of the arrested parties were brought by a file of men to the prison and there lodged.

Question. Did he present you a regular commitment from any civil officer acting under this State or the General Government?

Answer. He did not.

Question. Did you understand him to demand of you a place in the public jail of that county in which to lodge those persons?

Answer. Yes, sir.

Question. Do you know how long it was after those persons were put in prison before affidavits were filed against them?

Answer. I am inclined to think that it was on Thursday, two days after their arrest, that affidavits were filed against them.

Question. Did you ever see the affidavits that were filed against those parties?

Answer. I saw an instrument in writing purporting to be one.

Question. By whom were the affidavits made?

Answer. By a man by the name of Wingate Matthews.

Question. Was this Wingate Matthews a soldier?

Answer. He might have been; I could not say; he had been off a company; I think the Third Delaware had come home, and it was said he was discharged.

Question. Have you stated all you know in reference to this matter?

Answer. I know they had a guard placed at my door on Thursday after the election and refused me entrance into my house. I told them that I was the keeper of that house, and that I should go in, and they let me go in, or I went in.

Question. Do you know the purpose for which that guard was stationed at your door?

Answer. I do not; unless it was to guard those men who were in there. I came out and asked who placed them there. They told me they believed it was one Provost Lacey. I inquired of them if they knew where Major Burn was. They told me they did not, but supposed he was at the hotel. I then went in search of him. I wanted them taken away.

Question. How long were those persons who were arrested by the soldiers that day kept in prison?

Answer. I believe from Tuesday until Friday or Saturday morning.

Question. Had you, as Sheriff of the county, at any time during the last year, charge of any part of Sussex County's quota of the State arms?

Answer. I believe I had not. The Commissary had charge of them. He acted under the Governor.

Question. Do you know whether he retained possession of those arms up to the time of the last general election?

Answer. He did not up to that time. They were taken away from him.

Question. When and by whom were they taken?

Answer. I think it was in April of last year.

Question. Was it either during the April or October term of the Court previous?

Answer. I think so. They were taken away by a company of soldiers. All the arms, among which were two cannon, were taken. I do not know by what authority they acted. They were commanded, I understood, by Captain McCullough.

Question. Were there at any time during the last two years any organized volunteer companies in Georgetown, and if so will you state how many?

Answer. I think there were two companies at one time.

Question. About what time?

Answer. I think they were organized in 1861 or 1862, I do not remember exactly.

Question. Were both or either of those companies in existence at the time of the last general election?

Answer. One of them, I think, was disbanded. Perhaps both were disbanded.

Question. By whom were they commanded?

Answer. One was commanded by Captain Paynter, the other by Dr. Marshall.

Question. Do you know what was the cause of the disbanding of Captain Paynter's company?

Answer. I suppose it was because he was arrested, and the guns for which he had given bonds were taken away.

Question. How long was this before the last general election?

Answer. At the same time the guns were taken from the arsenal.

Question. Were Captain Marshall's arms taken from his company at the same time?

Answer. I do not think they were.

Question. Is it not understood that Captain Marshall's company still retain possession of their guns?

Answer. I do not know that they do. I know they have them there and can take them when they choose. They are at Mr. Ewing's hotel.

Question. At what time were the arms taken from Captain Paynter's company, and also from the arsenal at Georgetown?

Answer. It was in October, 1861.

Question. Do you know whether Captain Marshall had a large number of fire-arms sent to him just previous to the last election?

Answer. Arms were brought there for that company.

Question. To what political party do Captain Marshall and most of that company belong?

Answer. To the Union or Republican party.

Question. To what political party do Captain Paynter and most of the persons who constituted his company belong?

Answer. To the Democratic party.

WM. F. JONES.

ALFRED P. ROBINSON, sworn and examined.

By the Chairman:

Question. What is your occupation, and where do you reside?

Answer. I am an Attorney at Law, practising in Georgetown. My place of residence is in Sussex County, in this State.

Question. Did you vote on the day of the last general election?

Answer. I did, sir. I voted at Georgetown, in Georgetown

Hundred, in Sussex County.

Question. Did you observe anything unusual and different from what you had ever seen before, around the polls on election day?

Answer. Yes, sir; and what I never expected to see in the State of Delaware, and hope never to see again. I saw an armed force of men take possession of the window, or the polls, on that day.

Question. Do you know by whose command they took possession of the window?

Answer. A short time after I had voted, myself, I heard Mr. William Ellegood, who, I understood, was acting as the Provost Marshal on that day, say to one of the persons, "Officer, take a squad of men and take charge of that window," at the same time pointing to the window where the ballots were deposited.

Question. Who is William Ellegood, and what are his politics?

Answer. He belongs to the Union or Republican party, and it is generally understood that he voted the ticket of that party.

Question. Is he an active and violent politician?

Answer. He is a very active politician. I cannot say that he is very violent. He is generally considered one of the best politicians in the county.

Question. Will you state everything else that you know in reference to the presence of the soldiers in Georgetown on election day; when they came there, what they did, and when they left?

Answer. Very soon after the result of the little election was known, in our county there was a report in circulation that the government of the United States would send a military force into the county, to be present at the general election. I am not sure, but I think, it was on Monday night previous to the general election, one or more companies of mounted cavalry passed by my house into the town, and when I went into the town on the day of the election, I found this or some other cavalry company in front of the brick hotel then and now occupied by Adolphus P. Ewing; and as I went up to the window to vote, I walked by the side of the Court House, and as I approached the window where they were receiving the votes, one of these cavalry men, with his sabre hanging at his side, caught me by the left shoulder or arm and said that I must not go to the window. I told him that he had nothing to do there, and that I was going to the window to vote, and immediately went up to the window and voted. It was after I had voted, and not a great while after, that Mr. Ellegood ordered a squad of soldiers to take possession of the window. The place of voting at Georgetown is at the Court House, in the office occupied by the Sheriff of the County, at the east window of the office. There is a railing around the Court House some three feet high; this railing is about twenty-five or thirty feet from the window where the election was held. Both on the morning and afternoon of the election, I saw what I suppose you would call a mounted cavalryman, armed with a sabre, which was drawn, within the railing and next to the Court House and the place of voting, and marching up and down the length of the yard.

Question. Did the presence of the soldiers there produce great intimidation among the voters?

Answer. I think it did with a number of them. I am satisfied of the fact, that the presence of the soldiers caused a number of persons to leave the election ground earlier than they would otherwise have done. They left some time before the election closed. I know the fact, that up to the time that I voted, nor afterwards during the whole day, nothing had occurred to require the presence of an armed force from the government of the United States.

Question. Were the persons of whom you speak as having left the polls through intimidation, working and influential Democrats?

Answer. Yes, sir; I believe the most of them were; and they were all active Democrats upon the day of the election.

Question. Did the Republicans also appear to be intimidated by the presence of the soldiers?

Answer. No, sir.

Question. From your position as a lawyer, have you not always been an active and prominent Democrat, knowing all the principal plans and purposes of the Democratic party?

Answer. I have always been a Democrat. I cannot speak for my prominence in the party. I believe that I knew the plans and purposes of the party during the last campaign.

Question. Did you ever hear of an intimation of a desire or purpose on the part of the Democratic party to interfere with the polls on the day of the last general election, so as to prevent a fair election?

Answer. I never heard of such a report, except as coming from the Republican party.

Question. If there had been any such purpose, from your position in the party, would you not certainly have known it?

Answer. I think I should, sir.

Question. Will you state what you know in reference to volunteer companies in your town; how many, when they were organized, and when disbanded?

Answer. The first company organized in our town was, I think, a company raised by and was under the command of Caleb R. Layton, as captain. The company was called the "Sussex Guards," and was organized very soon after the John Brown raid in Virginia. This company, I believe, after furnishing themselves with clothes, was suffered to go to naught because they had not drilled within the time specified by the act of Assembly. Then there was another company formed under the command of Mr. Layton, or Dr. Marshall, I do not remember which. I know that Dr. Marshall subsequently had the command, and was captain of the company. There was also another company formed of which Caleb R. Paynter was captain. Mr. Paynter's company was furnished by order of the Governor, I believe, with guns from the armory at Georgetown. The company commanded by Dr. Marshall was furnished with Minnie muskets. Where those muskets came from I am unable to say.

Question. When was Captain Paynter's company disbanded?

Answer. It was either in the spring or fall term of the court in 1861.

Question. Do you know what caused the disbanding of that

company?

Answer.   Mr. Paynter was arrested and the arms taken from him by a government force.

Question.   Do you know whether Dr. Marshall's company was in existence at the time of the last general election?

Answer.   I do not think Dr. Marshall's company was in existence as an organized company at that time.

Question.   Had they possession of their arms at that time?

Answer.   I have understood that a portion of the arms of that company were in the possession of Captain John Waples, at Georgetown—I have heard so since the company was disbanded—and some of them in possession of Mr. Daniel J. Layton, who was a member of the company.

Question.   Were the arms of this company in Georgetown at the time of the last general election, and at the command of that company, so far as you understand?

Answer.   So far as I know it is generally understood that the arms which belonged to Dr. Marshall's first company are now in Georgetown or the neighborhood; but that the arms of the Home Guards, of which he is now the commander, are different, and I believe are kept, a portion of them, if not all of them, in the hotel occupied by Adolphus P. Ewing, and are used by the company every Saturday afternoon upon drill, I suppose.

Question.   Do you know to what political party Captain Marshall and the persons that constitute his company belong?

Answer.   To the Union or Republican party.

Question.   Do you know to what political party Captain Paynter and the persons who constituted his company belong?

Answer.   To the Democratic party.

Question.   Is it not understood that all the volunteer companies in Sussex County, commanded by Democrats, were disarmed previous to the last general election by order of the General Government?

Answer.   It was so understood. I would also state that at the time they took the arms from Captain Paynter's company, they took two cannon, one of which belonged to Gardiner F. Wright, and the other to George W. Green. Those cannon had been used for 4th July purposes.

Question. Is it not also understood that the volunteer companies, commanded by Republicans, retained possession of their arms?

Answer. It is so understood. I know the fact that at the time the arms of Captain Paynter's company were taken from them, those belonging to Captain Marshall's company were not taken from them.

ALFRED P. ROBINSON.

EDWARD WOOTTEN, sworn and examined.

By the Chairman:

Question. What is your occupation, and where do you reside?

Answer. I am one of the Judges of the Superior Court of this State, and I reside in Georgetown, in Sussex County.

Question. Did you vote on the day of the last general election, and if so, where?

Answer. I voted in Georgetown, in Georgetown Hundred.

Question. Did you observe anything unusual and different from what you had ever seen before, near to or around the polls that day?

Answer. I saw a considerable armed force stationed at the polls, and some thirty-odd of a cavalry company within about eighty or a hundred yards of the polls; there were sixteen stationed immediately at the window where the votes were received, with drawn sabres, and one on a horse, moving up and down the Court House yard, about from twenty-five to thirty feet from the polls, who also had a drawn sabre. They were there from a short time after the polls were opened until the election closed. There were also armed soldiers about eighty yards from the polls, who refused to allow me to go from the place where the election was held to my residence, until I had remonstrated with them for some time, when they finally allowed me to pass. I believe they did not allow anybody to pass around that part of the square.

Question. Were the presence and position of the military at the polls that day calculated to produce great intimidation among the voters there that day?

Answer. I have no doubt it intimidated, to a considerable extent, a very large portion of the Democratic voters; and I have understood, and have reason to believe, that it caused some eight or ten of the most active and useful members of that party to leave the town, who did not return for some day or two afterwards. I know that some of them left before noon, who stated to me that they were going because they were threatened with arrest, some three persons having been previously arrested and carried by the soldiers to the common jail of the county, one of whom was very soon released; the others were detained until the latter part of the week. After those arrests were made I went to the person who was called the captain, and told him that they were arresting men without any cause, and upon the statement of persons, if I was correctly informed as to those who made the charges or statements, who were men of little or no character, and who were not worthy of being believed. He replied, that there had been some arrests that morning without his knowledge, but there would be no more unless affidavits were made, showing a sufficient cause, and that affidavits would have to be made against those who had been arrested. Soon after one of the persons who came to me and said he was going away had left the town, I saw some six or eight of the cavalry company going pretty rapidly out in the direction of the Almshouse, where he resides as overseer. Report was that they had gone to arrest that person. After they had returned, it was said that he had made his escape and they did not find him. I never heard that they went after any other person, though I have no knowledge, except the general report, that they went after him. I understood that the soldiers told his wife that they went to arrest him. This, of course, was but rumor.

Question. From your position as a citizen in Sussex County, and also as a judge of the highest court in the State, did you think then, or do you think now, that there was any necessity for the presence of soldiers in this State, to preserve the public peace?

Answer. I have voted at every general election in the County for more than thirty years, and during that time have resided and voted in two different Hundreds, and I have never attended an election when it would not have been quite as necessary for the presence of an armed force, as at the last election. I have no hesitation in saying that there was no necessity whatever for the presence of troops for any such purpose. The laws of our State are amply sufficient to protect all our citizens in the free exercise of their elective franchise. The law makes it the duty, not only of the election officers, but of the Sheriff, Justice of the Peace, Constables, and all other peace officers, to preserve order and prevent breaches of the peace, at all elections; and they are clothed with ample power for that purpose, and no necessity was ever before supposed to exist for resort to other means.

Question. If there had been the necessity for the presence of troops in this State, what would have been the proper channel through which to have applied to the General Government for them?

Answer. I should suppose the Executive of the State, who, by the Constitution, is made commander-in-chief of the military forces of the State.

Question. Have you ever heard any gentleman holding high official position in this State advocate the bringing of military into this State on the day of the last general election?

Answer. I never did. I heard a gentleman holding such a position say, that it was represented to him that it was absolutely necessary, and if it was not done, Union men, as he called them, would not be allowed to vote, but would be driven from the polls and beaten as they were at the little election in Georgetown Hundred. I told him that there was no necessity for the introduction of troops there, by reason of anything which occurred at the little election, or for any other reason. He said if there was no necessity, there was a set of lying men in Sussex.

Question. What occurred at the little election?

Answer. I saw nothing like disturbance until about the time, the votes had all been taken in, but a few minutes before the time prescribed by law for closing the election, when a drunken man, who had been swearing and bragging on his manhood around the polls nearly all day, having at least on one occasion taken his coat off, challenging some one to fight; he was very abusive of the Democrats, swearing that he could whip any damned Democrat on the ground, I believe was his expression. No one seemed to take much notice of him until about the time of closing the election, when he succeeded in getting a fight. I had been sitting in a stand in the Court House yard, which had been used by political speakers, and about the time I was leaving, this occurrence took place. I went in, and succeeded, without any assistance from the Sheriff or other peace-officers who were present, in preserving order and preventing any further violence or breach of the peace, and in a very short time those who were present dispersed, the election having closed, and I did not see or hear of any other disturbance or breach of the peace; and the occurrence to which I have referred did not originate in any dispute or controversy at the polls, in reference to any vote, but solely from the indiscretions of a drunken man. I have rarely seen a more peaceable, quiet election, and have often seen much greater violence and disturbances at our elections.

Question. Did you ever hear of a desire or purpose on the part of the Democrats to interfere with the polls on the day of the last general election, so as to prevent a fair election, or do you believe that any such desire or purpose existed?

Answer. I never heard of any such desire or purpose being manifested. Judging from all that I heard said by the Democrats, they did not seem to think it necessary to resort to any such means. They said, and, I believe, thought, that unless there was some interference to prevent a fair election, their success was by no means doubtful. It was and still is my opinion that if there had been no interference by the introduction of troops, the Democratic majority in Sussex County would have been at least three hundred, and a majority of five hundred or more would not at all have surprised me.

On motion of Mr. Waples,

The Committee adjourned until 8 ½ o'clock to-morrow morning.

FRIDAY, February 6, 1863—9 o'clock, P.M.

The Committee met pursuant to adjournment.

Present—Messrs. Saulsbury, Slay, Williams, Waples and Horsey.

The examination of EDWARD WOOTTEN was resumed, he being recalled.

By the Chairman:

Question.   Was it generally understood that all the volunteer companies in this State, commanded by Democrats, had their arms taken from them previous to the last general election, and also that all the volunteer companies, commanded by Republicans, were permitted to retain possession of their arms up to that time?

Answer.   Such was the general understanding. I never heard it denied. The Governor commissioned officers for a number of volunteer companies, formed after his proclamation, about the month of April, in 1861, recommending the organization of such companies. Under the law of our State the commissions were issued to such persons as raised the requisite number to form a company, without reference to their political sentiments.

Question.   Will you state all that you know personally in reference to the organization and disbanding of any of those companies?

Answer.   There was a company formed in Georgetown some three years ago, or more, commanded by Caleb R. Layton, who was commissioned by the Governor—now Captain or Lieutenant in the regular army. During the session of the Legislature, in '61 he received, under the order of the Governor, about fifty-five Minnie muskets, which were taken from here to the Milford depot, where they lay until the month of April following. His company having been reduced below the number which entitled him by law to the arms, and then disbanded, the Governor made an order upon him to deliver them to the Commissary of Sussex County—the Governor writing to him at the same time, that when he increased his company to a sufficient number to entitle him to commissions and arms, he would give him an order for the same guns. He represented to the Governor afterwards that he had the requisite number of men. But the Governor declined, as he informed me, to issue commissions to his officers, until he complied with the order for the delivery of the guns to the Commissary. Upon his promise to do so, the Governor issued commissions, but the guns were not delivered. Shortly after, Mr. Layton received an appointment, I think, of Lieutenant in the regular army, and subsequently Dr. William Marshall was appointed Captain of the same company. The Governor told me, when he (Marshall) applied for his commission, he refused to issue it until his order for the delivery of the guns was complied with; that the object was not to deprive them of the guns, but to enforce his orders as the Executive and Commander-in-chief of the military forces in the State. Marshall went away and returned in a few days afterwards, and represented that he had delivered the arms to the Commissary; whereupon the Governor directed a commission to be issued to him and gave him an order for the same Minnie muskets, supposing from his representations that they had been delivered by him to the Commissary. I believe they never were delivered, but remained and still are somewhere in the county, in the hands of different persons. Dr. Marshall not long after his appointment as Captain of that company, went off, I understood, as Surgeon for the Third Delaware Regiment. I have no knowledge, myself, of that company's having drilled since he left it. I am not aware that it is kept together as a company.

Question. Have you any knowledge of the formation and disbanding of Captain Paynter's company?

Answer. Captain Paynter formed a company in the spring of '61, and was commissioned as Captain. Commissions were also issued to

Lieutenants, and some time afterwards he was supplied with inferior muskets from the arsenal of Sussex County, by the order of the Governor. That company drilled regularly, I think, during the summer of '61, and in October of that year, he was arrested by an armed force, said to have acted under the order or authority of the General Government, the company being commanded by Captain McCullough, I think his name was, who, I understood, went to the residence of Captain Paynter's mother some time after dark, and told Captain Paynter that he was directed by Major Andrews to take his arms. I was also informed, by Mr. Paynter, that he replied to Captain McCulloch, that he would deliver them to him as soon as he could collect them together, that they were in the hands of the members of his company, some of whom resided several miles in the country. Captain Paynter was arrested, and kept under arrest all night and nearly the whole of the next day, whilst his friends were collecting, as fast as they could, the arms, nearly, if not all of which, were delivered to Captain McCullough. At the same time the arms and accoutrements were all taken from the arsenal and carried off under the direction of Captain McCullough.

Question. I understood you to say that it was generally understood that all the volunteer companies in the State, which were commanded by Democrats, had been deprived of their arms previous to the last general election, and also that all the volunteer companies in the State, which were commanded by Republicans, were permitted to retain their arms up to that time. Do you now say, that so far as your personal knowledge extends, that was the fact?

Answer. Such was the general understanding, and, so far as my knowledge extends, it was true. I never heard it contradicted.

EDWARD WOOTTEN.

DANIEL J. LAYTON sworn and examined.
By the Chairman:
Question. Mr. Layton, where were you on Saturday previous to

the last general election?

Answer. I was in Washington and Baltimore.

Question. When did you go to Washington and to Baltimore?

Answer. I went down to Washington Friday afternoon, and back to Baltimore on Saturday afternoon.

Question. Did you go to Washington and Baltimore, or to either place, on business in relation to the bringing of soldiers into this State to be present on the day of the last general election?

Answer. I left home on Wednesday for the purpose of superintending the printing of tickets for the Union party, and was requested by the friends of that party to stop over at this place, (Dover,) and learn definitely whether the Delaware Regiments, or any portion of them, had been ordered home to vote, and if not, to urge that a military force be sent into this State, or rather into the lower portion of it, to preserve the public peace on that day; that although they had heretofore been opposed to the introduction of an armed force, yet from the increased partizan feeling, they deemed it necessary.

Question. Will you please state the names of the friends to whom you allude as having made this request of you?

Answer. Jacob Moore, John D. Rodney, I think, William Ellegood, Caleb S. Layton, and others whom I do not remember. I saw at this place, (Dover,) George P. Fisher, Esq., who, at that time, did not surely know whether the troops from this State, or any part of them, would be present on election day. I went up to Wilmington the same day, and there remained until Friday noon, attending to the printing of tickets. On Friday morning, intending to return on Saturday morning, some individuals met together and selected Colonel Henry S. McCoombs as a suitable party to proceed to Washington and secure the return of the Delaware Regiments, or as great a portion as possible, to this State, to vote at the general election.

Question. Did you converse with no person while you remained in Dover, except George P. Fisher, Esq., in relation to bringing troops into this State?

Answer.   I may have conversed with others on this subject.

Question.   Did you converse with any person in the town of Milford on the subject?

Answer.   I may have done so; I do not now recollect.

Question.   Who were the persons constituting the conference of which you have spoken as having been at Wilmington, at which Colonel McCoombs was appointed to go to Washington?

Answer.   I do not know. After he was selected as the person, I was requested by Governor Cannon, Colonel McCoombs, and others whom I do not now recollect, to accompany him. I accordingly did so.

Question.   Was not your father for many years a judge of the Superior Court in this State?

Answer.   I believe he was.

Question.   Is not Jacob Moore a member of the legal profession and a practising lawyer in your county?

Answer.   He is.

Question.   Do you know whether they, or either of them, were aware that if the presence of the military in this State, was necessary for the protection of the public peace, at a time when the Legislature was not in session and could not be convened, the Executive of the State was the proper channel through which to apply to the General Government for such protection?

Answer.   I cannot say what they knew; but I can say that I now think that they then believed it was useless so to apply.

Question.   Were you, or so far as you know, was Col. McCoombs the bearer of any message or letter from any person in this State to the Secretary of War, or any other person in Washington, in reference to the sending of military into this State, to be present on the day of the last general election?

Answer.   I believe, some time previous to Col. McCoombs' going down to Washington on the 31st of October, that there had been communications between parties in this State, whom I do not now know, and the Secretary of War.

Question. Did you or Colonel McCoombs, after your arrival at Washington, wait on the Secretary of War, and consult with him in reference to sending soldiers into this State?

Answer. I did not. I cannot say whether Colonel McCoombs did or not.

Question. When did you return from Washington to Baltimore?

Answer. On Saturday afternoon.

Question. When did you leave Baltimore?

Answer. Sunday afternoon or evening.

Question. Where did you go?

Answer. I went on board a steamer bound for Seaford, Delaware.

Question. Were there armed soldiers on board of that steamer?

Answer. I was requested by General Wool to accompany him. We went on board the steamer about five o'clock in the afternoon. When we went on board they were putting on board the boat a company of cavalry. We went on board, and the vessel soon after dropped out into the stream.

Question. Were there other steamers in company, having on board cavalry, or United States forces of any kind?

Answer. There was one that took on board a company of cavalry at an adjacent pier, and a third, together with the two already named, stopped at Fort McHenry, and took on board two companies of infantry.

Question. Were the three steamers, to which you have alluded, all that came into this State, so far as you know, with troops of any kind on board?

Answer. The three steamers referred to were the *John Tucker*, *Nelly Baker*, and a tug named the *Putnam*. Those three brought all the troops that were brought with him from Baltimore. No other steamers or gunboats accompanied them.

Question. How many troops came on board those three steamers?

Answer. Two full companies of cavalry, with their horses, amounting to two hundred, and two full companies of infantry; four hundred in all.

Question. Was Major-General Wool commander of the steamers?

Answer. Yes, sir; they were subject to his command.

Question. Had you been acquainted with Major-General Wool previous to your visit to Baltimore?

Answer. I first met him between Baltimore and Washington, on Saturday, as I came back from Washington.

Question. Who introduced you to him?

Answer. I believe I was introduced by Colonel James, of his Staff, or Colonel McCoombs, I cannot say which.

Question. Do you know whether Colonel McCoombs is colonel in the regular army or a colonel of the Delaware Volunteers?

Answer. He was appointed Colonel of the Fifth Delaware Volunteers, commissioned by the Secretary of War. There had been communications between the Secretary of War and Governor Cannon and George P. Fisher, in relation to sending troops into this State; and, as I understand, and believe it was the opinion up to that time of a large portion, if not the majority, of the influential men of the party (Union party), that no troops were needed; and as I was informed, Colonel McCoombs so informed the Secretary of War. On Friday previous to the election, or I might say that before I left home, these same parties, who had been opposed to the introduction of troops, were now convinced that it would be a measure to prevent disturbance and preserve the public peace, and therefore requested that a force sufficient be sent into the State. Colonel McCoombs then went down to Washington to request the Secretary of War to send troops into this State to be present on the day of the election, and also to permit the Delaware Volunteers to return home to vote.

Question. Who were the persons to whom you allude, as having been opposed to the introduction of troops, but subsequently became convinced that their presence was necessary, and accordingly made the request?

Answer. I believe all those I have heretofore named, viz.: Governor Cannon, George P. Fisher, Jacob Moore, Caleb S. Layton,

John D. Rodney, Colonel McCoombs, and others.

Question. Did you come all the way to Seaford, on the steamer, with Major-General Wool?

Answer. I did.

Question. What became of the troops after they arrived at Seaford?

Answer. They were distributed and placed under the charge of the Provost Marshals of the several Hundreds.

Question. With what political party were the gentlemen you have named as having made the request that troops be sent into this State connected?

Answer. The Union party.

D. J. LAYTON.

On motion of Mr. Williams,
The Committee adjourned until Monday evening at 8 o'clock.

MONDAY, February 9, 1863—8 o'clock, P.M.

The Committee met pursuant to adjournment.
Present—Messrs. Saulsbury, Hitch, Slay, Stubbs, Williams, Waples, and Horsey.

The examination of EDWARD WOOTTEN was resumed, he being recalled.

By the Chairman:

Question. Do you recollect to have heard any conversation in reference to the appointment of Provost Marshal in this State on the day of the last general election; if so, will you state what that conversation was?

Answer. I heard a conversation at New Castle, soon after the election, which arose from a conversation about the occurrence which took place at Georgetown on Saturday night before the election, in reference to the report which had been circulated that an American flag had been torn down, and it had been said that that was the cause of the introduction of troops into the county. I remarked that that could not have been the cause, for I heard a respectable gentleman say, after the election, that the commissions of two Provost Marshals were received on Friday previous to the election. Mr. George P. Fisher said that that was not so, that he knew that they were not made out until Sunday; that he helped to fill them up.

EDWARD WOOTTEN.

WILLIAM H. ROSS sworn and examined.
By the Chairman:

Question. Where do you reside?
Answer. In Sussex County, near Seaford.
Question. Did you vote on the day of the last general election, and if so, where?
Answer. I voted at Seaford.
Question. Did you observe anything unusual and different from what you ever saw before about the polls that day?
Answer. I did observe something very unusual, and what I had never seen before; I passed up to vote between two files of cavalry with drawn sabres.
Question. Did you ever see soldiers at the polls before?
Answer. Never.
Question. Will you please to state all you know about the arrival of troops at Seaford; when they came, when they left, and what they did while there?
Answer. I was told about 12 o'clock that some soldiers had already arrived there. I went down there and sought an interview with Colonel Wallace; I succeeded after a while in seeing the Colonel. My

object was to know what the soldiers were brought for. The Colonel gave me but little satisfaction, but said the soldiers were not brought there to prevent the Democrats from voting. I learned through the Colonel that General Wool was on his way up the Nanticoke river, with two or three boat loads of soldiers from Baltimore. When the boat arrived at Seaford, I made an effort to go on board to have an interview with the General. Colonel Wallace told me the General was engaged, and I could not see him then. After awhile the General came ashore, escorted by a number of citizens of Sussex County, who, I afterwards learned, were the Provost Marshals of the different Hundreds of the County. The General, with the Provost Marshals, went to Mr. Coulborn's hotel, at Seaford. Then I, with Dr. McFerran and Captain Wright, again endeavored to obtain an interview. Dr. McFerran and I succeeded in getting into the room where he was, surrounded with military officers and the Provost Marshals. When the Provost Marshals discovered we were in the room, several of them arose, and by their manners showed that they considered our entrance an intrusion, upon which we left the room. Mr. Coulborn then invited us into another room, where we were joined by a number of other gentlemen belonging to the Democratic party. Our object in meeting was to consult as to the best means of obtaining an interview with the General; and our only object in seeking such interview was to ascertain whether we could have a fair election. After consulting together for some time, I finally proposed to address a letter to the General, reminding him of having spent an evening with him about the year 1852 or 1853 at the St. Nicholas Hotel, in New York. All of the gentlemen present approved of my proposition. I accordingly wrote such a letter, and stated that I and others had been denied admittance into his room that evening, but, of course, without his knowledge, for no other reason, as I considered, than that of being Democrats. The letter was sent in by the landlord, John L. Coulborn. As soon as the General received it, he came out of the room into the passage, and sent for me. He professed to recognize me, and to be glad to see me, but said that he was then very much engaged and would see me again in a few minutes. This was about half-past five or six o'clock in the afternoon. I waited impatiently until ten o'clock at night. About that time I was asked, being hard of hearing, if I heard that? I replied, no; what is it? I was told the soldiers were going out of town singing the song of "John Brown's soul is marching on." I then proposed to go home, and told my Democratic friends that an interview with the General was unnecessary, as I considered the mischief then done. The gentlemen present insisted on my remaining, which I did until eleven o'clock, at which time General Wool came to the room. I introduced him to all present, and then asked him the object of bringing the soldiers to Delaware. I do not recollect his answer, except that it was his wish that we should have a fair election. The next day I was told by Silas C. Winwright and others that Mr. Hazzard, the Provost Marshal, would not allow certain persons to go to the window to vote. I took Winwright down to General Wool's room, and, on entering, asked the General if he did not assure me we should have a fair election. He said he did. I told him that I had been informed that the Provost Marshal had constituted himself both inspector and judge of the election, and that I considered the election an unfair one. I told the General that I wished he would instruct the Provost Marshal to let the judges of the election settle the question in regard to doubtful voters. He said he could not do it. I asked him why—if he appointed him he could instruct him as to his duty. He said he did not appoint him, that he had been appointed either by the President or the Secretary of War, and that he had no control over him. Indeed, said he, if I must confess, so far from the Provost Marshal being under my control, I am, for the time being, rather under his. Upon which I apologized for having interrupted him, and left the room.

Question. Was the presence of the military on the election ground calculated to produce great intimidation among the voters?

Answer. I think it was.

Question. Were you once the Governor of this State? If so, when were you elected, by what party, and how long did you serve?

Answer. I was elected Governor of this State by the Democratic party in 1850, and served a term of four years.

Question. Did you ever hear of a purpose or desire on the part of the Democrats to interfere with the polls on the 4th day of November last, so as to prevent a fair election?

Answer. Never.

Question. Are you not well acquainted with the people of this State?

Answer. Yes, probably as well as most men.

Question. Was there, in your judgment, any necessity for the presence of military at the polls, to preserve the public peace, on the 4th of November last?

Answer. Not the least in the world. I do not think it had entered into the mind of a Democrat in Sussex County to prevent a fair election.

Question. Were not the Democrats in that county sanguine of carrying the election, if the election was a fair one?

Answer. Yes, by a considerable majority.

WM. H. ROSS.

JOHN C. HAZZARD, sworn and examined.

By the Chairman:

Question. Where do you reside?

Answer. In Milton, Sussex County.

Question. Were you Provost Marshal on the day of the last general election?

Answer. Yes sir.

Question. From whom did you receive your commission as Provost Marshal?

Answer. Edwin M. Stanton, Secretary of War.

Question. Have you the commission here, sir?

Answer. Yes sir.

Question. Will you let us see it?

Answer. I do not know that it is necessary to show it.

[Presents the commission.]

Question. Are you acquainted with the handwriting in which this was filled up? Was this commission accompanied with instructions?

Answer. I got instructions from General Wool.

Question. By whom was this commission delivered to you?

Answer. By John D. Rodney.

Question. On what day?

Answer. On the 2^d day of November.

Question. Was the 2^d of November the Sabbath day?

Answer. I believe it was.

Question. Did you act as Provost Marshal at Milton on the 4th day of November?

Answer. I endeavored to do so.

Question. Had you command of the soldiers that were there?

Answer. They were under my charge, I believe.

Question. Did you direct what position they should occupy in reference to the window?

Answer. I directed Lieutenant Davis to allow one gentleman on each side of the window to challenge illegal votes, and if any difficulty arose in the crowd or assembly, no matter by which party it arose, to quash it if possible without using violence to either party; and for fear that other difficulties might arise after one had arisen, to place a portion of his soldiers on either side of the window, leaving a passage by which all persons or voters could go to the window and vote one at a time, and also to allow the said gentlemen that were already at the window for the purpose of challenging votes as aforesaid, to remain there, who were William V. Coulter on behalf of the Democratic party, and Caleb F. Morris on behalf of the Union party; that the soldiers were not placed at the window until as above stated, after a slight difficulty did arise, if my memory serves me right.

Question. Do you know by what conveyance the soldiers were carried to Milton?

Answer. Not of my own knowledge. I was informed by

Lieutenant Davis, that they went on the Railroad from Seaford to Milford, and then walked to Milton.

Question.   Do you know how far it is from Milford to Milton?

Answer.   It is called twelve miles.

Question.   Do you know whether the laws of the State do not prohibit our own militia from being at or near the polls under arms on election day under heavy penalty?

Answer.   I do not know. I am not lawyer enough to know the fact.

Question.   Do you not know that the laws of this State require the Justices of the Peace, Constables and other conservators of the peace to be present to preserve order at the polls on election day?

Answer.   I know that the Justices of the Peace and Constables are there, and that the law requires them to preserve order if they are there.

Question.   Do you know whether the Justice of the Peace and Constable from your hundred were on the election ground that day?

Answer.   I think I saw them several times during the day.

Question.   Did you not order the Constable not to interfere with anybody there that day?

Answer.   I have no recollection of making any remark to the constable or any other person touching a matter of that kind, or that could have been construed in that light.

Question.   Have not the conservators of the public peace under the laws of this State always been sufficient to preserve order on the day of the election, and do you not believe they would have been sufficient on the day of the last general election?

Answer.   Perhaps they might have been sufficient. I cannot say as to what might have arisen.

Question.   Were soldiers stationed around the ballot-box during the time of the tallying of the votes?

Answer.   There were some soldiers in the Academy—four or five, perhaps, at a time—to keep the audience quiet, so that those counting the votes might not be interrupted. They were there for that purpose and no other.

Question. By whose directions were they placed there?

Answer. I asked the Inspector if he had any objections to their being there, in order that they might have quiet. I believe he did not object. I then ordered the Lieutenant to place a few there for that purpose, to preserve order and nothing more.

Question. Was there more noise and confusion around the polls during the time of reading out and tallying the votes than is usual on election day?

Answer. Not when I was there. They seemed to be getting along very quietly during time I was down there. There might have been some noise and confusion during my absence.

Question. Was it from any manifestations of disorder or violence that you stationed the soldiers around the polls during the time the votes were being tallied?

Answer. It was only to prevent some persons that were intoxicated from keeping a noise and hurraing. Such noise might have prevented the officers from tallying out smoothly and quietly.

Question. Did you not think the civil authorities were sufficient for that purpose?

Answer. I did not know whether the civil authorities would remain there all the time or not. Hence my reason for giving the order that I did.

Question. Did you believe, then, or do you believe now, that there was greater necessity for the military to preserve order at the polls than had existed at previous elections?

Answer. I cannot say that I do or did. I will add that the soldiers or military were not there by request or solicitation of mine made to any person.

Question. Do you know at whose request or solicitation they were there?

Answer. No, sir. Neither did I know that there were to be any there until Monday evening previous to the day of the election.

Question.   Were you consulted in reference to your appointment as Provost Marshal before the commission was offered to you?

Answer.   No, sir. Neither did I ask for it.

Question.   When did the soldiers leave Milton?

Answer.   I think it was on Thursday after the election. I am not sure whether it was Thursday or Friday.

Question.   Do you know by whose order they left?

Answer.   They left by mine. They could have gone away the next day, but Lieutenant Davis requested to stay a day longer, stating that some of the soldiers' feet were sore, and that he would stay a little while longer himself, to visit some young persons with whom he was acquainted.

Question.   When did they go from Milton, and by what conveyance?

Answer.   They were directed to Milford first by wagons, and from there to Seaford, I presume, by cars.

Question.   By whom were the wagons furnished to convey them to Milford?

Answer.   The wagons were obtained by my solicitation from different citizens of the town.

Question.   At whose expense?

Answer.   At no one's expense. I believe I did pay two men out of my own pocket a small amount.

Question.   Were you commissioned as Provost Marshal for that day alone, or is your commission still in force?

Answer.   The commission does not say. It has never been rescinded.

Question.   From what source did you receive information on Monday that soldiers would be there?

Answer.   If my memory serves me right, I received, in the same envelope in which the commission came, directions on another slip of paper, directing me to go to Seaford by 2 o'clock in the afternoon on Monday, I think, to meet General John E. Wool. Over whose signature that was I believe I have forgotten. I think it was not over the signature of the Secretary of War, but am under the impression that it was over the signature of James R. Lofland.

Question. Do you know whether the Provost Marshals received compensation or pay for their services, or whether they are to receive such compensation or pay?

Answer. The language of the papers accompanying the commission, over the signature of Adjutant General Thomas, is that they shall receive — dollars per month.

Question. Do you understand from the language of the commission that you were, on the day of the election, and still are, under pay from the General Government?

Answer. I am not able to say whether I shall receive anything or not. One thing I do know, that I have not received anything.

JNO. C. HAZZARD.

On motion of Mr. Williams,
The Committee adjourned until 9 o'clock to-morrow morning.

TUESDAY, February 10, 1863—9 o'clock, P.M.

The Committee met pursuant to adjournment.
Present—Messrs. Saulsbury, Hitch, Cahall, Williams and Waples.

BENJAMIN WHARTON, sworn and examined.

By the Chairman:
Question. Where do you reside, and were did you vote on the 4th day of November last?
Answer. At Milton, in Sussex County.
Question. What is your occupation?
Answer. I keep a public house.

Question. Do you know whether the soldiers, who were there on the day of the election, interfered with or arrested any person residing in that town, or in that Hundred?

Answer. Yes, sir; I thought they interfered with me. I was arrested, for what cause, I have not found out. At the time, I was leaning on the banisters on the stairway, smoking a cigar. I was on the porch a while before dark on Tuesday evening the day of the election, talking with a couple of men, of whom I had borrowed some money to keep for them until the next day. While talking with those two men, a young man, dressed in marine's clothes, a soldier, I suppose, told me he would have no fuss around the house—those men were talking pretty loudly. I then asked him if he had any business with me. He said I would soon find out. I replied to him, and told him if he had any business with me to go about it—I had none with him. I then stated if his officers had any business with me, to go and tell them to come and see me themselves, not to send a young snotty nose like that. I had children in the house older than he was. Probably an hour after that, I was talking with another soldier that came to my house, stating to him concerning the conversation between the young man and me, in regard to my keeping less noise about my own premises. This man made a reply, that "He did right, and had it been me, I would have shot you." He also said to me: "Damn you, I will have you arrested any way." I had no further conversation with him. I think it was between the hours of seven o'clock and eight o'clock on the same evening that I was arrested, by some five or six of those soldiers, and taken to an old school-house in our village. While in the school-house, I was seated close to a ten-plate stove, and removed on the bench a little further back in a few moments afterwards. While sitting on the bench, a soldier said to a darkey, whom I think he called George, "Stay here a few moments, I am going as far as the door; put a stick of wood in the stove." The darkey obeyed the order, put a stick in the stove, and then turned round and laughed at me. I suppose I was placed under a darkey sentinel. I remained in the old school-house half an hour, it might have been three quarters, when I was told by one of the soldiers to walk as far as the door, that some person wanted to see me. I walked out of the door and met a gentleman who, I was informed afterwards, was called the 1st Lieutenant of the company, and, as he told me, Captain in charge at that time. I did not know his name. After getting out of the crowd, there were two other gentlemen, one of them being Mr. John C. Hazzard, the other I did not know. After going ten or fifteen yards from the school-house with those three gentlemen, we stopped and conversed together. Mr. Hazzard asked me what was the matter. I told him that I had been arrested for some cause or other, but could not tell what. He said that he heard of my arrest, and, not being very well, was in the act of retiring to bed, but came down to see why I was arrested, I think his words were. I then asked Mr. Hazzard if I ever interfered with him or his business. He answered, "No, you never did." I asked him if he ever knew me to keep a disorderly house, or interfere with any person's business. The answer was "No." Then the Lieutenant, I think it was, made the reply, and said that I was arrested through the intelligence of loyal citizens; that I had abused the soldiers. I told him, if he or any other man said so, he told a falsehood. Then he told me I could go home, and he would go a part of the way with me. He went as far as the old churchyard corner, being about thirty yards from where we stood at the time we were talking. We stopped on the corner of the churchyard; I thanked him very kindly for his kind offer; told him I did not require any guard, was no stranger in the village, and knew the way home.

Question.   Did you see any of the soldiers, present at Milton that day, interfere with Mr. Ponder, at his store, or any other place?

Answer.   No, sir; not that day, but the next. I did not see them do any thing, except I saw them go to the store; I saw them come out of the store; I met four of them on the corner of the street; at the corner of Mr. Ponder's dwelling. Said I, "Gentlemen, what is the great trouble." One of them made the reply, "We are going to arrest that damned Jim Ponder." I asked what that was for. He said that it was for some of his threats; he did not tell what the threats were. One young man, a soldier, said he did not think Mr. Ponder had ever made any such threats.

Another spoke up, and said, "Yes, he did, the damned son of a bitch; let us go and arrest him any way." At that time, Mr. Willard Saulsbury drove up in a carriage. Mr. Ponder came out of the store, met Mr. John F. Allen, and the 1st Lieutenant of the company, while crossing the street, halted a few moments to talk with them. He then invited the soldiers over to his house. The charge against Mr. Ponder, as I now remember, was not that he had made threats, but that he called them black Republicans.

B. P. WHARTON.

JAMES M. BAYNAM sworn and examined.

By the Chairman:

Question. Were you present at Milton, at the general election, on the 4th day of November last?

Answer. I was.

Question. Were there soldiers about the polls that day?

Answer. Yes, sir.

Question. Did you see those soldiers, or any of them, interfere with, abuse, or strike any citizen of that Hundred, when he was going to the polls that day?

Answer. I did see them interfere with more than one. I saw them strike a man three licks in the face, knocking him down, and kicking him, and tore the coat off him. I ran in, and caught hold of a couple of them, and told them, "For God's sake, not to kill him." They ordered me to hush; I did so at that time. A short time after that, I went across the ground; I heard a Republican and a Democrat in conversation; I saw an officer standing close by; he heard the conversation, and ordered the Democrat to hush talking. I found if he did not hush, he would be arrested; I caught him by the coat, and told him he had better walk away. In a few minutes afterwards, I walked around on the other side of the ground by the polls. While I was standing there, I saw Mr. James Ponder start to the window; I did not know at the time what he started for; I learned afterwards that it was to speak to Mr. William V. Coulter, and in going there, somebody tripped him, or he slipped and came near falling. I heard one of soldiers at the other end of the entrance halloo, and tell other soldiers to stamp him, repeating it, I think, three times. At that time the Provost Marshal was on the ground, but did not try to stop him. Mr. Hazzard did tell them to let him go before he was struck, but not afterward. Directly I saw one of the officers go up to Mr. Ponder, and talk with him; I do not know what Mr. Ponder said to him. In a few minutes I heard him call one of the soldiers to him, and tell him to stand there; that he wanted to go and see Mr. Ponder; that he wanted an explanation of what he meant; and he did go to Mr. Ponder. I think, as well as I recollect, I heard Mr. Ponder tell him, if he (the soldier) would attend to his business, he (Ponder) would attend to his. I never was at the polls at night after the polls were closed. My friends told me not to go up there, they were hunting for me to arrest me. I kept out of their way until they left the town.

Question.   Is not Mr. Ponder one of the principal citizens of the town, and a peaceable man?

Answer.   Yes, sir. He is a merchant and grain dealer, and one of the principal citizens of the town, and a peaceable, law-abiding man.

Question.   Did not the soldiers, who were at Milton, create all, or nearly all, the disturbance which took place that day?

Answer.   They created all the disturbance that I saw on the ground.

JAMES M. BAYNAN.

ROBERT L. LACY, sworn and examined.

By the Chairman:
Question.   Were you Constable at Milton during the last year, and at the time of the last general election?

Answer.   Yes, sir; and at the election before.

Question.   Were you present in Milton on the day of the last general election, in the obedience to the requirements of the law, as a conservator of the public peace?

Answer.   Yes, sir.

Question.   Do you recollect any instance there that day of a little disturbance, when you were endeavoring to preserve the public peace?

Answer.   I do. There was a Democratic wagon drove up from the Neck, having several persons in it. There was a Republican who got up on the wheel, I thought he was intoxicated; I put my hand on him and told him I wished him to get down, in obedience to my duty as constable. I wished him to raise no disturbance. He looked around at me, and kicked me down. I asked him why he did it. He said I had no business to put my hands on him. Mr. Hazzard, the Provost Marshal, came up in the time, and said I had no right to put my hands on any one—that I must keep my hands off. I told him I was only endeavoring to keep order. He went off and said no more to me.

Question.   Did you hear any threats there that day on the part of any person, that they would arrest, or cause persons to be arrested?

Answer.   I did; I heard the Lieutenant, in several cases, tell Democratic persons that they might think, but could not talk; and if they did not mind how they acted, he would have them arrested. Mr. Ponder, John Stokely, that I know of, and myself, were threatened with arrest.

Question.   Did not the soldiers, who were in Milton, at or near the polls that day, create the principal part of the disturbance which took place?

Answer.   They created all that I saw, except the case in regard to myself, of which I have spoken.

Question.   Would you not, in your judgment, from all that you saw, have had better order without the soldiers than you had with them?

Answer.   I thought we should have had fully as good order, if not better.

Question.   Were the persons you have named as having been threatened with arrest, guilty of any breach of the peace?

Answer.   They were not; they were active Democrats, and were only trying to get as many to vote their ticket as they could by fair means.

ROBERT L. LACEY.

WILLIAM V. COULTER, sworn and examined.

By the Chairman:
Question.   Where do you reside?
Answer.   At Milton, in Broadkiln Hundred, in Sussex County.
Question.   Did you vote on the day of the last general election, and if so, where?
Answer.   I did; in Milton.
Question.   How long have you been a voter?
Answer.   Forty-six years.
Question.   Did you observe anything on that day, at or near the polls, unusual and different from what you had ever seen before?
Answer.   Yes; I saw things that day which I never saw before, and hope I shall never see again. I was called on by my Democratic friends to stand at the window that day and see to the voting. I went down to the Academy in the morning where they vote. There were several soldiers standing around near the window. I asked what they were there for. John Allen, who was in soldiers' clothes, remarked to me that they were not to prohibit any one from voting. The window at which we vote was high, and it is necessary to have something to stand on. We put a box there. I was one of those who stood at the window on that box, and had a good chance to see what was going on. The election was opened; people commenced voting as peaceably as usual, and about fifteen or twenty had voted, when a lot of soldiers were brought by the Lieutenant and placed in two lines from the window. I saw no reason why they should be brought there. There had not been one word of disturbance. The people passed up and voted for a considerable time. Then came up a man who

was intoxicated and offered his vote. But he seemed to have a good deal to talk about. He had not broken the public peace. The Lieutenant at the outer end of those men told them to take him away. They ran up and took hold of him, and as he was backing out, they commenced striking him in the face with their fists, and finally got him down. He afterwards came up again to vote, and he commenced talking again in his way, doing nobody any harm. The Lieutenant told him if he did not vote that he should come away and not vote at all. He got his vote in finally. He was a Democrat.

Question. Do you know any citizen of Milton, a prominent Democrat there, who consulted frequently with you during the day, and who was interfered with and finally pushed down by the soldiers?

Answer. I can say this much: that the Democratic friends had not the same privilege to come and speak to me at the window that the Republicans had on their side of the window. For it seemed to me that those soldiers found out pretty soon who the Democrats were. Mr. James Ponder, who wished to speak to me about something, I do not recollect what, got up to me on the outside of the soldiers, between them and the steps. The fellow that stood next to me seemed to be Sergeant. As Mr. Ponder stepped back to go out, this soldier stepped back and jammed Mr. Ponder between himself and the steps. Mr. Ponder made a blunder and came near falling. Another soldier remarked he would like to catch that fellow. He said, "Yes; I wish I had broken his legs." They were taken away, and other fellows filled their place. The same soldiers did not remain all the time. They would have their bayonets out in the hands and rubbing them to make them brighter, and swearing that they would like to use them, and that they could drink a gallon of rebel's blood. Before the polls were closed, they wanted the window put down. I told them it should not be put down until the proper time. One of them told me if I did not put it down, he would vote. I told him if he did, he should vote over my body. The election was closed. I stepped off the box to go away. I heard somebody thumping on the window with their fingers. I turned round to see who it was, and it was Mr. Hazzard, the Provost

Marshal. The window was hoisted. I stepped back to it, and he asked the officers if it would not be best to put some soldiers in the house. I objected and it was not granted. I stepped off again. I heard some one thumping against the house or door, and it was Mr. Hazzard thumping at the door. They opened the door, and he went in. I did not get in. The door was pulled to while he was in there. He then came out and got some soldiers, and they went in.

Question. Did you believe, from your observation that day, and from your knowledge of the voters of that hundred, that there was any necessity for the presence of soldiers at the polls at Milton that day, for the preservation of the public peace?

Answer. None at all.

Question. Do you or do you not think that the presence of the soldiers there that day had the effect to intimidate Democratic voters?

Answer. I do. I saw an old gentleman, a Democrat, come up at the lower end of the file of soldiers at two different times. I was satisfied his object was to come up to vote. He turned off and went away. I beckoned to a gentleman to come up to me where I was, and told him to tell the man to come up and vote; that he should not be hurt. He came and voted afterwards.

Question. Would you not, in your judgment, have had a much fairer election, without the presence of the soldiers, than you had with them?

Answer. Yes. I think we should have had a fair election had it not been for them.

Question. Did not the presence of the soldiers there that day rather create trouble and disturbance than prevent it?

Answer. Yes, sir. I never saw such disturbance at an election before.

WM. V. COULTER.

On motion of Mr. Waples,
The Committee adjourned until 8 o'clock, P.M.

SAME DAY, 8 o'clock, P.M.

The Committee met pursuant to adjournment.

Present—Messrs. Saulsbury, Cahall, Hitch, Williams, Waples, Horsey, and Slay.

JAMES PONDER, sworn and examined.

By the Chairman:

Question. Where do you reside?

Answer. In Milton, Broadkiln Hundred, Sussex County.

Question. Did you vote on the day of the last general election, and if so, where?

Answer. I did; at Milton.

Question. Did you observe anything unusual, and different from what you had ever seen before at or near the polls that day?

Answer. We had soldiers at our polls, which is unusual and unprecedented.

Question. Will you please to state all you know in reference to the soldiers there that day; what they did when they came there; when they went away; under whose command they were while there, and everything you know in reference to them?

Answer. Very early on election morning, I was called up by a portion of my family to see soldiers march by. I immediately arose, went up to the Academy, the voting place in our Hundred. I found the soldiers in possession of the house, their arms stacked in front of the window where the votes are received. I went in search of the officers who had them in charge to ascertain the object of their presence. I succeeded in finding two persons who called themselves lieutenants, and John C. Hazzard, who, I afterwards learned, was the Provost Marshal for that Hundred. The said Provost Marshal introduced me. I asked them why we were honored with their presence. One of the lieutenants informed me that he was sent there by General Wool. I asked him what for. John C. Hazzard, I believe, replied to my interrogation. He said that threats had been made. I asked him what kind of threats, and if he did not know that we were a very civil and law-abiding people. He answered, "Well, there have been threats, and threats made." I then addressed myself to the Lieutenant, and said that I presumed we should have the rights of freemen, that we should vote and talk. He replied, that we might think, that our thoughts were our own, but should not be allowed to talk. I turned away; one of the Lieutenants remarked to the other, that that was a secessionist or rebel; the other replied, "Yes, I know him; I have heard of him before." I then went home to my breakfast, and returned to the voting place a short time before the voting began. After the polls had been open some fifteen or twenty minutes, I suppose, and the people were voting in their usual and quiet way, very suddenly, and almost by magic, there was a file of soldiers placed on each side of the window, and voters were directed to pass through the files of soldiers. Shortly after the soldiers were placed at the window, a man, by the name of Primrose, started up to vote; he stopped about midway, I suppose, said he wanted to read his ticket, and see if there were any negroes on it. That created a considerable sensation. Some were hallooing, "Go up and vote," and some hallooing, "Take him out." Meanwhile, some of the soldiers caught him from behind, while two or three were striking and kicking him in the front. This man had his ticket open, and it was a Democratic ticket. They finally succeeded in pulling him or knocking him down and tearing his coat. I remarked to some one standing by, "I thought it was a pretty state of affairs, and outrageous to force us to vote through soldiers." Shortly after that, one of the Lieutenants came to me, and wanted to know what were those remarks I had made in regard to the soldiers. I replied, that I had neither the time nor opportunity to quarrel with him; that if he had any business to attend to, he had better attend to it, and I would attend to mine; that I knew my rights, and was going to maintain them.

Question. Do you know of any instances of their interfering with individuals that day, other than those you have named—whether they arrested anybody?

Answer. There was not anybody arrested that day on the election ground. I heard of their threatening to do it during the whole day. They interfered in almost every instance when they saw Democrats talking with voters; for, by some means, they very soon learned who the Democrats were. I do not know of a single instance where they interfered with Republicans, and they did assist and were very willing to assist the Republicans on every occasion.

Question. Did their whole conduct there that day show that they were there for the benefit of the Republican party, and for the injury of the Democratic party?

Answer. It did, conclusively.

Question. Did their presence at the polls contribute to the preservation of the public peace?

Answer. It did not. We have very peaceable elections; at the Inspector's election, held about a month previous, at which there were nearly as many votes polled, it was very quiet and peaceable, and not a particle of disturbance during the day.

Question. Did the presence of the soldiers there produce great dissatisfaction and intimidation among the voters?

Answer. It did; it was with considerable difficulty that we could get some of our Democrats who were there to go up to the polls to vote.

Question. Was there any necessity for the presence of soldiers there to preserve the public peace?

Answer. Not a particle. The officers who are required by law to be on the election ground, were there in their official capacity to preserve order, and were able and competent to do it, so that every individual should have an opportunity to exercise the right of suffrage; and if there had been any necessity for soldiers, there was a Republican Home Guard organized in our town, still in possession of their arms, and under the command of one of the candidates for the State Senate on the Republican ticket.

Question. Did not their presence at the polls that day rather create difficulties than prevent them?

Answer. It did. I do not think there would have been a fight or any difficulty; indeed, there was none outside of the soldiers.

Question. Do you know whether the soldiers, at your place, were a part of Wallace's Maryland Home Guard, or some that came under General Wool?

Answer. They were part of Colonel Wallace's regiment, called Maryland Home Guards, as I understand.

Question. Did any portion of those soldiers visit you the next day, at your store, before they left?

Answer. On Wednesday morning there came three of these soldiers in my store, swearing that they would whip me, that I had called them Black Republicans. I told them that I had not called them anything; I had not spoken to them. I told them to be off and leave me, or I would try the virtue of the civil law on them. They told me there was no civil law; that they were soldiers, and that military law superseded every thing else. They went away, however, swearing they would arrest me, or have me arrested. Shortly afterwards I met the Lieutenant who had them in charge, and remarked to him that I had just been attacked by three of his soldiers. He asked what for. I told him they had charged me with calling them Black Republicans. He asked if I had. I said I had not, and if I had, I did not suppose it would be any cause for arrest. He remarked that General Wool had ordered him to arrest every person who called another a Black Republican; and advised me, if I did not want to get into difficulties, to keep my mouth shut. This was the same Lieutenant who had told me previously that we should not be allowed to talk.

Question. Was there any violence offered to you on election day by the soldiers, or during their stay in Milton?

Answer. I had occasion several times to speak with Mr. Coulter, who was stationed at the window at the polls, and in passing up behind the soldiers, they would step back and try to prevent me, and, on one occasion, pushed me down on the door-steps.

Question. Who was in command of the soldiers there that day?

Answer. I understood they were in charge of the Provost

Marshal, John C. Hazzard.

Question.   Was Mr. Hazzard an active and zealous partizan?
Answer.   He was—on the Republican side.

JAMES PONDER.

DAVID LOFLAND, sworn and examined.

By the Chairman:

Question.   Are you a Justice of the Peace?
Answer.   I was at the time of the last election.
Question.   Where did you reside?
Answer.   At Milton, Sussex County, Delaware.
Question.   Were you present at the polls on the day of the last general election, in obedience to your duty as Justice of the Peace, to aid in the preservation of the public peace?
Answer.   I was.
Question.   Were there soldiers also there?
Answer.   There were.
Question.   Was there any necessity for their presence there for the preservation of the public peace?
Answer.   I think not.
Question.   Did not their presence rather tend to create difficulty and disturbance than to prevent it?
Answer.   It did.
Question.   Were not the civil authorities fully adequate to the preservation of the public peace at the polls at Milton that day?
Answer.   I think they were. They always had been.
Question.   Did or did not the soldiers themselves create most of the difficulties that occurred there that day?
Answer.   They did.
Question.   Will you please to state, in as few words as you can, what was the general conduct of the soldiers there that day?

Answer. Their conduct appeared to be very imprudent. I heard them say or tell Mr. John Stokley that "He was a damned gray rebel. Damn him, they could eat him!" I saw them both kick and strike Theodore Primrose, and knock him down. Primrose told me that he was hurt very badly. I was on the ground at the opening of the polls, and remained there until the polls were closed. I then went home for my supper. After eating, I went immediately back to the Academy, where they were tallying the votes. They had just commenced. There were five soldiers in the house to guard the polls. The house was densely crowded. I did not stay in there long. When I came out at the door, there were five or six soldiers. I heard one of them say that they were going to arrest James Ponder that night. I went to Mr. Ponder's house, and told him of it. I advised him not to come out. I then went back to the Academy. Still there were several soldiers standing about the door. I went in and there were five or six soldiers in the house, around the place where they were tallying out votes. I remained there awhile, and went out again, and still the soldiers were about the door.

Question. Was the Provost Marshal present while they were tallying the votes?

Answer. He was there at times. He did not stay there long.

Question. Did he give any orders or directions, or make any inquiries during that time?

Answer. He inquired if there had been any misbehavior by any person in the house. I do not recollect hearing any answer made.

DAVID LOFLAND.

JOHN STOKLEY sworn and examined.

By the Chairman:

Question. Did you vote on the day of the last general election?

Answer. I did vote at Milton, Broadkiln Hundred, Sussex County.

Question. What ticket did you vote?

Answer. I voted the Democratic ticket.

Question. Were you active in exerting your influence for the party that day?

Answer. I tried to do all I could to secure the election for our ticket.

Question. Will you please to state whether the soldiers interfered with you?—and if so, what they said or did to you that day?

Answer. There was a contention over a vote. Robert Hazel, whose father I knew to be a Democrat, fell into the hands of the Republicans, and they appeared to intimidate him a good deal. I told him not to be scared, that if he wished to vote the Democratic ticket he should have a fair chance to do it. A soldier replied and asked, "What in the hell it was my business about his voting." Then a number of persons gathered around, with some more soldiers. I turned my back and walked off, and as I went off, the soldier called me "a damned gray rebel." I gave him no reply. I thought I had other business to attend to which was more important than to be quarreling with him.

Question. Did not the presence of the soldiers there that day rather tend to produce difficulty than to prevent it?

Answer. I thought so.

Question. Did the person, to whom you have just alluded, and about whose vote the difficulty occurred with you, vote that day?

Answer. I was informed that he did vote the Republican ticket.

Question. Do you know, or have you heard of any person who remained away from the election that day on account of the presence of the soldiers at the polls?

Answer. I heard that a man by the name of Sharp, and one by the name of Willy, would not come to vote because the soldiers were there. If they had been there, they would have voted the Democratic ticket, I presume. They always have voted that way, so far as I know.

JOHN STOKLEY.

On motion of Mr. Waples,

The Committee adjourned until to-morrow morning, at 9 o'clock.

WEDNESDAY, February 11, 1863—9 o'clock, P.M.

The Committee met pursuant to adjournment.

Present—Messrs. Saulsbury, Hitch, Cahall, Slay, Stubbs, Williams, Waples, and Horsey.

PETER CALHOON, sworn and examined.

By the Chairman:

Question.   Where do you reside?

Answer.   In Sussex County, Cedar Creek Hundred, on the road from Milford to Milton.

Question.   Were you a member of the last Legislature?

Answer.   Yes, sir.

Question.   Did the soldiers who went from Milford to Milton on the day of the last general election, stop at your house, and if so, did they commit any depredation on your property, and if so, state what it was?

Answer.   There was a set of armed men came to my house on Tuesday morning, a little before day, and marched around my house in the yard. This was very unexpected to me, and alarmed my family a good deal. The women were very much alarmed and confused, and expected that their intention was to take me away. When we got up in the morning, my daughters went to the milkhouse and found that it was stripped of butter, and even the cream which had been in the house was gone. They went off without committing other damage to my knowledge. I proceeded to Milton. They did not pay for the butter and cream which they took, neither did they ask me for anything to eat; if they had I should have given them something.

PETER CALHOON.

SHEPHERD P. HOUSTON sworn and examined.

By the Chairman:

Question. Where do you reside?

Answer. In Lewes and Rehoboth Hundred, within a mile and a quarter of Lewes.

Question. How long have you been a voter?

Answer. For thirty years.

Question. Did you see anything at or near the polls on the day of the last general election, unusual and different from what you ever saw before?

Answer. Yes sir. We had a company of cavalry there, numbering, I believe, between thirty and forty. They were, I think, about equally divided between the hotels. The Captain and about one-half of his men were at the United States hotel. The others were at the hotel where the election was held. They were not stationed at the polls. I observed Captain Cline near where the election was held, in conversation with Captain Lyons, which was the only time I saw Captain Cline near the polls.

Question. Do you know whether the soldiers who were at Lewes that day were Maryland Home Guards, under command of Colonel Wallace, or whether they were a portion of the troops brought over from Baltimore under command of Gen. Wool?

Answer. I had a conversation with Captain Cline on the day of the election. He informed me that they were Philadelphians, stationed at Baltimore, and came on with General Wool to Seaford.

Question. Do you know who had charge of the troops at Lewes that day after their arrival there?

Answer. Captain Cline told me that he was under the direction of Captain Lyons.

Question. Where does Captain Lyons reside?

Answer. In Lewes.

Question. Is he an active and violent partisan?

Answer.   I consider the Captain pretty violent in political excitement.

Question.   To what political party does he belong?

Answer.   To the Republican party.

Question.   Did the presence of the troops in Lewes, on the day of the election, produce any considerable excitement or intimidation among the voters there?

Answer.   Yes, sir; the Democratic voters were very much alarmed.

Question.   Are the two parties there pretty equally divided as to numerical strength?

Answer.   Yes, sir.

Question.   Was there any necessity for the presence of soldiers at the polls that day to preserve the public peace?

Answer.   None at all; we are a very quiet, peaceable set of men.

Question.   Did it not seem to be the general impression among persons of all parties, judging from their actions, that the troops were there for the benefit of the Republican party, and for the injury of the Democratic party?

Answer.   There can be no doubt, I think, about that being the object.

Question.   Do you know whether there was a volunteer company at Lewes previous to the last general election, and whether they retained possession of their arms up to the day of the election?

Answer.   Yes, sir. There was a company of Home Guards organized in the month of October, who, I believe, were drilled every Saturday. They were drilled and commanded by Captain John N. Burton. The Lieutenants were David Murray and Thomas W. Turner. The officers of the company are all Republicans, and the entire company, as far as my knowledge extends, are Republicans.

Question.   Was there any Democratic company in that Hundred having possession of arms on the day of election?

Answer.   No, sir.

Question.   Had not all the volunteer companies in your County, commanded by Democrats, so far as your knowledge extends, been deprived of their arms previous to the day of the last general election?

Answer. So far as my knowledge extends, they were.

Question. Were not all the Republican companies in your county, so far as your knowledge extends, permitted to retain their arms up to the day of the last general election?

Answer. So far as my knowledge extends, they were.

Question. By what authority was it generally understood that the Democratic companies had been deprived of their arms, and the Republican companies permitted to retain permission of their arms?

Answer. I believe it was generally understood that these orders came from the War Department.

SHEPARD P. HOUSTON.

LABAN L. LYONS, sworn and examined.

By the Chairman:

Question. Where do you reside?

Answer. In Lewes, in Sussex County.

Question. Were you at home all day on the Sabbath previous to the last general election?

Answer. No sir; I went to Georgetown.

Question. How long did you remain at Georgetown?

Answer. I left there late in the afternoon; I am not positive about that.

Question. Did you go immediately back to Lewes?

Answer. Yes, sir.

Question. Did you go to Georgetown that day for the purpose of consultation in reference to the introduction of soldiers into the State to be present on the day of the last general election?

Answer. No, sir.

Question. When did you first learn that soldiers were expected to be present in this State on the day of the election?

Answer.   When I got to Georgetown, I suppose at 11 o'clock, A.M., I found our people congregated together, and seemingly alarmed. They stated that on Saturday night a wagon had been attacked by the Democrats, and two or three men badly beaten, and that they should not go to the polls if they could not have protection; and that they had sent messengers to Washington to see if they could get troops.

Question.   Who were the persons who made these representations?

Answer.   Mr. Jacob Moore, Mr. William Ellegood, and others, whom I do not remember.

Question.   Did they state that the difficulty with the wagon, of which you have spoken, was the cause of their sending those messengers to Washington?

Answer.   I think that was what they stated.

Question.   Did you believe, from all that you saw and learned from those gentlemen, that that difficulty was really the cause of sending those messengers to Washington for the purpose of soliciting troops to be brought into the state?

Answer.   I do. I was surprised to find men so alarmed.

Question.   Did you learn at what time on Saturday night this difficulty occurred?

Answer.   I believe it was about 11 o'clock.

Question.   Have you ever been at Washington?

Answer.   Yes, sir.

Question.   Did you not know that it was utterly impossible to send messengers at 11 o'clock on Saturday night to go to Washington, in time to make arrangements and have troops brought into this State, and be present on the day of the election?

Answer.   I am not positive when they said they sent them. I suppose it was impossible; I gave that no thought at the time.

Question.   Do you not know that for some time previous to the day of the last general election, it was in contemplation among the leading members of your party to make an effort to have soldiers brought into this State, to be present at the polls on the day of the election?

Answer. No, sir; not to my knowledge; I never had a conversation of that kind with anybody.

Question. Had you never a conversation with anybody, or did you never hear a conversation between others, in which that thing was proposed and discussed?

Answer. I have heard a conversation in reference to bringing soldiers from our own County home to vote, but never in reference to introducing foreign soldiers into the State.

Question. Was it only for the purpose of voting that it was proposed to bring your own soldiers home?

Answer. That is the way I understood it.

Question. Were you the Provost Marshal for Lewes and Rehoboth Hundred on the day of the last general election?

Answer. I was special Provost Marshal.

Question. When did you receive your commission?

Answer. On Monday morning about three o'clock.

Question. By what means did you receive it?

Answer. By a messenger from Georgetown; his name was Martin; I am not certain whether his first name was William or George.

Question. Have you this commission with you?

Answer. No, sir.

Question. When was it dated?

Answer. I think it was dated the 2^{d} of November; I do not remember exactly.

Question. What day in the week did the second of November come on?

Answer. Sunday.

Question. Over whose signature was your commission?

Answer. Edwin M. Stanton, Secretary of War, I believe.

Question. Did you know the handwriting in which the commission was filled up?

Answer. No, sir; I did not.

Question.   Did you receive any letter or communication from any citizen of this State at the same time you received your commission?

Answer.   I received no letter; I think there was an order, on a separate piece of paper, to report to General Wool, at Seaford.

Question.   Over whose signature was this order?

Answer.   I believe it was James R. Lofland.

Question.   Have you that order with you?

Answer.   No, sir.

Question.   Will you please state its contents, as far as you can recollect?

Answer.   I am not able to state correctly, for it has passed off my mind; but I will state it to the best of my knowledge. Either it, or the commission, I am not able to say which, ordered me to report to General Wool, at Seaford.

Question.   Do you know for what object you were appointed Provost Marshal, and what were your duties?

Answer.   I do not know; I was appointed without my consent. I suppose the object was to take charge of the troops detailed for Lewes.

Question.   Did you take charge of those troops, and provide for their accommodation?

Answer.   I do not know that I took much charge of them; they went on ahead of me. I ordered them to stop at Georgetown until I came up, but it was late at night, and citizens from our place were there, and volunteered to guide them to Lewes.

Question.   What citizen or citizens were they who volunteered?

Answer.   I think it was John P. Marshall.

Question.   Do you know the purpose for which Mr. Marshall visited Georgetown that day?

Answer.   No, sir; I do not.

Question.   Of what political party is he a member?

Answer.   I believe he belongs to the Union party.

Question.   Did you, or did you not, bespeak accommodations for the soldiers at the two hotels at Lewes, either before or after their arrival?

Answer.   I do not remember exactly; I do remember that an arrangement was made, either by me or somebody else, to divide them between the hotels, one hotel not being sufficient to accommodate them all.

Question.   Do you know by whom the expenses of the soldiers at the hotels were paid, or whether they have been paid at all?

Answer.   They have never been paid. Bills were made out and sent to General Wool, but they have never been heard from.

Question.   Did you believe at the time of the last general election, or do you believe now, that there was any necessity for the presence of soldiers at Lewes to preserve the public peace?

Answer.   I do not think there was any great necessity.

Question.   I understood you to say that you never heard the subject of bringing soldiers into this State, to be present on the day of the last general election, proposed or discussed previous to your going to Georgetown on the Sabbath previous to the election—was I correct?

Answer.   I may have been present when some persons expressed a wish to have soldiers here. This was the first serious conversation I ever heard in relation to the subject.

Question.   I understood you to say that the disturbance at Georgetown, about eleven o'clock on Saturday night previous to the election, was the cause or pretext for the effort made to bring soldiers into the State, to be present on the day of the last general election—was I right?

Answer.   Yes, sir. That was what I understood to be the cause.

Question.   Did you request Captain Cline to station soldiers about the polls at Lewes on the day of election, or did you request him to cause the arrest of any citizen of that Hundred?

Answer.   I never saw Captain Cline from the time he left Seaford until Tuesday morning, the morning of the election. On Tuesday morning I called on Captain Cline, at the hotel. He asked me what I wanted him to do. I told him I did not want him to do anything but keep his men in order, and not let them get drunk, and stray about the town and commit any uncivil act. That if any emergency should arise in which I should want him, I would call for him.

Question. Did you call for him at any time that day, and request him either to station troops at the polls, or cause the arrest of any citizen of your County?

Answer. No, sir.

Question. Was there another Provost Marshal in Lewes?

Answer. Henry C. Maul, I think, is permanent Provost Marshal; appointed, I think, two or three months before the election.

Question. Do you know for what purpose he was appointed?

Answer. No, sir; I do not.

Question. Do you know what his politics are?

Answer. He is a Union man.

Question. Did you then, or do you now, expect to receive any compensation for your services as Provost Marshal?

Answer. No, sir. I did not, and do not expect to receive any. I was only special Provost Marshal for that day. I think the commission stated that I should receive — dollars per month, and expenses paid.

LABAN L. LYONS.

On motion of Mr. Williams,
The Committee adjourned until 7 ½ o'clock this evening.

SAME DAY, 7 ½ o'clock, P.M.

Committee met pursuant to adjournment.
Present—Messrs. Saulsbury, Cahall, Hitch, Stubbs, Williams, and Waples.

JOSEPH A. MCFERRAN sworn and examined.

By the Chairman:
Question. Did you vote on the day of the last general election; and

if so, where?

Answer. I voted at Seaford in Sussex County.

Question. Did you observe anything unusual and different from what you had ever seen before at the polls that day?

Answer. I did, sir.

Question. Please state what it was.

Answer. I saw a squad of United States cavalry, with drawn sabres, guarding the entrance to the polls.

Question. What was their position in reference to the polls?

Answer. They were drawn in line on each side of the window; their sabres were drawn; they were also mounted. I saw also an officer there called Provost Marshal—Rhodes Hazzard, a citizen of Seaford.

Question. Is Rhodes Hazzard an active and zealous partizan?

Answer. He is an active politician, in one sense of the word. He is a smooth, plausible man: one who is capable of doing the work of the Devil in the guise of an angel, in my opinion.

Question. To what political party does he belong?

Answer. He belongs to the Republican party, or, as they call themselves, the Union party.

Question. Had he charge of the soldiers at Seaford that day?

Answer. Yes, sir. I say "Yes, sir," because General Wool said so.

Question. Was the presence of the soldiers at the polls that day calculated to produce great intimidation among any class of voters?

Answer. I thought so. In fact, I may say it did, among all classes of Democratic voters. The opposite party were exultant over their presence.

Question. Was their position on horseback, with drawn sabres, as you have described, calculated to produce greater intimidation than could have been produced in almost any other way?

Answer. The position at the polls was the most threatening one they could have assumed.

Question. Will you please to state when the soldiers arrived at Seaford, by what conveyance they were brought, and everything that happened?

Answer. Colonel Wallace's regiment was there in the afternoon of Monday previous to the election on Tuesday. I suppose they came by the cars. I did not see. General Wool came in the afternoon of the same day by steamboats. He brought several companies of cavalry—I don't know how many.

Question. Will you please state whether you had an interview with him, and what happened at that interview?

Answer. When the boats first came to the wharf at Seaford, I, in company with some other gentlemen, sought an interview with him; but in consequence of his being occupied with the Provost Marshals of the different parts of the county, we were denied the privilege of going on board of the boat. Subsequently we sought an interview at the hotel; and there we were at first denied entrance into his room. Dr. Shipley went first. I went the second time; and then I was denied entrance into the room by Garret Layton, one of the Provost Marshals. I was told by Jacob Knowles, a strong Republican partizan, that it was of no use; that I could effect nothing; for the thing was all fixed. Afterwards Governor Ross sent a note to General Wool, asking an interview; which was replied to by General Wool in person, stating that he would see us as soon as he got at leisure. About 10 o'clock or 11 o'clock that night, after General Wool finished his business with the Provost Marshals and his officers, he came hurriedly into the room where we were, and after being introduced to several, we asked him what the object was in bringing troops into the county?—if they were to control the election? He answered that if it were so, he had nothing to do with it; but that to satisfy us he would go and ask "these gentlemen"—meaning, I suppose, the Provost Marshals. He went, and when he returned he said that they did not intend to interfere with legal voters. I asked General Wool what he meant by legal voters. He said he did not know, that he had nothing to do with it. He seemed to be in a hurry and left. Mr. Hazzard, the Provost Marshal, took it upon himself to decide whether votes were legal or not, constituting himself judge at the polls. I went to see General Wool on the day of the election in reference to a vote, refused by Mr. Hazzard, and stated to the General the law of our State in reference to challenged votes: that they should be decided by Judges appointed for that purpose. He said that he would see Mr. Hazzard that noon. He referred the matter to Mr. Hazzard and not to the Judge of the Election. I saw Mr. Hazzard drive a man from the polls before he arrived at the window. He was a Democratic voter, and told him that if he did not leave here he would arrest him, or words of like meaning. The man referred to did not vote that day.

Question. Was the presence of the military at the polls calculated to produce, and did it produce, a difference in the result of the election?

Answer. I think it did, sir, for this reason: The Democrats made no effort for at least an hour and a half after the polls opened. The doubt of what action the military were going to take prevented any effort on the party of the Democrats at the opening of the election. In fact, it was seriously debated whether or not it was not better to give up the contest on the night previous to the election, after our interview with General Wool.

Question. Were you not a member of the State Senate for four years previous to the present session?

Answer. I was, sir.

Question. By what party were you elected?

Answer. By the Democratic party.

Question. Are you not an active Democrat, knowing all the principal plans and purposes of the Democratic party?

Answer. I try to do all I can for the party. I think I am acquainted with the principles and purposes of the party; and if there are secrets, I am apt to know them.

Question. Did you ever hear of a purpose or a desire, on the part of the Democrats, to interfere with the polls on the 4th day of November last, so as to prevent a fair election?

Answer. No, sir; never.

Question. Were the Democrats of your County sanguine and confident of carrying the election by a handsome majority, if the election was a fair one?

Answer. They were, sir, by a majority of from five hundred to a thousand votes.

Question. Do you recollect what the Democratic majority, in your County, was at the little election?

Answer. No, sir; I do not.

Question. Was there, or was there not, a necessity for the presence of military at the polls, to preserve the public peace, on the day of the last general election?

Answer. No, sir; the civil authorities in our County have always proved sufficient to preserve the peace.

Question. Was it, or was it not, understood that all the volunteer companies in your County, commanded by Democrats, had been deprived of their arms previous to the day of the last general election?

Answer. It was so understood.

Question. Was it, or was it not, generally understood that the volunteer companies in your County, commanded by Republicans, were permitted to retain their arms up to the time of the last general election?

Answer. I never heard of a company, commanded by Republican officers, being disarmed. In fact, I saw the arms of the company at Bridgeville, last fall, in Mr. William Cannon's store—I mean the present Governor.

J. A. McFerran.

JOHN S. BACON, sworn and examined.

By the Chairman:

Question. Where do you reside?

Answer. In Little Creek Hundred, Sussex County.

Question. Did you vote on the day of the last general election, and if so, where?

Answer. I did; at Laurel, in Little Creek Hundred, and Sussex

County.

Question. Did you observe anything at or about the polls, unusual and different from what you had ever seen before on the day of the election?

Answer. I did, sir; I saw a portion of Captain Watkins' company of Colonel Wallace's regiment, of Maryland Home Guards, armed with muskets, loaded, and bayonets fixed, also a Provost Marshal, John L. Bacon.

Question. Who had command of those soldiers that day?

Answer. The Captain had the immediate command, but he said he was under the control of the Provost Marshal.

Question. Of what political party was the Provost Marshal understood to be a member?

Answer. Of what I would call the Republican party; of what they call themselves, the Union party.

Question. In what position were the military that day in reference to the polls?

Answer. They formed three sides of a square, the house in which the votes were received, and the adjoining fence making the other.

Question. Were the soldiers placed in any other part of the town that day?

Answer. They were placed in charge of two storehouses and two hotels.

Question. Who were the proprietors of the storehouses of which they took charge?

Answer. One was mine, the other was Isaac W. Sirman's.

Question. What are the politics of yourself and Mr. Sirman?

Answer. I am a Democrat; he is what is called a Union man, or Republican. The Captain said to me that he put the soldiers to watch me, and I must watch the liquor; meaning thereby, I suppose, to keep me from the polls, at least; he told me when he saw me at the polls, that I had violated his orders in leaving the store.

Question. Was there any proclamation of any kind made at the polls about the time the voting commenced, by the Captain or any other person?

Answer. The Captain said, about the time the polls were opened, that there should no one go inside of this square of soldiers to challenge voters—that that should be determined by the Inspector and Judges. Later in the day, a gentleman was talking to another one, requesting him to go forward and vote a white man's ticket, when the Captain said that he would arrest and compel that man to take the oath of allegiance, for no man should talk that way in his presence. He said our thoughts were our own, but our actions and words belonged to the government. The man was compelled to leave town to avoid arrest.

Question. Was the presence of the military at the polls and in the town that day, calculated to produce, and did it produce, great dissatisfaction and intimidation among any class of voters present that day?

Answer. It did, sir; among the Democratic voters.

Question. Did it produce a like intimidation among the Republican voters?

Answer. It did not; it made them sanguine and dictatorial.

Question. Was there, in your judgment, any necessity for the presence of soldiers, at Laurel, on the day of the last general election in order to preserve the public peace?

Answer. There was not, so far as the Democrats were concerned. All that the Democrats desired, was a fair election.

Question. Did the presence of the military there, in your judgment, conduce to the preservation of the public peace?

Answer. I think not; I think it would have been as quiet, so far as the polls were concerned; there might have been more noise off from the polls.

Question. Do you know whether any person was arrested there that day?

Answer. I saw three in charge of some soldiers, George M. Wootten was one, Hezekiah Matthews another, and a man by the name of Washington Cole.

Question. I think Mr. Wootten was arrested for urging his son to vote the Democratic ticket. I was not present. I do know why the others were arrested. The two that could vote were Democrats. The other was not entitled to a vote.

JOHN S. BACON.

STEPHEN GREEN, sworn and examined.

By the Chairman:

Question. Where did you reside at the time of the last general election?

Answer. In Broad Creek Hundred.

Question. Where did you vote?

Answer. I voted in the same Hundred.

Question. How long have you been a voter?

Answer. About fifty-one years.

Question. Did you see anything at or near the polls in Broad-creek Hundred, on the day of the last election, unusual and different from what you had ever seen before on election day?

Answer. I did. I never had seen soldiers at the polls before that. It was with difficulty that the Democrats could get to vote at all, until near night. Some left without voting, and returned again late in the evening; and some, I think, did not return at all that day.

Question. What position did the soldiers occupy in reference to polls?

Answer. There was a square formed at the end of the house where they received the votes, perhaps twelve feet square. There were three soldiers within that square during the day, and it was with very great difficulty that any of the Democratic voters could get within that square; frequently when they did enter, they were thrust back at the point of the bayonet. The Union party, I presume they go by that name, could get admittance, as certain individuals, who wore blue ribbons in their button-holes, were permitted to take any and several individuals at a time to go within that inclosure, and vote them at their will.

Question. Were there many persons who wore these blue ribbons, of which you speak?

Answer. I think there were eight or ten.

Question. Did they all belong to the same party, or were they members of different parties?

Answer. They all belonged to the same party.

Question. To what party did they belong?

Answer. The Union party.

Question. Was there any other person, except the soldiers you have named, permitted to remain within that inclosure during the day?

Answer. The Provost Marshal, Henry Betts, and Mr. James Scott, who, as I understood, was the Democratic Provost Marshal, were in there.

Question. Do you know what time in the day Mr. Scott went in this square?

Answer. I did not see him there before 1 o'clock.

Question. To what political party did Mr. Betts, the Provost Marshal, belong?

Answer. The Union party.

Question. Was he an active and violent partizan?

Answer. He was.

Question. Did you ever hear of a purpose or desire on the part of the Democrats to interfere with the polls, so as to prevent a fair election on the 4th of November last?

Answer. I never did.

Question. Was there, in your judgment, any necessity for the presence of military at the polls, to preserve the public peace on that day?

Answer. In my judgment, there was not.

Question. Was it generally understood by all parties there, that the military were present for the purpose of benefiting one party and injuring the other?

Answer. I believe that was the general opinion.

Question. For the benefit of which party was it understood that they were there?

Answer. For the Union party. As a proof of it, I had to become security to an old lady with an only son, who was afraid to suffer him to go to the election without my becoming surety for his safe return without injury.

Question. Did you, or did you not, see Mr. Betts several times that day take Democratic tickets from voters after they went into the square, and place Republican tickets in their hands?

Answer. I was standing close by the window where they received the votes, outside the square. I saw Mr. James Truit, an old gentleman, considerably under the influence of intoxicating liquor, who, I believed, intended to vote a Democratic ticket. When he approached the window where they received the votes, I saw Mr. Betts, the Provost Marshal, take the ticket out of his hand and read it. He retained that ticket, and ran his hand in his left pantaloons' pocket, took out another ticket, and placed it in Mr. Truit's hand, and immediately took him by the hand and held it to the window, and told him to vote it, and he did so. As to seeing him take a ticket from any other individual and exchange it, I did not see him, but I heard a number of others say he did do it.

Question. Did they, or did they not, that day, form their square by means of a rope?

Answer. Yes, sir.

Question. Were those men who wore blue ribbons permitted to take in voters across the ropes whenever they pleased?

Answer. They stepped over the rope just whenever they pleased. Mr. Jacob Knowles carried at least fifty across the rope, and there were others who could have done so, if they had been as active partizans.

Question. Were the Democrats also permitted to carry their voters across this rope?

Answer. They were not. I think we lost all the doubtful voters in consequence of their not permitting us to cross the rope.

Question.   Were any persons, except those gentlemen you have named as wearing blue ribbons in their button-holes, permitted to take voters across that rope?

Answer.   No, sir; with the exception of myself. I was permitted to pass over once.

Question.   Do you recollect any way by the side of the house in which persons were permitted to pass up and vote?

Answer.   At each corner of the house there was a small entrance, in one of which they would admit voters, the other was for them to return out.

Question.   Had all classes of voters the privilege to pass between those tents and the house?

Answer.   I thought not. I knew a number of persons who were trying to vote from early in the morning until 4 o'clock, before they succeeded. I think all their party had voted before a number of the Democrats got to vote at all.

Question.   Were the tents, of which you have spoken as one boundary of the space you have referred, the tents of the soldiers?

Answer.   Yes, sir.

Question.   Were you present at Broad Creek Hundred on the day of the little election?

Answer.   I was.

Question.   It has been stated that a man stood at the polls with a loaded revolver, threatening to shoot any Union man who attempted to vote. I desire to know if that was true?

Answer.   I was not there at the time. I understood the next day there was a quarrel between Mr. Dawson and some other man, and that Mr. Dawson drew his pistol in self-defence. I did not understand that he threatened to shoot any Union man who attempted to vote. I understood that it was a Democrat whom he threatened to shoot if he did not desist.

STEPHEN GREEN.

On motion of Mr. Hitch,

The Committee adjourned until 8 ½ o'clock to-morrow morning.

THURSDAY, February 12, 1863—8 ½ o'clock, A.M.

The Committee met pursuant to adjournment.

Present—Messrs. Saulsbury, Hitch, Cahall, Stubbs, Waples and Horsey.

JAMES H. BOYCE, of S., sworn and examined.

By the Chairman:

Question. Where did you vote on the day of the last general election?

Answer. In Laurel, Little Creek Hundred, Sussex County.

Question. Where did you spend the day?

Answer. I stayed at Laurel until 1 ½ o'clock.

Question. Please state what you saw at Laurel, of the action of the military?

Answer. I saw the military there. I did not pay a great deal of attention to their conduct. They were stationed around the polls: a part of them were around the polls, and a part of them at the stores and hotels.

Question. Did their presence there produce great dissatisfaction and intimidation among any class of voters?

Answer. Yes, sir; it did among the Democrats.

Question. Did it produce a like intimidation among the Republican or Union voters?

Answer. No, sir.

Question. Was there, in your judgment, any necessity for the presence of soldiers at the polls, at Laurel, to preserve the public peace, on the day of the last general election?

Answer. No, sir; there was not.

Question. Are you a Democrat?

Answer. I am, sir.

Question. Do you know all the principal plans and purposes of the Democratic party in conducting campaigns?

Answer. Principally so, sir.

Question. I ask you whether you ever heard of a desire or purpose, on the part of the Democratic party, to interfere with the polls, so as to prevent a fair election on the 4th of November last?

Answer. No, sir; I never did.

Question. Will you state what you saw and know of the action of the military in Broad Creek Hundred, and also of the conduct of the Provost Marshal there, on the day of the last general election?

Answer. The conduct of the Provost Marshal was to prohibit all Democrats from voting Democratic tickets that he possibly could, by keeping them off from the polls. I went up with some men to see them vote, and he told me that these men could not vote until he got ready or saw proper; that the power was in his hands, and he intended to use it. And at the time that I was up at the polls, he would call for men that wore the blue ribbons, at a distance of thirty or forty yards, and ask them if they had certain men in order for voting, and if so, to bring them along, and he would vote them. I asked him if he intended to let the Democrats vote that day. He made no answer, but Jacob Knowles asked me if I had come out there with the intention of taking the polls as usual. I told him I had not, but came out there to see that the Democrats should have a chance to vote. He pointed with his hand to the bayonets, and told me, "That is what protects us." Jacob Knowles seemed to be acting in concert with the Provost Marshal, William H. Betts, a member of the Republican party, I think, and a pretty strong partizan, so far as his knowledge extends.

Question. Do you know anything else in relation to the conduct of the soldiers at the polls, in your Hundred, on the day of the last general election there?

Answer. I was down to Mr. Edward Moore's on the morning of

the election, a hotel keeper in Laurel, and Captain Watkins brought up some eight or ten soldiers, halted them in front of the hotel, went in to see Mr. Moore himself, and said to him: "I want you to stay in here, and watch your liquors, and these two soldiers I place at your door are to watch you." Mr. Moore said to him: "Here are the keys, take them, and lock up." He said: "I shall not do it." Captain Watkins then went out of the store, and Mr. Moore followed him. Mr. Moore said to Captain Watkins: "I wish you would explain this matter to me, if you please." Said he: "When I say 'whoa' to a horse, I mean him to stop; when I say 'go on' to a horse, I mean him to start, and that is the plain letter of the law."

Question. For what purpose did he wish Mr. Moore to watch his liquors?

Answer. I do not know. I thought at the time it was to keep Mr. Moore from the polls.

Question. Was Mr. Moore an active and working Democrat?

Answer. Yes, sir.

Question. Do you also keep a hotel? Were there similar orders left at your house?

Answer. I suppose there were. I saw two soldiers placed at my door, and in order that I might not be prevented from going to the polls, I left and went to Mr. Moore's.

Question. Did you not feel yourself fully competent to take care of your liquors that day?

Answer. I did, sir. I always have been before and since.

Question. Is not Mr. Moore a good business man, and fully qualified to take care of his own interests?

Answer. Yes, sir.

Question. Do you know whether this Captain Watkins belongs to the Maryland Home Guards, under command of Col. Wallace?

Answer. I so understood.

Question. Did it seem to be generally understood by all classes, both in Little Creek and Broad Creek Hundreds, that the military were present at the polls in those places for the benefit of the Republican party, and for the injury of the Democratic party?

Answer.   That was the general understanding.

JAMES H. BOYCE, of S.

STEPHEN H. WARRINGTON, sworn and examined.

By the Chairman:

Question.   Did you point out to the military who were at Georgetown, on the day of the last general election, any persons to be arrested by them?

Answer.   Yes, sir; I pointed out Alfred Hart and Oliver Greenly.

Question.   By whose direction did you point out those men to be arrested?

Answer.   By direction of the Major.

Question.   Did you believe then, or do you believe now, that there was any necessity for the arrest of those men?

Answer.   I believe they ought to have been arrested if they were the men who tore the flag down. I did not know whether they ought to have been arrested or not.

Question.   To what particular flag do you allude?

Answer.   I mean the flag belonging to our Union party, which was torn down around Georgetown Square, opposite Stephen Halyard's Hotel. It was torn down from the wagon.

Question.   When was it torn down?

Answer.   On Saturday evening about—I do not remember the time—it was in the night.

Question.   Were you in the wagon?

Answer.   No, sir; I was in another wagon. I was in a wagon some three or four wagons behind. It was said, in an outcry by the men who were along, "One of our flags is torn down."

Question.   Had you more than one flag?

Answer. We had nearly a flag in each wagon.

Question. Do you know what the persons who were in the wagon, from which the flag was torn down, were doing with it?

Answer. I do not know; I never heard anybody say, except what I have heard up here from the witnesses.

Question. Do you say that you never heard anybody say, either before, at the time of, or after the occurrence, what was being done with the flag in that wagon?

Answer. I never did, to my knowledge.

Question. What were those wagons doing at the time it was said the flag was torn down?

Answer. We were going around the square.

Question. How often did you go around?

Answer. I think we went around two or three times.

Question. If that flag had been held in an erect, dignified position, as the flag of the Union ought to be carried, would it have been possible for anybody standing on the ground to have torn it down?

Answer. It was a very large flag, and, as it had a short staff, it might have been caught from the ground, even when standing erect.

Question. Did you tell the Major that the persons you pointed out to him for arrest, were the persons who tore that flag down?

Answer. I did not.

Question. Were you not all on a kind of a "spree" that night, driving fast around the square, and one party meaning to tantalize the other?

Answer. I do not know; we came into the meeting.

Question. Was it not a kind of a boast, as much as to say "Look at us! here we go?"

Answer. We wanted to go around to show the meeting.

Question. Have you not heard, over and over again, that the persons in the wagon were dropping the flag on the heads of persons as they drove along?

Answer. I do not remember.

Question. Did you not tell me last week, and do you not say now, that you believe that there was no necessity for the presence of soldiers, in Georgetown, to preserve the public peace?

Answer. I did not see any use of any soldiers until last little election. On that day there were Democrats who said that the men should vote as they wanted them to vote. Because Aaron Dodd, belonging to the Union party, went up and voted his sentiments—a Union ticket—against his nephew, who was running on the Democratic ticket for Assessor, then came up old Natty Vaughn—Captain Waples came up with him—and Alfred Hart, and Coulter Hart, and Oliver Greenly were there—Alfred Hart said that the men should vote just as they said. I do not know that there was any necessity for troops in this State on election day, and I might have told you so.

Question. If a parcel of men had been driving around the square, and striking you over the head with the flag-staff, would you not have caught hold of the flag?

Answer. I think it quite likely. I do not like to see one party put on another.

S. H. WARRINGTON.

EDWARD W. MOORE, sworn and examined.

By the Chairman:

Question. Where do you reside, and what is your occupation?

Answer. In Laurel, Little Creek Hundred, and Sussex County. I am now keeping a public house, and was in the same business at the time of the last general election.

Question. Will you state whether your house and premises were interfered with, on election day, by the military who were there?

Answer. On the morning of the election, Captain Watkins came down with a squad of infantry. Captain Watkins came in my house, asked me if I was proprietor. I answered that I was. He then told me that he desired me to sell no liquor on that day. It was a general prohibition, not confined to the soldiers. He remarked that he should leave me there to take care of that liquor, and that he should leave two soldiers to see that I obeyed his orders. I reached the keys down and requested Captain Watkins to close up. He said to me that he should not do it. I then said to him: "Captain Watkins, I will close up." "No, sir," said he, "you will not close up." He then went out of doors. I thought that I might have misunderstood him. I asked him, if I understood him to say that I should not close up. He replied by saying: "When I say to a horse, 'go,' I expect him to go; when I say to a horse, 'whoa,' I expect him to stop." He then left. He gave me no reason why he wished to confine me to the house that day.

Question. Did you desire to be out that day—and if so, what for?

Answer. I always have a desire to be out on election day, for the purpose of voting myself and seeing that other members of the Democratic party get to vote.

Question. Do you know who were the Inspector and Judges of the election?

Answer. William J. Windsor, Isaac Giles and John Moore, my father, were the Judges.

Question. Were there any directions given, or threats made that day, by Captain Watkins, to the Judges?

Answer. Not that I know of.

Question. Were you told by the Judges, or any of them, of anything said to them by Captain Watkins?

Answer. I heard one of the Judges say, on the day after the election, in conversation with him, that at the time a man by the name of James L. Davis, offered his vote, it was about to be refused. Captain Watkins present, said, unless that vote was received, he would smash the ballot-box. John Moore, my father, was the Judge who told me this.

Question. Of what political party is your father, John Moore, a member?

Answer. He is a member of the so-called Union party.

Question. Was he solicited by that party to act as their Judge that day?

Answer. I presume he was. He also held a commission as Justice of the Peace at the same time.

Question. Who is James L. Davis, of whom you have spoken?

Answer. He resides about Laurel. He is generally known as a foreigner. I do not know whether he has been naturalized or not.

Question. Was there, in your judgment, any necessity for the presence of military in Laurel, on the 4th of November last, to preserve the public peace?

Answer. I never believed there was any necessity whatever.

Question. Did it not seem to be the general impression and feeling of persons of all parties, judging from the conduct and actions of men, that the military were there for the benefit of the Republican party, and for the injury of the Democratic party?

Answer. So far as my observation extended, the so-called Union party seemed very much elated; the Democratic party seemed very much depressed.

E. W. MOORE.

JOHN L. BACON, sworn and examined.

By the Chairman:

Question. Were you the Provost Marshal for Little Creek Hundred, at the polls, on the 4th of November last?

Answer. I was special Provost Marshal; I do not know whether it was for that day simply, or whether it extends.

Question. From whom did you receive your commission as Provost Marshal?

Answer. From Hon. Edwin M. Stanton, Secretary of War.

Question. When was it delivered to you, and by whom?

Answer. I received it on Monday morning previous to the

election. It was contained in an envelope, handed to me by Benjamin Foukes.

Question. Was it accompanied by any order or directions?

Answer. There was an order signed by James R. Lofland. The order was to meet General Wool, at Seaford, on the afternoon of the same day.

Question. Have you your commission or order with you?

Answer. Yes, sir.

Question. Will you allow us to see it?

Answer. Yes, sir.

[He presents the commission.]

Question. Look at the handwriting in which the commission is filled up, and look at the handwriting over which the order to meet General Wool was given, and tell me whether there is not great similarity?

Answer. There is great similarity; but I never thought of it before.

Question. Will you look at the handwriting in which this paper is made out, and tell me if you are acquainted with it?

Answer. I do not, positively.

Question. Are you acquainted with George P. Fisher's handwriting?

Answer. I have some knowledge of it.

Question. Does not the handwriting in which this order is made out, very much resemble Mr. Fisher's handwriting?

Answer. It does.

Question. Will you please tell us the date of the commission?

Answer. It is dated November first.

Question. Did you meet General Wool at Seaford, in compliance with the order?

Answer. Yes, sir; and received from him instructions.

[The witness presents the instructions, which are as follows:

"Headquarters, Eighth Army Corps,
"Baltimore, Md., November 2^d.
"Captain Thomas Watkins, with 40 men, care of S. Provost for Little Creek,—

"Sir: You will proceed with John L. Bacon, Provost Marshal, and act strictly in accordance with his directions and instructions, taking care, in travelling through the country, that no depredations are committed, and no injury done to the inhabitants by officers or soldiers under your command; and that whatever is obtained by either officers or soldiers of the citizens, unless voluntarily given to them, be paid for. No coercion or intimidation will be allowed, unless advised and directed by the Provost Marshal.

"John E. Wool, Major-General."]

I then proceeded to Laurel, in Little Creek. On Monday night previous to the election on Tuesday, drew up and handed to Captain Watkins certain orders by which to govern his acts on the day of the election, which I offer to be recorded:

Orders of the Provost Marshal.

"Order 1st.—All liquor houses to be closed at 8 o'clock, A.M., and prohibit the sale of any intoxicating liquors whatsoever during the hours of voting. That the proprietor or proprietors of said establishments be placed as a guard over their respective places, attended each by two soldiers, who will see that this order is strictly obeyed, allowing, however, said proprietor or proprietors ample time for voting.

"Order 2^d.—That a guard sufficient for any emergency be placed at the places of voting, and that they preserve order at the same.

"Order 3^d.—And it is further ordered that, as the voters arrive in crowds, by wagons, or any other way whatsoever they may be grouped, you will order them to disperse, and decide for themselves their respective ways of voting.

"Order 4th.—That you will have an ample guard to be used as police, detailed for the purpose of preventing any assemblage in the streets, whereby disturbance may occur. That said force will disperse all crowds of boys and negroes collected around or near the polls.

"Order 5th.—That you will arrest any and all persons you may hear cheering for Jeff. Davis, or the so-called Southern Confederacy. That you will not allow your own men to be insulted by any one.

"John L. Bacon,
" Provost Marshal, of Laurel, Little Creek Hundred."

The foregoing is a true copy of the order handed to Captain Watkins.

Question. Was that order handed to him on the day of the election, or on the day previous?

Answer. On the night previous to the election the next day.

Question. Is that order a copy of the general order given by all the Provost Marshals?

Answer. I do not know whether any other Provost Marshal gave the same. This order was made out by myself.

Question. Who were the other Provost Marshals who met you at Seaford, on the day previous to the election?

Answer. Henry Betts, from Broad Creek; Garret Layton, from Bridgeville; William Ellegood, from Georgetown; Labal L. Lyons, from Lewes and Rehoboth; John C. Hazzard, from Broadkiln Hundred; Nathaniel Phillips, from Dagsborough; a man by the name of Conoway from Nanticoke, and Samuel Lacy, from Baltimore Hundred, were there. I understood there from these men themselves that they were Provost Marshals.

Question. Was it your understanding that you gentlemen met General Wool in your official capacity as Provost Marshals?

Answer. So far as it regarded myself, I did.

Question. Was there any form of oath given to the Provost Marshal, to be administered to voters on the day of the election?

Answer. There was not, to my knowledge.

Question.	Did you give to Captain Watkins any order except the one you have had recorded?

Answer.	No, sir; not to the best of my recollection.

Question.	Your name was mentioned by Mr. Wingate, in connection with a letter which he delivered to Colonel Wallace either on Saturday or Monday previous to the election. Have you any knowledge of that letter?

Answer.	I have a faint recollection that on Saturday previous to the election, I saw Mr. Wingate at the Laurel Station. I asked him if he had received a letter there that day, to the best of my recollection.

Question.	Who was the author of the letter to which you alluded?

Answer.	I supposed it would be from Governor Cannon, though I did not see him write it.

Question.	Why did you suppose that Governor Cannon would write a letter to Colonel Wallace?

Answer.	I did not suppose so. I saw Mr. Jacob Moore writing to Colonel Wallace when Mr. Cannon was present. I do not know who signed it. I understood it was to go to Colonel Wallace for troops to preserve the public order at the polls on election day. Mr. George Wootten was arrested that day, as I saw him in the hands of some soldiers. I know not for what cause, unless for being a little intoxicated, as he appeared to be. I afterwards interceded in his behalf, and got him released in time for him to vote, which he did. I presume he voted the so-called Democratic ticket. I did not see the ticket. I, also, during the day, chanced to meet Captain Watkins on the street. He asked me who was the owner of that carriage which went up to James Boyce's Hotel. I told him I did not know the carriage, but if he would point out the man he had reference to, I thought I could tell him. I asked him what was the trouble. He said he heard, or understood the man to hurrah for Jeff. Davis. I afterwards saw him in conversation with one Hezekiah Matthews, Jr. I heard Matthews acknowledge that he came in that carriage. I turned off and went down the street. I afterwards heard that said Matthews had been arrested. About night, I was waited on by a brother of said Matthews, called Henry Clay, to try to effect his release, as he would promise to take him off home himself, and would further vouch that he would make no more disturbance. They were both residents of Broad Creek Hundred. I also knew of one Washington B. Cole being arrested, who was a citizen of the State of Maryland, who was represented to me to be intoxicated. I also saw three other men there from Maryland; these are all I noticed.

Question. Is it not a very usual thing for persons to come over from Maryland into this State on the day of our election?

Answer. It may be, but not to my personal knowledge. I have seen but two, to the best of my recollection; and I have never seen a more quiet election than the last at our place.

Question. Do you not know, or was it not understood, that Captain Watkins and his men, who were at Laurel on the day of the last election, were a portion of Colonel Wallace's regiment of Maryland Home Guards?

Answer. It was so understood.

JOHN L. BACON.

On motion,
The Committee adjourned until 8 o'clock this evening.

SAME DAY, 8 o'clock, P.M.

The Committee met pursuant to adjournment.

Present—Messrs. Saulsbury, Cahall, Hitch, Slay, Stubbs, Waples, and Horsey.

GEORGE M. WOOTTEN, sworn and examined.

By the Chairman:

Question. Where did you vote on the day of the last general election?

Answer.   In Little Creek Hundred, Sussex County.

Question.   Were you interfered with by the soldiers that day?

Answer.   Yes, sir. I had been informed that my son said he would rather follow me to the grave than see me vote the Democratic ticket; so I mentioned it to him. While I was talking to him about that, he said: "I am as good a Democrat as you are." I told him he was a Black Republican, and if he wanted to see, just follow me, and he might see me vote a Democratic ticket. When I got out into the porch, I told him if he did not vote that way I would cut him off with a shilling. I afterwards called him a Black Republican, or something of that sort, when an officer slapped me on the shoulder, and told me I would have to stop that. When he got hold of me I shoved him off. He said: "Boys, take hold of him." I think I told him the property belonged to me. They said they did not care for that, and took me out of my own house. There were three of them; one having hold of each arm, and one behind me I did not see. He, or some other person, struck me over the head twice with a sword, I think it was, punched me in the back with a bayonet, I think. They got me up where their company was stationed, and put me in a smoke-house. There they kept me, I think, it may be about two or three hours. I had some company, Mr. Hezekiah Matthews; I was not satisfied to stay there.

Question.   Do you say all this was caused by your having remonstrated with your son for voting the Republican ticket?

Answer.   That is the only reason I know.

Question.   Do you say that the conversation with your son was in your own house?

Answer.   Yes, sir.

Question.   You had not broken the peace in any way?

Answer.   No, sir.

Question.   Did your son vote that day before you were released?

Answer.   I do not know; I suppose he did. I was nearly the last one that voted.

GEORGE M. WOOTTEN.

C. C. HART, sworn and examined.

By the Chairman:
Question. Were you at Georgetown, on Saturday evening before the election?
Answer. Yes, sir.
Question. Were you present at the time when it was said a flag was torn down there?
Answer. Yes, sir.
Question. Will you state all you know about the occurrence?
Answer. George Harris, my brother, and myself, probably one or two more, whom I cannot now name. Mr. Harris said to me: "Coulter, let us stand here and count those wagons as they go around; do you count the wagons, and I will count the carriages." We were standing and leaning up against the square-fence. The first time they came around they waved the flag over our heads, and knocked off my hat, and, I think, my brother's. The second time they went around, they hit my brother on the head with the flag-staff. He said to me: "If they do that again, I will tear them out of that wagon, *certain*." I said to him: "Don't you do it; it will cause trouble. I would not do it." I determined to pay a little attention to him when they came round again, because I was satisfied he would do it; but I had forgotten it, and the first thing I knew, I saw him hold of the end of the pole, and I think he tilted some half dozen out with the pole. I suppose by holding on to the pole or one another they were pulled out. It was rumored then all around the country that the Rebels had raised, and torn down the American flag and trampled it under foot; but there is not a word of it true; if there was a stitch in it torn, I did not see it. I think I was the first one that picked it up. That is about all.

Question. Had you, or your brother, been tantalizing or abusing them in any way when they struck you?
Answer. Not a word; we had not opened our mouths to them.
Question. What occurred afterwards?
Answer. I think they fought a little; they immediately jumped on

him. They made the attack. They ran to him as soon as they struck the ground. I do not think anybody was much hurt. He got hurt a little.

Question. Were you at the election on Tuesday?

Answer. A little while.

Question. How long did you stay?

Answer. About a half hour.

Question. Is it your habit to stay at elections so short a time?

Answer. Generally, I have been about the first one there, and the last one to leave.

Question. How came you to leave so early that day?

Answer. I think I should have been arrested if I had not left.

Question. Had you broken the public peace, or interfered with anybody?

Answer. No, sir.

Question. Why, then, do you think you would have been arrested?

Answer. I was told so by some of my friends; in fact, I saw them coming right at me. Mr. Lynch, Mr. Wingate, and others, told me that it was my turn next; that they were coming right after me. I did not want to go, but they pushed me right along and made me go. I went out home, and stayed there all the time the soldiers were there, except a portion of two nights. It was rather new business for me to be running away from anybody. They had arrested two of my brothers and my brother-in-law about twenty minutes before that. They put two of them in jail; they stayed there until Friday or Saturday morning.

Question. Were you a candidate, on the Democratic ticket, for Assessor for Georgetown Hundred at the little election?

Answer. Yes, sir.

Question. Were you elected?

Answer. Yes, sir; by a majority of one hundred and forty.

Question. What was the Democratic majority at the general election?

Answer. I do not know.

C. C. HART.

ROBERT LAMBDEN, sworn and examined.

By the Chairman:

Question.   Where did you vote on the day of the last general election?

Answer.   In Broad Creek Hundred, in Sussex County.

Question.   Were there any soldiers about the polls that day in that Hundred?

Answer.   Yes, sir; I think they said there were about forty or forty-five; I did not count them.

Question.   How were they stationed in reference to the polls?

Answer.   There was a ring drawn around the window, and staves driven down into the ground, and a rope on the staves from one to another, with the exception of about three feet at each corner of the house. There were soldiers stationed around outside of that line. One space was for the voters to go in; the other for them to come out. I suppose nine or ten soldiers walked back and forth around the circle for some two hours it may be, when they left, and others came in their place.

Question.   What was the object of their marching around?

Answer.   To keep people from crossing the rope, I suppose.

Question.   Was anybody permitted to remain inside of that circle?

Answer.   Mr. Betts, the Provost Marshal, the Lieutenants, and others were.

Question.   You say a portion of the voters were permitted to cross the rope. Who were they?

Answer.   I suppose from ten to twelve Republican leaders or prominent men on the ground, who had a piece of blue and white ribbons tied into the button-holes of their vests, were permitted to carry voters over the rope all the time. These men were David W. Moore, Jonathan Moore, Jacob Knowles, Curtis A. Conoway, John C. Cannon, Thomas Workman, and several others. I think Greenbury M. Truit, William W. Morgan, Jacob Cannon, and Clark Matthews, were there. All those persons were permitted to take voters across the rope. If they did not choose to go themselves, they would hand the voters over to Mr. Betts.

Question. Do you know to what political party all those gentlemen who had ribbons in their button holes belonged?

Answer. I believe I do, sir; I did not see them vote, but they are advocates of the Union party, as they call it, or the Republican party.

Question. Were Democrats also permitted to cross that rope, and go to the polls and vote, and take their friends up to vote?

Answer. No, sir.

Question. By what way or entrance were Democrats permitted to go up and vote?

Answer. At one corner of the house there was a way for going to the window; at the other, was the way for coming out.

Question. Had the Democrats equal privilege with the Republicans in going up to vote, even in the way at the corner of the house?

Answer. I do not think there were many Democrats or good Republicans went in until after the doubtful men on the ground had nearly all voted. I mean by good Republicans, those not doubtful. I stood at the way for going in from one to two hours with a doubtful man, and did not get in, and I left.

Question. Do you say that the Democrats were prevented from voting until the Republicans had nearly all voted?

Answer. There was very little voting at the way for going in until one or two o'clock.

Question. You have spoken of handing voters across the rope to Mr. Betts—what do you mean by that?

Answer. Those men who had the ribbon tied into the lappel or button-holes of their vest or coats, as I believe said, were admitted to go up to the ring, and go over, or put the men over the line, or go in at the way for going out. They would go to the line with their men, and hand them over to the Provost Marshal, who would take charge of them, take them to the window, and vote them.

Question. Did you see Mr. Betts at any time that day, when a Democrat would go up to vote, take a Democratic ticket out of his hand, and put a Republican ticket in its place?

Answer. I do not know that I did; I heard it so rumored: I did not see it.

Question. Are you not an active Democrat in your Hundred?

Answer. I vote the Democratic ticket.

Question. Are you not generally well acquainted with the purposes and plans of the Democratic party?

Answer. Pretty well acquainted.

Question. Did you ever hear of a purpose or desire, on the part of the Democratic party, to interfere with the polls on the day of the last general election, so as to prevent a fair election?

Answer. No, sir.

Question. Was there, in your judgment, any necessity for the presence of the military at the polls that day, for the preservation of the public peace?

Answer. I do not think there was.

Question. I will ask you, if, judging from the conduct of men of all parties, it was not generally understood that the military were present for the benefit of the Republican party, and for the injury of the Democratic party?

Answer. That is the general opinion in Sussex County. I have been told by several Republicans before the election, that it was doubtful whether myself and several other Democrats would get to vote. But I believe I met with no great difficulty when I was allowed to go to the polls. I suppose it was three or four o'clock before I got an opportunity to vote.

Question. Do you know whether any persons there that day were required to take an oath of allegiance before they were permitted to vote?

Answer. Yes, sir; I do. Jasper Dawson, Eggleston Moore, and Louder N. Hearn, I think, and several others were required to do so.

Question. Who administered that oath to them?

Answer.   I do not remember.

Question.   It was stated by the Governor, on his examination, that, on the day of the little election, he was informed that a person in Broad Creek Hundred stood with a loaded revolver near the polls, threatening to shoot any person who went up to vote the Union ticket; and he gave that as one of his reasons for asking the presence of military on the day of the general election. I ask you, if that was true?

Answer.   No, sir; I was by, and saw it. It was some fifteen or twenty feet from the window, I think, that Mr. King, a Democrat, and some other person, were in a dispute over a doubtful voter, whether he was entitled to a vote or something in that way. It was not of much amount; there were only a few words. Up stepped one Mr. Parker, and made a good deal of blowing, and was in the act of drawing, or did draw his coat, and as Mr. Jasper Dawson supposed, he was directing his mad spite at him. He came up close, raving and stamping. Mr. Dawson drew out his pistol, and told them to let him come on, or something of that kind. In a minute, I suppose, it was all over, and Mr. Dawson went one way, and Mr. Parker went the other. I heard that Mr. Parker was a Democrat; Mr. Dawson has told me several times, that it was an old grudge which had existed between him and Mr. Parker for three or four years. They were both Democrats, so far as I understood. It was not a political quarrel at all, as I understood it.

ROBERT LAMBDEN.

WILLIAM D. RICORDS, sworn and examined.

By the Chairman:

Question.   Did you vote in Broad Creek Hundred on the day of the last general election?

Answer.   Yes, sir.

Question.   Were there any soldiers stationed around the polls that day; and if so, state their position?

Answer.   They had a rope stretched so as to form a square, with staves driven down, and a rope from one to the other, leaving a space of about three feet at each end of the house. At one corner they went in, and at the other they went out. There was a soldier at each corner—one where they went in, and one where they went out. Those soldiers had muskets, and bayonets on their muskets; they were promenading backwards and forwards, with arms in their hands, from one corner of the rope to the other.

Question.   Were those soldiers under the command of any person?

Answer.   Yes, sir. After they were fixed in that position, I went up and asked one of the soldiers for the Captain. He told me that the Captain was busy. Then I stepped back to see him, and this soldier told me that he had just stepped out of the circle. I went about twenty yards from the circle, and I saw the Captain, and I asked him if the Democratic party were going to have a fair chance to vote. He told me they were. I asked him if we could not be permitted to place a man in the circle to challenge voters. He told me that it was not as he pleased, that I would have to go and ask Mr. Betts, the Provost Marshal. I then went to the circle, and called Mr. Betts to the line, and asked him if he would let us put a man in the circle. His answer was that I might come in. I told him I could not. Then he said that I might choose some man that was not noisy. I called on Mr. Henry R. Pepper. He said he could not. Then I called Mr. James Scott, who immediately got over. I think Mr. Scott had been over, it may be from two to three hours? I called him to the line, and asked him why he did not take a more active part in there than he did. His answer was, that he had no more to do or say in there than a dog, I think was his reply.

Question.   About what time in the day was Mr. Scott admitted into the square?

Answer.   It was about the time of the opening of the polls. He remained in there, it may be, until three or four o'clock, and possibly all afternoon.

Question.   What reason did Mr. Scott give for his having nothing more to do in there than a dog?

Answer. That the Provost Marshal would not let him have anything to say.

Question. How were the voters permitted to go to the window? Was it through the avenues of which you speak, or could they go over the line anywhere?

Answer. The Democrats had to go in the way in the corner.

Question. Did those of the opposite party have to go in and come out in like manner?

Answer. Not all of them. Any men that had the ribbon on their coats could bring up voters to the rope and call Mr. Betts, who would take them up to vote, through the square.

Question. Did you observe those men who wore those badges cross the line with voters, and take them up to the window to vote?

Answer. I did, frequently.

Question. To what political party did those men belong who wore those badges?

Answer. They called themselves Union men.

Question. Were they active and violent politicians?

Answer. Yes sir, they were.

Question. You spoke of Mr. Betts as being Provost Marshal. Is he an active politician?

Answer. Yes, sir; he is.

Question. To what political party does he belong?

Answer. He calls himself Union, or Republican.

Question. Do you know whether there were any bayonet charges made on that day by the soldiers upon the voters or citizens of the neighborhood?

Answer. Yes, sir. I saw them run their bayonets through John Pewsey's vest; he said it hurt him; they skinned his breast a little. I saw several others whom they pushed with their bayonets. I think I saw them push their bayonets into Mr. Bailey's clothes. I heard him say they did.

Question. Did you understand the causes which induced the

soldiers to push their bayonets into men's clothes, or was there no cause?

Answer. The cause was, as they said, to make them stand back so as to give them a chance to vote.

Question. So far as you were capable of judging from what you saw, did you think that both parties had equal privilege in getting to the polls?

Answer. No, sir. My reasons for so saying are that they wanted to get all the doubtful voters from the Democratic party. Mr. Culver was one of the doubtful voters, and William E. Cannon and myself were trying who should get his vote; and we agreed for him to say which ticket he wanted to vote, and he said he wanted to vote a Union Democratic ticket. I handed him my ticket and Mr. Cannon handed him his, and his cousin replied to him, "If that is the ticket now come and vote." He walked off with his cousin and Mr. Cannon, and I followed them. When they went up—Mr. Culver and Mr. Cannon—the bayonets were opened for them to go in; the bayonets were closed as soon as they got in. I told them they ought to allow me to go in too, but they would not allow me. I saw Mr. Cannon whisper into Mr. Culver's ear, and he voted the ticket he (Cannon) gave him.

Question. Do you know what the majorities were in your Hundred at the little election, and in favor of which party?

Answer. At our little election the Democratic majority was 153; at the general election, the Democratic majority was 121.

On motion of Mr. Hitch,

The Committee adjourned until to-morrow morning at 8 o'clock.

FRIDAY, February 13, 1863—8 o'clock, A.M.

The Committee met pursuant to adjournment.
Present—Messrs. Cahall, Hitch, Slay, Waples, and Horsey.
The Chairman being absent,
On motion of Mr. Waples,

Mr. Cahall was appointed Chairman, *pro tem.*

The examination of WILLIAM D. RICORDS was resumed, he being recalled,

By Mr. Cahall:

Question. Have not the Democratic majorities in your hundred always been greater at the general elections than at the little elections?

Answer. Yes, sir, they have.

Question. What, in your judgment, was the cause of the Democratic majority in your hundred, at the general election, being less last fall than at the little election?

Answer. It was caused by the soldiers. There were a great many persons who were afraid to go out on the day of the general election, because the soldiers were there. I took it upon myself to tell them to go out and vote.

Question. Was the vote polled as great as usual?

Answer. Yes, sir, greater. It was 611.

Question. Do you know any persons who were compelled to take the oath of allegiance before they were permitted to vote?

Answer. Yes, sir. Jasper Dawson was one; also Ebenezer Gray, Louder N. Hearn, and Eccleson Moore.

Question. Do you know who administered the oath to them?

Answer. Mr. Betts had it in his hand, I think, and handed it to the Judge. I think the Judge administered it.

Question. Did there appear to be great intimidation on the part of the Democratic voters at the polls that day?

Answer. Yes, sir, there did.

Question. You have been an active working man in the party for a good while, knowing all its principal plans and purposes in conducting campaigns, have you not?

Answer. Yes, sir.

Question. Did you ever hear of a purpose or intention on the part of any Democrat to interfere with the polls at the last general election, so as to prevent a fair election?

Answer.   No, sir.

Question.   If there had been such a plan or purpose on foot, do you not think, from your knowledge of the plans of the party, that you would have known it?

Answer.   Yes, sir; I should.

WILLIAM D. RICORDS.

The examination of ROBERT LAMBDEN was resumed, he being recalled.

By Mr. Cahall:

Question.   Do you know what the Democratic majorities were in Broad Creek Hundred at the little election last fall?

Answer.   Yes, sir. The Democratic majority was, I think, 153.

Question.   Do you recollect what the average Democratic majority was at the general election held in November following?

Answer.   Yes, sir. At the general election the Democratic majority was 121 or 122.

Question.   Is it generally the case in that Hundred that the majority is less at the general election than it is at the little election?

Answer.   No, sir. The Democratic majority is larger, generally speaking, at the general than at the little election.

Question.   What, in your judgment, was the cause of its being less at the last general election than it was at the little election preceding?

Answer.   I believe the Democratic majority was not as large as it would have been on account of soldiers being at the polls.

Question.   Did the presence of the soldiers at the polls seem to create much intimidation among the Democrats?

Answer.   Yes, sir; I believe there were a good many intimidated.

Question.   What, in your judgment, would have been the

Democratic majority in Broad Creek, if there had been no soldiers present, and no intimidation offered?

Answer. I believe the Democratic majority would have been at least 200; some place it at a larger number. William Brown, and one Mr. Neal, and Mr. Spicer, all Democrats, went home without voting. I think I saw some illegal votes. Mr. James Smith was under age, and voted. He had joined the cavalry company, and came down to vote. He worked with me up to some time last fall; he told me he would be of age this coming May, 1863. He voted the Union or Republican ticket.

ROBERT LAMBDEN.

JAMES SCOTT, sworn and examined.

By the Chairman:

Question. Where did you vote at the last general election in November last?

Answer. In Broad Creek Hundred, in Sussex County.

Question. Did you see anything there unusual, and different from what you had ever seen before at the polls?

Answer. Yes, sir; I saw soldiers there; I understood there were about forty. They were all armed with muskets and bayonets. They seemed to be under command of a Captain and a Provost Marshal both. There was a rope drawn so as to form a square in front of the window, and leaving an avenue at each corner of the house. Near the rope on two sides of the square, and about two or three feet from the rope, a mark was drawn on the ground, outside of which soldiers promenaded back and forth, and between which and the rope was the avenue through which Black Republican voters might go to the polls.

Question. Who was the Provost Marshal?

Answer. I think his name is William H. Betts.

Question. Were you admitted into the square of which you speak?

Answer. I was invited into the ring by the Provost Marshal.

When I was called in, I expected to have a white man's privileges, but I had none. At one time I stepped up to the Provost Marshal, and said to him: "This man who is going to vote is not a resident of Delaware; he belongs to Maryland." Mr. Betts said to me: "Dispute his vote." I did so; after which Mr. Betts came up and told the Judges they must take the vote, and let them know that if they did not take the vote, he would send a man in there who would take it; that he had the power and would use it. The vote was taken. I disputed John S. Smith's vote, as being a non-resident. Mr. Betts triumphed over us, and Smith voted. That evening he (Smith) tried to make fun of me, and let me know that I had disputed his vote, but he got it in, if he had no right. I challenged several others, whose names I do not recollect. They all voted. I do not remember a single Republican who tried to vote and failed.

Question. Who decided in regard to the legality or illegality of the votes—the Judges inside, or the Provost Marshal outside?

Answer. The Provost Marshal. There was an old man, being feeble, came in. The Provost Marshal ordered him out of the ring, and told him that he had no right to vote. He told him to wait and he would show him his tax receipt. He was about to turn him out of the ring. George W. Green told the Provost Marshal to wait and let the old man show his receipt. He took the receipt and read it, and said he: "I suppose you will have to vote." He did not show the receipt to the Judges at all. That is why I saw he was judge.

Question. Did the Judges refuse any voters brought up by Mr. Betts?

Answer. No, sir; I think there was a little contention over one.

Question. Were there any persons there wearing badges in their coats?

Answer. Yes, sir.

Question. Did they seem to be privileged over other persons?

Answer. Yes, sir; they could bring men over the rope when they chose.

Question. To what political party did they belong?

Answer.   To the Black Republican.

Question.   Did there seem to be an understanding, so far as you were capable of judging, between those men who wore badges and the Provost Marshal?

Answer.   Yes, sir; I believe they understood each other. They could bring men up to the rope and he would take them to the window.

Question.   Was this privilege allowed all persons?

Answer.   No, sir. I saw no Democrat have the privilege. The Democrats would come up to the avenue where they would have to wait, sometimes pushed back by bayonets. I saw Mr. Jacob Knowles bring a dozen men to the rope, when the Provost Marshal took them over the rope to the window.

Question.   Did you see the Provost Marshal offer any man money for his vote within that ring that day?

Answer.   I saw a man going up to the window to vote. The Provost Marshal called to him, and said something to him. The man then went up and voted, and as he came from the window Mr. Betts pulled out his pocket-book and gave him some "greenbacks."

Question.   Did there seem to be much intimidation on the day of the general election on the part of the Democrats?

Answer.   Yes, sir.

Question.   Were you admitted into that ring to challenge votes for the Democratic party, and if so, had you full privileges?

Answer.   I was admitted by the Provost Marshal, but I had no power. I was no more than a log of wood or a dog. I left the ring twice to go home, knowing that I was of no use there, but I was persuaded to go back by my friends. The Provost Marshal gave me no chance to do anything whatever.

JAMES SCOTT.

LOUDER N. HEARN sworn and examined.

By the Chairman:

Question.   Where do you reside?

Answer.   In Broad Creek Hundred, Sussex County.

Question.   Were you present at the election, and did you vote on the 4th day of November last?

Answer.   I was there and voted.

Question.   Did you observe anything about the polls unusual, and different from what you ever saw before on the election ground?

Answer.   Yes, sir; I did. There were soldiers, rifles, muskets, bayonets, and swords, more than I ever witnessed before on election ground.

Question.   How were the soldiers stationed at the polls?

Answer.   They had staves driven down into the ground, and a rope from one to the other, so as to form a square in front of the window where they receive the votes. On the outside of this rope, soldiers were promenading up and down all the time of voting.

Question.   Were any persons placed within the ring—if so, state who they were?

Answer.   Yes, sir; William Betts, said to be our Provost Marshal on that day, and some soldier, said to be a General, were in the ring.

Question.   Was Mr. Betts understood to have command of the soldiers there?

Answer.   It was understood so.

Question.   Who is Mr. Betts; what is his character; and what his politics?

Answer.   Mr. Betts is a son of Newfoundland Samuel Betts, as he is called; was raised near the Cedar Swamp. I think Mr. Betts generally does not stand very high. As to myself, if I had the weighing of him, I think I would try him on a three-cent piece first. He is generally pretty violent in politics. He belongs to the Republican party.

Question.   What did Mr. Betts do that day inside of the ring?

Answer.   He tried to intimidate the people. I supposed he knew my sentiments; that we were not, as we had heretofore been, of the same politics. When I was making my way up to the window, or to the gap-way, with a number of voters before me, the gap-way was closed, so I was informed, and voters were taken in on the other side. I stood there with my men, I think, near two hours, and they became very impatient, and commenced pressing towards the gap-way. Mr. Betts, Provost Marshal, seeing the situation I was placed in, gave orders to the soldiers to clear that gap-way. The soldiers came with their muskets and bayonets, and rushed the men, I suppose, some ten feet back from the gap-way, enough, at least, to squander all of my men. A short time after that I was looking around, and saw my men taken in across this rope. I called Mr. Scott, and asked him what way those men were voting. Said he: "Nothing crosses this rope but those who vote the Republican ticket." I mean by my men, men that I took there, and who I knew intended to vote the Democratic ticket.

Question.   You have stated that Mr. Betts had the entire control of the soldiers who were there that day—I ask you whether he used that power fairly and impartially between men of all parties?

Answer.   He had the power, but did not use it fairly and impartially.

Question.   Did not Mr. Betts use his whole power, as Provost Marshal, for the benefit of the Republican party, and for the injury of the Democratic party?

Answer.   I believe he did.

Question.   State what are the evidences of his partiality—whether he permitted persons wearing badges to cross the rope with voters, and denied that privilege to others?

Answer.   There was a gentleman, in the morning when I first came on the ground, came to me with a badge or ribbon and presented it to me. I asked him what was the intention of that. He commenced telling me that a man wearing this badge could have the privilege of voting. I told him no; I would not carry that thing in my pocket, let alone pinning it on my coat. I then went on to ask him further questions in regard to this badge or ribbon. He said that the greater part of it was, if a man should by chance get into a riot that day he might escape the bayonet. I told him I always had had my privilege there on the election day, and I hoped to have it that day; and I left him. This man was a son of Philip Matthews, and a Republican. Mr. Betts gave those gentlemen wearing badges privileges which he denied to other men. Mr. Betts, and his brother, and Jacob Knowles, or any of those men wearing badges, would bring men up to the rope and pass them right over. All these men wearing badges were Republicans, so far as I know them. Mr. Betts allowed no Democrat to go himself or take others across the rope to vote. I had not been in the habit of voting the Democratic ticket until the last election. I made up my mind some time before to vote the Democratic ticket; and if I had not before, I should have done so that day, merely from the partiality used on that day.

Question. Did not the presence of the soldiers there produce great dissatisfaction and intimidation among the voters?

Answer. Yes, sir. There appeared to be no show and no room for a Democrat to get to the polls until after the doubtful men were voted.

Question. Was it not generally understood, so far as you observed the conduct of men that day, that the soldiers were there for the benefit of the Republicans, and for the injury of the Democratic party?

Answer. I think it was so understood.

Question. Do you believe, as an old resident of that Hundred, being well acquainted with the people, that there was any necessity for the presence of soldiers at the polls to preserve the public peace?

Answer. No, sir; I do not; and further, I do not believe they would have been brought there if it had not been for the poll on the Democratic ticket on the day of the little election. It was an unusual thing for the Democratic ticket to get so large a majority at the little election as at the last little election.

The Chairman. State what the majority was.

The Witness. I think it was 154.

Question. Was it not generally understood that if there was a fair election, that majority would be very much increased at the general election?

Answer. Yes, sir; it was. The majority was 121 or 122; and, I believe, if we had had the same show as at the little election, our majority would not have been less than 175 of 180. The little election was a fair, quiet, and peaceable election.

Question. Was there any test-oath presented to you as a condition upon which you were permitted to vote?

Answer. Yes, sir. Mr. Betts presented me the oath when I went to the window to vote. William Betts let me know that I must take the oath before voting. I asked him why it was that I had to take the oath before voting. He said to me it was no time for argument. I said to him I wished I could believe he was as good a Union man as I was myself, and was at the same time still offering my vote at the window. He objected, except on condition of my taking the oath. Finally I made up my mind that I would not be driven away, and so took the oath. Mr. Betts directed the Judges not to take my vote until I had taken the oath. I believe the Judges would have received my vote without the oath, if they had been left to their own judgments.

Question. Who administered the oath?

Answer. Esquire Matthews, a Republican.

Question. Are you not quite as much interested in the Government, and have you not quite as much to lose by any injury to the Government as Mr. Betts?

Answer. I supposed a great deal more.

Question. Have you not as much to lose as a half dozen of such men?

Answer. I believe I have.

Question. Was the same test-oath presented to any other citizen of that Hundred?

Answer. My father-in-law, Ebenezer Gray, and Isaac Wootten, Isaac Tunnel, and Nathaniel King, were required to take the oath.

Question. Is not Mr. Gray, your father-in-law, an old gentleman of great respectability and wealth in that Hundred?

Answer. Yes, sir; he is.

Question. Are not the other gentlemen you have named as having been required to take the oath before they could vote also men of property and position in that community?

Answer. Yes, sir; they are.

Question. About what age is this Mr. Betts?

Answer. About thirty years old; possibly a little more.

Question. Do you know whether Mr. Betts considered it necessary that he himself should take a test-oath before voting?

Answer. I suppose not. I suppose he considered himself a pretty good patriot.

LOUDER N. HEARN.

WILLIAM H. BETTS, sworn and examined.

By the Chairman:

Question. Were you the Provost Marshal for Broad Creek Hundred on the day of the last general election?

Answer. Yes, sir.

Question. From whom did you receive your commission?

Answer. Hon. Secretary Stanton, Secretary of War.

Question. When, and from whom did you receive that commission?

Answer. On Monday before the election; Mr. Philips, I think, brought it to my house; I was not at home.

Question. Did you receive any instructions from General Wool at the same time you received your commission?

Answer. Yes, sir.

Question. Have you those instructions with you?

Answer. Yes, sir.

The Chairman. Let us see them.

[The witness presented the instructions, which are as follows:

"HEADQUARTERS, EIGHTH ARMY CORPS,
"Baltimore, Md., November 2ᵈ, 1862

"Captain Evans, with 40 men, commis'd offc'rs & privates, for Broad Creek,—

"SIR: You will proceed with William H. Betts, Provost Marshal, and act strictly in accordance with his directions taking care, in travelling through the country, that no depredations are committed, and no injury done to the inhabitants by officers or soldiers under your command; and that whatever is obtained by either officers or soldiers of the inhabitants, unless voluntarily given to them, be paid for. No coercion or intimidation will be allowed, unless advised and directed by the Provost-Marshal.

"JOHN E. WOOL, Major-General."]

Question.   Do you consider these as your instructions?
Answer.   I did. They were all I received from General Wool.
Question.   I see certain orders—by whom were these orders signed?
Answer.   James R. Lofland.
Question.   Look at the handwriting in which these orders are made out [presenting the paper containing the orders] and also the handwriting in which the commission was filled up, and tell me if they are not very much alike?
Answer.   I think they are pretty smart alike.
Question.   Do you not believe they are in the handwriting of the same individual?
Answer.   I think they are.
Question.   Did you receive any other instructions from General Wool, or any other person, which you have not exhibited?
Answer.   I received no written instructions.
Question.   Did you receive any verbal instructions from General Wool, other than what you have mentioned?
Answer.   I think he told me to preserve order; and if it became necessary to fire, to use no blank shots.

Question.   Did General Wool deliver you the form of an oath to present as a prerequisite for voting to citizens of your Hundred?

Answer.   No, sir.

Question.   Did you present a test-oath to any citizen of that Hundred as a condition of voting?

Answer.   Several persons were required to take the oath of allegiance.

Question.   Was it by your direction?

Answer.   Not entirely. There was a consultation held early in the morning by several persons—Mr. Jacob Knowles, Mr. Jonathan Moore, William E. Cannon, and others. These are Union men, otherwise called Black Republicans. Some of them, and, I believe, all, came to the conclusion that it would be nothing amiss to require the oath of allegiance of several persons who might be on the ground, and it was done.

Question.   Did you direct the Judges not to receive the vote of anybody until he had taken the oath?

Answer.   I said to the Judges that it had been decided that the oath of allegiance would be required of some individuals on the ground before they would be allowed to vote; and when those men came up to vote, that it was required of them, or words of like meaning.

Question.   Did you tell the Judges by whom it had been thus decided?

Answer.   No, sir.

Question.   By whom was it so decided?

Answer.   By the individuals I have mentioned in the consultation I just now referred to. The oaths were then administered by one of the Judges, Mr. Matthews, I believe.

Question.   To whom were those oaths administered?

Answer.   To Mr. Ebenezer Grey, Isaac Wootten, Isaac E. Tunnel, Louder N. Hearn, Nathaniel King, and, I think, Eggleston Moore, and perhaps others.

Question.   Are not those men to whom oaths were administered, large property holders and men of respectability in their communities?

Answer. No, sir; they are not. Some of them are pretty large property holders. There are some of them whom I do not know much about. It was represented that some of them did not stand well; at least, that they were not loyal.

Question. What is loyalty?

Answer. It is to support and maintain the Government with all their power.

Question. What is the Government?

Answer. I mean the Constitution of the United States; and in supporting the Government in crushing out Rebellion.

Question. Do you know, or were you informed previous to the last election, of any breach of the Constitution of the United States on the part of any of those gentlemen to whom oaths were administered?

Answer. I do not know what you mean by a breach of the Constitution. I do not know whether any of them had broken it or not. I do not know that they had a chance to break it.

Question. What were the politics of the Judge of the election who administered the oaths?

Answer. He was a Union man.

Question. By whom was that oath dictated?

Answer. I drew up the oath.

Question. Have you a copy of it?

Answer. No, sir.

The Chairman. State its contents.

The Witness. It was to support the Constitution of the United States, bear true faith and allegiance to the same, defend it against all its enemies, foreign or domestic. This was the substance.

Question. Did you consider that the consultation of which you have spoken gave you sufficient authority to have that oath administered to those men, as a condition upon which they were to vote?

Answer. I considered that I had sufficient authority without any consultation. I chose to hold a consultation before I did it, and others concurred in the same.

Question. From whom did you get the power to administer the oath?

Answer. If I got it at all, I got it from the same source I got my commission from.

Question. Did you consider that your commission and instructions gave you such authority?

Answer. I consider that they did. The reason why I did it was, that I heard certain individuals, for example, Henry Hudson, say that: "He would fight for Stonewall Jackson; he would vote for him; he would send him a beef it he could; he would render him and his cause any assistance he could if he had the chance." I did not consider *that* the language of any loyal man, and that taking the oath of allegiance would hurt no loyal man. Another man, by the name of Nathaniel King, I heard glorying and boasting over the defeat of the Government troops, and of the ability of the rebel leaders in their generalship, &c., saying that United States troops who were killed in battle were dead and in hell. I did not consider *that* the language of any loyal man. For example, again, Ebenezer Grey I heard say that he did hope that the rebels would take Washington, and used considerable of other language at the same time, which, I thought, was of a disloyal character. Another man, by the name of Jasper Dawson; I saw him stand at the election window, on the day of the little election, or perhaps within some three or four feet of it, with a drawn revolver, brandishing it up and down, in that way, [throwing his hand up and down,] and said: "Clear that window!" repeating it, perhaps, a third time, "I stand here, like Stonewall Jackson, on American soil!" I did not think *that* looked very loyal. Some of them said: "Get out of the way, he will shoot you!" I was standing within four feet of him, I guess, and nearly in front of him. This took place not later than 1 o'clock. I thought he had about sense enough to shoot. Previous to that, I had been standing on one side of the window, and he on the other, challenging votes. There were a good many persons around the window at the time. About the same time that he drew his pistol, there was a fuss knocked up between one Joseph Parker and Nathaniel King, which arose over, as I understood, Hilary Gray then and there having voted the Union ticket. Mr. Parker, if I understood his politics, was a Union man. I had it from his own mouth. The object of Parker in this fight was Nathaniel King and not Mr. Dawson. I was right by Parker. Near enough to him to have put my hand on him. King got mad because Grey voted the Union ticket; commenced abusing the Black Republicans, and afterwards launched out into the discussion before named about the Government troops. The window was cleared; so we considered; I for one; and the men driven off by this revolver.

Question.   When did Mr. Hudson make the remarks to which you have alluded, and in the presence of whom?

Answer.   He made it in Adolphus Ewing's hotel, in Georgetown.

Question.   Did you consider that the conversation you have attributed to the persons you have named, gave you the authority, as Provost Marshal, to direct that oath to be administered?

Answer.   I thought it was sufficient to require it; and I thought I had the authority, either with or without such conversation on their part.

Question.   What was the oath which you took as Provost Marshal?

Answer.   It was to support the Constitution of the United States, bear true faith and allegiance to the same; defend it against all its enemies, foreign and domestic, and something else I do not recollect. That was the substance of it.

Question.   Did you not know at the time, and do you not know now, that the administering of that oath to the persons you have named, was a direct violation of the Constitution of the United States and the Constitution of the State of Delaware?

Answer.   No, sir; I did not, and do not now know it.

Question.   Have you ever read the Constitution of the United States and the Constitution of the State of Delaware?

Answer.   Yes, sir; I have read them both.

Question.   By whose direction was it that certain persons wore blue ribbons in the lappel or button holes of their coats on the election ground that day?

Answer. I do not know. It was not at mine.

Question. Why was it that persons wearing those badges were permitted to cross the rope drawn there that day, also to take others across for the purpose of voting, whilst this privilege was denied to others?

Answer. They had not the privilege from me.

Question. Did they not do it?

Answer. There were some instances when those who wore the ribbons brought up men to the rope, and there were instances when others, who had no badges, brought up men to the rope. I did not know the men with blue ribbons who crossed the rope with their voters. There might have been some. I paid no attention.

Question. Do you know of any single instance that day when a Democrat was permitted to cross that rope and vote, or send a voter across the rope, to go to the polls and vote?

Answer. I think they crossed it in several instances. I do not recollect. Neither do I recollect a single one that crossed on the other side.

Question. If you do not recollect a single Democrat who crossed that rope for the purpose of going to the polls, how can you say that they did cross the rope?

Answer. There were men that crossed the rope, and in one instance a Democrat and Union man crossed together.

Question. By whose direction was the rope placed there?

Answer. I do not know; it was not by mine.

The Chairman. Mr. Betts, you will please sign your testimony.

The Witness. I am not through.

The Chairman. You are now at liberty to make any statement in explanation of your testimony, confining yourself strictly to the questions which have been propounded to you by the Committee.

The Witness. The troops were at the election, which everybody knows; and, in my opinion—as well as a great many others—we could not have voted that day, nor had an election, without the presence of those troops; and that there would have been bloodshed and murder in general on the election ground. There were some two or three bullies, out of Maryland, that came there, as we were informed, to help bully Union men from the polls, and prevent them from voting. James Henry West was one, and it is said there were two or three others that I did not see. Mr. Scott was in the ring and had full chance to challenge; and was not by me, at any time, prohibited from challenging votes that were illegal. There was an entrance at each corner of the house: one for going in and the other for coming out, and men of the so-called Democratic party did enter and vote at the place of going out about as regularly as those of the opposite party.

W. H. BETTS.

The examination of ROBERT LAMBDEN was resumed, he being recalled.

By the Chairman:

Question. Will you explain all you know in reference to the drawing of a pistol by Mr. Dawson, at the little election, in Broad Creek Hundred, last year?

Answer. On the day of the little election in Broad Creek Hundred, in Sussex County, I suppose it was about 12 o'clock, noon, Mr. King, and some other man besides Mr. Parker, got into a contention over some illegal vote. One Mr. Parker came up, and had something to say about the affair, and as Mr. Parker came up, Mr. Jasper Dawson had something to say about the affair. It was hardly a moment before Mr. Parker, who was in a perfect rage, was in the act of drawing his coat, or did draw it, to come to Mr. Dawson. I think one or two gathered around Mr. Parker, and two or three—Mr. King and others—were between Mr. Dawson and Mr. Parker. Mr. Dawson drew out a pistol, and told them to clear the way and let him come; that he knew at whom he (Parker) was directing his mad spite. He threw his pistol up and down, and as he did so, Mr. Rickets touched him, and told him to come off this way; that he would not do that. Mr. Dawson immediately put up his pistol, and stepped back towards the corner of the house. I heard no more contention over it that day, except that Mr. Parker made some threats about presenting Mr. Dawson for drawing the pistol on him. I do not think Mr. Dawson's pistol was out of his pocket more than one minute. Mr. Dawson jumped up and said, "He was a good Democrat, and stood on American soil." I am positive he said nothing about Stonewall Jackson. He might have said, "I stand as a stone wall on American soil." I will not be positive about that. Some one told me that Mr. Parker was a Democrat; I did not know the politics of the gentleman myself. Some two hours after that, I went to Mr. Parker, and told him I was sorry that the difference arose between him and Mr. Dawson, both being of one political party, as I had understood, and told him that I would let the matter rest.

Question. Did Mr. Parker admit that he was a Democrat?

Answer. I do not know that he made any reply. He did not dissent from my statement. I said to Mr. Solomon Short, one of the leaders of the Republican party, who was having something to say about the affair, that I did not think it was any of this business; that it was a mere Democratic quarrel, as I understood. Mr. Betts alleged to-day that Mr. Parker voted a Republican ticket at the general election. I do not know how he voted. If he did not vote a Republican ticket, it was not for the want of a chance.

Question. Is not Mr. Dawson a civil, gentlemanly man?

Answer. Yes, sir.

Question. Did Mr. Dawson, waving his pistol up and down in the air, as was described by Mr. Betts to-day, drive the people from the election grounds and cause them to go home?

Answer. He did not, sir. Mr. Dawson was standing from ten to fifteen feet from the window, with his back to the window, when the occurrence took place. Mr. Parker was ten feet, I suppose, from Mr. Dawson when the quarrel began.

Question.   After the difficulty between Mr. Dawson and Mr. Parker had subsided, did not the election continue peaceable and quiet until night?

Answer.   Yes, sir. The affair was quite short. I think there were few offering to vote. The whole difficulty did not last two minutes.

Question.   Did Mr. Betts act fairly and impartially, giving members of each party an equal chance to vote there on the day of the general election?

Answer.   He did not, sir, in my opinion.

Question.   Do you know anything about this Mr. Hudson, who was spoken of by Mr. Betts, as having said he would fight for Stonewall Jackson; that he would send him a beef, &c.—do you know the man?

Answer.   Yes, sir; I am very well acquainted with him.

Question.   Is he a prominent leading man in the Democratic party?

Answer.   He is a man of not much fortune but a good Democrat. He is a good working man in the Democratic ranks.

Question.   Do you believe, from all you know of Mr. Hudson, that he is a man that ever contemplated doing any harm to his Government?

Answer.   No, sir. I do not believe Mr. Hudson would do any harm to his county. Mr. Hudson is a man that takes occasionally a little too much liquor, and if he had the conversation that has been represented here by Mr. Betts, he must certainly have been drunk; for I do not believe the man would say such things when sober.

Question.   Are you acquainted with Mr. Ebenezer Gray?

Answer.   Yes, sir; I know him when I see him.

Question.   Is he not one of the most reliable men in your section of country?

Answer.   I believe Mr. Gray is one of the most reliable men we have in our Hundred.

Question.   Did you ever hear him charged in his own neighborhood with being an enemy to his country?

Answer.   I have never heard any charge of that kind against him. I do not live in his neighborhood.

Question. Are any of the persons spoken of by Mr. Betts, as having said things derogatory to the Government, men who would be feared by persons in their own neighborhood as designing any harm to their Government?

Answer. I do not know what the man said to Mr. Betts, but I would not fear any citizen of Broad Creek Hundred doing any harm to the Government. The Government, I think, is perfectly safe, so far as they are concerned.

Question. Are you well acquainted with Mr. Betts?

Answer. I have known Mr. Betts ever since 1855; I never had any dealings with him. The character he has borne since he has been Provost Marshal has been pretty bad. The people in Broad Creek Hundred are generally very much opposed to his doings as Provost Marshal.

Question. You recollect that Mr. Betts testified that the avenue for voters to come out from the window was open equally for members of both parties to go up and vote—was this statement true?

Answer. There might have been some afflicted Democrats admitted into the way for going out, but for the Republican party it was a very open thoroughfare. It was not, neither was any other place equally open for Democrats as for Republicans.

Question. Was it true, as represented by Mr. Betts to-day, that a number of armed bullies from Maryland were at the polls in Broad Creek Hundred for the purpose of aiding the Democrats in taking possession of the polls, and driving the Union men away?

Answer. If there were any there, I did not know it at the time, and heard no talk of it then or since, until I heard Mr. Betts say so to-day.

Question. If there had been such a combination between the Democrats of your Hundred and the people of Maryland, from your position in the Democratic party would you not certainly have known it?

Answer. Yes, sir; I believe I should.

Question. Is it true, as represented by Mr. Betts, that if it had not been for the presence of soldiers at the polls, the Democrats would have taken forcible possession of the polls, and that there would have been murder and bloodshed in general?

Answer.   No, sir; I do not think there would have been murder or bloodshed. I think we should have had as quiet an election as usual.

Question.   Did you ever hear of a desire or purpose, on the part of the Democrats, to interfere with the polls, so as to prevent a fair election?

Answer.   No, sir; I did not, and do not think the idea was entertained by any Democrat of the Hundred.

Question.   Were not the Democrats sanguine and perfectly confident that, if there was a fair election, they would have a large majority in the County?

Answer.   Yes, sir. A good many prominent Democrats in the County estimated the majority from 500 to 1000.

ROBERT LAMBDEN.

The examination of LOUDER N. HEARN was resumed, he being recalled.

By the Chairman:

Question.   Did you hear the testimony of Mr. Betts, the Provost Marshal, from your Hundred, to-day?

Answer.   I did, sir.

Question.   Was it true, as represented by him, that all parties had an equal chance to vote, and that he acted impartially towards all parties on election day?

Answer.   No, sir; I think not. As I before stated, the Democratic party was apparently kept away from the window by the Republican party and by the soldiers as long as they well could to give them any time to vote.

Question.   Did not the whole conduct of Mr. Betts on that day show that he was acting with great partiality, and endeavoring to promote the interests of the Republican party by unfair means, and the injury of the Democratic party?

Answer. Yes, sir; and his conduct was very overbearing.

Question. Are you not very well acquainted with the people in Broad Creek Hundred?

Answer. I am very well acquainted with the people of that Hundred generally.

Question. Did you ever hear of any combination between the Democrats of that Hundred and bullies of Maryland, as was described to-day by Mr. Betts, to take forcible possession of the polls, and drive Union men away?

Answer. No, sir; I never did, until I heard it so stated by Mr. Betts himself, to-day. I do not think there ever was such a thing thought of or intended by the Democratic party.

Question. Is it true, as was represented by Mr. Betts, that if it had not been for the presence of the soldiers at the polls, the Democrats would have taken forcible possession of the polls, and that there would have been murder and bloodshed in general?

Answer. I would think not. I am confident nothing of the kind was intended.

Question. Were not the Democrats in Sussex County, previous to the election, sanguine and perfectly confident that, if the election was a fair one, they would elect their ticket by a large majority?

Answer. Yes, sir; that appeared to be the opinion and the general talk amongst the most of the leading Democrats. It was also my own opinion.

LOUDER N. HEARN.

On motion,

The Committee adjourned until 8 o'clock on Monday evening next.

MONDAY, February 16, 1863, 8 o'clock P.M.

The Committee met pursuant to adjournment.
Present—Messrs. Saulsbury, Hitch, Slay, Stubbs, Williams, and Waples.

HENRY W. LONG, sworn and examined.

By the Chairman:
Question.   Where did you reside at the time of the last general election?
Answer.   In Baltimore Hundred.
Question.   Did you vote in that Hundred on that day?
Answer.   Yes, sir.
Question.   Did you observe anything there unusual, and different from what you had been in the habit of seeing on election day?
Answer.   Yes, sir; there was a cavalry force there, which was unusual.
Question.   How were they stationed in reference to the polls?
Answer.   They were drawn up in a half circle in front of the polls, they were armed. During the time of voting, their arms were at their sides; after the polls were closed, they drew their sabres, and were ready for a charge. They were mounted.
Question.   Were there much intimidation and dissatisfaction among any class of voters there on account of the presence of the soldiers?
Answer.   Yes, sir; I think there was.
Question.   Did this intimidation and dissatisfaction exist equally among members of both parties, or was it confined to one party?
Answer.   It was confined to one party—the Democratic party.
Question.   Was the intimidation so great as to make some of the active working members of the Democratic party timid and fearful to exert themselves?
Answer.   I think some were a little, but not to so great an extent

as one might suppose.

Question. Was there any person who stayed away from the polls on that day on account of the presence of the soldiers?

Answer. Not that I know of.

Question. Who had command of the soldiers there that day?

Answer. They were commanded by the Lieutenant. One Samuel Lacey was Provost Marshal. In placing them at the polls, the Lieutenant was under the direction of the Provost Marshal.

Question. Was there any person within the circle of which you speak?

Answer. There were some. The Provost Marshal went in the circle when he pleased or wherever he pleased.

Question. Was he taking a very active part about the polls?

Answer. Yes, sir; he was a very active man.

Question. From your observation of his conduct that day, do you think he was striving to have a fair election, and to give every man an opportunity to vote, no matter what were his politics—or was he working for the benefit of one party in particular?

Answer. I think the intention was for the benefit of one party—the Republican or Abolition party.

Question. How long has Mr. Lacey been a resident of your Hundred?

Answer. I do not exactly know—long enough to entitle him to a vote. He had been there more than a year, I think.

Question. If the people of your Hundred had been going to choose a man who would have acted fairly in reference to the election, is Mr. Lacey the man they would have selected when they wanted fair play shown?

Answer. Not the sensible portion of the men in Baltimore Hundred.

Question. Is he, or is he not, a bitter, prejudiced, and vindictive man?

Answer. He is, when he has authority.

Question. Was there fair play shown at the polls that day?

Answer. Not in my way of thinking.

Question. Was there any necessity for the presence of soldiers at the polls on that day for the preservation of the public peace?

Answer. No, sir; not any; because, at the little election, we had a full turn out, the fullest ever known in that Hundred, and we never had a more peaceable election. That is why I think so.

Question. What was the majority in that Hundred at the little election, and for which party?

Answer. I have forgotten what the majority was, but it was for the Republican party.

Question. It was stated by the Governor, in his testimony, that he had been informed by numerous citizens that there was a combination between the Democrats of your Hundred and certain citizens of Maryland, headed by one Curtis W. Jacobs, to come into that Hundred, and take possession of the polls, and that that was one of the reasons why he sent for troops. I desire to ask you whether that statement is true?

Answer. I think there was no truth whatever in it; because, if there had been such an intention, I think I should have known it. I never heard any such thing, except as coming from the Republican party. I think it was a base falsehood, got up by some of that party. I never saw a Democrat who knew anything about it.

Question. Were the Democrats of your County, previous to the election, sanguine and perfectly confident of carrying the election in that County by a large majority, if there was no interference?

Answer. Yes, sir; that was the calculation by all that professed to know anything about it with whom I talked. It was also my own calculation.

Question. From your observation of the voters in Baltimore Hundred, was it not generally understood by men of all parties there that day, that the soldiers were there for the benefit of the Republican party, and for the injury of the Democratic party?

Answer. Some few Republicans undertook to justify the presence of the soldiers by saying that their presence was necessary. But it was generally understood that the real design of having them there was to benefit the Republican party and to injure the Democratic party.

Question. Do you believe that the Republican party was benefitted, and the Democratic party injured by the presence of the soldiers?

Answer. Yes, sir; I do think so.

Question. Were there any persons arrested in your Hundred on the day of the election?

Answer. Yes, sir; there were eight. Curtis W. Jacobs and George Hudson, from Maryland; Captain John James, Charles D. Bennett, Charles Stephens, John Hudson, Elisha Bryan and myself, from Baltimore Hundred.

Question. To what political party did the citizens of Baltimore Hundred, who were arrested, belong?

Answer. John Hudson had his ticket altered to vote a part of each ticket. I do not know how Charles Stephens voted. The rest were all Democrats I know.

Question. Had these persons voted before they were arrested?

Answer. I think they had, all but John Hudson.

Question. What time in the day were the arrests made?

Answer. Curtis Jacobs and Captain John James were arrested some time in the forenoon. The others were arrested about two hours before sundown.

Question. Had these persons, who were arrested, been guilty of any great disorder, or any breach of the public peace?

Answer. Not that I know of.

Question. For what were they arrested?

Answer. I do not know.

Question. Were they confined?

Answer. They were placed in a house with a guard at the door.

Question. How long were they kept in confinement?

Answer. I do not know how long two of them, Mr. Jacobs and Captain James, were confined. The rest were confined about two hours.

Question. Do you know by whose order the arrests were made?

Answer. By order of the Provost Marshal I suppose. I did not hear him make the order, but that was the general understanding.

Question. How many persons were there from Maryland, that day, at your election?

Answer. Four that I know. I do not know of any more. William B. White and Henry W. Poole, besides those I have mentioned, were there.

HENRY W. LONG.

JOHN W. JAMES, sworn and examined.

By the Chairman:

Question. Where did you vote on the day of the last general election?

Answer. In Baltimore Hundred.

Question. Did you see anything unusual, and different from what you had ever seen before at or about the polls on that day?

Answer. Yes, sir; a company of cavalry was there.

Question. Were they armed?

Answer. Armed.

Question. Were they mounted?

Answer. Yes, sir.

Question. How many of them were there?

Answer. I think there were some forty or fifty. I did not count them.

Question. Under whose charge were they?

Answer. Under the charge of Samuel Lacey.

Question. Who is Samuel Lacey?

Answer. Provost Marshal.

Question. How long had he been a citizen of your Hundred?

Answer. I think about a year on the day of the election.

Question. To what political party did he belong?

Answer. To the party styled the Republican party.

Question. Was Mr. Lacey an active and violent partizan?

Answer. He appeared to be so, especially on that day.

Question. If the people of Baltimore Hundred had wanted to select a man who would have acted fairly and impartially, and secured to every man his rights, irrespective of party, is Mr. Lacey such a man as they would have fixed upon?

Answer. I do not think any Democrat or one half of the Republican party would have chosen such a man as that.

Question. Did he act fairly and impartially towards the members of all parties there that day, endeavoring to secure to every man his rights?

Answer. No, sir; I do not think he did. He arrested me very soon after I got there. He did not know whether I had voted or not; but I had voted.

Question. Had you been guilty of any breach of the public peace, or any other cause for which you ought to have been arrested?

Answer. I did not think so. I asked him what authority he had to open a way through the crowd, which was all I said to him. He immediately ordered them to arrest me. I did not know that he was Provost Marshal.

Question. It was stated by the Governor of the State, when giving in his testimony, that one reason for his soliciting troops to be present on the day of the election was, that he had been informed by various persons, residents of Baltimore Hundred, upon whom he could rely, that there was a combination between certain Marylanders—I think, about twenty—with one Curtis Jacobs at their head, and the Democrats of your Hundred, to take possession of the polls and prevent Union men from voting—will you please to state whether there was any truth in that statement?

Answer. I am well acquainted with Curtis Jacobs; he puts up at my house, or my brother's, every time he comes up to his farm. If there had been any such talk, I think he would have told me or my brother. I never heard him mention any thing about such a company on the day of the election; nor did I ever hear talk of such a thing among the Democratic party. I heard some of the Republican party talking such talk. I think it was more to influence the election on their side than anything else.

Question   Were not the Democratic party in your County perfectly sanguine and confident of carrying the election in that County by a large majority, if there was no interference with the election?

Answer.   That appeared to be the opinion of the sensible part of them, I believe.

JOHN W. JAMES.

SAMUEL W. LACEY, sworn and examined.

By the Chairman:

Question.   Where do you reside?

Answer.   I reside in Baltimore Hundred.

Question.   How long have you been a resident of that Hundred?

Answer.   On Wednesday night next at eight o'clock, if you want the precise time, I shall have been there a year and three months.

Question.   Were you Provost Marshal for that Hundred on the day of the last general election?

Answer.   I was.

Question.   By whom were you appointed?

Answer.   I suppose I was appointed by Edwin M. Stanton, Secretary of War. I received my commission through and by a man of the name of Isaac T. Dunning.

Question.   Is your commission still in force?

Answer.   I consider it still in force. I have it with me.

Question.   Will you allow me to see it?

Answer.   Yes, sir.

[Witness presents the commission.]

Question. Were there any orders accompanying the commission?
Answer. Yes, sir.

[Witness presents the orders.]

Question. Will you please to look at the handwriting in which the commission was filled up, and also the handwriting in which these orders were made out, and tell me whether you think they are the handwriting of the same person?

Answer. I think they are both the handwriting of James R. Lofland.

Question. Did you receive, from General Wool, or any other person, the copy of an oath to be administered on the day of the election to voters?

Answer. I did not. I received an oath to be taken by myself, which was all the oath I did receive.

Question. Have you a copy of the oath you took yourself?
Answer. I have not.

Question. Do you recollect the substance of that oath?
Answer. I do not, precisely. I had to make oath that I had never been in the rebel army; had never taken up arms against the General Government; that I had never supported treason in any form, &c.

Question. Who administered that oath to you?
Answer. I think that Esquire William Hazzard, Justice of the Peace and Notary Public, did, on the 3^d day of November.

Question. Are you a Justice of the Peace or Notary Public?
Answer. I never have been yet.

Question. Do you hold any office under the General Government, or under this State, which authorizes you to administer oaths?
Answer. I consider I do.

Question. What office is it which you hold which empowers you to do thus?
Answer. The office of Provost Marshal.

Question. Is there anything in the commission which you received from Mr. Stanton, as Provost Marshal, which gave you authority to administer an oath?

Answer. Well, I do not know what you might consider; I suppose you saw it.

The Chairman. I am only asking what you thought. You have a right to put your own interpretation on it.

The Witness. I consider that I had a right under present circumstances.

Question. Will you allow me to see that commission again a moment?

Answer. Yes, sir.

[The witness presents the commission, which is as follows:

"War Department, Washington City, D.C.
"November 1st, 1862.

"Samuel W. Lacy:

"Sir: You are hereby appointed Special Provost Marshal for Baltimore Hundred, Delaware, under General Orders No. 140, from this Department. Immediately on receipt hereof, please to communicate to this Department, through the Provost Marshal General, your acceptance or non-acceptance; and with your letter of acceptance, return the oath herewith enclosed, properly filled up, subscribed, and attested.

"Your headquarters will be at Tunnell's store, and you will make such arrangements, when absent on duty, that any communication from this department may reach you without delay.

"Edwin M. Stanton,
"Secretary of War."]

Question. Did you administer an oath to any citizen of Baltimore Hundred on the day of the last election?

Answer. I administered the oath of allegiance.

Question. To whom did you administer such oath?

Answer. I do not recollect; there were five or six. I believe Curtis W. Jacobs, from Maryland, was the only one from that State. Captain John James, Charles Bennett, Elisha Ryan, I think, Captain Henry Long, John Rust, John Hudson, I think, and another person, whose name I forget. These are all I recollect.

Question. Have you a copy of the form of oath you administered?

Answer. I have not with me.

Question. What was the form of oath?

Answer. I do not recollect exactly.

The Chairman. State its substance, as well as you can recollect.

Witness. I do not recollect much about it; it is down in writing, but I have not got it with me.

Question. Had you the form of oath in writing at the time?

Answer. I had.

Question. Had you it before you?

Answer. No, sir; I had committed it to memory, I think, as nearly as I could.

Question. Do you say that you do not now recollect the oath you administered?

Answer. I say that I do not recollect all of it.

Question. Do you recollect any part of it with sufficient distinctness to relate it?

Answer. I might relate some of it.

Question. Will you please relate what you do remember?

Answer. I can remember thus far. For instance, suppose I was swearing Captain Henry Long, it would run thus: "Captain Henry Long, you solemnly swear on the Holy Evangels of Almighty God that you will bear true allegiance"—I forget the balance of it. It closed up with, "So help me God." I did not require them to kiss the Bible or any other book.

Question. By whom was the form of oath, which you administered, given to you?

Answer. Lieutenant Walters gave it to me, and I wrote it down.

Question. Will you sign that testimony?

Answer.   I hardly think that is my testimony.

Question.   Is that not the testimony as you gave it to the clerk?

Answer.   It is the testimony as I gave it to the clerk.

The Chairman.   Sign it, or refuse to sign it; take your own choice.

Captain Samuel W. Lacey.

On motion,
The Committee adjourned until 8 o'clock to-morrow morning.

Tuesday, February 17, 1863, 8 o'clock A.M.

The Committee met pursuant to adjournment.
Present—Messrs. Saulsbury, Hitch, Cahall, Williams, and Horsey.

The examination of Henry W. Long was resumed, he being recalled.

By the Chairman:

Question.   Will you please to state, as nearly as you can recollect, what the oath was which was administered to you by Captain Samuel W. Lacy?

Answer.   While I was under guard, Dr. Holloway told me that he had been to Samuel W. Lacey and told him that I would take the oath to support the Constitution of the United States in order to be released. Lacey came into the guard room where I was, and asked me if I wanted to see him. I told him, "No, damn you; I do not." I asked him if he wished to see me. He said, "Not in particular." I told him that I wanted to know what I was arrested for. He said I had been talking treason. I told him, if I had, I wanted him to say wherein I had done so, and to prove it. He asked me then if I was ready to take the oath of allegiance. I told him I should not take the oath of allegiance to support the present administration; that I would take the oath to support the Constitution of the United States, and nothing else. He told me to raise my right hand. The oath that I took was this: "Henry W. Long, you do solemnly swear, upon the Holy Evangels of Almighty God, that you will support the Constitution of the United States." He was going on to swear me to bear true allegiance to the Government. When he said these words I told him to stop; that I should take no oath but to support the Constitution of the United States. He then administered the oath as I have related it above, and that was all the oath I took. Then I was released.

HENRY W. LONG.

The examination of JOHN W. JAMES was resumed, he being recalled.

By the Chairman:

Question.   Did Mr. Lacey administer an oath to you on the day of the last general election?

Answer.   Yes, sir. But I have no recollection of what it was. It was such an oath as I thought at the time that I could safely take.

Question.   Did he profess to swear you on the Holy Evangels?

Answer.   I think he did.

Question.   Did he require you to place your hand on the Bible or Testament and kiss it?

Answer.   No, sir. He told me to hold up my right hand. He first read his authority, which was his commission. Then he said he would swear me before he would let me out. He held his commission in his hand at the time he swore me.

Question.   Something has been said about the presence of citizens from Maryland at your polls on the day of the last general election—is such a thing unusual at your polls?

Answer.   No, sir. The States are very near together at that place, and they frequently come over to our polls, and, I understand, that persons from this State frequently go to their election.

Question.   Has the presence of the citizens of Maryland at your polls ever caused any disturbance of which you are aware?

Answer.   None to my recollection.

JOHN W. JAMES.

ISAAC GILES, sworn and examined.

By the Chairman:

Question.   Did you vote on the day of the last general election—and if so, where?

Answer.   I voted on that day in Little Creek Hundred, and in the town of Laurel.

Question.   How long have you been a voter?

Answer.   I have been a voter about thirty-four years.

Question.   Did you observe anything unusual, and different from what you had ever seen before on the day of the election?

Answer.   Yes, sir; quite unusual. I saw a company or part of a company of soldiers armed, said to be the Maryland Home Guards.

Question.   State all that you know in reference to bringing soldiers into this State, how they were stationed in reference to the polls, under whose charge they were, what they did, the effect of their presence on the election, and everything you know in reference to them.

Answer.   Some two or three weeks before the election, and a very few days after Mr. Fisher and Mr. Smithers spoke in the town of Laurel, I, being at Laurel, was informed by William Hitch, the present State Senator, that there was a man from Milford, a stone-cutter, by the name of Read, I think, at Laurel, on the day when Mr. Fisher and Mr. Smithers spoke, who offered to bet from one to five hundred dollars that the Republican or Union party, whatever he termed it, would carry the State and the Legislative branch in two of the counties; and also that a man at Laurel, by the name of John Moore, a Justice of the Peace, was authorized to take a bet of that kind. I called on the said Moore, and told him that the bet would be taken, provided there were no soldiers brought into the County, and the people were suffered to have a fair election. He replied that they would take the bet, but would make no conditions. Not being disposed to take the bet without conditions, I retired. From that time up to the election, it was rumored that there were to be soldiers at the polls. We, fearing the effect it would have by intimidating persons from coming to the polls, tried to convince the people that none would be there. There was a meeting held at Laurel, by each party, between the time Mr. Fisher was there and the election. The Democratic meeting was the largest meeting I ever knew to be held in that place by any party, and there was no quarreling, or fighting, or any disturbance of any kind. The Union or Republican meeting which took place after this, on the Saturday before the election, was the largest that I ever saw of that party in that place. I saw or heard of no quarreling, or fighting, or disturbance of any kind, except a man by the name of Ellis, from North West Fork Hundred, whom I frequently heard going through the crowd called the Democrats rebels. He came where I was sitting, on Nathaniel Horsey's porch, and called me and Horsey damned rebels, and repeated it several times, saying: "If you do not hear, damn you, I will make you hear." But we, suspecting that he had been set on by others for the purpose of getting up a row or fuss, to be used as an excuse for bringing soldiers into the County, made no reply to him whatever. On Monday, after we had learned that the boats had come up the river bringing the soldiers, we received a message from Ex-Governor Ross, stating that he thought there would be no intimidation, that the people would be allowed to vote their sentiments. We then posted men on horseback, through the Hundred, conveying that intelligence, that is, that there would be no intimidation, and persuading the people to come to the polls; and on that night, Monday night previous to the election, I was informed, by a man by the name of Ellis, who said that he, that afternoon, had been told by a man by the name of White, who was riding on the horse of the Provost Marshal of that Hundred, that if he went to the polls the next day to vote the Democratic ticket, he would be arrested. On arriving at Laurel on the morning of the election, I saw the soldiers parading in the streets, and while I was yet in my carriage, I saw them rush into a store, and drag out a man. I heard the Captain say to the men: "Take him to the guard house." They took him down the street. I did not see what they did with him. I then went down to the house where the election was held, the election not being then open. Shortly afterwards, Captain Watkins came down with a squad of soldiers, said to be forty or fifty. He went up to the house where the votes were received, and ordered the people to fall back, or rather pressed them back, and formed a square probably thirty by fifty feet in front of the window, and ordered all persons outside of the square. He then made a speech, in which he said there was to be no intimidation, and that they must take care how they talked; that their thoughts belonged to themselves, but their words and actions belonged to the Government. I immediately asked him if persons would be admitted at the window inside of the square for the purpose of challenging votes. He replied: "No; that is the duty of the Judges." In a few moments, there came a message to me from the Inspector, requesting me to go into the house. I had before declined acting as Judge, but at his earnest request I then accepted, and was sworn in, together with the other Judge. Shortly afterwards the polls were opened, and on the opposite side of the street, some thirty or forty feet from the window, the members of the Democratic party appeared to be mostly standing. The opposition, or Republican, or Union party, appeared to be collected at the north of the window. When the polls were opened, they commenced coming from the Democratic ranks one or two at a time, according to directions from the front of the window and also from the other side, where the opposite party were standing. It continued so but a very short time, when I saw, but did not hear, a conversation between the Provost Marshal (John L. Bacon) and Captain Watkins, and immediately the Captain said there should be no more crossing the line in front from where the Democrats were standing; observing, at the same time, that he wanted to mix up the votes to give some trouble to the Clerks in tallying them. After that time no person was admitted to cross the line in front, but voters were admitted on the extreme right. There was a man came up to vote, and his vote was advocated by the Republican party, and objected to by me on the ground of his not having paid his tax. I cannot give his name, but I recollect the circumstance perfectly well. He offered to make oath that he had paid a tax within two years in Little Creek Hundred. On examining the books of the two last collectors, I could not find his name therein. I contended he had no legal right to vote. Captain Watkins ordered the Inspector to swear the voter and take his vote, and he did so. Shortly afterwards another man, by the name of William S. Hearn, came up to vote. His residence was not objected to. He produced a receipt for having paid a tax in 1861, in the Hundred. His vote was objected to on the ground that another man by the same name had already voted on the opposite side, and showed a tax receipt for 1862, and that there was but one name of that kind on the books. The Inspector and myself had decided to receive the last mentioned vote, when the Captain ordered him to go out of the ring, just as the Inspector was about to take his vote, and he was not permitted to return, and did not get to vote. Shortly afterwards another man came up to vote. I do not recollect his name, and his vote was objected to by the Provost Marshal, on the ground that he had not paid a tax within two years. But after the late Collector was sent for, it was proved that his tax had been paid within two years and paid by the Provost Marshal. He voted. Shortly after that a man by the name of James L. Davis, came up to vote. Being an Englishman, I demanded his naturalization papers, or proof thereof. The Captain came up shortly afterwards and asked me what the contention was. I told him that the man was a foreigner, and I demanded his naturalization papers or proof of his naturalization. He says: "You require impossibilities." He then said to the Inspector: "Take the vote, or I will smash the ballot-boxes and the whole damned concern!" The Inspector held out his hand, trembling, and said to the voter: "Hand here your ticket," and put the vote in the box. When I remonstrated with him for so doing, he remarked that he was forced to do it. The Judge on the other side said I had better be quiet, and take what we could get, for we should get some majority any way.

The Captain at the time he told the Inspector to take this vote, remarked: "You admitted the vote of a damned Dutchman, and you shall admit this." The Dutchman alluded to had some time before voted. When he came to the window, I did not know him. I had never seen him before, to my recollection. I did not know that he was a Dutchman or foreigner of any kind. When he handed his vote to the Inspector, I asked him if he had paid a tax within two years. He pulled out a receipt which showed that he had, and showed it to me. He then said he had another paper he would show me, if I wanted to look at it, and pulled it partly out of his pocket. I, not thinking that he was a foreigner, could not think of any other paper that he needed, and said to him: "I do not want to see any other papers." John Moore, also, the other Judge, said he was all right, that he worked in the tanyard for Mr. William Delany; and I am fully satisfied, from what I have since seen and heard, that the paper he offered to produce to me was his naturalization papers. His vote was not objected to by anybody. No other foreigner voted in the Hundred to my knowledge. Another man by the name of Ferbush came up to the polls to vote. His residence was not objected to. He produced the required tax-receipt, but his vote was objected to by the Provost Marshal on the ground that it was said he had been convicted of felony in Maryland. After I stated that the conviction alluded to in our Constitution meant a conviction under our own Constitution and laws, and not those of any other State, and further that there was no proof of any conviction before us, the Inspector and myself decided to receive his vote. The other Judge objected. Immediately Captain Watkins drove him out of the ring, and ordered him not to come back again. He consequently did not get to vote. A young man came up to vote, who was a Democrat. His vote was objected to on the ground that he was under the age of 21 years. About the same time, I heard a voice from the crowd calling on me to send for Levin Twilly who would prove this man's age. Our men were very seldom over the line, while some of their men had free admission all the time. The name of the young man alluded to was Henry Rhodes, who was born in one of my tenant-houses, not more than one-fourth of a mile from my house, and near the age of one of my children, and knowing his age myself, and fearing that if the case was delayed by calling Twilly, the young man would be driven out of the ring, and would not get to vote, his vote was admitted on my own knowledge, when a man standing inside of the lines in front of the window, by the name of Jacob Morine, kept abusing me, swearing that the man alluded to was under age, and that he would not believe me if I swore to it, and was allowed to continue doing so by the Provost Marshal. Morine was a very active man in the Republican party.

Question. I state that the Governor of the State, in relating his testimony to the Committee, stated, in substance, that he had asked Colonel Wallace to place soldiers at the polls on the day of the general election, in Baltimore Hundred, Broad Creek Hundred, Little Creek Hundred, and Dagsborough Hundred, and gave, as his reason for so doing, that there had been a combination, as he had been informed by a number of respectable and reliable men, between a number of Secessionists in Maryland, headed by one Curtis W. Jacobs, and a number of Democrats in Delaware, to take possession of the polls, and drive Union men away, and prevent them from voting—I ask you sir, whether the statement is true?

Answer. I do not believe it has any foundation in fact. I think I have the confidence of the Democratic party in Sussex County. I never heard it intimated by a single member of the party. But on the other hand, I did hear Dr. John Fowler, of Maryland, say, about one week before the election, that he heard William Lennard, a Colonel of the "Purnell Legion," say, that they must send soldiers to Delaware, that the Delaware election must be carried for the Administration.

Question. I ask you whether the presence of soldiers at the polls, at Laurel, on the day of the election, had the effect to produce great intimidation and alarm among the Democratic voters, and great satisfaction and confidence among the Republicans voters?

Answer. I have no doubt but that many members of the Democratic party were greatly intimidated, and did not do what they would have done but for such intimidation. I observed that men, when they came to the window to vote, were trembling, while on the other hand, the opposite party appeared buoyant, frequently insulting and threatening to have the Democrats arrested.

Question.   Did, or did not, the Provost Marshal, John L. Bacon, and Captain Watkins, take possession of the window, to the exclusion of everybody else, as challengers?

Answer.   No person of the Democratic party, excepting in one or two instances, was admitted to the window as challengers, while the other party had four or five there at a time for that purpose. When our men did come, as they did only in a few cases when I would call persons for that purpose, it was only by the permission of the Provost Marshal and Captain Watkins that they could come. The Provost Marshal always gave orders through Captain Watkins; he acted all the time in an electioneering manner. Frequently when I called persons for this purpose, they were not permitted to come.

Question.   Did not the whole conduct of the Provost Marshal and Captain Watkins on that day, show that they were acting for the benefit of the Republican party, and for the injury of the Democratic party, instead of making an effort to insure a fair election, and equal chances to members of all parties?

Answer.   Their principal object appeared to be the benefit of the Republican or Union party. They did make some effort to keep the peace.

Question.   Was there any necessity for the presence of the military at the polls that day to preserve the public peace?

Answer.   I think there was not. I have never known the people in our Hundred or County more quiet in any political campaign.

Question.   Were not the Democratic party in Sussex County perfectly sanguine and confident of carrying the election in that County by a large majority, if there was no interference, and was that not your own individual opinion?

Answer.   The Democrats of the County were certainly sanguine and confident of carrying the County, provided we had a fair election. I never heard a single Democrat express himself otherwise, and it certainly was my own opinion.

Question. Was it not the interest, as well as the desire, of the Democratic party to have a fair, peaceable, and quiet election?

Answer. It certainly was the interest and desire of the Democratic party to have a fair and quiet election; and so far as I could understand, every prominent member appeared to be making exertions to that effect.

Question. Was there any attempt, on the part of the Democrats, at Laurel, that day, to break over the lines formed by the military, and take forcible possession at the polls?

Answer. None that I saw or heard of. I was at the window, and observed the crowd in front of the window all day, and saw no such attempt. Persons may have accidentally stepped over the lines.

Question. Was there anything occurred that could have justified the Provost Marshal, or any other reasonable person, in forming the opinion that there was any such intention or purpose?

Answer. There certainly was not, so far as anything I have seen or heard. I believe that if they had been disposed to have done so, they would have found no difficulty in doing it.

Isaac Giles.

On motion of Mr. Waples,
The Committee adjourned till 8 o'clock P.M.

Same Day, 7 ½ o'clock, P.M.

Committee met pursuant to adjournment.
Present—Messrs. Saulsbury, Hitch, Cahall, Slay, and Williams.

George W. White, affirmed and examined.

By the Chairman:

Question. Where did you vote on the day of the last general election?

Answer. In Cedar Creek Hundred, Sussex County.

Question. Will you please to state all you know in reference to the presence of soldiers there that day, what they did, what the effect of their presence on the election, and how you managed to get rid of them, and all that you know in reference to them?

Answer. On election morning, I walked a part of the way to Cedar Creek. When I went into the room where they held the election, I found William Lofland, late Sheriff of Sussex County, who, at that time, resided in Georgetown Hundred, sitting at the table, putting characters and names upon what they call Union tickets, what I call Republican tickets. I was looking at him before he saw me. He looked up and saw me, and asked me what in hell I was doing there so soon in the morning. I told him I was about my own business. I then asked him if he would give me the privilege of asking him what he was doing with those tickets, and why he was not at home in his own Hundred. He then said to me: "George, you had better stay in the house to-day." I asked him, "Why should I stay in the house?" He then said to me, "You had better stay in the house." I asked him, "Why so?" He said: "We are going to have a company of soldiers here to-day." I asked him who he meant by "we." He said: "We, the Union party." I said to him: "Duck (this was his nick-name,) do you mean that?" "Yes," he said, "I do mean it." And he said further, "We do not intend to see any jarring or forcing men up to these polls; if you do, there will be bloodshed here to-day." I then asked him if he or his party intended to form a line with the soldiers before our window. He said: "Yes, we do." I asked if he meant to do so positively. He said: "Yes, just as soon as they come on the hill." I then told him that if he or his party did form a line before that window that day, I was going to stay in the house, and act as one of the Judges of that election, and if I was sworn as such, and the soldiers formed a line before that window, that, with the consent of our Inspector, a Democrat, we would lower that window. He asked if I meant it. I told him just as sure as he believed there was a God in heaven I would do it, if you arrest me in five minutes afterwards. He said that would be done if the window was lowered. There was no more said until the soldiers came. They came within about twenty steps of the window, formed a line, and stacked their arms. Then the Lieutenant was requested to move his company to what we call a barn-yard at the end of the house. There they remained until the polls were closed. The soldiers did not interfere at all with the election.

Question.   What was your reason for telling Mr. Lofland that you would put down that window if the soldiers formed a line in front of it?

Answer.   It was because I saw no occasion of insurrection or invasion which required them to form a line.

Question.   What would have been the effect of the election in that County by your shutting down the window and not taking the votes?

Answer.   There would have been no election in that Hundred. The votes there would not have been counted.

Question.   What was the majority in that Hundred, and for what party?

Answer.   I think it was 122 for the Republican party, so far as the Governor was concerned.

Question.   The holding of no election in that hundred would have increased the Democratic majority 122 votes, would it?

Answer.   I think it would, so far as the Governor was concerned.

Question.   Was it understood to be in view of the fact that the Republicans had a large majority in that hundred, and that you had given notice as a Judge of the election, that if soldiers were formed in line in front of the window you would close the window and hold no election, that the soldiers were removed from the presence of the voters, and sent into the barn-yard as you have named?

Answer.   It was so understood.

Question.   Do you know whether the captain or Lieutenant of the company, or whoever had them in charge, was reproved for not forming a line in front of the window, and if so, by whom?

Answer. I can not say personally myself. I am not sure, but I am inclined to think William D. Fowler told me that the Captain or Lieutenant was met on Milford bridge, after walking five miles from the election with his company, by James R. Lofland, who was Provost Marshal, I think, for the State. He asked the Lieutenant if he did form a line at Cedar Creek, before the window. He told the Provost Marshal that he did not. Lofland asked him why he did not do it. He said he saw no cause for it. Mr. Lofland then said to him, "I believe that you are a traitor and a secessionist." He then said to Mr. Lofland that that was the third time he had been called such, and that he had belonged to the United States service for the past eight years. He (the Lieutenant) then pulled out of his pocket a revolver and said to him, that if he repeated the same words he would blow a ball through him. This is all I know.

GEO. W. WHITE.

WILLIAM A. SCRIBNER, sworn and examined.

By the Chairman.
Question. Were you a candidate upon the ticket at the last election for the Legislature from Cedar Creek Hundred, Sussex County?
Answer. I was, sir.
Question. Were you present at the election on that day, in Cedar Creek Hundred?
Answer. I was, sir.
Question. Please to state what you know in reference to the presence of the soldiers at the polls that day, what position they occupied in reference to the polls?
Answer. I left home about 8 o'clock in the morning. I overtook the soldiers about half way from Milford to Cedar Creek. I got to Cedar Creek, I suppose, about forty minutes, perhaps, before they got there. They walked up about thirty or forty yards from the place of voting, then halted and stacked their arms. The Lieutenant left. He went in the house,

I think, or around the house, and was gone some five or ten minutes. When he come back he ordered his men to take up their arms and march. He took them in a barnyard at the end of the house. They remained there as long as I stayed at Cedar Creek. I do not think any of his men were out of the yard during that day until they left to return to Milford. I saw a Lieutenant in the yard. I went up to him and asked him if the Democratic party was going to have a fair chance to vote there that day. He told me that was his intention, to let every man have a fair chance to vote. I told him that was all we asked. I saw him once or twice, in the afternoon, up stairs, looking out at the window right over where they were voting, when there was a good deal of pulling and hauling, but he never interfered. I left there about fifteen or twenty minutes before the polls closed.

Question. Do you know why he assigned his troops a position in the barn yard?

Answer. I do not.

WILLIAM A. SCRIBNER.

On motion,

The Committee adjourned until 8 ½ o'clock to-morrow morning.

WEDNESDAY, February 18, 1863—8 ½ o'clock, A.M.

Present—Messrs. Cahall, Slay, Stubbs, Waples, Williams and Horsey.
The Chairman not being present,
On motion,
Mr. Cahall was appointed Chairman, *pro tem.*

HENRY RIDGELY sworn and examined.

By Mr. Cahall:
Question. Where did you vote at the last election?

Answer.   In Dover, sir.

Question.   Were there any armed soldiers at the polls that day; if so, please state their position in reference to the polls, and all you know in reference to the matter?

Answer.   Yes, sir. There were armed soldiers in the town that day. They were drawn up on the south side of the square, about 100 yards, I suppose, from the place of voting, some time before the voting commenced. They were said to be a portion of the Maryland Home Guards, and remained drawn up in the same place during the whole day except at two or three intervals. During these intervals they made two charges across the Court House pavement, where the votes were taken in. At the first charge, I was struck twice: once immediately in the breast with a bayonet, and also in the left side.

Question.   What was the occasion which induced the soldiers to make these several charges of which you speak?

Answer.   The cause of the first charge, as I understood, was from a very unprovoked attack of Mr. George P. Fisher, on Mr. Joseph Wicks, both of this place. The cause of the second charge I did not know. I heard of it afterwards, but cannot speak of my own knowledge.

Question.   Was there, in your judgment, any necessity for the presence of soldiers at the polls in Dover on that day, in order to preserve the public peace, and to insure a quiet election?

Answer.   No, sir; not the slightest necessity.

Question.   Did there appear to be much intimidation among the voters at the polls on that day, and if so, what political party seemed to be most intimidated?

Answer.   In my opinion, there was intimidation that day on the part of the Democratic voters.

Question.   Do you think that intimidation was sufficient to make a difference in the result of the vote on that day—and if so, to what extent?

Answer.   I think it did make a difference in the result of the vote and in favor of the Republican party. I cannot say to what extent.

Question. Have you not been an active Democrat for a number of years, and in the confidence of the Democratic party, knowing all its principal plans and operations in conducting campaigns?

Answer. Generally speaking, I have, I believe, sir.

Question. Did you ever hear of a purpose, or an intention, or a desire, on the part of any Democrat, to interfere with the polls at the last election, so as to prevent a fair election?

Answer. No, sir. There seemed to be a strong desire, on the contrary, that everything should pass off peaceably and quietly.

Question. If there had been such a purpose or intention, do you not think that you would have known it?

Answer. Yes, sir; I took the trouble to inquire and to ascertain if any such desire was entertained by any member of the Democratic party, so that I might prevent it with what little influence I possessed.

Question. What induced you to make those inquiries—was it from the report circulating through the Union or Republican party?

Answer. The reason that I made the inquiries was, that if there was any desire exhibited on the part of the Democratic party to disturb the public peace on the election day, it would give the leaders of the Republican party a pretext for bringing troops here on the election day, of which I had heard flying rumors for some time.

Question. Under whose command were the soldiers at the polls that day? Who was the Provost Marshal?

Answer. I do not know of my own knowledge, but I understood that Napoleon B. Knight was Provost Marshal for the town, and, of course, the troops were under his command.

Question. Was it under the command of Napoleon B. Knight that the several charges were made that day upon the voters at the polls?

Answer. I do not know, sir. I do not know by whose order the charges were made.

Question. Who is Napoleon B. Knight, and to what political party does he belong?

Answer. He is said to be a Major in the Delaware Cavalry, and a very short time before the election joined the Republican party.

Question.   Do you know anything else bearing upon the subject of this investigation—if so, please state it?

Answer.   I was particularly struck, on the election day, with the remarkable good order observed by the residents and voters of East Dover Hundred. The most troublesome and disorderly men in the town on that day, were men dressed in the uniform of United States soldiers, and said to belong to the Fourth Delaware Regiment. They seemed to be nearly all drunk, cursing and swearing, and threatening almost everyone they met. They made frequent attacks upon the peaceable citizens of the place, and not the slightest effort was made, that I could see, to keep them in order by the Maryland Home Guards who were in the town that day. One case, in particular, came under my own immediate notice. A man came running near me, on the Court House pavement, pursued by another dressed in the uniform of a soldier. The man who first came near me, seemed very much frightened, while the soldier was cursing and swearing. I stepped in front of the soldier, and asked him what he meant by pursuing that man? He said he wanted to kill the damned secessionist. I asked him if he knew the man was a secessionist. He said "No, and he did not care." I believe I only recollect seeing one man who lives in East Dover Hundred, and who belongs to the Democratic party, and who was drunk and at all troublesome, and he was soon carried off. I saw, at another time, several of these men, dressed in United States uniform, beating Draper Voshell most inhumanly, and no effort was made by the Maryland Home Guards to stop it. At another time, I saw Robert Mitchell, an old man, said to be between eighty and ninety years of age, lying on the pavement of the County Building under the feet of those Maryland Home Guards, apparently very much hurt, and unable to get up. In my opinion, if these men were sent here on election day to prevent disturbance and preserve the public peace, they utterly failed in doing it. I think that if they had kept these drunken soldiers in order, our own civil officers would not have been called upon to preserve order among the residents of this Hundred, because their interference would not have been needed.

Question. Was there any person besides yourself that received any bodily harm during any of the charges?

Answer. Yes, sir. Robert Mitchel, whom I have already named, William M. Jester and James A. Clifton.

Question. Were they in any manner disturbing the public peace?

Answer. I did not see them when they were struck. I was not, myself, when I was struck.

H. RIDGELY.

The examination of ISAAC GILES was resumed, he being recalled.

By Mr. Cahall.

Question. When you were before the Committee last you spoke of several illegal votes having been cast in your hundred. Can you name any other illegal votes cast in that hundred; and if so, state the circumstances under which, and in favor of what political party they were cast, and all you know in reference to the matter.

Answer. There were two votes in addition to those I have before named that I have no doubt were illegal. One of them was by a man of the name of Luther Legat, who had formerly been a resident of the Hundred, but some six or eight months before the election, having shot a man by the name of Aaron Gordy, absconded from the State and lived with his concubine in Maryland. This proof was offered at the window, but the Captain of the company (Watkins) commanded the Inspector to swear the voter as to his residence, and take his vote. He did so. The other voter alluded to—his name was Machelon Ralph—after the death of his mother moved into Maryland with his bed and other chattels, and resided with his brother, he being unmarried and much afflicted. But some two or three months before the election he had returned to Delaware, leaving his bed and other chattels in Maryland, and resided with his brother-in-law. His vote was offered, and objected to by myself as one of the Judges. The Captain, after hearing the case, commanded the Inspector to swear him as to his residence, and receive his vote. The voter being a man of a very weak mind, took the oath and voted. The Englishman by the name of Davis, before alluded to be myself, of whom I had demanded his naturalization papers or proof thereof, I have since ascertained had no naturalization papers and was not naturalized. All three of these men voted with the Republican party.

Isaac Giles.

WILLIAM M. JESTER, sworn and examined.

By Mr. Cahall:
Question.   Where did you vote at the last general election?
Answer.   In Dover, Delaware.
Question.   Did you see anything unusual, and different from what you had ever seen before, connected with the voting that day, and if so, state what it was?
Answer.   I did. On the morning of the election there were armed soldiers in town, said to have come from Salisbury, Maryland, called Home Guards of Maryland. They were formed in line early in the morning on the south side of the green, in front of Nathaniel B. Smithers's office.
Question.   Did those soldiers offer intimidation to the voters—and if so, state the manner in which that intimidation was offered?
Answer.   I do not know that they attempted to prevent any person from voting, but there was intimidation among the Democratic party, and a great deal of complaint on account of its being unusual and, as they considered, unnecessary. I do not know under whose command they were, myself. I saw them make a charge, in the afternoon, across the pavement in front of the polls, in which they struck me, standing on the pavement near the polls, and injured me very seriously. I was confined about six weeks—there were eight weeks during which I could not attend

to business—attended by Dr. Saulsbury. James A. Clifton was struck, while standing at my side, in the same charge. While I was lying on my back, one of the soldiers thrust a bayonet at me, and was seen by John Penington and others. I saw the gun, with the bayonet on it, at my side as I lay on my back. They kicked my hat and wig off into the middle of the road.

Question. What were you and Mr. Clifton doing at the time you were struck?

Answer. We were standing near the polls when the charge was made, I with my back to the soldiers, and did not see them until they were within a few feet of my back with their bayonets. I had no chance to escape then. There was a little disturbance created by the men of the Fourth Delaware Regiment. I was standing looking at this affair, talking to nobody, when they made the charge and struck me.

Question. Was there any disturbance of any kind which would have rendered a charge necessary upon the voters that day?

Answer. None at all; and had it not been for the soldiers, we should have had as peaceable an election as we ever had, in my judgment. I say so, because, at the little election, we had not a particle of disturbance.

Question. Was it generally understood that the soldiers present that day were in confidence with the Republican party, and not in confidence with the Democratic party, and was their presence considered to promote the one and injure the other?

Answer. That was the general opinion, and also my own opinion. And my reasons for that opinion, on my own part, were these: I conversed with Mr. Charles B. Day, early in the morning, in reference to the soldiers being here, and asked him what they were here for. He did not answer me. I told him I was afraid they had come to interfere with the election. He said not at all, that we would have as quiet and as full an election as we had ever had.

Question. Who were the disorderly people in the town of Dover that day, so far as you had an opportunity of judging from observation?

Answer.   The soldiers who were called "Fourth Delaware" soldiers. They behaved very badly. They created the disturbance, on account of which the charge was made when I was injured.

Question.   Do you know whether there was any effort made by the Maryland Home Guards to keep the men of the Fourth Delaware Regiment, who were present on this occasion, in order, and prevent the disturbing the public peace?

Answer.   I do not think there was. But I believe they were both colleagued to do violence—both the Maryland Home Guards and the men of the Fourth Delaware Regiment.

Question.   Did Mr. Day give any reason, or state by what authority the Maryland Home Guards were brought here?

Answer.   He did not. I asked him why, and by whom, and for what purpose they were brought here. I told him I was afraid they had come to interfere with the election. His answer was: "Not a bit of it; you will have as peaceable and as full an election as you have ever had." He did not answer my question directly; but I inferred from his conduct that he knew at whose solicitation they were brought.

Question.   About how many Maryland Home Guards do you suppose there were here that day?

Answer.   I would suppose about forty or forty-five.

Question.   Do you, in your judgment, believe that the presence of the soldiers at the polls that day had an influence upon the result of the election—and if so, in favor of what political party?

Answer.   If it had an influence, and I think it had, it was in favor of the Union or Republican party.

Question.   Was it because the energies of many of the working men of the Democratic party were impeded and embarrassed so as to induce them to do less for the party on that day than they otherwise would have done?

Answer.   Yes, I think it was; the working men of the party were intimidated. As to my part, I thought I was like a man who was stealing what belonged to him. I felt justified in doing so.

Question.　Who is Mr. Day?

Answer.　He is a lawyer of this town, and an active politician. I believe, at this time, an officer under the General Government, and a law-partner of Mr. Fisher, who was a candidate for Representative in Congress at the last election. I would say, in addition to what I have said, in reference to my position in reference to the disturbance which was the pretext for the charge of soldiers in which I was hurt, that I was standing on the State House pavement near the polls, while the disturbance happened on the other side of the County road, on the pavement of the County Building, some sixty feet from me.

W. M. JESTER.

On motion,

The Committee adjourned until 7 o'clock this evening.

SAME DAY, 7 o'clock P.M.

The Committee met pursuant to adjournment.

Present—Messrs. Cahall, Hitch, Slay, Stubbs, Williams, Waples, and Horsey.

JESSE P. CONAWAY, sworn and examined.

By Mr. Cahall:

Question.　Where did you vote on the day of the last general election?

Answer.　In Nanticoke Hundred, at Coverdale's Cross Roads.

Question.　Were you Provost Marshal at the polls on that day?

Answer.　Yes, sir.

Question.　Were you commissioned—and if so, from whom did you receive your commission?

Answer.　Yes, sir. I received it from General Wool, I believe.

Question.　By whom, and when was that commission delivered to you?

Answer.   On Monday morning, I think, by Mr. William L. Cannon, the son of Governor Cannon, and Mr. Wadman.

Question.   Have you that commission with you?

Answer.   No, sir.

Question.   Did you receive any other communication with that commission?

Answer.   Yes, sir. I did receive a paper, at Seaford, from General Wool.

Question.   Have you that paper with you?

Answer.   No, sir.

Question.   Can you recollect its contents?

Answer.   I could not.

Question.   Do you recollect upon what subject it was bearing?

Answer.   I could not answer.

Question.   Had you any soldiers under your command at Coverdale's Cross Roads that day?

Answer.   Yes, sir; there were about twenty under my command. I do not know where they were from. They were delivered to me on the election ground on Tuesday morning by a young gentleman by the name of Willy, who came with them.

Question.   What did you do with those soldiers while under your command at the polls?

Answer.   I did nothing. I appointed two men, one of each party, at the window, and also at the gate. Josiah Marvel was one, S. A. Lambden was the other. They were there to keep the peace.

J. P. CONAWAY.

NOBLE CONAWAY, sworn and examined.

By Mr. Cahall:

Question.   Where did you vote at the last general election?

Answer. At Coverdale's Cross Roads, in Nanticoke Hundred.

Question. Did you see anything unusual, and different from what you had ever seen before at the polls—if so, state what it was?

Answer. I saw some soldiers there, something which I never saw before at the polls.

Question. Will you please to state their position in reference to the polls?

Answer. Two stood at the gate; one on each side of it. There were two on horseback inside of the yard. There were two gates, one where we went in to vote, and another where we came out. There was another walking up and down the yard all the time. He was said to be Lieutenant. I did not know.

Question. Were those soldiers armed?

Answer. They had their swords. I do not know whether they had pistols or not. They were cavalry.

Question. Do you know by whose order those soldiers were placed there?

Answer. They were under the control of Jesse P. Conaway. He and the Lieutenant agreed they should not be around the yard or gate. Isaac Fisher let them know that the soldiers should be put there; that they were sent there for that purpose. As well as I recollect, Isaac Fisher said to Mr. Conaway, the Provost Marshal: "Those soldiers were sent here for that purpose, and if you do not put them there, I will make you look out."

Question. Who is Isaac Fisher, and to what political party does he belong?

Answer. He used to belong to the Whig party, and two years ago last fall, he was a Lincoln man, and what party he belongs to now, I do not know. I rather suppose he belongs to the Republican party.

Question. Is he an active and violent politician?

Answer. He does all he can.

Question. Did the presence of the soldiers at the polls produce much embarrassment on the part of any of the voters?

Answer. I should think it did. It did so much that some would not go to the polls, and some, after they went, would not vote.

Question. To what political party did those persons belong who were induced to go away without voting?

Answer. To the Democratic party.

Question. Do you consider that the presence of the soldiers at the polls that day affected the result of the vote?

Answer. Yes, sir; I should think it did. Their presence injured the Democratic party. I do not know that it injured the Republican party.

His
NOBLE X CONAWAY.
mark.

Attest: JOHN O. SLAY.

MINOS CONAWAY sworn and examined.

By Mr. Cahall:

Question. Where did you vote at the last general election?

Answer. At Coverdale's Cross-Roads, in Nanticoke Hundred, Sussex County.

Question. Did you see anything unusual, and different from what you had ever seen before at the polls—if so, state what it was?

Answer. I saw cavalry, equipped, and armed with swords and pistols, guarding the polls.

Question. Do you know at whose solicitation those soldiers were brought there and placed at the polls?

Answer. I heard Nathaniel Conaway say that he and several other gentlemen, viz: William Ellegood, Jacob Moore, Judge Layton and Jesse P. Conaway, signed a petition to have them brought into the State of Delaware.

Question. Do you know to whom they petitioned?

Answer. I do not.

Question. Do you know when it was they signed the petition?

Answer. He told me that they signed the petition the day after the little election.

Question. Did you understand for what purpose they petitioned for soldiers to be brought into the State, and to be here on the day of the general election?

Answer. I understood it was to carry the election for the Republican party.

Question. Did you hear Nathaniel Conaway express himself in regard to the soldiers, and for what purpose they were to be brought?

Answer. Mr. Conaway told me, "They are to keep the Democrats at a distance."

Question. Did the presence of the soldiers at the polls on that day produce much intimidation?

Answer. I should think it did.

Question. Was that intimidation so great as to produce an effect upon the result of the vote—and if so, in favor of what party?

Answer. It did. I should think in favor of the Republican party.

Question. Who is Nathaniel Conaway, and to what political party does he belong?

Answer. He belongs to the so-called Republican party. He was formerly 'Squire of Nanticoke Hundred.

Question. Is he an active and violent partizan?

Answer. I should think he was.

Question. Do you know to what political party those persons you have named, as having petitioned for soldiers to be brought into this State, belonged?

Answer. To the so-called Republican party.

Question. Do you know whether they are active and violent politicians?

Answer. I should think they were.

Question. Do you know anything else connected with the subject of the soldiers being at the polls in Nanticoke Hundred on that day—if so, please state what it was?

Answer. I saw a gentleman put out of the yard and prohibited from voting. I cannot say to what party he belonged. He was put out by the soldiers, at the command of the Provost Marshal. I do not know the cause.

MINOS CONAWAY.

JOSIAH P. MARVEL, sworn and examined.

By Mr. Cahall:

Question. Where did you vote on the day of the last general election?

Answer. In Nanticoke Hundred, at Coverdale's Cross-Roads.

Question. Do you know anything in reference to soldiers being at the polls on that day—if so, please state what it was?

Answer. On arriving at the election, on election morning, we found about twenty cavalry, I suppose, armed with swords and pistols.

Mr. Cahall. Please state their position in reference to the polls.

Answer. On opening the polls, the Lieutenant ordered the way cleared; one or two cavalrymen rode inside of the yard, and remained on their horses, with drawn swords; a couple of soldiers were at the gate, with their swords crossed, through which the voters had to pass. Other soldiers were behind the crowd in the road.

Question. Did their presence create much intimidation among the voters that day?

Answer. Several of the active, prominent Democrats were very much frightened, and took very little part in the election, while the Republicans appeared to have things pretty much their own way.

Question. Do you know of any person so intimidated that day by the presence of the soldiers that he went away without voting, or any one who was taken away by the soldiers?

Answer. Peter Hitchins was put out of the yard because they thought he was going to vote the Democratic ticket, as I thought. This was the way it originated. He was then offered something less than five minutes, I think, to vote which way he pleased. Whereupon he left the yard, and in a few minutes returned to vote, and was then put out of the yard by the soldiers, at the command of the Lieutenant, I think. Mr. Hitchins voted the Democratic ticket at the little election.

Question. Was it generally understood that the soldiers were present at the polls for the benefit of the Republican party, and for the injury of the Democratic party?

Answer. I believe it was.

Question. Was that the effect the soldiers had?

Answer. Mr. Jesse P. Conaway, the Provost Marshal, and the Lieutenant, acted very honorably and impartially, I believe; but the leading Republicans were very overbearing, and used such language and threats as to intimidate a great many of the Democrats, which produced quite a different result in the election from what it would have been if we could have voted as we had been accustomed to vote. I think the difference would have been twenty votes to the Democratic party, if there had been no soldiers.

Question. Do you not consider that you would have had as peaceable an election, if not more so, without the soldiers than you had with them?

Answer. I do not know that we would. I think it would have been about the same.

Question. You have been an active Democrat for a number of years, did you ever hear of a purpose or design on the part of any Democrat to interfere with the polls, so as to prevent a fair election?

Answer. I have not.

Question. Do you know of any one who was arrested on that day because he voted a Democratic ticket?

Answer. Henry Smith told me that some of the leading Republicans promised to release him from the army if he would vote a Republican ticket. He voted a Democratic ticket. A Republican went up with him, thinking he would vote a Republican ticket, but he voted a

Democratic ticket, whereupon he was immediately arrested by the cavalrymen.

Question.   Do you know anything else bearing upon this subject—if so, please state what it is?

Answer.   At Charles Jones' store, about a week before the election, Jacob Moore took me out at one side, and said: "Well, Josiah, what are you going to do with us at this election." Said I: "I think the Democrats will give a majority; what do you think will be the result?" Said he: "We will beat you 200; and if one thing occurs, which I think will, we shall beat you 500." I considered that bearing on or having reference to military interference.

Question.   Who is Jacob Moore, and to what political party does he belong?

Answer.   He is a lawyer in Georgetown, and belongs to the Republican party.

By Mr. Williams:

Question.   What led you to infer that Mr. Moore had reference to the military?

Answer.   I had heard rumors and reports that they would have military at the polls.

JOSIAH P. MARVEL.

On motion,
The Committee adjourned until to-morrow morning at 9 o'clock.

THURSDAY, February 19, 1863, 10 o'clock, A.M.

The Committee met pursuant to adjournment.
Present—Messrs. Saulsbury, Hitch, Slay, Stubbs, Williams, and Waples.

SAMUEL W. FISHER, sworn and examined.

By Mr. Cahall:

Question. Where do you reside?

Answer. In Nanticoke Hundred, in Sussex County.

Question. Were you present at the polls on the 4th day of November last, at the general election, and did you vote?

Answer. I was, sir; and did vote.

Question. Did you see anything unusual, and different from what you had ever seen before at the polls?

Answer. I did, sir. There were cavalry there. I do not know where they were from. They stood at two small gates—two soldiers on horseback at a gate, with drawn swords. They did not admit more than one at a time through the gate that I know of. Their swords were crossed in front of me as I attempted to enter.

Question. Did you see any violence offered to any citizen by the soldiers on that day?

Answer. I did, sir. One man—Peter Hitchins, he called himself—was thrown out of the yard by them. He went in again, and was thrown out the second time. He did not get to vote that I know of. I do not know to what political party Mr. Hitchins belonged—he claimed to be a Democrat in their presence. I do not know that that was the cause of his being thrown out. I think it was not.

Question. Was there much intimidation on the part of any of the voters there that day in consequence of the presence of soldiers?

Answer. There seemed to be considerable.

Question. Was that intimidation sufficient to change the result of the election to any considerable extent; and if so, in favor of what political party?

Answer. I think it was, to some extent, in favor of the Republican party. The working men of the Democratic party were not aware of the soldiers being there, therefore were much surprised, and thought they would be partial to the Republican party. From that fact, they were discouraged, and did not work for some considerable time—some of them expressing themselves that it was of no use, that it was a gone thing with us. And that is why we lost considerable, as I think.

Question.   So far as you were capable of judging, did the soldiers act in concert with any party; and if so, with what party?

Answer.   In my judgment, they did; in concert with the Republican party.

Question.   Do you, in your judgment, believe that there was any necessity for the presence of soldiers at the polls on that day, in order to preserve the public peace?

Answer.   I do not.

Question.   Do you know anything else bearing upon this subject of investigation? If so, please state what it was.

Answer.   I do not.

Question.   Was it not the interest, as well as the desire, of the Democratic party, to have a peaceable election on that day?

Answer.   It was, sir.

Question.   Was it not the expectation, and was it not your opinion, that the Democratic majority would have been considerably more than it was, provided you had had a peaceable election, and no interference on the part of the military?

Answer.   It is my opinion that we should have had a considerably larger majority, probably from ten to fifteen more in our Hundred.

SAMUEL C. FISHER.

The examination of JESSE P. CONAWAY was resumed.

By Mr. Cahall:

Question.   You have stated, in the former part of your testimony, that you were commissioned as Provost Marshal for Nanticoke Hundred, I ask you if, in your judgment, you believe there was any necessity for the presence of soldiers at the polls on that day, in order to preserve the public peace, and secure a fair election?

Answer. I heard some of the other men say they were going to stand at the window with their pistols. But what their meaning was I could not answer.

Question. Do you not think that the civil authorities would have attained that object much better than the soldiers?

Answer. I could not say, positively.

By Mr. Saulsbury.

Question. Do you, or do you not believe, from your knowledge of the people of the hundred, and from your presence at the polls on the 4th of November last, that there was a necessity for the presence of the military at the polls to preserve the public peace?

Answer. I did not see any necessity myself. In my judgment, I could not see any necessity.

By Mr. Williams.

Question. Who were the men who threatened to stand at the polls with their pistols?

Answer. Manlove D. Hill said, "I am going to stand at the window." He did not say anything about a pistol. William E. Fleetwood said, "I am going to take my pistol and go to the window," but he did not say what he was going to do with it. He did not say he was going to carry the pistol in his hand.

By Mr. Cahall:

Question. From your acquaintance with Mr. Fleetwood, and his general character, do you believe that he had any serious intentions of preventing a fair election on that day?

Answer. I do not know whether that was his intention or not. I should not suppose that he wanted to injure anybody. He is a man who, like other persons, talks a great deal in fun.

J. P. CONAWAY.

The examination of Minos Conaway was resumed.

By Mr. Cahall:

Question. You have spoken, in a former part of your testimony, of knowing or hearing of certain persons in Sussex County petitioning for soldiers to be sent into this State, to be present at the polls on the 4th day of November last. Did you hear any one of those gentlemen express himself in relation to that subject, prior to the general election, and if so, please state what it was?

Answer. I heard Judge Layton remark in conversation, the next morning after the little election, that the Republican party had been beaten at the little election, and that the Democrats had a majority of the Inspectors, and that the Republican party must have some force to carry the election, or else the Republican party would be beaten more at the general election.

Question. Did he (Judge Layton) say that he believed that there had not been a fair election at the little election, and that it would be necessary to resort to any extraneous means at the general election, in order to secure a fair election?

Answer. He did not. He gave no reason further than that they were beaten. I would say further that he thought he was talking to a Republican, when he was talking to me—I having been introduced to him by a Republican friend of his. The Judge was left in the dark as to my politics. The conversation then ended.

Question. Did you hear any expression of regret from any gentleman after the result of the voting was announced at the general election, belonging to the Republican party, that if they had known that the contest would have been so close, how easily they might have produced a different result; if so, state who it was, and what the conversation was, as nearly as you can recollect?

Answer. I heard Mr. S. A. Lambden say, "if we had only known the contest would have been so close, how easily we could have carried the election."

Question.   Did you infer from that conversation how he meant that they could have carried the election?

Answer.   I presumed from the tenor of the conversation, that he meant by a military force.

Question.   To what political party does S. A. Lambden belong?

Answer.   To the so-called Republican party.

MINOS CONAWAY.

AARON B. MARVEL, sworn and examined.

By Mr. Cahall:

Question.   Where do you reside?

Answer.   I resided in Dagsborough Hundred on the day of the last election.

Question.   Were you present at the polls in that hundred on that day, and did you vote?

Answer.   Yes, sir.

Question.   Was there anything unusual or different from what you had ever seen before at the polls on the day of the general election?

Answer.   Yes, sir. There was a lot of soldiers there—they had possession of a store-house. They kept a guard before the door, two soldiers walking up and down. I think they said there were forty. The two who kept guard were armed with muskets or rifles, with bayonets, and then there was a number of them mingling in the crowd of voters, armed with bayonets.

Question.   So far as you were capable of judging, from observation, were these soldiers in confidence with any political party, and acting in concert with them, in order to influence the voters at the polls?

Answer.   Yes, sir, they were in concert with the so-called Republican party.

Question.   Did you understand where these soldiers came from, and under whose command they were, on that day?

Answer.   I understood, I think, they came from Seaford, and that they were a part of the soldiers under Gen. Wool—they may have been the Maryland Home Guards. At all events they were not citizens of our own State. While at the polls they were under the direction of Nathaniel H. Phillips, the Provost Marshal, as he himself told me.

Question.   Who is Nathaniel H. Phillips; and to what political party does he belong?

Answer.   He belongs to the Republican party.

Question.   Is he an active and violent politician?

Answer.   Yes, sir.

Question.   Did the presence of the soldiers produce much intimidation among any class of voters at the polls on that day; if so, state to what political party they belonged?

Answer.   I think they did produce intimidation among the Democratic voters.

Question.   Was that intimidation sufficient to produce a marked difference in the result of the vote on that day, and if so, in your judgment, to what amount and in favor of what party?

Answer.   I think it did, to the amount of forty or fifty votes in that hundred, in favor of the Republican party.

Question.   Was there, in your judgment, any necessity for the presence of soldiers at the polls on that day, in order to preserve the public peace and secure a fair election?

Answer.   No, sir.

Question.   You have been a Democrat for a good many years, and in confidence with the Democratic party, knowing all its plans and purposes in conducting political campaigns. I will ask you if you ever heard of a purpose or design on the part of any Democrat to interfere with the polls at the last general election, so as to prevent a fair election?

Answer.   I have always been a Democrat, and I never heard of any such intention or design—*never*.

Question.   If there had been such a design entertained, do you not believe that you would have been cognizant of that fact?

Answer.   I think it is very certain that I should.

Question.   Was there any person arrested or intimidated in your hundred on that day, so as to prevent him from expressing his sentiment at the ballot-box?

Answer.   I think there were some persons arrested. There was a wagon with a number of voters, about eight or ten, who were arrested by the soldiers as soon as they drove up. Part of those voters jumped out of the wagon, and three of them were arrested and put in the soldier's headquarters, and kept there until the afternoon. The men arrested were Benjamin Roach, William N. Bailey, and Joseph Fisher. We then, by solicitation, got them released and they voted. The charge against them was that they carried what the soldiers called a secession flag. I will state that the flag was one used during the campaign of President Polk's election. One of the voters became so much frightened that he went home, and we had to send to his home after him to come and vote, which he did.

Question.   Were you a candidate, on the Democratic ticket, at the last general election—and if so, for what office?

Answer.   I was—for the office of Sheriff for Sussex County.

Question.   Were you elected—and if so, by what majority?

Answer.   I was, by twenty-one majority.

Question.   Did you consider that the free and honest expression of the people of your County?

Answer.   No, sir.

Question.   What do you consider would have been your majority, could the voters have had free and uninterrupted access to the polls?

Answer.   I do not think it would have been less than three hundred in the county.

Question.   Do you consider this difference was caused by the soldiers acting partially and in concert with the Republican party?

Answer.   I do.

Question.   As a candidate on the Democratic ticket for Sheriff, did you not thoroughly canvass your County during the last campaign?

Answer.   I did, pretty well.

By the Chairman:
Question.   Was it not the calculation of all the leading Democrats in the County, previous to the election, and was it not also your own opinion that, if there was no interference by the military, the Democrats would carry the County by the large majority?
Answer.   It was.
Question.   Was it not, therefore, the interest, as well as the desire of the Democrats, that the election should be a peaceable and fair one?
Answer.   It was.
Question.   From your knowledge of the people of your County, and their temper previous to the last campaign, did you believe there was the slightest necessity for the presence of the military in any part of your County to preserve the public peace on the election day?
Answer.   None whatever, in my opinion.

AARON B. MARVEL.

On motion,
The Committee adjourned until 8 o'clock, P.M.

SAME DAY, 8 o'clock P.M.

The Committee met pursuant to adjournment.
Present—Messrs. Cahall, Hitch, Williams, Waples, Horsey, Stubbs and Slay.
The Chairman not being present.
On motion of Mr. Waples,
Mr. Cahall was appointed Chairman, *pro tem.*

JOSEPH MARVEL, sworn and examined.

By Mr. Cahall:
Question.   Where were you on the 4th day of November last?

Answer.   I left my home for the election ground, in Dagsborough Hundred, I suppose, about 9 o'clock in the morning.

Question.   When you arrived there, did you see anything unusual, or different from what you had ever seen there before?

Answer.   Yes, sir. We arrived, about fourteen of us, in a wagon. We saw about forty soldiers there. They had bayonets in their hands. We had not got within 125 yards of the place where they deposit the votes, when the soldiers came running at us in two lines. They said to us: "Give up the wagon and flag!" We did so. We had no contention. The boys handed the flag right out to them. A number of them, I do not know how many, jumped on it, and stripped it from the pole; some of the others caught hold of our mules hitched to the wagon, some others caught hold of four of our men and took them down to the place near where we voted, their headquarters, I suppose, and put them in there. After they put our men in there, they went in and loaded their guns. I saw one of them walking in the crowd, having his gun, with a cap on it, already cocked and ready for shooting. I did not know what he was going to do. I slipped up and voted in a hurry. I believe some of our party ran clear home. One of them ran, or walked, about six miles, I believe. Another ran about two miles, so they said. People kept coming to me, and telling me that I was the owner of the wagon, and had better leave. I then went to Georgetown and remained all night and until 9 o'clock next morning. I thought if I went home, they might come there after me and get me, and it would make a big fuss.

Question.   Did those men in the wagon leave without voting?

Answer.   I do not know whether they voted or not.

Question.   Did you learn the cause which induced the soldiers to attack your wagon and arrest the men?

Answer.   I have heard causes, but I do not know whether they were so or not. The soldiers said we had a secesh flag. Jacob Moore helped to contribute money for the flag; also, myself and the present Sheriff, Aaron B. Marvel. It was made six years ago and more. Jacob Moore is a lawyer in Georgetown, and at that time belonged to the Democratic party. He now belongs to what some call the Republican party.

By Mr. Williams:
Question.   What kind of a flag was it?
Answer.   It was a red, white and blue flag. There was but one star—it had faded.
Question.   Was that flag, when it was made, intended for an American flag?
Answer.   It was intended for that purpose, and nothing else. So considered by us all. The soldiers, when they attacked the wagon, jobbed their bayonets at the boys' feet, they said. They stuck them into the wagon.

By Mr. Cahall:
Question.   Did you learn from whence those soldiers came?
Answer.   They were there when we got there. I do not know what time they came. I do not know where they were from—people said they were from Seaford.
Question.   Did they produce much intimidation?
Answer.   Yes, sir; it was a new thing with us. The Democratic party were intimidated. The Republican party seemed to be very well pleased. They laughed at me about it, anyhow.
Question.   How long did you remain at the polls?
Answer.   I guess I did not stay more than two hours.
Question.   Did you leave because you were intimidated by the soldiers?
Answer.   Yes, sir.

JOSEPH MARVEL.

JACOB M. HILL, affirmed and examined.

By Mr. Cahall:
Question.   Where do you reside?

Answer.	In Dover, Kent County.

Question.	Where were you on the 4th day of last November?

Answer.	I was in and about the polls.

Question.	Were you the Deputy Sheriff of Kent County at that time?

Answer.	Yes, sir.

Question.	Did you witness the presence of soldiers about the polls on that day?

Answer.	There was a squad of soldiers, said to be part of the Maryland Home Guards, Colonel Wallace, marched up in front of Nathaniel B. Smithers' office, there they stacked their arms. Some time during the day, there was some contention near the polls about a voter. I think his name was Chapman. I was standing near the State House steps. I saw there was a rush through the crowd, and at the head of that posse, I observed George P. Fisher. He came up, parting the crowd, and shoved some man—I do not know who he was—against me, and knocked me down on the steps of the State House. He was followed by five or six soldiers, with side arms, belonging to the Fourth Delaware. Immediately afterwards, there was a fight commenced outside of the crowd. I immediately ran out, and commanded the peace. In getting through the crowd to where the fight was, I found some four or five of the Fourth Delaware beating a man who, I think, was Captain Benn. I pulled the soldiers away from him after some contention. I think, in the course of two minutes, there was a charge made by the soldiers, with fixed bayonets, right through the crowd in front of the State House.

Question.	Did the soldiers, on that day, act in concert with you as a civil officer in preserving the public peace?

Answer.	No, sir; altogether to the contrary. Several times they took hold of me, and told me if I did not desist, they would lick me. Whereupon I said to them: "Pitch in, I shall endeavor to keep the peace as long as I am able to do it." Some of them told me that nothing but my gray hairs kept them off. I told them, "That need not be any excuse."

Question.	Do you consider that the presence of the soldiers, on that day, contributed to the preservation of the public peace, so as to secure a fair and quiet election?

Answer. No, sir; I think to the contrary. Without their presence, there would have been no difficulty in keeping the peace, so far as I know the people, and, I think, I know them pretty well.

Question. Who were the persons creating the most disturbance of the public peace on that day at or near the polls?

Answer. The soldiers belonging to the Fourth Delaware, with the exception of one or two drunken men.

Question. Do you believe that you would have had less difficulty, as a civil officer, in preserving the public peace, if the soldiers had not been there?

Answer. Yes, sir; I do.

Question. Was it generally understood, and did you understand, from what you saw and heard, that the soldiers, on that day, were in the confidence, and acted in concert with any particular party?

Answer. Yes, sir; they acted in concert with the Republican party.

Question. What evidence have you of that fact?

Answer. I saw Mr. George P. Fisher, the present Representative in Congress, and a candidate at that time for re-election to that office, and other prominent members of the Republican party mixing with them, and bringing the Fourth Delaware up to the polls to vote. It was understood that the other soldiers present were entirely under the control of the Republican party.

Question. Did the presence of the soldiers produce much intimidation among any class of voters on that day?

Answer. I am not prepared to say—not so far as I could see. A man, by the name of William Mahle, a Dutchman, was arrested the night before, and carried out to the camp ground of the Delaware Cavalry, and detained there until six o'clock on the day of the election after the polls had closed.

Question. Do you know upon what charge he was arrested?

Answer. I understood that he had a fight with some person in a lager beer saloon the night before the election. He was very much beaten up himself when I saw him. He has the reputation of being a very influential Democrat among his associates.

Question. How long have you been a voter?

Answer. I have been a voter since 1819.

Question. You are in the confidence of Democratic party, knowing all its principal plans and operations for conducting political campaigns—did you ever hear of a purpose or design on the part of any Democrat to interfere with the polls at the last general election?

Answer. No, sir; so far from that, it appeared to be the desire of the party that any man, who was entitled to a vote, should have a chance to do so without interruption.

JACOB M. HILL.

On motion,
The Committee adjourned until 9 o'clock to-morrow morning.

FRIDAY, February 20, 1863—9 o'clock, A.M.

The Committee met pursuant to adjournment.
Present—Messrs. Saulsbury, Hitch, Slay, Williams, and Waples.

CURTIS W. JACOBS, sworn and examined.

By the Chairman:

Question. The Governor of this State, in giving in his testimony to this Committee, stated, in substance, that one reason for his asking that soldiers should be present at the polls on the day of the last general election in this State was, that he had been informed, by a number of reliable persons in Baltimore and other Hundreds, that a number of Secessionists from Maryland, amounting to fifteen or twenty, to be headed by Curtis W. Jacobs, had entered into arrangements with the Democrats in Delaware, to take possession of the polls in Baltimore Hundred, and prevent Union men from voting. I ask you, sir, whether this statement was true, or whether there was the shadow of foundation from such a statement?

Answer. The whole statement, sir, so far as it applies to myself, or anyone else of my knowledge, is false *in toto*; false in its conception, and in all of its details. I never conferred with any man in Maryland or Delaware, with the view of doing what the Governor of this State has alleged I intended to do.

Question. Are you not a property holder in Baltimore Hundred, and well acquainted with the people of that Hundred?

Answer. I am, sir.

Question. Are you not frequently in that Hundred for the purpose of attending to your business there?

Answer. Yes, sir; I average from once to twice every week in the year.

Question. Were you present at the election in that Hundred on the 4th of November last—and if so, state for what purpose, and all that occurred while there, so far as you were informed?

Answer. I was present at the election in Baltimore Hundred for the purpose of attending to my legitimate business, which had no reference to the election or its result in any manner. On the day before the election, I rode up to my farm in Cedar Neck, where I had hands at work, and the next morning rode back to the voting place to transact business with two men, whom I named to the Provost Marshal and the Lieutenant by whom I was arrested. I had scarcely got upon the ground, when the Lieutenant told me, "You must leave, or you will be arrested." He granted, however, that I could see the two men on business, and take them off the ground. While in that act, the Provost Marshal, Samuel W. Lacey, came up, and told me I should leave at once, or be arrested, which I did, in company with the two men aforesaid. When at the distance of between 200 and 300 yards from the voting place, and out of view of it, the Lieutenant, Walters, I think his name was, with a number of cavalry, overtook me, and arrested me. Walters was a Lieutenant of the 13th Pennsylvania Cavalry, stationed at Baltimore. This was about ten o'clock in the day. I was confined in an old store-house from then until half-past four o'clock in the afternoon. I requested to know of the Provost Marshal for what I was arrested. He gave me no satisfactory answer, but intimated at different times in the day that the charges against me were quite serious, and that there would have to be a thorough investigation of my case, when I might possibly be released at the close of the polls, or sent on to General Wool, in Baltimore. I asked him to confront me with the witnesses or persons who had made any charges against me, which he declined. I never heard any charge against me up to the time of my arrest, and had no suspicion that they intended to arrest me; nor do I now know for what I was arrested.

Question. Did you see any other person arrested that day, or hear the Provost Marshal order the arrest of any person?

Answer. Yes, sir; I saw and heard both the order and arrest of Captain John James.

Question. Please to state when and where, and for what he was arrested?

Answer. He was arrested on the 4th of November last, near the voting ground. I heard no cause for his arrest, except that he questioned the authority of Mr. Lacey, the Provost Marshal, to arrest me. I was under arrest at the time that Captain James was arrested, and on my way back to the voting place, in charge of Lieutenant Walters, a number of persons in the crowd exclaimed, "There goes the old rebel. We have got the old secessionist at last." "Are you not glad?" said one to another. "We will now have the election our own way." Others exclaimed, "Put him in the stable, cow-house, hog-pen; take him out in the field and shoot him, he is not fit to live." I will do the Lieutenant justice to say, that when I appealed to him, as his prisoner, to stop such insulting language, that he did so.

Question. Will you please to state at what time, and under what circumstances, Captain James and yourself were released?

Answer. Captain James, I think, was released about 12 o'clock in the day. He complained of being ill himself, and had left a child at home, and said that he did not know Mr. Lacey had any authority to make arrests. Because of that statement Mr. Lacey released him.

Question. Did Mr. Lacey administer, or pretend to administer an oath to Captain James; if so, please state what it was?

Answer. Mr. Lacey told Captain James that he would have to take an oath. Captain James told him that he was willing to swear to support the Constitution of the United States and the laws. Mr. Lacey told him to hold up his right hand (in this way) and repeated over certain words, to which Captain James assented, and was so released. As near as I can remember, the words were, "You, John James, do solemnly swear on the Holy Evangels of Almighty God, that you will support the Constitution of the United States, and the laws thereof," and if there was any other verbal pledge (for oath I did not consider it), I have no recollection of it.

Question. Did Mr. Lacey propose to administer to you a similar pledge, as a condition of your release?

Answer. He did sir, at about 4 ½ o'clock in the afternoon. I had told Mr. Lacey during my confinement, that I had at different times sworn to support the Constitution of the United States, and the laws thereof, in an official capacity, and had no reluctance to do so then, if the oath were properly administered, but that I could not swear to anything beyond that. He then released me in the same manner that he did Captain James.

Question. I ask you whether your object in seeing the persons, on business, mentioned in the previous part of your testimony, was not to secure a debt from one of them which had been contracted a few days previous, and to make arrangements with the other in reference to a house which he was building for you?

Answer. Yes, sir; that was my business; and one of the persons was a very strong, active Democrat.

Question. You have stated that you are well acquainted in Baltimore hundred, and are there once or twice a week for transacting business. Will you please to state the nature and extent of your business?

Answer. Agriculture, sir, exclusively—such as draining and reclaiming waste lands. I own a considerable body of land in the Cedar Swamp, of which I have already reclaimed enough for several settlements, which are doing well. About fifteen hundred acres I purchased for $2.12 ½ an acre, which I have reclaimed, and have in a successful state of cultivation. I have cut one canal which cost me $2200.00 dollars, between four and five miles in length.

Question. Are you not also engaged in reclaiming and clearing another tract of swamp land in Baltimore Hundred?

Answer. Yes, sir. I am, near Cedar Neck, on which I built a house and made a new settlement in 1862, and that accounts for the other man, John Rust, whom I wished to see at the polls, as he built the house on contract, and I had previously understood he wanted additional material and some money. That is why I wished to see him.

Question. Are there not ties other than business and pecuniary interests which bind you to the people of this State, and cause you to feel an interest in all which interests them?

Answer. There are, sir. My father and mother's bones are now deposited in her soil. My brothers and sisters lie buried here. I was born and reared in Delaware. My wife was born in Delaware. My wife's father was born and raised in Delaware. These are ties nearer and dearer than monied or business interests.

Question. I ask you, in view of your familiarity with the people of Baltimore Hundred, and your knowledge of their temper and disposition previous to the last election, whether there was, in your judgment, any necessity for the presence of the military at the polls to preserve the public peace?

Answer. None under the sun.

Question. Do you know, or have you heard whether any person in Baltimore Hundred was prevented or deterred from voting on the 4th of

November last?

Answer.   I understood Mr. John Hudson was arrested and detained until after the polls had closed, and thereby denied the right to vote. I also was told by Mr. Thomas Taylor, the Collector of Baltimore Hundred, that he did not vote at that election, because he was assured by the Republican party that if the Democrats got the power, Delaware would secede, and that he wanted no secession.

C. W. Jacobs.

On motion,
The Committee adjourned until Monday next, at eight o'clock, P.M.

Monday, February 23, 1863—8 o'clock, P.M.

Committee met pursuant to adjournment.
Present—Messrs. Saulsbury, Hitch, Cahall, Waples, and Horsey.

James A. Clifton, sworn and examined.

By the Chairman:
Question.   Where did you vote on the day of the last general election?
Answer.   I voted in Dover.
Question.   Did you see anything unusual about the polls that day?
Answer.   I certainly did, sir. I saw armed soldiers, with their guns, bayonets, revolvers, and swords.
Question.   Did they commit any violence upon the citizens of the town or the voters here that day?
Answer.   They did. In the first place, I saw a disturbance created by the Fourth Delaware, upon Mr. Charles Brown. I saw that several of them were striking at him, running him backwards and striking at him—five of them, to the best of my recollection—and he had no assistance.

John Klingler was the foremost one of them. He is Sergeant in the Fourth Delaware, I think. I was well acquainted with him, and I had an idea that if I could get to speak to him, he would instantly stop. I said to him: "For God's sake, do not strike an old gray-headed man like that." He replied: "Damn you, I will strike you as quick as I will him;" and he accordingly did so. I received several blows from him. Others behind him, whose names I heard, but do not now remember, were also striking at me. Mr. Brown, seeing that they had the advantage of me, assisted me in getting rid of them.

Question.   What was the cause of this assault on Mr. Brown?

Answer.   I did not exactly know, myself. I think there had been a charge of bayonets previous to that time. I do not think there was one just at the time.

Question.   Do you know whether, later in the day, there was a bayonet charge upon the voters of this Hundred?

Answer.   Yes, sir; there was. In about five minutes after I got rid of the soldiers of the Fourth Delaware by the tree, Mr. Jester and I walked towards the County Building. We were standing by the curb of the State House pavement in the street. There was some excitement at the door of the County Building. One of the voters was intoxicated, and appeared to be noisy, and his friends were taking him away. He was not committing any violence upon anybody. As we were paying attention to the noise in front of the County Building, I heard a rumbling at my feet—behind me, rather. I said to Mr. Jester: "Look out," and, as I spoke, I turned, and received a bayonet charge in my side. I fell, and afterwards another one came on my left side, and stuck in the ground. I believe I knew no more until the occurrence was over. I was taken into Mr. Eli Saulsbury's office.

Question.   Had you been guilty of any breach of the peace, or were you making any noise, or creating any disturbance at the time?

Answer.   No, sir; I had not, and was not speaking to any one.

Question.   Who was commanding the soldiers at the time that charge was made?

Answer.   Napoleon B. Knight, to the best of my knowledge,

under orders of George P. Fisher.

Question.   Who is Napoleon B. Knight?

Answer.   He is Major in the Delaware Cavalry, I believe.

Question.   Do you know whether he was Provost Marshal for this place on that day?

Answer.   I understood that he was.

Question.   Do you know whether, at the time the charge was made of which you speak, when you were knocked down and a bayonet thrust into your side, any other citizen of the town or the Hundred was injured?

Answer.   Yes, sir. William M. Jester fell at the same time I did.

Question.   Were you seriously injured?

Answer.   I was. For three weeks I was not able to work; but I passed around and attended to hands, except during the first three days, during which I was in doors the most of the time, and unable to attend to any business.

Question.   Had you any conversation with George P. Fisher in reference to this matter at any time afterwards? If so, state when.

Answer.   I had, on the same day of the election. He came to my house with the intention of having me arrested, as he said he understood that I intended to kill him after night. I had a friend that said to Mr. Fisher, and told him that he did not think that I said it, as he was with me during the time I was hurt, and if I had said such a thing, that I would say it again. Mr. Fisher asked me: "Did you say so?" I said: "I had not." I told him I had not said anything of that kind concerning him. I told Mr. Fisher I considered he acted very meanly in bringing those soldiers here in the first place, and in the second place in giving them the orders to charge down the pavement on civil and private citizens. He said: "I did not do it." I told him: "You did do it; I am satisfied of it." I do not think there was any other conversation.

Question.   Did Mr. Fisher tell you that he did not know the soldiers were to be here on that day, or did he not?

Answer.   No, sir; he did not tell me that.

Question.   Have you entirely recovered yet from the injury you received that day?

Answer.   No, sir; I suffer severely with a pain in my side frequently.

Question.   Where were the headquarters of the soldiers stationed in this place that day?

Answer.   I believe I do not know.

Question.   Do you, or do you not, know whether the soldiers were in front of Mr. Smithers' office, and there stacked their arms?

Answer.   I saw arms stacked there, and some were passing in and out from the office.

JAMES A. CLIFTON.

WILLIAM C. ELIASON, sworn and examined.

By the Chairman:

Question.   Where do you reside?

Answer.   In Smyrna.

Question.   Were you Provost Marshal for Duck Creek Hundred on the 4th of November last?

Answer.   Yes, sir.

Question.   From whom did you receive your commission?

Answer.   Edwin M. Stanton.

Question.   Have you your commission with you?

Answer.   Yes, sir.

Question.   When did you receive that commission?

Answer.   If the election was on the 4th, I received it on the 3d, and by mail. I received it on Monday.

Question.   What were your duties under that commission?

Answer.   The commission states for itself. My duties were as the instructions said, to settle all riots, to take up deserted soldiers, and to keep the peace.

The Chairman.   Allow me to see that commission. Are you

acquainted with the handwriting in which that commission was filled up?

The Witness.   No, sir.

The Chairman.   Look at the handwriting in which that commission is filled up and the handwriting in which those orders [pointing to them] are written, and tell me whether there is not great similarity between them.

The Witness.   There is some similarity.

Question.   Do you not believe they are the same?

Answer.   I would not say so.

Question.   When were you first informed that you were desired to act as Provost Marshal on that day?

Answer.   On the 3^d of November, about nine o'clock, A.M., I received the first intimation.

Question.   Was the commission conveyed to you from above, or was it from below?

Answer.   I think it was from below.

Question.   Had you never been consulted in reference to your appointment as Provost Marshal previous to receiving your commission?

Answer.   No, sir.

Question.   When did you first learn that soldiers were expected to be present on the election day?

Answer.   I never learned it until about ten o'clock on the 3^d of November.

Question.   Had you never been consulted in reference to the propriety or impropriety of bringing soldiers into this State, to be present on the day of the election, previous to that time?

Answer.   Yes, sir. I cannot state when.

Question.   By whom were you consulted in reference to that matter?

Answer.   Nunus Coverdale.

Question.   Had you never been consulted by any person except Nunus Coverdale?

Answer.   No, sir.

Question.   Were you, or were you not, present at a meeting or meetings of several gentlemen in this town, or some other place in this County, previous to the last general election, when the subject of bringing into this State was proposed and discussed?

Answer.   I think I could say I had been at three or four meetings where that subject was discussed.

Question.   Where were those meetings?

Answer.   One of them was in James Hoffecker's store, in Smyrna. Another, I think, was in Edwin Wilmer's office, in Smyrna. Another, was in George P. Fisher's dining-room, in Dover. There were some persons in Mr. Hoffecker's drug store. I do not know whether the subject was talked about.

Question.   Do you recollect about the time of meeting in George P. Fisher's dining-room, in Dover, of which you speak?

Answer.   I should think a week or ten days before the election.

Question.   State, if you please, as nearly as you can recollect, who were present at that meeting?

Answer.   Mr. Fisher, Thomas L. Sutton, Nunus H. Coverdale, a man by the name of Taylor, a merchant in this County, Charles H. B. Day, who are all I recollect at present. There were a half dozen more there. Several were there whom I do not know. It was decided then that we did not want any soldiers, and at all the meetings I was at, the decision was that we wanted no soldiers. I contended that we had need of soldiers, and we could not have a peaceable election without soldiers.

Question.   Did you believe then, and do you believe now, that soldiers were necessary to be present at the polls to preserve the public peace?

Answer.   Yes sir.

Question.   Were the soldiers present in the town of Smyrna on that day?

Answer.   Yes, sir.

Question.   Under whose charge were they?

Answer.   Under my charge, as Provost Marshal.

Question.   Where did they come from?

Answer.   They were the Sixth New York. There were no others there as soldiers.

Question.   Were not Colonel Wallace and a portion of his men there?

Answer.   They were there in uniform, but not as soldiers.

Question.   Had they their arms with them?

Answer.   No, sir. They might possibly have had revolvers, but I did not see them. They had no arms that I saw.

Question.   What time on the election day did Colonel Wallace leave Smyrna?

Answer.   He left there about eleven o'clock.

Question.   Do you know the purpose for which he (Colonel Wallace) visited Smyrna that day?

Answer.   As a friend of mine—he and his men.

Question.   Had they no other purpose in going to Smyrna, except to pay you a friendly visit?

Answer.   No, sir.

Question.   How many of Colonel Wallace's command were present with him that day?

Answer.   I think there were four, besides himself.

W. C. ELIASON.

DANIEL F. EWELL, sworn and examined.

By the Chairman:

Question.   Where do you reside, and what is your occupation?

Answer.   I reside in Smyrna. I am now engaged in the ministry.

Question.   Were you in Smyrna on the day of the last general election?

Answer.   I was, sir.

Question.   Did you observe anything unusual, and different from what you had ever seen before in this County on the election day?

Answer. I did sir. I saw quite a number of men, in uniform, and with the implements of war, in front of the polls—something what I never saw before.

Question. Were you acquainted with any of the military officers who were present that day?

Answer. I was acquainted with Colonel Wallace, whom I met on the street.

Question. Had you any conversation with him, if so, please state what it was?

Answer. I met Colonel Wallace on the street, and after the common salutations, inquiring for the health of himself and his family, I inquired of him for my brother-in-law, Captain Graham, in Colonel Wallace's regiment. He told me he was well and his family were well. I invited the Colonel to dine with me that day. He excused himself by saying that he was stopping with Mr. Clements, and had to leave in the 11 o'clock train, to look after his men down the road, I think was the expression he used. I inquired of him if there were many of his regiment in Smyrna, and who of them. He told me there were none but his staff, naming Mr. Poulson, Dr. Phelps, and I think some others, but they were men I was not acquainted with. That was the amount of the first interview I had with Colonel Wallace that day. At the suggestion of a friend I afterwards waited on Colonel Wallace, and asked him if he felt free to tell me what those soldiers were brought there for. He answered: "Certainly, they are here in case of a riot to put it down. My orders from General Wool are, that in case of a riot to clear the streets summarily, and I shall do it; and persons on the side-walks will be in danger; they will be considered as aiders and abettors." I then asked the Colonel if he had not sufficient control over the soldiers to keep them within bounds, so that they might not make a disturbance. He then pointed to some men in uniform, without arms, and said that he had no control over those men, that they were Delaware soldiers, who had come home to vote, and were not under military law. I gave it as my opinion that there was no danger of a riot or disturbance unless that class of men commenced it. He said, "In case of a riot it will be no time to inquire who commenced it, that the streets will be cleared." I then asked him if those soldiers were to interfere with the election. He answered, "They are not; every man will be allowed to vote his sentiments." I expressed my regret that he had not sufficient authority or control over certain persons I saw in the street, for fear there would be trouble. I expressed my fears, especially, for two gentlemen and their property, that I was afraid in case of trouble they would suffer. I named them. He said they had heard all that, and were willing as good men and loyal citizens to risk all, and to assume all responsibilities, and that Mr. Eliason was in command. I then asked him a second time. "Do I understand you that those soldiers will not interfere with any body's voting?" He said they would not. That is nearly all that passed between us. He said, during the conversation, that threats had been made. I do not recollect whether he said by the secessionists or Democrats, or whether he said by anybody, to take possession of the polls and to have things their own way. I think he said, "We are determined to let them know they cannot do these things." In conclusion I said to him, "If Mr. Eliason is in command, and the soldiers are not to interfere with anybody's voting, you may leave without any fear of trouble here," and bade him good-bye.

Question. Did I understand you to say that Colonel Wallace told you, in case of a riot, it mattered not by whom commenced, whether soldiers or citizens, that the streets would be cleared, and that persons on the side-walks would be in danger; that these were the orders given to him by General Wool, and that he intended to carry them out?

Answer. I stated that Colonel Wallace said, that in case of a riot, the streets would be cleared summarily, and that it would be no time to inquire who commenced, that his orders from General Wool were, that in case of a riot to clear the streets summarily, and he said that it would be done, and that persons on the side-walks would be in danger; that they would be considered as aiders and abettors.

Question. Are you positive that he said that the orders which you have stated were given to him by General Wool?

Answer.   Yes, sir.

Question.   Did you understand from Colonel Wallace that he had command of the soldiers until they were handed over to the Provost Marshal?

Answer.   I am positive he said, "My orders from General Wool," &c., from which I inferred that he was the commander. That was the impression made on my mind; and after he left, the command was transferred to Mr. Eliason. When I first met him in the street, he remarked to Mr. Eliason—they were together, looking over to the crowd near the window: "Why, they seem pretty quiet for so large a crowd." Mr. Eliason remarked: "They are more so than what they were when I went for you." This also strengthened my opinion that he was in command.

Question.   How long have you lived in Smyrna?

Answer.   I moved there, I think, the 24th day of last March. I have been preaching at Smyrna Station two or three years.

Question.   Are you pretty well acquainted with the people about Smyrna and in the neighborhood?

Answer.   I think so; pretty well.

Question.   From your general knowledge of the people in that neighborhood, did you believe before the election, or do you believe now, that there was any necessity for the presence of the military on election day, to preserve the public peace or insure a fair election?

Answer.   I do not, sir.

Question.   From what you heard and knew of the opinions of persons residing in your neighborhood, was it not the settled opinion that, if the election was a fair and peaceable one, there would be a large Democratic majority in this County?

Answer.   That is my impression, and seemed to be the impression of those whom I heard talk on the subject.

Question.   In view of this state of facts, was it not the interest of the Democratic party that there should be a fair and peaceable election?

Answer.   That is my impression; it seemed so to me. All that I ever heard express an opinion, thought if they could only vote their sentiments, the Democratic party would succeed.

D. F. EWELL.

On motion,
The Committee adjourned until 8 o'clock to-morrow morning.

TUESDAY, February 24, 1863—8 ½ o'clock, A.M.

The Committee met at 8 ½ o'clock.
Present—Messrs. Saulsbury, Cahall, Hitch, Waples, and Horsey.
No witnesses being present.
On motion,
The Committee adjourned until 1 o'clock this afternoon.

SAME DAY, 1 o'clock, P.M.

Present—Messrs. Saulsbury, Cahall, Hitch, Waples, Williams, and Horsey.

AYERS STOCKLY, sworn and examined.

By the Chairman:
Question.   Did you vote on the day of the last general election; and if so, where?
Answer.   I voted at Smyrna.
Question.   How long have you been a voter?
Answer.   I believe my first vote was cast at Smyrna in 1824—38 years ago.
Question.   Did you observe anything on that day unnatural, and different from what you had ever seen before on election day around the

polls?

Answer. Yes, sir. I observed, for the first time, a party of soldiers, with arms in their hands, near the polls; they took their station on the opposite side of the street from the polls; and so far as I observed, they remained there quietly during the time of voting.

Question. Do you know under whose charge these soldiers were?

Answer. I cannot say that I do know. I was informed that they were under the charge of William C. Eliason, as Provost Marshal.

Question. Is Mr. Eliason an active and zealous partizan?

Answer. I am not acquainted with Mr. Eliason's habits, but I think it is understood that he is an active politician of the Republican party.

Question. Do you know about what time the soldiers arrived in Smyrna on the day of the election?

Answer. I do not know with certainty. While I was at my breakfast that morning, a messenger came and told me that they were there, and requested my presence up town. I went, and with Mr. George W. Cummins, called on Mr. James R. Clements, at his house, to learn, if we could, by whose agency, and for what purpose, they were brought there. Mr. Clements could give us no information, he said, but stated that some of the officers were at breakfast there, and that he would introduce us to them, if we would wait and see them. This was declined, and we left the house. Afterwards, Mr. Clements came down town, and had a conference with Mr. Cummins and myself. At that time he averred that he had no knowledge of their coming, but that Mr. Eliason had gone to Seaford the day before, he did not know for what object, but supposed it had some reference to the presence of the soldiers. He went to Seaford on Monday before the election. I think Mr. Clements informed us that General Wool was at Seaford, and that Colonel Wallace was at Smyrna. He offered us an introduction to Colonel Wallace which we declined. I heard and saw nothing more of the soldiers until I saw them marching down the street, with Mr. Eliason at the side of the Captain at the head of the squad. They were placed nearly opposite the place of voting.

Question. You have stated that you have been a voter in the town of Smyrna for the last thirty-eight years. I ask you whether, from a residence of so long a time in that town, you are not well acquainted with the character and disposition of the people of Duck Creek Hundred?

Answer. I think I am, sir.

Question. I ask you, sir, whether, in your judgment, there was any necessity for the presence of the military there, on election day, to preserve the public peace or insure a fair election?

Answer. In answer to that question, I would say, emphatically, there was not the slightest necessity, in my judgment; and in confirmation of that opinion, I would add that no voter's right to vote was interfered with by the soldiers, as far as I know.

Question. I will ask you whether it was, or was not, the general opinion of persons in your Hundred, that, at a fair election, the Democrats would carry the County by a large majority at the last election?

Answer. So far as I heard an opinion expressed, that seemed to be the opinion of a large majority, at least of those whom I heard speak on the subject.

Question. I ask you, sir, whether in view of this fact, it was not the interest of the Democratic party that there should be a fair and peaceable election?

Answer. Of course it was.

A. STOCKLY.

JAMES R. CLEMENTS, sworn and examined.

By the Chairman:

Question. Did you vote on the day of the last general election; and if so, where?

Answer. I voted at Smyrna.

Question. Do you know anything in reference to the presence of soldiers at or near the polls on that day?

Answer. I saw soldiers there on the opposite side of the road—opposite the hotel.

Question. When did you first learn that soldiers were expected to be there that day?

Answer. I was told by Mr. William C. Eliason, the day before, that they were to be there.

Question. Was that the first intimation you had that soldiers were expected to be there on the day of the election?

Answer. I think not, sir. I heard it intimated five or six days previous to that.

Question. From whom did you receive that intimation?

Answer. To the best of my recollection it was from Mr. Eliason, and perhaps others, but I do not remember any one except Mr. Eliason.

Question. Do you know, or have you ever heard, at whose solicitation, or through whose agency, soldiers were brought into this State to be present on the day of the election?

Answer. I do not.

Question. Were you ever present at a meeting, or do you know of a meeting of several gentlemen in this county, at which the subject of bringing soldiers into this State, to be present on the day of the election, was proposed and discussed?

Answer. I never was at such a meeting, and do not know of any such meeting.

Question. Do you know who was the Provost Marshal for Duck Creek Hundred on the day of the last general election?

Answer. I heard on the morning of the election that Mr. William C. Eliason was.

Question. Had you any conversation with any of the military officers who were at Smyrna that day?

Answer. I had.

Question. With whom?

Answer. With Colonel Wallace, his Adjutant, Dr. Phelps, and

Mr. Poulson.

Question. Where did these conversations occur?
Answer. At my house, in a public manner.
Question. Were those officers your guests on that day?
Answer. Yes, sir.
Question. At about what time did they arrive at your house, sir?
Answer. About 2 o'clock in the morning.
Question. In the conversations which you had with Colonel Wallace, or any other of the officers, was it proposed by him or any of them to arrest any citizen of your town on that day?
Answer. No sir.
Question. Was the arrest of Mr. Temple, who was then candidate for Congress, spoken of by Colonel Wallace or any other person there?
Answer. Yes.
Question. Please state what was said in reference to it, as nearly as you can recollect, and by whom?
Answer. One of the company, Mr. Thomas L. Poulson, Chaplain of the regiment, asked, in a jocular manner, "How will it do to arrest Mr. Temple?"
Question. What reply was made to that question?
Answer. That it would not do to attempt such a thing.
Question. By whom was that reply made?
Answer. I think, by myself.
Question. Was it proposed or spoken of to arrest Mr. Bewley, or Mr. Gootee, who were candidates for the Legislature, or Mr. Voshell, who was a candidate for the Levy Court?
Answer. No, sir.
Question. Was there or was there not, in your judgment, any necessity for the presence of the military at Smyrna to preserve the public peace or insure a fair election?
Answer. There was.
Question. Were not the civil authorities in Smyrna sufficient to have insured that result without the presence of the military?

Answer.   I am not prepared to say that they were.

Question.   Had not the civil authorities always been sufficient for that purpose heretofore?

Answer.   They had not exercised it if they were.

Question.   I ask you, sir, whether there was greater necessity for the presence of the military on the last election day than at previous elections?

Answer.   I judged the necessity from the previous election.

Question.   I am requested to ask you whether the name of Mr. Bewley was not mentioned at your house, and at your breakfast table, in connection with the subject of arrests?

Answer.   Not that I recollect, in my presence.

Question.   Mr. Clements do I understand you to say that in your judgment there was necessity for the presence of the military in Duck Creek Hundred, on the 4th of November last, to preserve the public peace at the election, and insure a fair election, and that the civil authorities would not have been adequate for that purpose?

Answer.   The civil authorities heretofore had not been adequate. I believe it was necessary to preserve order.

JAS. R. CLEMENTS.

JOHN M. DENNING, sworn and examined.

By the Chairman.

Question.   Did you vote on the day of the last general election, and if so, where?

Answer.   I voted in Smyrna.

Question.   Were there armed soldiers at or near the polls on that day?

Answer.   I believe there were, but I did not notice them.

Question.   Do you know when the soldiers arrived in Smyrna?

Answer.   I do not.

Question.   When did you first learn that there was a purpose or intention to bring soldiers into this State, to be present on the day of the election?

Answer. I never learned it at all. I never heard it.

Question. Were you never present at a meeting in this town, or any other place in this county, when the subject of bringing soldiers into this State was discussed?

Answer. No sir, not to be in any part of the State on election day.

JNO. M. DENNING.

On motion of Mr. Williams,
The Committee adjourned until 7 o'clock this evening.

SAME DAY, 7 o'clock P.M.

The Committee met pursuant to adjournment.

Present—Messrs. Saulsbury, Cahall, Hitch, Slay, Waples, and Horsey.

JOSEPH P. COMEGYS, sworn and examined.

By the Chairman:

Question. Mr. Comegys were you present at the election in this town on the 4th of November last?

Answer. Yes.

Question. Did you see anything unusual and different from what you had ever seen before, at or near the polls that day? If so, state what it was?

Answer. I did. I saw a military force, at different times during the day, sometimes at, and at other times near the polls. They were armed with muskets and fixed bayonets.

Question. Did you see them make a charge that day upon any of the citizens of the town or hundred?

Answer. I did, on two occasions, see them make a charge upon the people at and about the polls, nearly all of whom I believe were citizens of the town and hundred.

Question. Was there, in your judgment, any necessity for either of those charges?

Answer. None, whatever.

Question. Did not the soldiers themselves, or their presence, occasion most of the difficulty and trouble which occurred around the polls?

Answer. I was not at the polls often during the day, and cannot say what occasioned most of the trouble, but I know that their presence excited a great deal of comment and bad feeling. I think there was an unusual degree of the latter, on that day. The only difficulty I saw at the polls, independent of the usual contest of words on such occasions, was when the person in command of the military attempted to induce the officers of the election to receive a vote, which they afterwards rejected. In speaking here about difficulty, I do not intend to include the charges of bayonets, of which I have before spoken. At the time of the attempt to have the vote referred to taken, there was considerable difficulty, though, as I recollect no actual violence.

Question. Who was the person having command of the military to whom you have alluded?

Answer. His name, he told me, was Comegys, and he informed me that he resided at Greensborough, in the State of Maryland; and that his force was a part of Colonel Wallace's command, under General Lockwood.

Question. Did you appeal to any one that day, who you supposed had the power to stop the difficulty here, at or about the time of either of the bayonet charges to which you have alluded, to use his influence for that purpose?

Answer. I did, although I cannot now say at what particular time it was, though it was in the afternoon, according to my recollection.

Question. Please state to whom it was that you made the appeal, and what answer you received?

Answer. I made the appeal to Mr. George P. Fisher, and I understood him to say, according to my present recollection, that he had no power to do so.

Question. So far as your observation went, did you think the soldiers were acting in concert with either of the political parties, and if so, with which?

Answer. I considered they were acting in concert with the Republican party, because the Democrats, so far as I heard any expression, were hostile to their being here, and they were under the command, as the officer before named informed me, of Major Napoleon B. Knight, as Provost Marshal, who is himself a member of the Republican party. And I also consider that they were acting in concert with the Republican party, because I believed then and believe now that they were brought here at the instance of leading Republicans, and that their object in bringing them here was, in some way, to promote the interests of their party. And furthermore I never heard any but opponents of the Republican party object to their being here, or complain of anything that was done by them on that day.

Question. Were you not born and raised in this town or neighborhood, and have not lived all your life here, and are you not well acquainted, not only with the people of this town and Hundred, but of the whole County?

Answer. I was born in the neighborhood of this town, in St. Jones' Neck, in this Hundred. I have never lived out of the Hundred, nor more than six years of my life out of the town. I am well acquainted with the people of this town and Hundred, and generally with the people in this County.

Question. I ask you whether, in your judgment, there was any necessity for the presence of the military either at this place, or any other voting place in this County, on the day of the last general election, to preserve the public peace, or insure a fair election?

Answer. Not the least, in my judgment.

Question. I ask you, Mr. Comegys, whether, from all your means of ascertaining the state of public opinion previous to the last general election, it was not generally conceded that, if the election were a fair one, the Democrats would carry this County by a large majority?

Answer.   So far as I know, it was.

Question.   In view of this fact, was it not the interest of the Democratic party that the election should have been a fair and peaceable one?

Answer.   I consider that it is the true interest of all parties, at all times, that the elections should be fair and peaceable.

Question.   Do you know anything else bearing upon this subject?

Answer.   I do not think I know anything else of importance, except the fact that the immediate commander of the troops who were here, told me that he was under the orders of Major Knight, as Provost Marshal, and that if he ordered him to do so, he should take possession of the polls.

Question.   I will ask you whether you had not fears, about the close of the election, that there might be an attempt, on the part of the military, to take possession of the ballot-box?

Answer.   I cannot say that I had fears of that description, though the presence of the military and the fact that they seemed to be acting in concert with the Republicans, inclined me to think that there might be some difficulty in polling all the votes in the Hundred.

Question.   I ask you whether, in your judgment, the presence of the military was not calculated to produce great intimidation among a certain class of voters?

Answer.   I rather think it was.

J. P. COMEGYS.

DANIEL C. GODWIN, sworn and examined.

By the Chairman:

Question.   Mr. Godwin, where did you vote on the day of the last general election?

Answer.   I voted in Dover.

Question.   Did you observe anything unusual, and different from what you had been in the habit of seeing, at or near the polls that day?

Answer.   I cannot say that I observed anything but what I had been in the habit of seeing, except that armed military were here at the polls.

Question.   Were you at or about the polls much of the time during that day?

Answer.   I was, during a portion of the day. Being somewhat unwell, I remained in my office, perhaps, more than I should have done if I had been in good health.

Question.   Did you observe the conduct of the military pretty closely?

Answer.   I cannot say that I did especially so. I saw that they were at and around the polls. They seemed to be taking considerable interest.

Question.   I ask whether, from your observation, they appeared to be acting in concert with either of the political parties—and if so, with which?

Answer.   I thought they were, and had no doubt but that they were acting in concert with the Republican party, as it was generally supposed they were brought here to answer their purposes.

Question.   Did you notice any acts of outrage or violence, on the part of the military, towards any of the citizens of this town or Hundred?

Answer.   Upon one occasion, during the day, whilst coming out of my office, I saw quite a crowd, and heard considerable strife about the window where the votes were being taken. What occasioned it, I knew not; but saw Mr. Jacob Hill, Jr., attempting to escape from the crowd, and being pursued by three or four soldiers, one or two of them with drawn bayonets. He was running in the direction of Mr. Baker's hotel at the time. I saw one of them pick up a bat and throw at him, whereupon he, in turn, threw a bat or stone at the soldier. They pursued him so closely that he was compelled to make his escape as best he could. I considered at the time that he was in danger of being seriously wounded, if not killed. Whereupon I snatched a stick from the hands of a gentleman standing by, threw off my shawl, and went to his rescue. I think there were four of them close at his heels when I came up with them. I struck at one of them with a stick, overhandedly. He dodged the lick, and turned upon me with his bayonet pointed at me. I invited him to come on, and told him I was ready for him. He, however, left me, and started again in pursuit of Hill, with one other soldier, the other two having "backed out." I followed them around the corner, they being still in pursuit of Hill, and saw them run him into the store of Pratt & Shockly. I followed, and found them with their bayonets drawn upon Hill behind the counter. I again drew the stick over their heads, and told them if they persisted, I should knock them in the head. In the meantime, others came to the rescue, they desisted, and after a little parleying, left the store, stood upon the pavement outside, and threatened what they would do if he came out of the store. In the meantime, the father of Mr. Hill came in. He and myself left the store-room, in company with his son, and walked back towards the State House, without any further interference on the part of the soldiers, or any one else, indeed.

Question.   Were you present at either of the bayonet charges that were made that day?

Answer.   I was not, sir.

Question.   I ask you, sir, whether the presence of the soldiers was not calculated to produce, and did not produce, great intimidation among a portion of the voters here that day?

Answer.   My opinion was, that such was the design.

Question.   Are you not well acquainted with the people, not only of this Hundred, but of this County?

Answer.   I have a pretty general acquaintance with the people in Dover Hundred, and generally in the County, more especially in the lower part of the County, where I was engaged in public business for twenty-five years, or more.

Question.   I ask you whether, in view of your knowledge of the people in this County, and of their temper previous to the last general election, there was any necessity for the presence of the military, either here or at any other voting place in this County, to preserve the public peace, or insure a fair election, on the 4th of November last?

Answer.   I can say, unhesitatingly, no: not the least necessity, in my judgment.

Question.   What was the general impression, previous to the last election, as to the result of that election in this County, if there were no military interference?

Answer.   The general opinion, so far as I had an opportunity of learning, was that the County would give a very large Democratic majority.

Question.   Was it not, therefore, the interest of the Democratic party that the election should be a fair and peaceable one?

Answer.   I should think so.

On motion,
The Committee adjourned until to-morrow morning at 9 o'clock.

WEDNESDAY, February 25, 1863—9 o'clock, A.M.

The Committee met pursuant to adjournment.
Present—Messrs. Saulsbury, Cahall, Hitch, Slay, Williams, Waples, and Horsey.

JOHN W. WALKER, sworn and examined.

By the Chairman:
Question.   Had you ever a conversation, previous to the last election, with any person, in reference to any purpose of carrying this State at the last election by military aid?

Answer.   I had, sir, frequently.

The Chairman. Please state with whom that conversation happened?

The Witness. The Conversation occurred with Mr. John A. Morris, of the city of New York, in the city of Wilmington, where I reside and voted. Mr. Morris also resides in the city of Wilmington, and has done so for the last fifteen months.

The Chairman. Please relate that conversation as nearly as you can recollect it.

The Witness. We were frequently in conversation in reference to the politics of Delaware some time previous to the nominations of the party for the State and County officers, and I always claimed 1500 majority for Delaware for the Democrats, and he as often replied that we would not get any majority, and told me I knew nothing of what was going on in the country. He said his father was an intimate friend of William H. Seward, and that there was an arrangement being made by which the party would be defeated. That the present administration wanted the vote of a slave State to sustain it. That they would carry Delaware at all hazards. That if the influence of money failed, they would use the military.

Question. Did Mr. Morris give you to understand that he obtained this information from his father, as the intimate friend of William H. Seward, the present Secretary of State of the United States?

Answer. He did not say directly that he derived it from him, but that he had got it from a reliable source, and remarked that his father was intimate with William H. Seward. That is about the language.

JOHN W. WALKER.

JAMES S. HAZZARD, sworn and examined.

By the Chairman:
Question. Where do you reside?
Answer. In the town of Dover. I have resided here fifteen

months.

Question. What political party were you associated with previous to the nominations for Governor and Representative in Congress last year?

Answer. With any and all parties opposed to the Democratic party.

Question. Had you any conversation, about the time of these nominations, with any leading gentlemen of the opposition to the Democracy?

Answer. I had, sir.

The Chairman. Please state with whom, and what the conversation was, and when it occurred.

The Witness. George P. Fisher and Caleb Smithers, of New Castle County, Collector for the port of New Castle. Mr. Fisher called at the shop where I worked, and asked me if I could keep a political secret. Said I: "You know I never divulged one." Said he: "We are going to carry Kent County." Said I: "Impossible, for, in fact, the Democratic party carried it two years ago by about some four hundred or five hundred majority." Said he: "We will let them concentrate their forces in Sussex County, and then we will carry Kent if by the point of the bayonet." I believe that is all the conversation I had with Mr. Fisher. On the morning after the Republican nomination of the State officers, Mr. Caleb Smithers called at the shop. He asked me how I liked the nominations. I told him: "Not at all." He remarked that it was just the thing which suited New Castle County, and gave his reasons why—that the influence of Mr. Cannon would carry Sussex County for the Republican party, that New Castle was sure for 1200 majority, and by that means Mr. Bradford would be claimed as United States Senator in the place of James A. Bayard, and that Willard Saulsbury had already said enough in the United States Senate to be treated as Jesse Bright, of Indiana, had been, by expulsion; and if not, he would be so provoked, that he would say something to cause his expulsion, and in his place, the Governor would appoint Nathaniel B. Smithers.

Question. Had you not previously been very intimate with Mr. Caleb Smithers, during your residence at Frederica, where he also previously resided?

Answer. Very intimate; particularly politically.

Question. Had you any conversation with James R. Lofland on this subject?

Answer. Yes, sir; trifling in its nature. The conversation with him was in reference to the election of officers, and not to the presence of military. But I omitted one thing in my conversation with Mr. Fisher, which I will state. He said: "We have a trail laid for us (meaning the Republican party) to carry the State of Delaware; all it wants is the match to be applied, and that will surely be done."

Question. Did you understand him to mean by "the match," military interference?

Answer. I judged that was his meaning.

JAMES S. HAZZARD.

ELI SAULSBURY, sworn and examined.

By the Chairman.

Question. Where did you reside, and where did you vote on the day of the last general election?

Answer. I resided in Dover and voted in Dover.

Question. Did you observe anything at or near the polls in Dover, different and unusual from what you had ever seen before?

Answer. When I came down the street on the morning of the election, I observed a company of armed men near Baker's hotel. After some little time, the company of soldiers that I first saw, I think, were marched out of town, and, I understood, were going to Hazlettville. Shortly afterwards, I observed other armed soldiers on another part of the public square, I think in the neighborhood of the office of Mr. Nathaniel B. Smithers. They seemed to rendezvous at that point, at least

I observed them there at different times during the day. I also saw a number of the members of the Fourth Delaware Regiment, whom I had seen enter the town the evening previous, with their arms. During the day, I observed members of the Fourth Delaware Regiment, as I thought, endeavoring to create disturbance at the polls, and in the neighborhood of the polls. I saw them at one time make an attack upon some citizen. I saw Mr. Charles Brown interfering for the protection of the citizen. I think that Jacob M. Hill, the Deputy Sheriff of the County, and other persons interfered for the purpose of protecting the citizen, and maintaining the peace. I saw, among the number, the son of Jacob M. Hill, and I saw him chased by some four or five of the members of the Fourth Delaware Regiment, one of them, I think, carrying a stick or club, one I think, had a bayonet in his belt. One, I saw throw a part of a brick at young Mr. Hill, who had to dodge to prevent being hit. I started towards him for the purpose of rendering some assistance, if I could, in his protection; and about that time I heard noise and confusion in front of the polls, and, looking in that direction, I saw the soldiers that had previously been in front of Mr. Smithers' office, charging quite rapidly, with fixed bayonets, upon the crowd. They charged across the pavement, and halted in line, and loaded their muskets in the presence of the people, and within thirty yards of the polls, and after a short time moved to another position. I saw the same soldiers make a second charge, during the afternoon, across the pavement in front of the polls. I saw an old man knocked down on the pavement. I heard of Mr. Jester and Mr. Clifton being injured. Mr. Clifton was subsequently brought into my office. I will state further, that while the old gentleman, to whom I refer, was lying upon the pavement, I saw the Deputy Sheriff endeavoring to command the peace, and protect the old man; and I heard members, or a member, of the Fourth Delaware Regiment cursing the Deputy Sheriff, and using threatening language towards him. And all the difficulty that I saw on that occasion grew out of the conduct of the soldiery present on the election ground.

Question. I ask you whether, in your judgment, there was any necessity for either of the bayonet charges to which you have alluded?

Answer. Not the slightest. But I believe the charges were maliciously ordered, for the purpose of intimidation and injury to the members of the Democratic party present.

Question. I ask you whether, from your observation, most of the disturbance around the polls during the whole of that day was not occasioned by the presence of the military?

Answer. I think most, if not all, of the disturbance was occasioned by their presence and conduct.

Question. Do you know who was in command of the military here that day?

Answer. The soldiers of the Maryland Home Guards were under the immediate charge of an officer, by the name of Comegys—a Lieutenant, as I understood—but subject, as I understood, to the orders of Napoleon B. Knight, as Provost Marshal.

Question. Will you please to state who Napoleon B. Knight is, and what are his politics?

Answer. My first acquaintance with Napoleon B. Knight was some time in the summer or fall, I think, of '61. His father and family reside in the County. He informed me, I believe, at our first interview, that he had been in the State of Georgia, engaged as a teacher in a school, that his school had been broken up by some of the students having gone to the war, and that he had returned at the instance of his friends. His views upon the question of secession differed from my own so much, that I did not desire to cultivate his acquaintance. I found him to be a gassy young man, entertaining the extreme Southern view on the right of secession, and, though courtesy compelled me to tolerate his presence when he came into my office, I found his visits neither pleasant nor profitable.

Question. Do you know whether any person was held under arrest during the day of the election, and until after the polls closed, who was entitled to a vote at this place?

Answer. I understood that William Mahle had been arrested,

and had been taken to the camp or rendezvous at the Agricultural Fair Ground, and I determined to ascertain, if possible, if he was held legally, and by authority; and for that purpose, I approached the Hon. George P. Fisher, then standing on the steps at the Court House door, and asked him if he was the commandant of the camp or rendezvous. He informed me that he was. I then stated to him that I had been informed that one of the citizens of our town had been arrested, and carried to the camp and was there detained. I stated to him that I did not desire his release if he had been rightfully arrested or was rightfully detained, but I appealed to him not to suffer our fellow-citizen to remain under arrest improperly, so as to deprive him of his right to vote. He then stated to me that he knew nothing about the matter, and that the camp, for that day, was under the command of Major Knight, as he called him. I went then to Napoleon B. Knight, and inquired of him if the camp or rendezvous at the Fair Ground was under his control and charge. He stated that it was not. I said to him that Mr. or Colonel Fisher—I do not know what term I used—had informed me that he had charge of it for the day. He said he was not apprised of that fact, but if Mr. Fisher desired to put it under his control, he could do so. I then appealed to him to have William Mahle discharged from arrest and confinement, so that he might exercise the right of voting; but he, like Colonel Fisher, seemed to be ignorant of the arrest and detention of Mahle, and seemed disposed, as I thought, not to interfere for the release of Mr. Mahle. Mr. Mahle was not released so as to be able to vote, but was released in thirty minutes, as I understood, after the polls were closed.

Question. I ask you whether you were not, during the last campaign, and whether you have not been, for a number of years, an active member of the Democratic party, knowing all its principal plans and purposes in conducting political campaigns?

Answer. I have taken a tolerably active part in political matters in this State for a number of years; and in the last campaign especially I took a very active part. I believe I enjoyed the confidence of the party, and knew its secrets and plans of operation.

Question. I ask you whether you ever heard of a purpose or desire, on the part of the Democrats, to interfere with the polls on the 4th of November last, so as to prevent a fair election?

Answer. I never heard of any such purpose or desire, nor do I believe that the Democratic party of the County in which I have lived, or in the State, would have permitted any interference with the polls so as to prevent a fair election.

Question. Were you not a member and regular attendant of the Democratic Association of this town during the last political campaign?

Answer. I was. I believe I attended nearly all its meetings, and frequently addressed the Association.

Question. It has been reported in this town, that at a meeting of that Association on the night previous to the election, it was proposed and determined to bring a number of stout able-bodied men to the polls sufficient to take possession thereof, and to take such possession. I ask you whether there is any truth in this statement?

Answer. I was present at the meeting of the Association, on the night previous to the election, and I pronounce any such statement unqualifiedly false. No such committee was appointed or proposed at that or any previous meeting of the Association. There was, however, a committee appointed for the purpose, as I understood, of hunting up Democratic voters, and taking them to the polls, and seeing that they got an opportunity to vote. I was present when the committee was appointed, and know that there was no purpose to interfere with the rights of any other man in casting his vote.

Question. From your observation of the conduct of the military on election day, were they apparently acting in concert with either of the political parties; and if so, with which?

Answer. They seemed to be entirely under the control of the Republican party, and ready to do the bidding of the leading men of that party in the town. I will state further that the whole conduct of the leading Republicans in the town showed conclusively to my mind that they understood the object of the presence of the soldiers to be to aid them in carrying the election. Whereas the members of the Democratic party regarded the presence of the soldiers as designed and calculated to injure the election of the Democratic ticket.

Question. I ask you whether you are not well acquainted with the people of this County, and with their temper and disposition, especially previous to the last election, and whether, from such knowledge, you believe there was any necessity for the presence of the military either at this place or any other voting place in this County, on the 4th day of November last, to preserve the public peace, or insure a fair election?

Answer. I have a pretty general acquaintance with the people of this County, and understood, as I think, the temper and disposition of the people during the last campaign. I addressed, I believe, political meetings in every Hundred but one in the County, and had a good opportunity, during the campaign, to learn the views and feelings of the people of the County, and from my knowledge and observation, I am satisfied that there was not the slightest necessity for the presence of troops, either to protect the public peace, or to insure a fair election. Nor do I believe that they would have been desired or have been present, had it not been that the Republican party desired and believed that by their introduction into the State, they could secure the election of the Republican ticket.

Question. I ask you what was the general opinion, previous to the last election, in regard to the probable result of that election, if there should be no military interference?

Answer. I think the general impression among the Democrats was, that the Democratic ticket would be elected by a majority of not less than 500, and, perhaps, 1000.

Question. I ask you whether, in view of this fact, it was not the interest as well as the desire of the Democratic party, that the election should be a fair and peaceable one?

Answer. I conversed with no Democrat but who seemed confident that we could carry the Democratic ticket by a large majority if the election should be a fair one. And I conversed with none who expressed any other desire than that the election should be fair. It was therefore regarded as the interest of the Democratic party that the election should be perfectly fair.

ELI SAULSBURY.

On motion,
The Committee adjourned till 8 o'clock P.M.

SAME DAY, 8 o'clock, P.M.

The Committee met pursuant to adjournment.
Present—Messrs. Saulsbury, Cahall, Hitch, Horsey and Williams.

HENRY FLOWERS, sworn and examined.

By the Chairman:

Question. Where do you reside?

Answer. I reside in the town of Dover.

Question. Did you vote on the day of the last general election?

Answer. No, sir, I did not.

Question. Did you start to go to the polls with that intention?

Answer. I started to go to the polls with that intention.

Question. How near the polls did you get?

Answer. To the corner of Mr. Baker's Hotel.

Question. What was the reason that you did not get closer to the polls?

Answer. The reason why I did not come to the polls was because, just at the time, soldiers were in the act of making a charge, and I thought if I could not come to the polls as I always had done before in my life, I would not come at all to vote.

Question. Did you return to your place of business?

Answer. I did sir. I turned right around and went home.

Question. Were you deterred from coming to the polls on account of the presence of the soldiers there?

Answer. That was why I returned home.

Question. What ticket did you intend to vote if you had got to the polls?

Answer. The Democratic ticket.

HENRY FLOWERS.

JOHN B. PENINGTON, sworn and examined.

By the Chairman:

Question. Where do you reside, and where did you vote on the day of the last general election?

Answer. I reside in the town of Dover, and I voted at the voting place in Dover Hundred, East Election District.

Question. Were you one of the Judges of the election on that day?

Answer. I was.

Question. Did you observe anything unusual and different from what you had ever seen before at the polls?

Answer. I did. I saw on the day of the general election above referred to, the presence of persons pretending to act under and by authority of the general government, armed and equipped as infantry, apparently, and in fact, exercising or attempting to exercise the control of the election, or in other words, intimidating voters from approaching the polls.

Question. Do you recollect any instance when the officer in command attempted to influence the vote of any person there?

Answer. My impression is that some time during the day, the individual who acted as the military officer in command of the squad of soldiers about the polls on that day, came up to the polls with a person whose name I think was alleged to be Heathers, and claimed the right for him to vote, which was refused by the officers of the election.

Question. Was the person to whom you allude as the commander of the soldiers, a citizen of this State?

Answer. He was not to my knowledge, and was, as I have been informed, a citizen of the State of Maryland.

Question. Do you recollect any bayonet charges which occurred that day?

Answer. I do. There were some two or three charges of the soldiers, or persons pretending to be acting as soldiers, made with fixed bayonets upon the voters at and about the polls on the day of the election, before referred to, which came under my observation. Immediately after, as I now recollect, one of the charges, they came to a halt, and in pursuance of an order made in my hearing by the person who exercised the command over them, loaded their muskets in my presence, and within some forty feet of the place at which we were receiving the votes of the electors for Dover Hundred, East Election District. Subsequently another charge of bayonets upon the voters of said district was made by the same persons acting as soldiers as aforesaid, immediately or directly across the pavement in front of the place where the votes were being received, in a northerly direction, and towards the house in which is kept the records of the County. In making this last charge they came in contact, or rather passed over a certain Mr. William M. Jester, who was at that time standing with his back towards the south, and looking in the direction of the County Building above alluded to, evidently at a number of persons congregated in front of the building near the door, and was at the time taking no part in any discussion that may have been going on, or in the least interfering or attempting to interfere with the free exercise of the right of any person to vote on that day; when, without any intimation on his part, as I believe, he was run over, knocked down, or fell, perhaps, to avoid being knocked down by the soldiers before alluded to, and thrust at by some one of them with a fixed bayonet in passing over him, and in the knocking him down and passing over him, quite a severe wound or bruise was inflicted upon one of his legs, which caused him to be confined to the house for some time, as I believe, and to limp in walking for several weeks.

Question.　　Mr. Penington, I will ask you whether, as a Judge of the election, having full opportunity to see and know all that was going on in the crowd, there was any necessity for either of the bayonet charges to which you have alluded?

Answer.　　There was not, unless that necessity arose from a fixed determination in the minds of those persons who were instrumental in bringing the troops into this State, on the day of the said election, and of those persons having charge of the same, to thwart and defeat the rights guaranteed to the voters of this State by the Constitution thereof, of a free and impartial expression, by means of their ballots, of their preference for the candidates presented for their support.

Question.　　I ask you, as an election officer, and, as such, having a peculiar interest in the preservation of good order about the polls, whether the presence of the military was necessary to preserve the public peace, or to insure a fair election; and whether their presence did, in the slightest degree, contribute to such result?

Answer.　　I have been a voter, voting in the town of Dover, at and since the general election in November, 1854. At no time, during that period, has there been any disturbance at any of the elections, which the civil authorities have not been able to suppress; and more especially have they been able to more effectually to do so since the division of the Hundred into two election districts, made prior to the general election of 1860. This was evidently apparent from the very quiet and tranquil manner in which the election for Assessor and Inspector was held, in the month of October, 1862, just previous to the general election of 1862—the election for Assessor and Inspector aforesaid being conducted so harmoniously that it was a general remark that not an angry word was uttered by any of the parties on that day, nor, as I believe, was there any vote challenged. I say, therefore, most emphatically, that there was no necessity for the presence of soldiers on that day, at or near the polls in the district in which I acted as an officer, in order to secure the free and untrammelled right of any elector, to cast his vote as he saw proper, but that in my opinion the presence of the military or soldiers above referred to conduced, by intimidation and threats of arrest, to prevent a fair and honest expression of the electors on that day.

Question. Do you remember any other material fact?

Answer. I do not, unless an application which was made by two or three gentlemen, whose names I do not now recollect, but in which I united, to George P. Fisher, who was supposed at that time to have the power or authority to order the release or discharge of a certain William Mahle, who was at that time, as I was informed, a prisoner in charge of persons who were then acting as the first battalion of Delaware Cavalry; to which Mr. Fisher replied that Mr. Mahle would be released at 6 o'clock on the evening of the day on which the application for his release was made. This application was made some time between the hours of 4 o'clock and 5 o'clock, and I think about twenty minutes past 4 o'clock on the day of the last general election in this State, immediately at or in front of the door through which the votes of the electors were received—I, standing on the inside of the partition or division separating the officers of the election from the electors outside, and Mr. Fisher and the gentleman upon the steps just outside of said partition or division.

Question. At what time did the polls close, and the voting cease that day?

Answer. The polls closed at 5 o'clock, P.M., the hour fixed by the law of our State for closing the general election. The voting ceased, or I should say, there were no votes offered for some time prior to the closing of the polls.

JOHN B. PENINGTON.

JOHN BROWN, sworn and examined.

By the Chairman:

Question. Were you the Inspector for the East Election District of Dover Hundred, on the 4th of November last, the day of the general election?

Answer.   I was.

Question.   Did you desire or solicit, as the presiding officer of the election, the presence of the military at or near the polls, to preserve the public peace or insure good order?

Answer.   I did not, sir.

Question.   Were you consulted in reference to the placing of soldiers at the polls?

Answer.   Not at all, sir.

Question.   Was there, in your judgment, any necessity for their presence to insure a fair election?

Answer.   I did not think so at the time, nor since.

JOHN BROWN.

WILLIAM MAHLE, sworn and examined.

By the Chairman:

Question.   Did you vote on the day of the last general election?

Answer.   No, sir.

Question.   Please to state why you did not vote?

Answer.   I was arrested about two o'clock in the morning. About 1 o'clock in the morning, I started down town to look for a friend of mine in Mullen's hotel. I saw him there. He told me he would meet me in Graver's lager beer saloon. When I started up from Captain Mullen's, I saw a squad of soldiers coming up the Bank Lane. I walked up to the corner of the Green. I met Samuel Moore. I asked Samuel where those soldiers came from. He told me he did not know. We walked up to Mrs. Reed's, and I saw George Fisher ahead of the soldiers. He marched them over to Baker's hotel. They went in the parlor. Mr. Moore told me: "Let us go in Baker's bar-room." We went in. George P. Fisher was standing at the head of the counter. One of the officers was bringing the soldiers out, six at a time, and treated them to anything they called for. After they got through with the soldiers, I asked Mr. Moore if he would take a drink. He said, yes. We both took a drink, I started for home. When I got up to the lager beer cellar, I went down to see if my friend was there according to promise. I was there about fifteen minutes. Mr. John Camac, and his son John Camac, and Charles Camac, and Caleb Hall came down in the cellar. They were down about ten or fifteen minutes before they raised any row down there. Young Camac was talking about William Temple, abusing him first one thing and then another. I told them that Mr. Temple was a better man than George P. Fisher ever was. He wanted to know what I meant by it. I told him that Mr. Temple was a white man. He said, "Bill Mahle, do you believe that Mr. Fisher is a negro man?" I told him I did not say that. Then he struck me, and while he struck me, he made a motion to draw his side arms, then I knocked him down. He told me I was arrested. I told him I would not go with him. He got his brother, Charles Camac, and Caleb Hall to help him. I still told him I would not go; they took me there by force, up to Isaac Baker's Hotel. Charles Camac called Major Knight; he came down and wanted to know "what was the matter." Camac told him he had arrested me. Major Knight asked him what for. He told him what I did. Major Knight told John Camac that he had no right to commit me to the camp for those reasons; that I had not done anything. He told John Camac, though, to take me up to Nathaniel B. Smithers. When we got up there he called Smithers, and Smithers came down in the entry of his house; he wanted to know what was the matter. John Camac told Smithers the same he told Major Knight. Smithers told Camac to take me to the camp. I asked Smithers what right he had to send me to the camp, or anywhere else. If I had done anything, that we had a civil law in Delaware, and I would be willing to be tried by it. He never gave me an answer. They took me out to the camp and put me in one of those tents, put a guard over me until between 11 and 12 o'clock, and then one of the officers came to me and asked me if I would not like to come out. I told him yes. He said then that I could get out, provided I would go in and vote a good Union ticket. I told him to go to hell, a damn son of a bitch; I shall lie here and rot before I would vote the Union ticket, I meant the

Republican ticket. He told me that I was a damn rebel. I told him that I was a better Union man than he ever was; that I was a Democrat. He kept me there until 6 o'clock in the evening, then discharged me.

WILLIAM MAHLE.

On motion,
The Committee adjourned until 9 o'clock to-morrow morning.

THURSDAY, February 26, 1863, 9 o'clock, A.M.

The Committee met pursuant to adjournment.
Present—Messrs. Saulsbury, Cahall, Hitch, Slay, Stubbs, Williams, Waples and Horsey.
No witnesses being present,
On motion,
The Committee adjourned until 1 ½ o'clock, P.M.

SAME DAY, 1 ½ o'clock, P.M.

The Committee met pursuant to adjournment.
Present—Messrs. Saulsbury, Hitch, Slay, Stubbs, Williams, Waples and Horsey.

DAVID HARRINGTON, affirmed and examined.

By the Chairman:
Question.   Did you vote on the day of the last general election, and if so, where?
Answer.   Yes sir. I voted at Hazlettville, in Dover Hundred, West Election District.
Question.   Were there armed soldiers around the polls at that place on that day; if so, how many, as near as you can judge?

Answer.	Of the 4th Delaware, I think there were between twelve and fifteen. Of the New York soldiers, I do not know the exact number, I suppose there were between thirty and forty.

Question.	Were they dressed in uniform and armed?

Answer.	Yes, sir; with guns and bayonets on them.

Question.	By whom were they conducted to Hazlettville?

Answer.	I do not know.

Question.	Under whose charge were they?

Answer.	Moses Rash assumed to be the Provost Marshal there that day; the name of the Colonel I do not know.

Question.	Were they understood to be under the charge and subject to the command of Moses Rash as Provost Marshal?

Answer.	Yes, sir; the town was under martial law that day; it was so proclaimed by the Colonel, or the person who claimed to be acting as Colonel.

Question.	Who is Moses Rash, and what is the character which he bears in that neighborhood.?

Answer.	Moses Rash was, at that time, a farmer. His character in the neighborhood is considered, I think, to be that of a very overbearing man. He calls himself a Republican.

Question.	Did you hear Moses Rash say anything about his powers as Provost Marshal? If so, state what he said, as nearly, in his own language, as you can recollect it.

Answer.	He said if they did not clear those windows, that he would close the polls; that he had more power than any twelve men there were on that ground. I will state that at that time he had shown no authority for his power. I did not know then that he was Provost Marshal. It was at the time or just after the soldiers of the Fourth Delaware were making a charge upon the voters at the polls.

Question.	Was the charge, to which you allude, made with fixed bayonets?

Answer.	Yes, sir. They came running up to the polls in what they call "double quick."

Question. By whose command was that charge made?

Answer. I do not know. There were a number of voices, but I could not distinguish them. The voices were: "Clear the window!" "Stick the bayonets in them."

Question. What was the occasion or pretext for that charge?

Answer. It was a contest about the vote of a man by the name of Masculin Foreakers. At the time of this contest over Mr. Foreakers, I was opposite the window, in the crowd, such as usually collect around the window. I walked out of the crowd, not wishing to be in a fuss, when I heard some one say: "Run, Fourth Delaware, and clear those windows!" I immediately turned round and saw them running towards the windows. Before they got to the window, I walked down opposite a post at the side of the window. I thought at the time that some one would be hurt, for they continued hallooing: "Stick the bayonets in them!" and "Clear the window!" While in that position, standing at that post, the soldiers came up. A man, by the name of Thomas Downham, who was in front of the Fourth as they came up, stood by the side of me; he reached out his gun with a bayonet on it, being ordered to do so by some one—I think, Daniel George—and was punching with his bayonet a man by the name of John Smith. I said to him: "Soldier, (for at that time I did not know who he was,) do not kill the old man, for he will get out of the way as soon as he can;" and at that moment some one ordered him to stick his bayonet in him, and, I believe, that was Daniel George; but there were other voices. At that moment, seeing his gun being thrust forward, as I supposed, into the old man's stomach, and believing that he would kill him, I took hold of the gun with my left hand, to prevent the thrust, at which moment he stepped back and swore "He would be G—d d—d, if he would not stick it into me," with his bayonet drawn back, and, at the same time, Daniel George told him to run it into me, while in that drawn position. In self-defence, I took my pistol from my pocket, and put it in about two feet from his nose, and told him to "Do it, you son of a bitch, and I will blow your brains out!" He stood motionless a few minutes with his gun, when another soldier, by the name of Wesley Jackson, standing partly behind Mr. Downham said, "Take care, I'll stick the bayonet in him!" At that moment, I advanced a step, caught hold of Mr. Downham's gun with my left hand, put my pistol partly over Downham's shoulder, told Jackson, if he stuck that bayonet in me I would blow his brains out. At that time the people closed in around the polls and the soldiers soon withdrew.

Question. Who is Daniel George, of whom you have spoken, as having told the soldiers to stick their bayonets into the people?

Answer. He is a farmer and a Republican, and, in our neighborhood, generally considered a liar.

Question. Is he a military officer?

Answer. No, sir.

Question. Under what authority did he claim to give that command?

Answer. He claimed no authority.

Question. I ask you whether that charge by the soldiers of the Fourth Delaware was, in your judgment, necessary to prevent violence, or insure fair play at the polls?

Answer. Not at all, sir. There was no attempt of violence, more than, as I have said, there was contention over Mr. Foreakers—each party claiming him. I heard him say that he intended to vote a Democratic ticket, holding, at the time, a Republican ticket in his hand. He was very drunk.

Question. At what time did the soldiers of General Wool's command arrive there?

Answer. I suppose about 10 o'clock.

Question. Did Moses Rash assume, as Provost Marshal, to have command of them also after their arrival?

Answer. He did, sir; for he did not show any authority until they did arrive. He took from his hat a piece of paper, said to be from General Wool, which was read by the Colonel, and at that time proclaimed the town to be under martial law.

Question. If the people of Dover Hundred West Election District had desired to select a Provost Marshal to preserve good order at the polls, and insure a fair election, is Moses Rash such a man as they would have fixed upon for that purpose?

Answer. I believe, sir, he would have been the last man in the whole Hundred that would have been selected for that purpose by the majority of the people of the Hundred.

Question. Is he such a man as would be trusted by the people to perform any important public duty?

Answer. I think not, sir.

Question. What disposition was made of the soldiers after the arrival of that portion of them said to belong to General Wool's command?

Answer. They were stationed in single file, I think to the number of ten or twelve on each side of the window, and persons who wished to vote had to go between their bayonets to get to the polls to vote.

Question. Did the soldiers appear to be in the confidence of, and acting in concert with either one of the political parties; and if so, with which?

Answer. I did not understand the New York soldiers to show any preference either way. The members of the Fourth Delaware, who were there, seemed to be in the confidence and acting in concert with the Republican party.

Question. I ask you whether it was not generally understood that the soldiers were brought there and were present for the benefit of the Republican party and the injury of the Democratic party?

Answer. That was the opinion of the Democratic party; it was also my impression that the Republican party thought the same, from the fact that they came and went and acted as the Republican party bade them.

Question. Did they make any arrests there that day?

Answer. They did, sir, make one that I saw. I heard of two others.

Question. What did they do with the persons arrested?

Answer. Mr. Walker, the one I saw arrested, sat upon the fence with a guard of soldiers around him.

Question.   Did they produce great intimidation and dissatisfaction among any class of voters there?

Answer.   They did, sir; with the Democrats; for I heard one man say, who was a Democrat, that he would not go between those soldiers to vote, and would not for some time. He was finally prevailed on to go.

Question.   Did their presence appear to give confidence and satisfaction to the Republican voters?

Answer.   It did, sir.

Question.   How long did the soldiers remain at the polls that day?

Answer.   I do not know. I suppose they remained there until the polls were closed.

Question.   Were you not an active Democrat, enjoying the confidence of the Democratic party in that District during the last political campaign?

Answer.   I was, sir, to the best of my knowledge.

Question.   There is a rumor in circulation, that the Democrats of West Dover Election District had entered into combination with a number of Democrats from Maryland to come to the polls in that Hundred, armed, and take possession thereof, and prevent Union men or Republicans from voting. I ask you, sir, if there is any truth in any such rumor?

Answer.   I believe that rumor to be utterly without foundation, and entirely untrue.

Question.   From your position in the party, if there had been any such combination or purpose, would you not certainly have known it?

Answer.   I believe that I should.

Question.   What was the general opinion, in your neighborhood, previous to the last general election, as to the probable result of the election in your District and in this County, if there was no military interference?

Answer.   The prevailing opinion among persons in my Hundred was, that the Democratic party would get a majority of from 800 to 1000 in the County. The lowest estimate that I ever heard made in our Hundred was 100 Democratic majority for that Hundred. Others claimed 125 and 150.

Question.   What was the majority in your Hundred at the general election?

Answer.   It was from 53 to 55.

Question.   Do you believe that the presence of the military there made a difference in the result of the election in favor of the Republican party, as great as the difference would be between a majority of 53 or 55 and 100?

Answer.   I do, sir. I believe we should have got 100 majority.

Question.   I ask you, sir, whether in your judgment, there was any necessity for the presence of the military at the polls to preserve the public peace, or insure a fair election?

Answer.   I do not believe there was, sir.

DAVID HARRINGTON.

THOMAS J. MARVEL, sworn and examined.

By the Chairman:

Question.   Where do you reside, and where did you vote on the day of the last general election?

Answer.   I reside in West Dover Hundred, and voted at Hazlettville.

Question.   How long have you been a voter?

Answer.   Thirty-two years.

Question.   Did you observe anything at or near the polls, at Hazlettville, on the 4th of November last, unusual, and different from what you had ever seen at elections before?

Answer.   Not for the first half hour, and then a military force, armed with guns and fixed bayonets, came up in double-quick time. The first I knew of them, I saw them forming in line about twenty yards from the polls. I stepped down that way to see. I saw Moses Rash, as the commanding officer, ordering them in line, and I heard him say to them: "Forward—march!" after they were in line. They marched towards the polls, but had made but a few steps, when he hallooed to them: "Double-quick time!" and they came running to the polls, and made a bayonet charge. As they got near the polls, he told them to charge, and others hallooed out: "Stick the bayonets in them!" Just at that time I put my hand on Daniel George's breast, who was hallooing: "Stick it in them!" and asked him why he did not tell them to quit it, instead of telling them to stick their bayonets into people. The next thing I saw, Moses Rash motioned with his arms, and told them to withdraw, and they did so.

Question. Who is Moses Rash, of whom you speak as having had command of the soldiers, and what is his character in the neighborhood?

Answer. Moses Rash is a man that never could take care of himself, let alone anybody else; and has always been said to do the dirty work of his party.

Question. Is he such a man as the people of your Election District would have selected as an officer to secure a fair election?

Answer. He could not have been elected by any means, by the majority of the people, for that purpose.

Question. Did the presence of the soldiers there produce great intimidation and dissatisfaction among any class of voters?

Answer. It did among a certain part of the Democrats—timid men, I mean.

Question. Did their presence appear to give confidence and satisfaction to the Republican voters?

Answer. It did, almost beyond measure.

Question. Was it generally understood, so far as you could judge, by persons of all parties, that the soldiers were there for the benefit of the Republican party, and the injury of the Democratic party?

Answer. It was understood to be for that purpose, and no other.

Question. Have you not, all your life, been an active Democrat, enjoying the confidence of the Democratic party, and knowing all its principal plans and purposes in reference to political campaigns?

Answer.   Yes, sir.

Question.   I ask you whether you ever heard of a purpose or desire, on the part of the Democrats, to interfere with the polls on the 4th of November last, so as to prevent a fair election?

Answer.   I never did.

Question.   It has been rumored that there was a combination previous to the last election, by the Democrats of your District, with a number of persons from Maryland, to go armed to the polls in your Hundred to prevent Union men or Republicans from voting. I ask you if there was any foundation for this rumor?

Answer.   None that I know of. I do not believe there was any such design.

Question.   If there had been any such purpose, from your position in the Democratic party, would you not certainly have known it?

Answer.   I believe I should certainly have known it.

Question.   Mr. Marvel, from your acquaintance with the people of West Dover Election District, for a period of more than thirty years, and from your knowledge of their temper and disposition previous to the last election, do you, or do you not, believe that there was any necessity for the presence of soldiers there on the last election day, to preserve the public peace, or insure a fair election?

Answer.   I do not believe there was any necessity.

Question.   What was the general opinion in your section of country, previous to the last election, as to the probable result, if the election was a fair one?

Answer.   It was generally supposed that the Democrats would give a majority of 800 in the County, which was also my own opinion.

Question.   In view of this state of facts, was it not the interest of the Democratic party that the election should be a fair and peaceable one?

Answer.   It was the interest of the party more than I ever thought before, to have a fair and peaceable election. It was the unanimous desire of the Democratic party, as I understood, that we should have a fair and peaceable election.

Question. Will you please to state whether, at any time after the election, you were interfered with, and deprived of your liberty, by any portion of the soldiers who were present at Hazlettville on the day of the election, or by any other soldiers?

Answer. The day after the election, I was arrested in the town of Dover, by a part of the soldiers who had been at Hazlettville, under the order of Moses Rash. When they walked up to me, Moses Rash pointed to me and said: "That is the man." The Colonel then said: "Take hold of him!" I asked them what I had said or done, that they should arrest me. Moses Rash replied that I would find out, and immediately told the soldiers to take hold of me, and they did so. They took me in front of Baker's Hotel, and kept me there about fifteen minutes. Then he (Rash) said to the soldiers: "Fetch that man this way." They took me from there to the Dover Depot; there they guarded me for fifteen minutes, I suppose; they then put me aboard the cars. Rash said to me as we went to the cars: "Mr. Marval, I never expected to have this done; but you ought to know that the Government (or Administration—I do not know which term he used) has got some power yet." After they put me aboard the cars, they carried me to Seaford, Delaware. When we arrived at Seaford, they put me aboard of a steamboat, the *John Tucker*. I was placed under guard in the front of the boat, on deck, exposed to the weather, which was cold, and remained there all night. In the morning, they took me in, and apologized for keeping me out all night, saying they had forgotten me. They used me as cleverly as they could, as long as they kept me. They took me from Seaford to Vienna, said to be twenty miles. When we got to Vienna, the boat broke, and they had to telegraph for relief. I asked them, while they were telegraphing for relief, to telegraph for me; that I did not believe any one had sworn against me. They said they had telegraphed for me. I did not ask them, and they did not tell me, whether they got any answer respecting me. They brought me back to Seaford, and turned me over to Provost Marshal Rhodes Hazzard, who told me I could come home.

By Mr. Cahall:

Question. Did you learn at that time, or have you learned since, upon what charge you were arrested, and taken to Seaford, and thence to Vienna?

Answer. I learned of no formal charge.

Question. Did you learn, while under arrest, and on board the steamboat, *John Tucker,* in whose employ that boat was, and at what cost?

Answer. I learned, from the Captain, that it was in the employ of the Government at a cost of $3000 a day.

Question. You spoke, in a former part of your testimony, of being delivered over to Rhodes S. Hazzard, Provost Marshal, at Seaford—did he release you, and did he give you any reason for so doing?

Answer. Colonel Morris, one of the men on board of the boat, handed me a piece of writing which contained my release, on condition of my reporting myself to Mr. Hazzard, the Provost Marshal at Seaford, within a reasonable time, whenever he should call me. He then asked me to sign the paper, which I did. He then handed the paper over to the said Mr. Hazzard, who told me I could go home.

Question. How many days was it from the time you were arrested in Dover, until you reached home again?

Answer. I was arrested on Wednesday, and reached home the Tuesday following.

THOMAS J. MARVEL.

JOHN C. CARSONS, sworn and examined.

By the Chairman:

Question. Did you vote on the day of the last general election; and if so, where?

Answer. I voted at Hazlettville.

Question. Did you observe any outrages committed by the soldiers who were there, upon any of the citizens of that Hundred?

Answer. I thought I did. The first knowledge I had of the soldiers coming, was on the afternoon previous to the election. I met a soldier of the Fourth Delaware, by the name of James Cochran, a boy raised in that neighborhood, on that day. He told me he had orders to report himself at the election. I asked him what for, and he went on to say, that they were called to keep order. I told him I did not think there was any need of that. This talk led me to believe there would be some interference at the election. I went to the election, and saw soldiers there. After I had been there some time, there was some fuss arose at the polls. I did not consider it any unusual disturbance. At the time, I was standing in the road in front of the building where the votes were taken. The fuss was over Masculin Foreakers, who has always been a Democrat, according to my understanding, and I think I have known him. It was known that he could not read, and, I suppose, they just wanted to see if he knew what he was going to vote. About this time, I heard them halloo for the soldiers. I heard Mr. Rash, about that time, declare that he would clear the polls. The soldiers came running, and charged on the men at the polls. I was standing, at the time, in front of the building in the middle of the street; not having anything to defend myself, I stood still, and let them pass by. At this time, they gathered up between myself and the window, so that I could not exactly see their operations. About that time, I was called off by Mr. Eli Kenton, a voter of our Hundred, and stood with him a few minutes, and then returned to the polls. By that time the soldiers had got back into the middle of the street, about where I had been standing. Then I heard them talking about sending after the other soldiers. I then turned my attention to the voters, telling them to hurry up and vote before the other soldiers came, that I feared we would not get to vote at all.

Question. Do you know Moses Rash, of whom you have spoken as having been in command of the soldiers, and as having declared that he intended to clear the window?

Answer. I do.

Question. How far did he live from you at that time?

Answer. Not over a mile.

Question. What character does Mr. Rash bear in that neighborhood?

Answer. I would not like to take him for an example.

Question. Is Mr. Rash a man who enjoys the confidence of the people of that neighborhood?

Answer. I think not.

Question. Is Mr. Rash a man who enjoys the confidence of the most respectable portion of his own party in that neighborhood?

Answer. I think not.

Question. Is not Mr. Rash a violent, blustering, and fussy man, always in quarrels and lawsuits in his neighborhood?

Answer. So far as I know, he is.

Question. Is he not a violent, prejudiced, and bitter partizan of the Republican party?

Answer. I think he is.

Question. Is Mr. Rash a man such as the people of your Hundred would have selected as an officer, to secure a fair and impartial election?

Answer. I do not think he is.

Question. Mr. Carsons, from your observation of the soldiers there that day, was it not apparent that they were acting in concert with and for the benefit of the Republican party?

Answer. It was.

Question. Was there, in your judgment, any necessity for the presence of soldiers at Hazlettville, on the 4th of November last, to preserve the public peace, or secure a fair election?

Answer. None at all. I believe we might have voted in peace at any time during that day without them.

Question. I ask you if the presence of the soldiers did not occasion most of the difficulty and trouble which occurred there that day?

Answer. I believe it did.

JOHN C. CARSONS.

On motion,

The Committee adjourned until eight o'clock, P.M.

SAME DAY, 8 o'clock, P.M.

The Committee met pursuant to adjournment.

Present—Messrs. Saulsbury, Hitch, Slay, Williams, Waples and Horsey.

PHILEMON SCOTTEN, sworn and examined.

By the Chairman:

Question.   Mr. Scotten, where did you vote on the day of the last general election?

Answer.   At Hazlettville, in West Dover Hundred.

Question.   Will you please to state whether you observed any outrages committed by the soldiers who were present there, upon the voters of that District?

Answer.   I did. The soldiers there of the Fourth Delaware made a bayonet charge on the people at the polls. They stuck a bayonet in me, but did not hurt me much, but would have done so, if I had not warded it off. They stuck a bayonet into my face.

Question. What was the cause of their sticking their bayonets into you?

Answer.   I suppose they had orders from the Provost Marshal to do so.

Question.   Had you been guilty of any disorderly conduct or breach of the peace?

Answer.   No, sir; I had not.

Question.   Did you hear Moses Rash order that charge?

Answer.   No, sir; I did not hear him. I heard others say they heard him order the charge. I heard him say that he would clear the window, and saw him when he went off to do it.

Question.   Did he claim that he had the right to drive the voters away from the window?

Answer.   He said he had the power, but he did not show any power when he came there.

Question.   Did you hear him threaten to close the polls that day?

Answer.   Yes, sir.

Question.   Did he claim that he had the authority to close the polls, and stop the election?

Answer.   Yes, sir; he said so.

Question.   What kind of a man is Moses Rash?

Answer.   I can hardly tell you; he does not bear a very good character among the people as a general thing, so far as I have heard of him.

Question.   Is he such a man as the people would be likely to select as Provost Marshal to secure a fair election and equal rights to members of all political parties?

Answer.   No, sir; I should judge not.

Question.   Is he a peaceable, quiet, and orderly man, or is he himself a blustering, quarrelsome, and domineering man?

Answer.   He is anything else but a peaceable, quiet man, so far as I know him.

Question.   Is he not a man that would use any official position he might be intrusted with for the promotion of his own ends, and the benefit of his own political party?

Answer.   I think so.

Question.   Did not the soldiers there that day appear to be acting in concert with the Republican party, for the benefit of that party, and the injury of the Democratic party?

Answer.   Yes, sir; I think so.

Question.   Did their presence produce much intimidation among any class of voters there?

Answer.   Yes, sir; among some of the Democrats. There was one man, by the name of William Jones, whom we had work to prevail on to go up between the bayonets and vote.

Question. Did, or did not, their presence appear to give confidence and satisfaction to the Republican voters?

Answer. Yes, sir; it seemed to please them very much, so far as I heard.

Question. Was there, in your judgment, any necessity for the presence of soldiers at the polls at Hazlettville, to preserve the public peace, or to insure a fair election?

Answer. No, sir; I could not see that there was any.

Question. Did not their presence there occasion most of the difficulty that occurred about the polls that day?

Answer. Yes sir.

Question. Was not their presence calculated to produce a great deal of excitement and bad feeling between the members of the two parties?

Answer. Yes, sir; it was, I think. It created a good deal of bad feeling with me, I know.

Question. It has been rumored that there was a combination between the Democrats of Dover West Election District, and certain persons in Maryland, to go armed to the polls, and drive Union men or Republicans away. I ask you, sir, if there was any truth in any such rumors?

Answer. No, sir; I do not think there was any truth in it. I live close to the Maryland line, and if there had been any truth in it, I should have been apt to have heard it.

PHILEMON SCOTTEN.

CHARLES BROWN, sworn and examined.

By the Chairman:

Question. Mr. Brown, where did you reside on the day of the last general election in this State, and where did you vote?

Answer.   I resided in Dover, and voted at the State House.

Question.   How long have you been a voter?

Answer.   Forty-four years.

Question.   Did you observe anything at or near the polls on that day, unusual and different from what you had ever seen before at elections? If so, please state what it was.

Answer.   I saw a number of men in United States uniform, some of them with side-arms—perhaps all—and revolvers, busy at the polls; and, in two instances, assaulting unarmed citizens. Several of them, perhaps six or seven at a time, striking, beating citizens; and, in one instance at least, that number had a citizen down on the ground, striking at him, and stamping him with their feet; one, at least, crying: "Kill the damned secessionist!" I interfered to prevent the man from being killed, and with the assistance of some others enabled him to escape. Some time after, I saw several of these soldiers around another man, trying to pick a quarrel with him. I went to the man, took him by the arm and attempted to lead him away to prevent another disturbance. These soldiers, or men in uniform, immediately commenced an attack; pursuing the man and striking at him for some distance, until a number of citizens assisted to take the man off the ground. While the soldiers were beating and stamping the first-mentioned man lying on the ground, the acting Sheriff, Mr. Hill, came to the spot, and called upon them to keep the peace. Several of the soldiers began cursing him, and threatening to serve him in the same manner. About this time, a company of soldiers, said to belong to the Maryland Home Guards, who had been standing in line in sight of the polls, some fifty yards off, I suppose, charged bayonets, as I supposed, upon the soldiers that were assaulting the citizens; but instead of doing so, they charged obliquely to the right, when they came near the spot, upon the people at the polls, where I have no recollection at this time of having any disturbance at that time. During the day, immediately after the charge of the soldiers I think, I went to Dr. Jump, and told him those soldiers were making great disturbance, which might become serious, and lead to bloodshed. He told me he had nothing to do with their being there, and had no control over them. I then went to Colonel George P. Fisher, and told him that I knew he had authority over the soldiers present, that he would be held responsible for the disturbance and violence that had taken place, and which might, in the end, prove serious, and begged of him to have them taken away, that I was perfectly satisfied that all would go on harmoniously if such were done. He told me he held himself responsible for their presence, and declined to give any orders for their removal. Not only have I never seen such proceedings at elections, but I never saw before a man in uniform, or a man armed with any kind of arms, at an election. I might say the particular cause for my asking those gentlemen to have the soldiers removed was, that after the charge of the Maryland Home Guards upon the people at the polls, they formed in line near the polls, some thirty or forty yards off, I presume, and appeared to load their arms with ball cartridges.

Question. Did you witness more than one charge of bayonets that day?

Answer. I think there were two.

Question. I ask you whether, in your judgment, there was any necessity for either of those charges?

Answer. Except the first charge was made for the purpose of driving off the soldiers who were maltreating the citizens, I saw no cause for the use of any force whatever, civil or military.

Question. I will ask you whether, from your observation, most, if not all, the trouble that occurred at the polls in this place, was not caused by the soldiers themselves?

Answer. All that I saw was, and I was at the polls nearly all day. I went late in the day to Major Knight, and told him, in the presence of several of them, that he could see that the drunken soldiers were creating all the disturbances, and begged of him, as I had done of Colonel Fisher, to have them sent away. He gave me no satisfaction, but shortly after, a number of them collected in a group near where he was, and with three cheers for the "Delaware Fourth," marched off towards Mr. Baker's Hotel, and I saw no more of them. I may mention that the first one of those attacks of the soldiers upon an unarmed citizen grew out of an apparent attempt of some Republican gentlemen to force an old man (I think they called him Mr. Chapman—I am not acquainted with him,) up to the polls to vote their ticket, which he seemed to be resisting.

Question.   From your observation of the conduct of the soldiers, was it, or was it not, apparent that they were acting in concert with one of the political parties; and if so, with which?

Answer.   I saw abundant evidence to satisfy me that they were brought there by the party opposed to the Democratic party, to aid it in the election then going on.

Question.   Have you not, all your life, been a Democrat, and were you not active in the last political campaign, enjoying the confidence of the party, and generally consulted in reference to its plans and purposes?

Answer.   I can say, to the first part, that I have never acted in any single instance in my life with any other than the Democratic party, and I believe that I have enjoyed its confidence fully throughout all that time, and think I have known most, if not all, of its plans and intentions, as much so as any other individual.

Question.   I ask you, in view of these facts, whether you ever heard the intimation of a purpose or desire, on the part of the Democrats, to interfere with the polls on the 4th of November last, so as to prevent a fair and impartial election?

Answer.   I never did. I might say further, that in the forty-odd years I have been connected with the Democratic party, I never heard in its secret council, or elsewhere, or knew of any desire or intention to interfere with elections by force or fraud of any kind. I wish that to be put down under the solemnity of the oath I have just taken.

Question.   Did you not frequently meet and address the Democratic voters in this County, in almost every section of the County, during the late political canvass, and had you not an opportunity to understand the temper and disposition of the Democratic voters of the County previous to the last general election?

Answer.   I should think I had, to a considerable extent.

Question. I ask you, in view of this fact, whether, in your judgment, there was any necessity for the presence of the military at the polls, on the 4th of November last, either at this or any other voting place in this County, to preserve the public peace, or insure a fair and impartial election?

Answer. I saw or heard nothing anywhere, calculated to induce the belief in the mind of any one that any extraordinary force, or force of any kind, would be required anywhere, to keep the peace or to insure a fair election. And although it was reported for some time before the election that the friends of the Administration of the General Government intended to bring United States soldiers into this State for the purpose of carrying the election, I refused to believe it until their arrival had actually taken place.

Question. Did you see any person, on the day of the election, interfere with any voter, and attempt to prevent him from voting his sentiments, and induce or coerce him to vote contrary to his sentiments?

Answer. I have stated the case of Mr. Chapman. On another occasion, Mr. James L. Heverin called my attention to an apparent controversy between a Lieutenant, with the United States uniform on, (I think it was mentioned that he was a son of John W. Cullen,) and a young man in United States uniform. The Lieutenant seemed desirous of persuading him to vote the ticket, as he said, in favor of the Government. The private, as I understood him, said he had always voted the Democratic ticket. The Lieutenant said to him that that ticket was against the Government, and that he had sworn to support the Government, and must vote a ticket to support it, or that he must not vote the Democratic ticket—I do not remember exactly which phrase he used. I did not see the end of the controversy, but I understood from Mr. Heverin that the young man voted the Republican ticket. I do not know the fact.

Question. I will ask you what was the general estimate, previous to the last general election, as to the probable result of that election in this County, if there was no interference by the military, and the election was a fair one?

Answer.   The estimates were various; but I think it was the general impression that there would be one thousand majority for the Democratic party, and especially that a large majority was expected after the little election.

Question.   I ask whether, therefore, it was not the interest, as well as the desire of the Democratic party, that the election should be a perfectly fair and peaceable one?

Answer.   Certainly. In this County, and in Sussex County, where I was during the canvass, their hopes of greatest success there, and in the State, by Democrats, was in a fair, full, and peaceable election.

CHARLES BROWN.

On motion,
The Committee adjourned until 8 ½ o'clock to-morrow morning.

FRIDAY, February 26, 1863—8 ½ o'clock, A.M.

The Committee met pursuant to adjournment.
Present—Messrs. Saulsbury, Cahall, Hitch, Slay and Waples.

LAZARUS TURNER, sworn and examined.

By the Chairman:
Question.   Mr. Turner, where do you reside, and where did you vote on the day of the last general election in this State?
Answer.   In Broad Creek Hundred, Sussex County.
Question.   Will you please to state whether there were soldiers at or near the polls on that day; and if so, what position they occupied in reference to the polls?
Answer.   There were soldiers there, and they pitched tents around the house where the votes were received. They formed a line, and a

portion of them occupied the space within the line. A portion of the soldiers were stationed on the outside of the line. They kept guard at the place of entrance. When we first opened the election, the place of entry was exactly opposite the window, but that was soon closed. I soon found that I could not be admitted there. They had then changed the place of entrance, and I saw several go in thereat, and before I could get there, that place of entry was closed. I then went to the third place of entry, as I supposed; there I remained trying to be admitted in to vote, for at least two hours, but was not able to enter. Then I became disgusted at the conduct and determined on leaving the place, and did leave, and got some hundred yards from the place of voting, and was followed up by several of my friends and persuaded to return, and did return, and made another attempt to get in at the place of entry in order to vote, and still did not succeed. I got more than ever disgusted, and determined to leave for home, and I did go home without voting. After getting home and resting a few minutes, I went back to the place of entry I had formerly left when I started for home. I there found several persons standing near the same position I left them in when I started for home. They let me know that they had been trying to vote—the main body of these persons were Democrats—during the whole of my absence, and had not succeeded.

Question. What time in the day did you get to vote?

Answer. I think it was near four o'clock.

Question. What time in the morning was it when you first attempted to vote?

Answer. Very soon after the opening of the polls. I have usually been, for a number of years, Judge in the house. On those occasions I usually waited until a later time to vote.

Question. You have stated that you have usually been a Judge of the election. Had you not, as Judge of election, a good opportunity to observe and understand what was going on outside?

Answer. So far as the conduct of people at the window was concerned, I had.

Question. How long have you been a voter?

Answer. Forty-two years.

Question. I ask you, sir, whether you ever, in your life, saw or heard of so much difficulty in voting as there was in your place on the day of the last general election?

Answer. So far as the Democratic party was concerned, I never did.

Question. You have stated that you stood in one position at the place which you understood to have been fixed as a place of entrance for the voters to the polls, making efforts to get to the polls to deposit your ballot. I ask you whether, during that time, any other person was admitted, and did go to the polls and vote?

Answer. They were at it all the time—of the opposite party.

Question. Do I understand you to say that there was no difficulty in members of the Republican party getting to the polls during this time?

Answer. I saw none, because they would take them over the rope, or wherever they pleased. They could enter in any position.

Question. I ask you whether all the difficulty in getting to vote was not confined to the Democrats?

Answer. I think it was.

Question. I ask you whether the soldiers who were present there were not acting in concert with the Republican party, for the benefit of that party, and the injury of the Democratic party?

Answer. It had that appearance to me.

Question. I ask you whether the Republicans did not appear to be confident and jubilant at the presence of the soldiers, and whether the Democrats did not appear to be dissatisfied, depressed, and intimidated by their presence?

Answer. I answer that in the affirmative.

Question. Mr. Turner, you have stated that there were persons permitted to remain within the space inclosed by the line which was drawn around the voting place. I will ask you who those persons were?

Answer. There were certain persons who went in and out of this space when they pleased, and took whom they pleased. These persons, who had this liberty, had badges or ribbons of different kinds, blue and red, in the button-holes of their coats.

Question.   Were those persons members of both political parties, or were they confined to one party?

Answer.   One party—what they call the Union party. They call themselves Republicans. I call them Whigs, that being the old name by which we knew the opposition.

Question.   I ask you, sir, if Henry Betts was not also permitted to be in that ring during that whole day whenever he saw fit?

Answer.   He was stationed in there all the time I was about the polls.

Question.   Was he acting as Provost Marshal, and, as such, had he command of the soldiers who were there?

Answer.   He was acting as such; he held that position.

Question.   Are you well acquainted with Henry Betts?

Answer.   Not intimately.

Question.   What kind of a man is Henry Betts understood to be, so far as your knowledge extends, in Broad Creek Hundred?

Answer.   He is a very strong party man.

Question.   I ask you whether he is such a man as the people of Broad Creek Hundred would have selected for the office of Provost Marshal, if they had desired an officer to secure a fair and impartial election?

Answer.   I should say, far from it.

Question.   I ask you if he is not understood to be a man who would use any official position he might occupy for the promotion of the interests of his own political party?

Answer.   It is my idea that he would.

Question.   You have stated that so far as the Democratic party was concerned, you never saw as much difficulty in voting at any other election as at the last general election. Do you mean by that, that the Democratic party created and gave difficulty that day?

Answer. There was no trouble occasioned by the Democratic party. The difficulty appeared to be occasioned by the soldiers, in conjunction with the Republicans, who seemed to be trying to prevent the Democrats from voting, thus occasioning the difficulty.

Question. I ask you whether you ever knew at any election, previous to the 4th of November last, of any persons of any party having the least trouble in getting to vote?

Answer. I have seen difficulties in voting at the window frequently, by unruly persons causing some pulling and hauling; but I never before saw a concentrated effort, on the part of members of one party, to prevent members of the other party from voting.

Question. Have you not been all your life-time a Democrat, and do you not enjoy the confidence of the Democratic party, knowing all its principal plans and purposes?

Answer. I have always been a Democrat. I never voted any other ticket, and I think I do enjoy the confidence of the Democratic party, and generally know its principal plans and purposes.

Question. I ask you if you ever heard the intimation of a desire or purpose, on the part of the Democrats, to interfere with the polls so as to prevent a fair election, on the 4th of November last?

Answer. I did not.

Question. It has been stated by the Governor of the State, in his testimony before this Committee, in substance, that he wrote to Colonel Wallace to place a portion of his command in Broad Creek Hundred, Little Creek Hundred, Baltimore Hundred, and Dagsborough Hundred, on the day of the last general election to preserve the public peace at the polls, and that he also solicited the Secretary of War to send troops into this State for a similar purpose; and gave, as his reason for so doing, that he was informed by a number of reliable persons in Baltimore and other Hundreds, whose names he could not recollect, that there was a combination by the Democrats of Baltimore Hundred, with certain Secessionists, amounting to fifteen or twenty, in the State of Maryland, headed by one Curtis W. Jacobs, to come into Baltimore Hundred on the day of the last general election, and prevent Union men from voting; and also that he understood there was a man, whose name he did not recollect, who stood at the polls in Broad Creek Hundred on the day of the little election, with a drawn revolver, threatening the Union men, alleging that they should not vote. I ask you whether the facts stated by the Governor as his reasons for making this request, were or were not true?

Answer. On the day of the little election alluded to in that question, there was a certain man, by the name of Jasper Dawson, with a pistol drawn. I was in the house, confined with the other Judge, and near the close of the little election I saw Mr. Jasper Dawson with a pistol, but I think the most of the voting was over at that time, and that they raised a fuss outside of the window within three or four feet of it. I do not think it was to prevent any person from voting. I heard no threats that Union men should not vote. I think the fuss had no relation to politics. I considered it an outdoor fuss. I do not know whether they were both of the same political party, or of different parties. I never heard the least syllable of the combination between the Democrats of Delaware and the Secessionists of Maryland referred to.

Question. If there had been such combination, from your position in the Democratic party, would you not certainly have known it?

Answer. I think I should have been most likely to have heard something of it.

Question. Mr. Turner, was there, in your judgment, any necessity for the presence of the military in Broad Creek Hundred, or any other voting place in Sussex County, on the day of the last general election, to preserve the public peace, or insure a fair and impartial election?

Answer. I should not suppose there was in the least.

Question. I am requested to ask you, Mr. Turner, whether, in your judgment, the presence of the soldiers in Broad Creek Hundred produced any difference in the result of that election from what it would have been if they had not been present; and if so, in favor of what political party, and to what extent?

Answer. I think it did make a difference. I think the Democratic party would have received from thirty to forty more votes than they did. I mean that thirty or forty of those who voted the Republican ticket would have voted the Democratic ticket had not the soldiers been present, which would have made a difference in the result of from sixty to eighty votes in favor of the Democratic party.

LAZARUS TURNER.

JAMES L. HEVERIN, sworn and examined.

By the Chairman:
Question. Mr. Heverin, did you see, on the day of the last general election, or hear any military officer in the service of the United States interfere, or attempt to interfere, with any voter in Dover Hundred, to prevent him from voting in accordance with his own political sentiments, and to force him, by threats or otherwise, to vote against his declared political sentiments?

Answer. I believe I did. I saw Lieutenant Hezekiah Cullen, a son of John W. Cullen, ask James Steel, a member of his company, and a private, to show him his ticket. He handed him his ticket, and Cullen said: "This is a Democratic ticket." He replied: "I never voted anything else, except at the last little election." Said Cullen then tore up the Democratic ticket, and gave him a Republican ticket, with a flag on the back of it, and said: "You must vote that;" caught hold of him, and said: "Come along." I remarked: "We are not under martial law here." He said: "I will show you;" and then said: "Come on," with an air of tyrannical authority. I think I said to Steel: "Stop, I will give you a ticket." From that Steel hesitated, and Cullen caught hold of him, and pulled him up to the polls, and he voted the ticket that Cullen gave him, which was, I have no doubt, a Republican ticket, because it had a flag on the back of it, and the Democrats had no tickets of that kind. Steel told me just previously that he wanted to vote a Democratic ticket.

Question. Is Hezekiah Cullen a man of substance and position in the community, having a greater interest and larger stake in the welfare of the community than a majority of the voters of this Hundred?

Answer. I think not. He is barely of age, if he is of age; and previous to being commissioned, was entirely dependent on his father.

Question. Did the presence of the soldiers in this Hundred and County, on the 4th of November last, contribute to produce a fair and impartial election, or did their presence contribute to prevent a fair and impartial election?

Answer. I think they contributed to prevent a fair and impartial election. I think it made a difference in the result of the election of sixty votes against the Democratic party in the Hundred, and of several hundred in the County. I do not think any better plan could have been devised to defeat the Democratic party.

J. L. HEVERIN.

On motion of Mr. Williams,

The Committee adjourned until half-past eight o'clock, P.M., on Monday next.

MONDAY, March 2, 1863, 8 o'clock, P.M.

The Committee met pursuant to adjournment.
Present—Messrs. Saulsbury, Hitch, Slay, Horsey and Waples.

NUNUS H. COVERDALE, affirmed and examined.

By the Chairman.

Question. Mr. Coverdale, were you at any time previous to the last election, consulted in reference to the propriety of bringing soldiers into this State, to be present at the election?

Answer. I was, sir.

Question. By whom were you consulted?

Answer. It would be out of my power to state all by whom I was consulted. I can recollect some of them. Nathaniel B. Smithers, Hon. George P. Fisher, Mr. John Fletcher Clements, and others. These are all I can recollect at this time.

Question. Where were you at the time you were consulted?

Answer. In the Hon. George P. Fisher's parlor.

Question. Were you sent for to come here for that purpose?

Answer. No, sir.

Question. Were you ever sent for to meet those gentlemen, or any other gentlemen, to consult in reference to that subject?

Answer. No, sir.

Question. Was the time, to which you have alluded, at which you were consulted in Mr. Fisher's parlor, the only time that you were consulted in reference to that subject?

Answer. The same subject was spoken of on another occasion in the same place, and by nearly the same persons.

Question. What opinion did you give those gentlemen in reference to the propriety of bringing soldiers into this State, to be present on the election day?

Answer. The opinion that I gave was, that I thought it would not be proper to send troops, but afterwards I rather changed my opinion, after seeing the effect the troops had at the polls.

Question. Do I understand you to say, that previous to the election, at the times when you were consulted, you gave it as your opinion that it would not be proper to send troops into this State to be present at the polls, and that you only changed that opinion after having seen the effect of the soldiers at the polls?

Answer. Yes, sir.

Question. Were you a candidate upon the Union ticket at the last election; if so, for what position?

Answer. I was a candidate for Representative to the General Assembly.

The Chairman.   Mr. Coverdale, we are through with your examination, please to sign your testimony as you have delivered it to the Committee.

The Witness.   I request a copy.

The Chairman.   Certainly, you can take a copy.

N. H. COVERDALE.

PARIS T. CARLISLE, sworn and examined.

By the Chairman:

Question.   Were you Provost Marshal for South Murderkill Hundred on the day of the last general election?

Answer.   I was.

Question.   When did you receive your commission as Provost Marshal?

Answer.   I do not know the date, it was several days before the election.

Question.   From whom did you receive the commission?

Answer.   It had Edwin M. Stanton's name on it.

Question.   Have you the commission with you?

Answer.   No, sir; I did not bring it.

Question.   Was there an order accompanying the commission directing you to report to General Wool, or any other person?

Answer.   There was.

Question.   From whom was that order?

Answer.   Major James R. Lofland, Provost Marshal General.

Question.   Did you notice the handwriting in which your commission from Mr. Stanton was filled up?

Answer.   I did not, particularly.

Question.   Do you recollect whether it was the same handwriting as that of the order from James R. Lofland?

Answer.   Not having noticed it particularly, I could not say on oath.

Question. Were you consulted in reference to your appointment as Provost Marshal before you received the commission?

Answer. No, sir.

Question. Were you ever consulted, previous to the election, in reference to the propriety or necessity of bringing armed soldiers into this State, to be present on the day of the last general election?

Answer. No, sir.

Question. Were you ever present when the subject of the introduction of troops for that purpose was discussed or spoken of?

Answer. I might have heard it spoken of in the stores. I never was in any meeting.

Question. Did you believe previous to the election, or do you believe now, that there was any necessity for the presence of armed soldiers at the polls in South Murderkill Hundred, to preserve the public peace, or insure a fair election?

Answer. I did.

Question. Why did you believe that soldiers were necessary in South Murderkill Hundred on the day of the election, to preserve the public peace or insure a fair election?

Answer. At our previous elections there has always been a great deal of difficulty for peaceable citizens to vote, and under the extra excitement, I thought it necessary.

Question. I ask you whether you recollect any previous election at which the citizens of that Hundred were prevented from voting their sentiments?

Answer. I remember where men had to be dragged away from the polls to give them room to get up to vote.

Question. Is it not a usual thing, in closely contested elections, for each party to make an effort to get their votes into the box at as early an hour in the day as possible?

Answer. I believe it is.

Question. I ask you whether the strife incident to this effort was not the only difficulty you have heretofore seen at the elections in your Hundred?

Answer.   Yes.

Question.   I ask you, sir, whether there was any difficulty at the little election, which was the last election previous to the general election on the 4th of November, sufficient to require the presence of an armed soldiery at the polls, to preserve the public peace or insure a fair election?

Answer.   There being troops there at the little election, we had it very quiet, hence I cannot say.

Question.   Were the troops, that were at Felton on the day of the little election, brought there for the purpose of preserving the public peace, and were they placed under the command of a Provost Marshal, or any other officer or person, who was a citizen of that Hundred, and a voter at that place?

Answer.   I only know that they were there, and that we had a very quiet election.

Question.   Please to state, if you know, for what purpose they were there?

Answer.   I think I answered that in the former question, when I said I only knew that they were there.

Question.   Do you mean to say by that, that you do not know the purpose for which they were there?

Answer.   I do.

P. T. CARLISLE.

JONATHAN CARROW, sworn and examined.

By the Chairman:

Question.   Where do you reside, and where did you vote on the day of the last general election?

Answer.   In Camden, North Murderkill Election District.

Question.   Were there armed soldiers in Camden, at or near the polls on that day?

Answer. Yes, sir.

Question. How far were they stationed from the polls?

Answer. About fifty feet, I should judge.

Question. Had they their arms when stationed fifty feet from the polls?

Answer. No, sir; their arms were stacked near by them.

Question. Do you know where the soldiers, of whom you have spoken, were from?

Answer. From New York, I understood the officers to say; they did not say of what regiment.

Question. Were any other soldiers there?

Answer. None in arms; there were a few of one of the Delaware regiments there, to vote, I suppose. I am not certain whether they belonged to the Fourth Delaware or not.

Question. Are you sure that the Delaware soldiers, who were present, had not their side-arms?

Answer. I do not recollect seeing any with their arms.

Question. Who was Provost Marshal there that day, having charge of the soldiers?

Answer. William Lord.

Question. Will you please to state who Mr. William Lord is, and what are his politics?

Answer. He is the son of Edward Lord, in Camden; his politics are of the Union party, professedly.

Question. Are you not, and have you not been for many years a member of the Democratic party, enjoying the confidence of the Democratic party, and knowing all its principal plans and purposes, in reference to political campaigns?

Answer. Yes, sir; I presume so.

Question. Did you ever hear an intimation of a purpose or desire, on the part of the Democrats, to interfere with the polls on the 4th of November last, to prevent a fair and impartial election?

Answer. No, sir; I never have.

Question. If there had been any such purpose, from your position in the Democratic party, would you not certainly have known it?

Answer. I certainly should.

Question. I ask you whether, in your judgment, there was any necessity for the presence of the military in North Murderkill Hundred, or at any other voting place in this County on the 4th day of November last, to preserve the public peace, or insure a fair and impartial election?

Answer. None whatever, in my opinion.

Question. I ask you whether their presence was not calculated to produce and did not produce great dissatisfaction and intimidation among the voters of one of the political parties?

Answer. I should suppose that it was calculated to produce that effect, and did produce it among the voters of the Democratic party.

Question. Had their presence the same effect upon the Republican voters?

Answer. No, sir. I thought some of them seemed to be overbearing and tyrannical.

JONATHAN CARROW.

ELIJAH B. REGISTER, sworn and examined.

By the Chairman:

Question. Mr. Register, do you reside in Camden, in North Murderkill Hundred, and did you vote in that place on the day of the last general election?

Answer. Yes, sir.

Question. Were there armed soldiers at or near the polls at any time during the day; if so, please state how near to the polls, and how many there were of them, as nearly as you can judge?

Answer. I think, perhaps, about forty or fifty feet, and I think about forty or fifty men.

Question. Do you recollect whether, at any time during the day, they were drawn up in a position to charge upon the voters in front of the polls?

Answer. There was a disturbance arose at the polls in regard to a vote about to be taken from Garrett Luff, residing at this time, and at that time—I cannot say how long before, perhaps five or six months—in Washington. During the disturbance, some person, I know not whom, called to the officer; I know not what was said to him; immediately they fell into rank, with their arms at charge, and came up within, I suppose, ten feet of the crowd. I stepped myself up towards them and importuned the officer—a Captain, I suppose—not to advance any further, that the disturbance at that moment was a difficulty between two men not concerned in the election, in my opinion. At that instant, William P. Lord, said to be the Provost Marshal, stepped up by the side of me, and ordered them to return to their station, and they did so.

Question. Who is William P. Lord, of whom you have spoken as Provost Marshal for Camden on that day, and what are his politics?

Answer. He is a son of Edward Lord. I believe from what I can learn, he is with the Republican party. I never have questioned him.

Question. Was the presence of soldiers calculated to produce, and did their presence produce great dissatisfaction and intimidation among any class of voters in Camden on that day?

Answer. I think it did, generally among the Democrats.

Question. Did their presence produce the same effect upon the Republican voters there that day?

Answer. I think not. They appeared to be better satisfied than the Democrats did.

Question. Did not the Republicans generally appear to be rejoiced and jubilant at the presence of the soldiers?

Answer. I cannot say that I witnessed anything like great rejoicing among them.

Question. Have you not been for many years an active Democrat, enjoying the confidence of the party, and knowing its principal plans and purposes?

Answer. I have always been a Democrat, and been in good fellowship with them; not very active in the cause, and therefore I cannot say how I stood.

Question. Did you ever hear the intimation of a purpose or desire, on the part of the Democrats, to interfere with the polls on the 4th of November last, so as to prevent a fair and impartial election?

Answer. No, sir.

Question. I ask you whether, in your judgment, there was any necessity for the presence of the military at the polls in your hundred to preserve the public peace or insure a fair and impartial election?

Answer. I think not, sir.

E. B. REGISTER.

JOHN F. CLEMENTS, sworn and examined.

By the Chairman:

Question. Mr. Clements, where do you reside, and where did you vote on the 4th of November last?

Answer. I reside in Camden, and voted in Camden, North Murderkill District.

Question. Were there armed soldiers at or near the polls in Camden that day; if so, state as nearly as you can judge how many there were?

Answer. Yes, sir; there were armed soldiers there; about forty, I think.

Question. Do you know where they were from?

Answer. They told me that they were from Fort McHenry.

Question. Do you know of what State they were citizens?

Answer. They said that they were of the Sixth New York Battery of Heavy Artillery.

Question. What were they armed with when they arrived at

Camden?

Answer.   I think they were Springfield rifles with bayonets.

Question.   Do you know by what conveyance they were brought to Camden?

Answer.   I think, sir, by the cars.

Question.   Do you know about what hour they arrived there, and on what day?

Answer.   They arrived there on the 3^d day of November, between 11 and 12 o'clock at night, I think.

Question.   Do you know where they went upon their arrival at Camden, and upon whom they called to furnish them with quarters?

Answer.   They called upon me, sir, to furnish them quarters. I conducted them to the Academy, and there made them as comfortable as I could.

Question.   Were you a Trustee of the Academy?

Answer.   No, I think not. I was one of the School Committee, who generally had charge of the Academy.

Question.   Had you previously obtained permission of the Trustees or Committee to quarter the soldiers in the Academy?

Answer.   I had not; but I knew that most of them were Union men, and I knew that it would be all right.

Question.   Do you know why they called upon you to furnish them with quarters?

Answer.   I do not, sir.

Question.   Had you learned, previous to their arrival, that they would be in Camden that night, or at any other time?

Answer.   I had, sir.

Question.   When did you learn it, sir?

Answer.   I do not remember, but I think it was two or three weeks before the election that it was supposed they would be there.

Question.   From whom did you receive the information, two or three weeks previous to the election, that it was supposed they would be there?

Answer. I do not remember precisely whom, but there was a number of us consulted together relative the necessity of bringing troops into our State on the day of the election, so as to secure a fair, peaceable, quiet election, as some of the peace men had been buying a great many revolvers, and having brought from Philadelphia a great many buckshot, and a considerable amount of bars of lead.

Question. Will you please to state, as nearly as you can recollect, the names of the persons to whom you have alluded, and with whom you state you consulted in reference to bringing soldiers into the State for the purposes you have stated, and in consideration of the causes which you have related?

Answer. I do not know that I could. I talked with the Union men generally, and they with me. I could not give you their names.

Question. Do you, or do you not, recollect the names of any of the persons to whom you have alluded?

Answer. Yes; I can tell you some of them.

The Chairman. Please to state them as far as you recollect them.

The Witness. I talked with Mr. George P. Fisher, Mr. Charles H. B. Day, Mr. Edwin Wilmer, I think, Mr. Nathaniel B. Smithers, Mr. James R. Lofland, and others.

Question. I ask you whether, at the consultations with the persons you have alluded to, it was determined to make an effort to procure the introduction of United States troops into this State, to be present on the day of the election?

Answer. Yes, sir; for the purpose of securing a fair election.

Question. How was it determined that the effort should be made, and through whose instrumentality?

Answer. I cannot say.

Question. Was there any person fixed upon, through whom the effort should be made?

Answer. I do not know what person was fixed upon for that purpose.

Question. Do you know who did make the request?

Answer.   I do not.

Question.   Have you never heard by whom the request was made of the Secretary of War, or of any other person having command of any portion of the United States troops, to send soldiers into this State for the purpose before alluded to?

Answer.   I believe, sir, that hearsay is no evidence in Court.

Question.   Do you decline to say whether you have heard by whom the request was made, of persons alluded to in the foregoing question, to send troops into this State, to be present on the day of the election?

Answer.   I think, sir, that I have answered as much as I know on that subject.

Question.   I ask you, sir, whether George P. Fisher ever told you, or said in your presence, that he had solicited, or intended to solicit, of the Secretary of War, or any other person, the sending of troops into this State, to be present on the 4th of November last?

Answer.   I do not now remember.

Question.   I ask you when you first learned definitely that troops would be present in this state on the election day?

Answer.   I learned it conclusively and positively on the 3^{d} and 4th of November.

Question.   From whom did you learn it?

Answer.   I first learned it from Captain William Lord, and then by seeing the troops.

Question.   You have stated that the reason of your determining, in conjunction with the persons you have before alluded to, to make an effort to bring troops into this State, to be present on the day of the election, was that some of the peace men had purchased and had brought here a large number of revolvers, and a large quantity of buckshot, and a considerable amount of bar lead. Will you please to state the names of the peace men to whom you allude?

Answer.   Well sir, as far as the buckshot and lead, I will give you the particulars. I was in Philadelphia, at Charles C. Babbitt's store, saw a bag or two of buck shot, and I suppose from twenty-five to fifty pounds of bar lead. I asked the book-keeper whose lead and buckshot that was. He told me that it was to go down to your neighborhood, to Willow Grove, and belonged to Ezekiel Cooper, merchant at Willow Grove. I do not remember all the persons who had revolvers. Edward Carrow had one, I had one, Dr. Saulsbury says he had one, Jonathan Lowber, a Union man in Camden, had one; I think I heard William Carrow say that he had a pistol or revolver. These are all. Mr. Simpson says he sold a large number of pistols.

Question.   Of what political party is Mr. Simpson a member?

Answer.   He is a good Union man, but would sell revolvers to peace men.

Question.   You have alluded to buckshot and lead which you saw in Philadelphia, and were, as you learned, for a merchant at Willow Grover; I ask you whether, as a merchant, you have not and do not sell shot and lead, and powder too?

Answer.   I sell powder, but have never sold a pound of lead or a pound of buckshot to my knowledge. I sell squirrel shot.

Question.   Have you never sold or bought balls for pistols or guns ready moulded?

Answer.   I have not. When I bought my pistol a man gave me a half pound of balls, and I have got them yet.

Question.   I ask you whether you know any individual in Camden, among those to whom you have alluded, who has more than one or a pair of revolvers?

Answer.   I do not think I know of anybody who has more than one.

Question.   You have stated that you own a revolver yourself. Do you not accord to every other citizen the same right and privilege to purchase and own a revolver that you claim for yourself?

Answer.   I do, most assuredly; but I suppose I never should have owned one if they had not become so common since the so-called Democratic party brought on this rebellion.

Question.   I ask you, sir, if you mean to assert, under the solemnity of the oath you have taken, that the Democratic party did bring on this rebellion?

Answer.   I believe, sir, that it was mainly through their instrumentality.

Question.   I ask you, sir, whether revolvers are not as common among the members of one party as the other?

Answer.   They may be. Those Peace men may have bought them—the Union men may have bought them in self-defense.

Question.   I ask you, sir, if you mean to assert that Peace men, as you call them, did first purchase revolvers, and that Union men bought them in self-defense?

Answer.   I bought mine, sir, in self-defense, and will defend myself, and I am willing for everybody else to do the same.

Question.   I ask you, sir, whether you had ever been attacked and threatened with injury by the use of fire-arms by any one?

Answer.   I have not, sir.

Question.   Why, then, do you call the purchase of a pistol self-defense?

Answer.   It is very natural for a man to want to defend himself; and why did Dr. Saulsbury buy one?

The Chairman.   That is not answering my question.

The Witness.   If anybody were to attack me, I should use a pistol, if it were necessary. I would not attack anybody.

Question.   I ask you, sir, whether you were afraid of being attacked and injured by any Peace man in Camden, or elsewhere?

Answer.   No, sir; I am afraid of no man that lives.

Question.   I ask you whether the reason of the request made to the Secretary of War to send troops into this State, by yourself, or any other person, or in conformity with the determination which you have stated that you and others came to, to make the application for troops before referred to, was because you were afraid that the Peace men, to whom you have alluded, with the revolvers, to which you have alluded, by the use of Mr. Cooper's buckshot and lead, to which you have alluded, would interfere with the polls on the 4th of November last, to prevent a fair election?

Answer. I did not make any request to the Secretary of War—do not know who did; but I believe it was the only way that we could have secured a fair, honest election.

JOHN F. CLEMENTS.

On motion of Mr. Waples,
The Committee adjourned until 8 ½ o'clock to-morrow morning.

TUESDAY, March 3, 1863—8 ½ o'clock, A.M.

The Committee met pursuant to adjournment.
Present—Messrs. Saulsbury, Hitch, Stubbs, Waples and Horsey.

GEORGE G. HARMON, sworn and examined.

By the Chairman:
Question. Dr. Harmon, where did you reside on the day of the last general election?
Answer. I resided in Camden.
Question. Were there armed soldiers at or near the polls in Camden that day; if so, state how many?
Answer. There were a part of a company, I suppose about forty. I suppose they were within twenty-five yards of the polls; their muskets were stacked.
Question. Do you know whether, at any time during the day, they were drawn up in a position to charge upon the voters in front of the polls?
Answer. They were. At one time, I noticed they were ordered to form in line, and did so. They were marched up, bayonets charged,

within twenty feet of the polls.

Question. Were they understood to be in charge of a Provost Marshal, and subject to his order?

Answer. That was the understanding.

Question. Who was the Provost Marshal having charge of the soldiers there?

Answer. William P. Lord.

Question. Will you please to state who William P. Lord is, and what are his politics?

Answer. He is a citizen of Camden, and a son of Edward Lord. He was, up to a few months previous to the election, a very active Democrat. At the time of the election, he was a Republican.

Question. Was the presence of the soldiers in Camden calculated to produce great intimidation among any class of voters?

Answer. It was.

Question. Was there, in your judgment, any necessity for the presence of the military at the polls in your Hundred on election day, to preserve the public peace, or insure a fair election?

Answer. None, whatever.

Question. Was it not generally understood, among voters of all parties, that they were brought there for the benefit of one political party, and for the injury of the other?

Answer. It was.

Question. For the benefit of which political party was it understood that they were brought there?

Answer. The Republican party.

Question. I ask you if their presence had the effect to give assurance and confidence to the Republican party, and to produce dissatisfaction and intimidation among Democrats?

Answer. It had.

Question. It has been represented to the Committee that a large number of revolvers were purchased in Camden, by what were called Peace men, and that some two or three bags of buckshot and some bar-lead had been sent to a Mr. Cooper, a merchant, at Willow Grove, and this has been assigned as a reason for asking that troops be sent to be present on election day. I ask you, sir, whether there was an unusually large number of revolvers bought in Camden by the Democrats, and whether there was any design to use either revolvers or Mr. Cooper's lead, to prevent a fair election on the 4th of November last?

Answer.   I have no knowledge of but one revolver being bought in Camden immediately preceding the election, and that was bought for sale by a Democratic merchant, and it is my impression that it was sold to a Republican. I recollect seeing an unusually large number of revolvers, mostly in the hands of the three months' men, discharged soldiers—men who almost universally supported the Republican party at the election. I know nothing of the purchase or sale of any shot or lead by Mr. Cooper. There was no intention, on the part of the Democrats, to make use of any unusual means to carry the election.

Question.   Are you not an active Democrat, enjoying the confidence of the party, knowing all its principal plans and purposes?

Answer.   I have always been an active Democrat, and have supposed that I enjoyed the confidence of the party.

Question.   I ask you, sir, whether you ever heard the intimation of a purpose or desire, on the part of the Democrats, to interfere with the polls on the 4th of November last, to prevent a fair and impartial election?

Answer.   I never heard any intimation of the kind.

Question.   I ask you, sir, whether, from your position in the party, if there had been any such purpose, you would not certainly have known it?

Answer.   I should.

Question.   What was the general estimate, previous to the last election, as to the probable result of that election, provided there was no military interference?

Answer.   It was supposed that the State would go largely Democratic.

Question.   In view of this fact, was it not the interest, as well as the desire of the Democrats, that the election should be a perfectly fair and peaceable one?

Answer.   It was.

GEO. G. HARMON.

EDWARD LORD, sworn and examined.

By the Chairman:

Question.   Mr. Lord, where did you reside on the day of the last general election, and where did you vote?

Answer.   In Camden.

Question.   How long have you resided in Camden?

Answer.   Since 1841—about twenty-two years.

Question.   Were there armed soldiers at or near the polls on that day?

Answer.   There were. I understood that there were forty.

Question.   I ask you whether there was, in your judgment, any necessity for the presence of the military there, to preserve the public peace, or insure a fair election?

Answer.   In my opinion, there was not.

Question.   What is your business or occupation in Camden, Mr. Lord?

Answer.   Mercantile business.

Question.   I ask you whether, from a residence of twenty-one years, being all that time engaged in the mercantile business, you had not an opportunity to be, and were not well acquainted with the people of your Hundred, and with their temper and disposition previous to the last election?

Answer.   I am acquainted with the larger part of the people of Murderkill Hundred.

Question.   Do you believe that there was the slightest disposition or purpose, on the part of the Democrats, to interfere with the polls on the 4th of November last, to prevent a fair and impartial election?

Answer.   I do not.

Question.   I ask you what was the general estimate, so far as your knowledge extends, previous to the last election, as to the probable result of that election, if there was no military interference?

Answer.   I am not a great politician myself, but, from what I learned, it was the general opinion that the whole State would go Democratic.

Question.   In view of this fact, was it not the interest, as well as the desire of the Democrats, that the election should be a perfectly fair and peaceable one?

Answer.   It was.

Question.   Do you know the position which the soldiers occupied in reference to the polls that day?

Answer.   I should judge they were from twenty to twenty-five yards from the polls.

Question.   Do you know whether they were drawn up in position, at any time during the day, to charge upon the voters in front of the polls?

Answer.   Only from hearsay.

Question.   Was it not generally the understanding and feeling among the people, that the soldiers were brought there for the benefit of one party, and for the injury of the other party?

Answer.   It was.

Question.   For the benefit of which party was it understood they were brought there?

Answer.   The Republican party.

Question.   I ask you, sir, whether their presence did not give confidence and assurance to the Republican party, and did not produce dissatisfaction and intimidation among the Democrats?

Answer.   I think it did give great dissatisfaction among the Democrats, and intimidate them.

Question.   Is it not customary for merchants, in this section of country, to sell powder and shot, and all material that is used in gunning, through the country?

Answer. Yes, sir.

EDW'D LORD.

ANDREW J. CALLEY, affirmed and examined.

By the Chairman:

Question. Where do you reside, and where did you vote on the day of the last general election?

Answer. I reside in North Murderkill District, and voted at Camden.

Question. Did you observe anything unusual, and different from what you had ever seen before, at or near the polls on that day?

Answer. I saw a lot of soldiers stationed about forty or fifty feet from the polls. I also saw a man going about there, to and from the polls, whom they called Captain Reynolds, who had side-arms on. He seemed to be an officer of some description. I also saw another man who was said to be from the Fourth Delaware Regiment, with his musket and bayonet on it, standing within four feet of the window all day, when the voting was going on. Some one asked him, in my presence, why he kept his gun in his hand all day. He replied that that was his order. All this, that I have related, is very unusual at elections.

Question. Do you know whether, at any time during the day, the soldiers were drawn up in position to charge upon the voters in front of the polls?

Answer. There was a contention raised over Garrett Luff's vote. The contention was, that he had no right to a vote; that he had left the State some twelve or eighteen months before that. His family had left eight or nine months before. While contending over that vote, there was a difficulty raised between two men, which drew a crowd around them, which is nothing unusual. My attention was then drawn to the crowd; consequently I stepped from the window. When I returned back to the window, there were six or eight soldiers drawn up in line in front of the window, with their guns, with bayonets on them, pointing to the ground. I put my hands to the guns, passed between them, and went back to the window. They remained there some ten or fifteen minutes. They were ordered back then, to their old station, by some one, I do not know by whom. That was the only charge I saw that day.

Question.   I ask you, Mr. Calley, whether it was, or was not, the general understanding and feeling among the people, that the soldiers were there for the benefit of one of the political parties, and for the injury of the other?

Answer.   It was most assuredly understood that they were there for the benefit of what is termed the Union party.

Question.   I ask you whether their presence did not produce great dissatisfaction and intimidation among Democrats, and did not give great confidence and assurance to the Republicans?

Answer.   It did give great dissatisfaction to the Democrats generally, and, to a large extent, intimidation. It was even thought that our election officers were intimidated, by those who are better judges than I am. The leaders of the opposite party were very sanguine of success.

Question.   Have you not always been identified with the Democratic party, enjoying its confidence, and understanding all its principal plans and purposes?

Answer.   I have the best reason in the world to believe so.

Question.   I ask you, sir, whether you ever heard the intimation of a purpose or desire, on the part of the Democrats, to interfere with the polls on the 4th of November last, so as to prevent a fair and impartial election?

Answer.   I have not, anywhere or at any time. I did hear insinuations from Mr. John F. Clements, that we would have to be held still, and he would hold us still on that day. Owing to a difficulty that occurred at a previous general election, between Mr. Clements and an active member of the Democratic party, he (Mr. Clements) said that there would be a power brought to bear on you—meaning the

Democratic party; that the same thing would not occur again.

The Chairman. State the difficulty to which you have alluded as having occurred between Mr. Clements and an active Democrat at a previous election.

The Witness. At our window generally one party takes one side of the window, and the other party the other side. William Dyer, a Democrat, got on the opposite side of the window from what we claimed. It was by accident; at least he did not know which side had been appropriated to us. Hence Mr. Clements gave him a heavy push, and put him on the other side; and that created the difficulty, which ended in a few minutes and without a lick struck.

Question. Was there, in your judgment, any necessity for the presence of the military at the polls in Camden, to preserve the public peace, or insure a fair election?

Answer. There was not. I will state that I never saw a more quiet time than there was at our Inspector election, held the previous month. I think we polled within twenty-five votes of what we did at the general election.

Question. What was the general estimate, previous to the general election, as to the probable result of that election, provided there was no military interference?

Answer. In our voting district we should have had, and would have had, and ought to have had, seventy majority. We got about twenty-four or twenty-five. It was generally understood that the State would go Democratic. It was generally supposed that this County would give, at the least calculation, 800 or 900 Democratic majority.

Question. I ask you whether, in view of these facts, it was not the interest, as well as the desire of the Democratic party, that the election should be a perfectly fair and peaceable one?

Answer. It was. Hence the advice was generally given, if one of the opposite party spits in your face, do not return the insult until the election is over.

A. J. CALLEY.

CALEB AARON, sworn and examined.

By the Chairman:

Question. Where do you reside, and were did you vote on the day of the last general election?

Answer. I reside in Dover West Election District, and voted at Hazlettville.

Question. What was your occupation at the time of the last general election?

Answer. I was engaged in the mercantile business at Hazlettville.

Question. There was been a report in circulation among the members of the party opposed to the Democratic party, which has come to the knowledge of this Committee, that on the day of the last general election there were a large number of guns and other fire-arms deposited in your store by the Democrats of your Hundred and a number of persons from Maryland, with a view of being used for the purpose of taking possession of the polls, and preventing a fair election. I ask you whether this report is, or is not, true?

Answer. It is not true. There were five guns in my store; four of them I had there for sale. The other belonged to a young man who had been gunning in that neighborhood that morning, and came to my store and there left his gun. As for those guns being for the protection of the polls, I do not suppose the Democrats thought of such a thing.

Question. Did you ever hear the intimation of an intention or desire by the Democrats, or by any person from Maryland, to interfere to prevent a fair election on the 4th of November last?

Answer. I did not, sir.

CALEB AARON.

On motion, the Committee adjourned until 1 ½ o'clock, P.M.

SAME DAY, 1 ½ o'clock, P.M.

The Committee met pursuant to adjournment.

Present—Messrs. Saulsbury, Cahall, Slay, Stubbs, and Waples.

ANDREW J. WRIGHT, affirmed and examined.

By Mr. Cahall:
Question.   Where did you vote on the day of the last general election?
Answer.   At Felton, in Murderkill South Election District.
Question.   Did you see anything there unprecedented by anything which you had ever seen before at a general election?
Answer.   I did, sir.
The Chairman.   Please state what it was.
The Witness.   I saw a number of armed soldiers at the polls. They were drawn up, a number forming a file on each side of the window, through which the voters had to pass, in order to deposit their votes in the ballot-box.
Question.   Did their presence produce much intimidation to any class of voters on that day?
Answer.   It did. There were a considerable number of members of the Democratic party who were intimidated by their presence.
Question.   Were there any class of voters exultant at their presence; and if so, to what party did they belong?
Answer.   There were. The faces of the most prominent Republicans beamed with joy and exultation at their presence.
Question.   From your observation, did you consider that the soldiers acted in concert with any particular party?
Answer.   They obeyed the orders of those who had the command of them, so far as I was able to judge.
Question.   Under whose command were they?
Answer.   They were under the command of Captain Smith, of the Sixth New York Battery, who reported himself to, and was under the command of Paris T. Carlisle, Jr., who was Provost Marshal for the day.
Question.   Who is Paris T. Carlisle, Jr.?

Answer.   He is a resident of Frederica, and a son of Paris T. Carlisle.

Question.   Is he an active and violent politician?

Answer.   He is, sir.

Question.   To what political party does he belong?

Answer.   To a party styling itself the Union party in Delaware, but a party more particularly known as the Abolition party of the North.

Question.   How long have you resided in South Murderkill Hundred?

Answer.   Nineteen years.

Question.   From your knowledge of the temper and disposition of the citizens of South Murderkill Hundred, did you believe that there was any necessity for the presence of soldiers at the polls on the 4th day of last November, the day of the general election, in order to secure a peaceable, quiet, and fair election?

Answer.   From my knowledge of the voters of South Murderkill Hundred, I know that there was no necessity for their appearance at the polls that day.

Question.   Have you not been, and are you not now, an active member of the Democratic party, knowing all its principal plans and operations in conducting political campaigns?

Answer.   I have ever been and am still a Democrat; and I think I have been generally acquainted with the principal plans and operations in conducting campaigns.

Question.   Did you ever hear of a purpose or design, on the part of any Democrat, to interfere with the polls at the last general election, so as to prevent a fair election?

Answer.   In all my intercourse with the members of the Democratic party, I never heard any one mention anything of the kind.

Question.   Do you not believe that the ends of justice would have been more fairly and easily attained without the presence of soldiers than with them on that occasion?

Answer.   I do.   A. J. WRIGHT.

HENRY WHITAKER, affirmed and examined.

By Mr. Cahall:

Question. Where do you reside, and where did you vote on the day of the last general election?

Answer. I reside in Frederica, and I voted in Felton, South Murderkill Hundred.

Question. Was there anything unusual or different at the polls that day, from what you had ever seen before at an election?

Answer. There were United States soldiers there. I had never seen the like before. They were armed with rifles with bayonets on them. I do not know whether they had side-arms, except the captain, who had. Before there were any votes cast, they were marched up to the window and formed what we might term a square, by placing their bayonets at the side of each window, leaving a space of six or eight feet inside this square, and then locked their bayonets one in another, and extending ten or twelve feet from the window. At the end of the gateway, where voters came in, two soldiers were stationed with their bayonets crossed, and no voter was allowed to come in, until the order was given to the soldiers to raise their guns, and let them in. Some few old men were let in at the side of the window. I believe all the balance of the voters went in at the gateway, at which stood the soldiers, except a portion of the Fourth Delaware Regiment, who were marched up early in the morning, by one purporting to be one of their officers, and tickets handed to them, and were let in at the side of the window where the old men, of whom I have spoken, were let in.

Question. Did you understand why this preference was shown to those who came in at this side of the window?

Answer. I do. In reference to the soldiers, I do. A part of them wanted to vote Democratic tickets, as they had always done. They were marched up, two by two, and votes placed in their hands. They could have come only one at a time, and nobody with them, if they had gone in at the gate. That is the reason why this preference was shown to them.

In reference to the old men voting at the side of the window, I requested the Provost Marshal of the day that that courtesy might be extended to the old men, and he granted it. There was generally a crowd at the gateway.

Question.   Did you know at whose instance the soldiers were placed at the polls?

Answer.   Paris T. Carlisle, Jr., was Provost Marshal.

Question.   Did the presence of the soldiers on that occasion produce much intimidation among any class of voters at the polls on that day?

Answer.   It did, sir; among the Democratic Party.

Question.   Did not the presence of the soldiers rather defeat than produce a fair election?

Answer.   I thought so; and am certain it did, knowing what I do about the voters of that Hundred.

Question.   Are you not well acquainted with the citizens of South Murderkill Hundred, knowing their temper and disposition?

Answer.   I am.

Question.   Do you consider the presence of the soldiers was necessary on that occasion in order to secure a peaceable, quiet, and fair election?

Answer.   I do not.

Question.   Do you consider that the presence of the soldiers made any marked difference in the result of the vote on that day; and if so, in your judgment, to what extent?

Answer.   I do. About forty-one votes in favor of the Republican party.

Question.   Did you ever hear of a purpose or design, on the part of any Democrat, to interfere with the polls, so as to prevent a fair election?

Answer.   I never did, sir. I am in my forty-eighth year of age, and I have spent all my life in that Hundred, except about eight years.

HENRY WHITAKER.

On motion,

The Committee adjourned until 7 ½ o'clock, P.M.

SAME DAY, 7 ½ o'clock, P.M.

The Committee met pursuant to adjournment.

Present—Messrs. Saulsbury, Hitch, Cahall, Williams, and Waples.

THOMAS B. BRADFORD, sworn and examined.

By the Chairman:

Question. Did you vote on the day of the last general election; and if so, where?

Answer. I voted at the polls in Dover East Election District.

Question. Did you observe anything unusual, and different from what you had ever seen before at or near the polls on that day?

Answer. I saw a large number of armed soldiers on the green near the polls. I saw them in the afternoon charging with fixed bayonets upon the citizens; and I saw an old gentleman, by the name of Mitchell, prostrate on his back, who had been knocked over at the time of one of the charges, on the end of the Court House pavement near the polls. I noticed also, on the County building pavement, just after Mr. Mitchell had been thrown down, quite a number of soldiers, said to be of the Fourth Delaware regiment, under the command of, I believe he was called, Lieut. William Warner. They were quite disorderly. Deputy Sheriff Hill was endeavoring to command the peace, and, as a citizen, I came to his rescue, as some of those soldiers were attempting to resist his authority. As a matter of opinion, I could say that I thought there would have been more order and peace if the soldiers had not been there. I saw, at the same time, Colonel Fisher, candidate for Congress, and at that time Representative in Congress from this State, taking, as I thought, quite an active part in leading on the military when they charged upon the citizens.

Question.   You have spoken of charges. Did you see more than one bayonet charge?

Answer.   Yes, sir; two. The first one I noticed started from the immediate neighborhood of Mr. N. B. Smithers' office, and halted a little south of the elm-tree in front of the Court House.

Question.   Was there, in your judgment, any necessity or justification for either of the bayonet charges, of which you have spoken?

Answer.   None, whatever; and no excitement or disturbance that could not have been allayed almost immediately if the soldiers had not been here. I regarded the presence of the soldiers and their conduct as a gross outrage upon the rights and privileges of the voters.

Question.   Did not the soldiers themselves create most of the excitement, and cause most of the difficulty which occurred here on that day?

Answer.   In my opinion, they most assuredly did.

Question.   Did, or did not the soldiers appear to be acting in concert with and for the benefit of one of the political parties; and if so, with which?

Answer.   I certainly thought so, and believed that they were subject to the bidding of prominent leaders of the Republican or so-called Union party.

Question.   As far as you had an opportunity to observe, was it not the opinion and feeling of the voters of both parties, that the soldiers were brought here for the benefit of the Republican party, and the injury of the Democratic party?

Answer.   I have not a doubt but the Republicans, very many of them, approved of the soldiers being brought here to promote the interest of their party at the election. And, I believe, that very many, if not all, the Democratic voters regarded the coming of the soldiers, to be present at the polls, as designed to interfere with a fair and free election, and therefore to injure the candidates running on the Democratic ticket. I know that many persons of the Democratic party, or voting that ticket, sought the opportunity to vote as soon as the polls were opened, fearing there might be an attempt early in the day to prevent free and easy access to the polls. I, myself, voted immediately upon the opening of the polls.

Question. Was there, in your judgment, any necessity for the presence of the military at the polls, or at any other voting place in this County, to preserve the public peace, or insure a fair and impartial election?

Answer. None whatever, judging from anything I either saw or heard before or on the day of the election.

Question. As far as you had an opportunity to learn or judge of public sentiment, what was the general impression, previous to the last election, as to the probable result of that election in this County and this State, if there was no military interference?

Answer. So far as I heard, the friends of the Democratic party believed that their whole ticket would succeed in Kent and Sussex Counties, by sufficient majorities to make certain the election of the Democratic candidate for Governor and Representative in Congress, and the success of the Democratic County tickets in both Kent and Sussex.

Question. In view of this state of facts, was it not the interest of the Democratic party that there should be a fair, full, and peaceable election?

Answer. I should think so, decidedly; and I never heard a member of that party desire anything else than a full and free expression of the popular will through the ballot-box on that day.

THOMAS B. BRADFORD.

VINCENT C. GILPIN, sworn and examined.

By the Chairman:
Question. Where did you reside in the months of October and November of last year?
Answer. In the city of Wilmington.
Question. Were you the Mayor of that city at that time?

Answer.   Yes, sir.

Question.   Were you at home on the 2d of November, being the Sabbath previous to the last election?

Answer.   I was in the city of Wilmington.

Question.   Were you at church on that day at any place in the city of Wilmington?

Answer.   I was, sir.

Question.   While at church, did you, or did you not, receive a letter or note, inviting you to an interview with certain gentlemen from this County?

Answer.   I did not. I received a note, but not from this County. I received a note from Colonel Henry S. McCoombs, of New Castle County.

Question.   If it is proper, and you are at liberty, will you please to state the purport of that note?

Answer.   The purport of the note was, that he wished me to call at his house, as he wished to see me on business, but I do not recollect whether that business was stated in the note or not.

Question.   Did you go?

Answer.   I did, sir.

Question.   Will you please to state whether you met any other gentlemen there than Colonel McCoombs; and if so, who?

Answer.   I met Mr. George P. Fisher, Mr. Nathaniel B. Smithers, and, I believe, a gentleman by the name of Lofland—James R. Lofland, I presume.

Question.   Did you learn by what conveyance they went to Wilmington on that day?

Answer.   No, sir.

Question.   Will you please to state for what purpose they were in Wilmington, and upon what subject they wished to consult you?

Answer.   They wished to consult me on the subject of having a military force in Wilmington on the day of the election, in order to keep the polls open, and free of access—whether I wished a force for this purpose. I replied that I did not wish any military force in Wilmington; that I was satisfied in my own mind that, with the police force, I could keep better order than I could with a military force, and that I required no military force to keep order.

Question. Was there a military force sent there, and stationed at the voting places in the different Wards on that day?

Answer. There was in several Wards, to my knowledge. I did not visit all the Wards.

Question. Do you know by whose order that military force was sent there, and distributed as you have described?

Answer. I do not.

Question. Do you know whether there were Provost Marshals appointed for the different Wards having charge of the soldiers?

Answer. I do not know whether there really was or not. My request was, at the time this thing was spoken of, that there should be no military there. I do not know—there may have been some Provost Marshals mentioned at the time; but I was not under the impression that there would be any Provost Marshals, because I was not under the impression that there would be any military there.

Question. What reply did Mr. Fisher, Mr. Smithers, Mr. Lofland, or Colonel McCoombs make to your remonstrance against sending a military force to the city of Wilmington, or rather to your assurance that you did not desire or need such a force?

Answer. None, that I recollect, sir.

Question. Was there anything said in that interview in reference to the placing of soldiers at the different voting places of the several Hundreds of New Castle County, outside of the city of Wilmington?

Answer. There was.

The Chairman. Please to state what was said in reference to that subject as nearly as you can recollect.

The Witness. They asked me what number of persons I thought would be required at certain polls in the County. I replied, I did not know; having no knowledge of any difficulty that might occur at those polls.

Question. Do you recollect which of those gentlemen asked that question?

Answer. I do not, sir. But I presume it was a general question.

Question. Was there anything said at that interview in reference to the bringing of armed soldiers into Kent and Sussex Counties, to be present at the polls on the day of the election?

Answer. There was, sir.

The Chairman. Please state what was said as nearly as you can recollect.

The Witness. Those gentlemen said there would be so many soldiers required at one place, and so many at another. I do not remember exactly what they said. I did not charge my mind with anything not relating to the City of Wilmington.

Question. Did you learn at that interview, or have you learned since, whether Colonel McCoombs had been in the city of Washington to solicit or make arrangements for the bringing a military force into this State, to be present on the day of the election?

Answer. That was my impression at the time.

Question. Did you derive that impression from anything that you learned from any of those gentlemen?

Answer. That was my impression from the general tenor of the conversation which I had with the gentleman, at that interview.

Question. Did you learn whether definite arrangements had been made for the introduction of troops into this State, to be present at the polls on the 4th of November last?

Answer. I did.

Question. Did you learn by whom that arrangement was made?

Answer. My impression is now, sir, by Colonel McCoombs.

Question. Did you learn at whose solicitation Colonel McCoombs went to Washington to complete that arrangement?

Answer. No, sir.

Question. Did you learn at that interview, or had you heard

before, or have you learned since, whether any citizen of this State had, previous to Colonel McCoombs' visit to Washington, solicited of the Secretary of War, or any other officer having charge of any portion of the military forces of the United States, the sending of such force into this State for the purposes before named?

Answer. No, sir.

Question. Were the soldiers armed that were placed at the voting places of the different Wards that you visited?

Answer. They were armed with musket and bayonet.

Question. Did the presence of the military at the polls in the city of Wilmington conduce to the preservation of good order?

Answer. No, sir.

Question. Do you not think that your regular police force would have preserved better order than the military force did?

Answer. Yes sir.

Question. Do you know of any instances of outrage or disorder that was produced in that city by the presence of the military on that day?

Answer. I cannot answer that question directly. My impression is, if the military had not been there, there would have been much less difficulty in preserving order than there was.

Question. Mr. Gilpin, are not the civil authorities, in your judgment, adequate to the preservation of the public peace, as well on the election day as all other days, not only in the city of Wilmington, but throughout the State?

Answer. In regard to the City of Wilmington, I would say they were. As it regards the State, I have no knowledge.

Question I am requested, by a member of the Committee, to ask you to what political party you have formerly been attached?

Answer. I, sir, am a "Bell and Everett man," if you know what political party that is.

By Mr. Williams:

Question. What ticket did you vote last fall?

Answer.   I voted what was called the Union ticket.

By the Chairman:

Question.   Was there anything said at the interview, to which you have before alluded, in reference to placing soldiers at the voting places in Kent and Sussex Counties under the charge of Provost Marshals?

Answer.   There was, sir, in a general conversation.

Question.   Will you please to state, as nearly as you can recollect, that conversation?

Answer.   It was in reference to selecting parties who would be suitable for that office. I do not recollect who the parties were; they were gentlemen I had no knowledge of.

Question.   Was it determined whether they should be all members of one political party?

Answer.   I do not know; for I did not know the politics of any of those gentlemen at all outside of the city of Wilmington.

Question.   Do you know with what political party Colonel McCoombs is understood to be connected?

Answer.   He was originally a Bell and Everett man. I presume he is what they call a Union man at the present time.

V. C. GILPIN.

On motion,

The Committee adjourned until half-past eight o'clock to-morrow morning.

WEDNESDAY, March 4, 1863, 9 o'clock, A.M.

The Committee met pursuant to adjournment.

Present—Messrs. Saulsbury, Cahall, Hitch, Williams, and Waples.

JOHN A. BROWN, sworn and examined.

By the Chairman:
Question.   Where do you reside, and where did you vote on the day of the last general election?
Answer.   I reside in Christiana Hundred, and voted at Fleming's tavern, near the Brandywine banks.
Question.   Please to state whether you saw anything unusual, and different from what you had ever seen before at or near the polls in that Hundred on that day?
Answer.   I did. There were seventeen armed men at the polls on the morning of that day, belonging to the Fourth Delaware Regiment. On the morning of that day, by particular request, I went to the polls quite early. Shortly after I arrived there, Mr. Moses Journey came down from Camp Dupont quite excited, and said that he had been ordered from the grounds, under threats of arrest if he did not do so, by Colonel Grimshaw, who charged him with being there to influence the soldiers in regard to the election to come off on that day. I immediately rode up to the camp; as I arrived there I met, I should judge, about one hundred armed men, some of whom stated to me that they were going to Wilmington to vote, and take care of the rebels. I went up to the camp ground, and saw a squad of seventeen men brought up to Lieutenant-Colonel Tevis' tent, and there supplied with seven rounds of ball cartridge, and then, under command of the said Colonel, started for the polls of Christiana Hundred. After they left, I went round through the different tents, and inquired if there were any voters left there. I found several, and, I think, they all said they had been asked the question, how they voted. They answered, the Democratic ticket, but were refused the privilege of going home to vote. I followed those seventeen men to the polls; they were brought up to the stoop near the voting window, where there was somewhat of a crowd, (not more than usual,) and nothing to hinder any individual from going up to deposit his ballot. The Colonel in charge ordered those near the window to stand back, when an

altercation immediately ensued between the Colonel and Mr. Patrick Haughy, concerning his authority to drive the voters from the polls. The altercation was getting very bitter between those two particularly, when I suggested to Mr. Henry Dupont, that we have those men vote as there was a plenty of opportunity, the window being clear, at the same time calling the one at the head to deposit his ballot, and he did so. The others immediately followed, putting in their votes, several of whom unrolled them, and asked the Lieutenant-Colonel if their vote was the right kind. Fifteen of the seventeen voted; the other two who had voted at the little election, by swearing their votes in on age, did not offer to vote on that occasion. That was about all.

Question.   How did the fifteen, that you have named, vote?

Answer.   They evidently all came there with tickets in their pockets, and those who showed their tickets, voted the Union ticket. While the altercation was going on, there was an opportunity to have handed those men other tickets, and I was informed that two or three were supposed to have voted the Democratic ticket.

Question.   Was there, in your judgment, any necessity for the presence of the military in that Hundred on that day, to preserve the public peace, or insure a fair election?

Answer.   Not the least.

Question.   Was there any other person, other than the regular military commander, who appeared to have charge and control of the soldiers that day?

Answer.   Not directly of the soldiers, but the Colonel appeared to get his orders from Mr. Henry Dupont. At intermission for dinner, the Colonel went to Mr. Dupont, and asked him some questions relative to the soldiers. Mr. Dupont's answer was: "We have no use for you here this afternoon." After those soldiers voted, they went outside of the voting place, loaded their muskets, and there waited quietly for any orders that they might receive.

Question.   Did the soldiers, during their stay at the polls, appear to be acting in concert with and for the benefit of either of the political parties; and if so, which?

Answer. It was very evident that they were brought there for the benefit of the Republican party, and so far as could be done, were prevented from holding any consultation with members of the Democratic party previous to their voting. During the altercation between the Lieutenant-Colonel and Mr. Haughy, Mr. Haughy asked the Colonel if he was a voter in this State. He said: "No." He then asked the Colonel if he was a citizen of the State. He answered in the negative. Then, said Haughy, I am both a citizen of the State and a voter, and I do not intend to be driven from the polls.

J. A. BROWN.

GEORGE READ RIDDLE, sworn and examined.

By the Chairman:

Question. Mr. Riddle, where did you vote on the day of the last general election?

Answer. In the Fifth Ward of the city of Wilmington.

The Chairman. Please to state all you know in reference to the presence of the military in that or any other Ward of that city, what their conduct was at the polls, and what effect their presence had upon the result of the election?

Answer. I know very little of any Ward, other than the Fifth. I had occasion to visit the City Hall, which was one voting place for the Fourth Ward, where the Collector of Taxes was stationed. In the Fifth Ward I went to vote early, but found a file of soldiers, with muskets and bayonets, before the window. They afterwards stacked arms, and voted all who had receipts. There were four of the soldiers who knew me, who were assessed, but had no receipts. I sent to the Collector money for their receipts, and was enabled only to procure one. Late in the afternoon, finding that some of these soldiers were likely to vote the Democratic ticket, they were ordered by the officer in command to the headquarters, and there detained, with the exception of the one whose receipt I obtained, until after the polls had closed. This one, according to his own statement, had scaled a high fence in order to get to the polls. At the First Precinct of the Fourth Ward, I saw a great many soldiers loitering about, but was not there long enough to know what they did. So far as the military were concerned, I believe they prevented, directly, to some extent, but indirectly, to a greater extent, fair expression of public sentiment in Wilmington; directly, they encouraged soldiers to vote contrary to their known previous predilections; indirectly, they emboldened persons disposed to commit frauds upon the ballot-box, but for which frauds Wilmington city, in my opinion, would not have given one hundred and fifty majority for the Republican ticket, instead of which it gave, according to my present recollection, about six hundred.

Question.   Was there, in your judgment, any necessity for the presence of the military, either at the voting places in any of the Wards in the city of Wilmington, or at the voting places in any of the Election Districts in this State?

Answer.   So far as the city of Wilmington is concerned, I can speak positively—there was no necessity. The only disturbance in the Fifth Ward was produced by the soldiers being there. So far as the State is concerned, my opinion is, that no necessity existed anywhere for the presence of the military.

Question.   I ask you whether you have not represented the people of this State in Congress, and whether, in the different canvasses for election to that position, you did not become intimately acquainted with the people in every section of the State, enabling you to judge correctly in reference to the necessity for the military interference above alluded to?

Answer.   I have represented the people of this State in Congress for four years. I have canvassed this State from one extremity to the other on several occasions, and think, at one time, I had as general an acquaintance with the people of Delaware as any man in the State. A more quiet and orderly people I never knew, and hence, I consider that any military exhibition at the polls, while it was not only contrary to the spirit and letter of our laws, was unwise, impolitic, and calculated to do nothing but harm.

GEO. READ RIDDLE.

JAMES M. WATSON, sworn and examined.

By the Chairman:

Question.   Where did you vote on the day of the last general election?

Answer.   At the First Precinct of the Fourth Ward. I was one of the Judges of the Election.

Question.   Will you please to state all that you know in reference to the presence of the military at the polls in that Precinct, or at any of the voting places in any of the Wards of the city of Wilmington; what their conduct was at the polls, and what effect their presence had upon the result of the election?

Answer.   I know nothing of my own personal knowledge of any of the Precincts, except the one where I was Judge—the First Precinct of the Fourth Ward. There were a considerable number of military there during the early part of the day, and continued around and about the polls, near the window and in the crowd. There were several slight disturbances which took place there in the early part of the day. Later in the afternoon the disturbances became more general, which, so far as I could see, appeared to be produced by the volunteers who were present with their arms, encouraged by several persons of the Abolition party who were about the window. Between three and four o'clock in the afternoon, I think, the disturbance became very general, when a file of soldiers marched up to the window, led there by Colonel Grimshaw. They marched directly up to the window, and planted their flag right before the window. Previous to that time, there was a very general fight, or mob, in which the military were the principal participants, using their swords, bayonets, and guns. I think they were only prevented from doing personal injury by the compactness or denseness of the crowd, which was composed of members of both political parties. One man, whom I saw, drew his sword, and raised it as though he were going to use it over their heads, and was only prevented from using it by the blade of his sword being seized by the hands of two or three persons, who prevented him from using it. After that, the soldiers were brought there in a body, and dispersed the crowd, and cleared the ground in front of the polls, and formed into files, with a space between the files of soldiers. Then they were ordered to load their guns, which they did. Those parties who were on the steps, members of the Republican party, cried out that the polls were being cleared, and men could come up and vote. That occurred about four o'clock. Those who voted after that time had to pass through these files of soldiers up to the window. But a few votes were polled after that. No one came forward after that that I personally knew to be a Democrat. We doubtless lost some votes by reason of the soldiers. I believe there would have been no disturbance at the polls that day had the military been kept away, and that the Democratic party would have had a larger vote. I would further state that the Mayor, with his police, possessed ample power to quell any disturbance without the assistance of the military. I think there is no doubt the Mayor would have done justice to the citizens.

By Mr. Williams:

Question.   Was there any disposition manifested by the Democrats to prevent Union men or Republicans from voting?

Answer.   None at all, that I saw or knew.

Question.   What party had a majority at that Precinct, and to what extent?

Answer.   What is termed the Union party had a majority, I think, of 155.

Question.   How long have you been a resident of the First Precinct of the Fourth Ward?

Answer.   Over six years.

Question.   Have the elections held in that Precinct, during your residence there, been quiet and orderly?

Answer.   As a general thing they have been quiet and orderly—more so than at the election held on the 4th of November last.

JAMES. M. WATSON.

On motion,
The Committee adjourned until eight o'clock to-morrow evening.

THURSDAY, March 5, 1863—8 o'clock, P.M.

The Committee met pursuant to adjournment.
Present—Messrs. Saulsbury, Cahall, Hitch, Slay, Waples, and Williams.

WILLIAM H. TAYLOR, affirmed and examined.

By the Chairman:
Question.   Where do you reside?
Answer.   I reside in Mispillion Hundred, Kent County, when I am home.
Question.   Where were you on the 4th of November last, the day of the general election?
Answer.   I presume I was at Prospect, if that was the day of the general election.
Question.   Were you Provost Marshal for Mispillion Hundred on that day?
Answer.   I was Special Provost.
Question.   What were your duties as Provost Marshal?
Answer.   It is impossible to tell you at a word. I don't know that I could tell you at all.

Question.   Did you act in the official capacity of Provost Marshal there that day?

Answer.   I tried to, sir.

Question.   Do I understand you to say, sir, that you acted in the official capacity of Provost Marshal, and do not know the duties of that position?

Answer.   I cannot state the whole duties as they were put down to me.

The Chairman.   Please to state the duties of Provost Marshal, as you now understand them, and as far as you can recollect them.

The Witness.   I could not state them.

Question.   What is the reason you cannot state them?

Answer.   I cannot state them, because I do not remember them.

Question.   From whom did you receive your commission as Provost Marshal?

Answer.   It was signed by the Secretary of War, Edwin M. Stanton.

Question.   When was it dated?

Answer.   I do not know.

Question.   When did you receive it?

Answer.   The probability is, that it was not more than a week previous to the election?

Question.   Was it so much as a week previous to the election?

Answer.   I do not know how long it was before the election.

Question.   Did you receive that commission by mail, or by the hands of some individual?

Answer.   A private individual.

Question.   From whom did you receive it?

Answer.   My impression is, that I received it from James R. Lofland.

Question.   Where were you at the time you received your commission?

Answer.   I think I was in the cars.

Question. Did you not receive that commission from the hand of James R. Lofland in the cars between Harrington and Milford, on the Sunday previous to the election?

Answer. It is impossible for me to say. I do not remember whether it was between Harrington and Milford, or between Harrington and Farmington. It might have been at Harrington.

Question. Did you receive that commission on the Sunday previous to the election?

Answer. I did not receive it in the day-time at all.

Question. Did you not receive that commission on the night of the Sunday previous to the election?

Answer. My impression is, I did.

Question. What did you do, as Provost Marshal, at the polls in Mispillion Hundred, on the day of the election?

Answer. I tried to keep order as the main thing.

Question. What means did you use for the preservation of order on that day?

Answer. It is almost impossible to answer that question. I do not remember the whole routine throughout.

The Chairman. Only state what you do know.

The Witness. In the first place, there was a difficulty at the window—I ordered Captain Graham to clear the window. In another instance, there were a couple of men quarreling—I ordered Captain Graham to preserve order. I interfered myself in several instances when men were quarreling, and would take one of the parties away.

Question. Were Captain Graham and the soldiers of his command, subject to your order on that day?

Answer. They were subject to my orders on that day.

Question. What was the difficulty at the window, to which you allude, at the time you ordered Captain Graham to clear the window?

Answer. The difficulty at that time was, that the Democrats had taken possession of the window.

Question. At what time in the day was this?

Answer. It was very early in the morning, as soon as the polls were open.

Question. How had the Democrats taken possession of the window?

Answer. They had collected around the window, so that the Union people could not get to vote. Some of the influential Union men asked that they should have half the window. The reply to that, by Charles Williamson, was: "Wait until we get done voting;" or "When we get done voting, you can vote."

Question. Had the Democrats done anything more than to press their way to the window, as is usual on the day of the election, to vote?

Answer. Yes, there was an unusual effort made by them.

Question. What do you mean by an unusual effort?

Answer. I mean more than common—more than they formerly did on similar occasions.

Question. I ask you if the effort they made consisted of anything else than to get to the window to deposit their own ballots?

Answer. I thought it did; that was the reason I gave the order.

Question. What did they do that you thought it consisted in anything else than the usual effort to deposit their ballots?

Answer. I cannot say what they did. It was impossible for me to see all that was done.

Question. If you did not see anything that the Democrats did, except the usual efforts incident to voting, why did you order Captain Graham to clear the window?

Answer. I cannot answer that question in the way it is put.

The Chairman. Answer it in your own way.

The Witness. I cannot say all that was done. I have not said that I did not see anything that was done. The question reads as if I had said I did not see anything that was done.

Question. What did you see that was done?

Answer. It is impossible for me to say all that was done.

The Chairman. Please to state any one thing that was done.

The Witness. I saw them take possession of the polls. That, and the reply of Charles Williamson, were the principal things I acted upon in having the polls cleared.

Question. What do you mean by "taking possession of the polls," and what acts did they do in taking such possession?

Answer. They refused to yield one-half of the window when they had it in their possession.

Question. Do you mean that they did anything more than to press up around the window to vote?

Answer. I have answered that question.

The Chairman. You have not. I tried to get you to answer it, but you have not answered it yet. I ask you now how you answered the question?

Answer. I have said in substance, the taking possession of the window, and Williamson's reply, and the conduct outside.

Question. Who were the Democrats that took possession of the window?

Answer. I remember Charles Williamson for one. Charles Eutin was at the window. There were others, but I do not remember them.

Question. I ask you whether there were not Union men or Republicans in the crowd around the window?

Answer. There might have been. I did not see any one in the crowd around the window.

Question. I ask you whether there is not a large Democratic majority in Mispillion Hundred, and if so, whether from that fact it is not perfectly natural that there should have been more Democrats than Republicans around the window?

Answer. There is a majority of Democrats in our Hundred. It is natural for them to have the largest share of the window, but it is not common to refuse to give any of the window until they get done voting.

Question. I ask you, sir, whether Mr. Williamson did not tell you that as soon as the persons who were at the window voted, they would retire and give place to others?

Answer. He did not tell me so.

Question. I ask you if he did not say, "as soon as we vote we will come away," or words to that effect?

Answer. He did not say so to me, nor in my hearing, nor did I hear him say so.

Question. What were the exact words that he did say?

Answer. I cannot say the exact words he did say. I have previously stated, in substance, that his reply in giving us one-half the window was, "wait till we get done voting," or "when we get done voting you can vote."

Question. I ask you if Mr. Williamson did not say, in substance, "that as soon as we"—meaning the persons at the window—"get done voting, we will get away and you can come?"

Answer. I did not hear him if he said so.

Question. I ask if that was not the meaning of his language?

Answer. I do not know what his meaning was. I took him at what he said.

Question. I ask you if you mean to say, upon your oath, that Mr. Williamson said to you in substance, or used language to convey the impression to your mind, that the Democrats did not mean to allow Union men or Republicans to go to the window until all the Democrats of that Hundred had voted?

Answer. That question is so lengthy I can scarcely comprehend it at all.

Question. You have spoken of a difficulty or quarrel which occurred at a later period in the day, when you say that you ordered Captain Graham to quell it or stop it—I forget your language. I ask you what that difficulty was?

Answer. It was a quarrel. It was between Alexander Johnson and George Ralston.

Question. I ask you what the quarrel occurred about?

Answer. I do not know that I could say what the quarrel occurred about. My impression was that it occurred in regard to Mr. Johnson's voting a young man who was said to be under age. My impression is that the young man's name was Mark Johnson. That was my impression.

Question.   How far from the window were the parties engaged in the quarrel?

Answer.   I do not know; perhaps twenty feet.

Question.   I ask you whether you placed or directed a file of soldiers to be placed on each side of the window on that day?

Answer.   That was not the order I gave to Captain Graham. I gave Captain Graham order to place his men in the shape of a V at the window, leaving an opening for voters to pass in and vote.

Question.   I ask you, sir, whether voters had free access to the polls after the soldiers were placed at the window?

Answer.   They had not access as they had at the commencement, for several to be at the window at a time, but were admitted to vote nearly as fast as they could receive their votes.

Question.   I ask you whether any person was permitted to remain within the space formed by the files of soldiers which you have described?

Answer.   I was permitted to be in there.

Question.   Was any other person allowed to remain in there?

Answer.   Not a great length of time. On several occasions, when waiting to vote, persons were permitted to remain in there.

Question.   I ask you whether Democrats and Republicans were permitted equally to go to that window with doubtful voters on that day?

Answer.   The answer is, I did not see any person want to vote the ticket that he did not vote.

Question.   I ask you, sir, whether Republicans were not generally admitted to go to the window with what is called doubtful voters, and whether Democrats were not generally refused that privilege?

Answer.   The Republicans voted as many doubtful voters as they could, as far as I saw them, and the Democrats were not refused, to my knowledge, in voting any one they could.

Question.   Did you not yourself take advantage of your position within the file of soldiers to take ballots from the hands of voters, with which they had been furnished previous to going within the space formed by the files of soldiers, and place other ballots in their hands in their stead?

Answer. I did not give to any one inside the file of soldiers a Union or Republican ticket, and take a Democratic ticket from any one inside the file of soldiers, nor prevent him from voting the same kind of ticket he had in his hand, or with the same names on it, to the best of my knowledge.

Question. Do you mean by that answer to say that you did not give to any voter on that day a ticket, after he had gone within the space above referred to?

Answer. No, I do not mean to say that. I mean to say that I did not take from the hands of any voter inside the file of soldiers a Democratic ticket, and give to him, in its place, a Republican ticket. I was called on several times for tickets, and generally gave them to persons asking.

Question. You have stated that in the morning you claimed one-half of the window for the Republican voters. Did you consider it consistent with fairness and with your duty as an officer selected to insure a fair election, to remain yourself within the space formed by the file of soldiers, and there furnish tickets to voters, while you denied the same privilege to Democrats, or to any one selected by them for that purpose?

Answer. I did not deny any one from distributing tickets to any one. I do not know, nor never have heard it suggested before, that any Democrat was appointed or refused to give tickets to any one when called upon, and as my duty as an officer, I deemed it necessary to stay with and by the soldiers the most of the day, which I did.

Question. Did you order the arrest of any person there that day?

Answer. I did not.

Question. I ask you whether you did not order the arrest of Alexander Johnson?

Answer. I did not—that I am able to prove. I will make an effort, at any rate, if it is necessary.

Question. Was there any person arrested there that day?

Answer. The soldiers had in charge, or did arrest, a young man by the name of Hardesty.

Question. By whose order was Mr. Hardesty arrested?

Answer. Not by mine. By whose, I do not know.

Question. I ask you if you had charge of the soldiers there that day, whether you did not consider it your duty to prevent the arrest of citizens of that Hundred, unless upon your order?

Answer. It was impossible for me to prevent that which had taken place. Mr. Hardesty was arrested before I knew it, and I conversed with Mr. Hardesty, and he confessed or said he did not mean to say what he was proven to have said about the soldiers, and interceded in his behalf for his release.

Question. What was proven that Mr. Hardesty had said about the soldiers?

Answer. I do not know. I was told that he asked where those negroes (meaning the soldiers) were going, as they went to dinner—or called them negroes.

Question. I ask you, sir, whether the soldiers had not negroes, or a negro with them as waiter?

Answer. They had one negro with them as a waiter, I presume.

Question. Did not Mr. Hardesty allege that all he said was to ask, when he saw the negro going to dinner with the soldiers, "Where is that negro going?"

Answer. I do not know; he did not say so to me.

Question. Do you know whether a number of tickets headed "Democratic tickets," on which the names of the Republican candidates were printed, did not come out of the box while the votes were being "tallied"?

Answer. I do not know. I was there only a short time during the reading out, and have heard of only one such ticket, and that ticket, I am satisfied, was voted by the man who wanted to vote just such a ticket.

Question. Do you know whether any tickets of that description were distributed among the voters that day?

Answer. I do not know to what extent they were distributed, but know of several persons having such tickets.

Question. Did you yourself distribute any tickets of this description?

Answer. My impression is, I did, in the morning before the polls were open, to Outen Anderson, at his own request.

Question. Was Outen Anderson a candidate on the Republican ticket?

Answer. I believe he was.

Question. Was Mr. Anderson the only person to whom you gave those tickets?

Answer. My impression is, I gave them to several parties for distribution.

Question. Mr. Taylor, will you please to sign the testimony you have given to the Committee? If you desire a copy of it, you can have it by making the copy yourself, at such time as it is convenient to the Committee to allow you to make it.

Answer. I am willing to sign it when I get a copy.

Question. Do you refuse to sign the testimony?

Answer. I refuse to sign it until I get a copy.

Question. I ask you, sir, if that is your testimony as it has been read to you by the Clerk?

Answer. It is.

Question. Do you refuse to sign the testimony?

Answer. Until I get a copy.

The Chairman. The Sergeant-at-Arms will see that the witness appear at the bar of the House to-morrow morning.

[Upon reflection, the witness signs the testimony.]

W. H. TAYLOR.

On motion,

The Committee adjourned until 8 ½ o'clock to-morrow morning.

FRIDAY, March 6, 1863—8 ½ o'clock, A.M.

The Committee met pursuant to adjournment.
Present—Messrs. Saulsbury, Hitch, Slay, Stubbs, and Williams.

ALEXANDER JOHNSON, sworn and examined.

By the Chairman:
Question.   Where do you reside, and where did you vote on the day of the last general election?
Answer.   I reside in Mispillion Hundred, and voted at Prospect, the place of holding elections in that Hundred.
Question.   How long have you lived in Mispillion Hundred?
Answer.   I have lived there all my lifetime, except two or three years, and have never voted anywhere else only at the elections of one year.
Question.   Did you see anything at or near the polls on that day unusual and different from anything you ever saw before at the polls on election day; if so, please state what it was?
Answer.   I did, sir. On my arrival at the place of voting, which was after the polls opened, I saw, immediately in front of the window, many soldiers with guns in their hands, for the purpose, as was said, to keep the peace during the time of voting.
Question.   Had the presence of the soldiers the effect to preserve the public peace that day?
Answer.   I cannot say that it had.
Question.   How were they stationed in reference to the voting place?
Answer.   There were two files of soldiers placed immediately in front of the window, which formed an alley for the voters to pass through to the window to vote.
Question.   Was there any person permitted to remain within the space formed by the file of soldiers?

Answer. There was. William Henry Taylor, who was said to be Provost Marshal, remained inside of the alley. No person else was permitted to remain in the alley, only as men would pass up to vote, others were allowed to go with them, but to remain only while the person with whom they went was depositing his vote.

Question. Had members of all political parties equal privileges to go to the window with their friends, or with doubtful voters, and see that their ballots were deposited?

Answer. I answer, no. My reasons are, that I saw men passing in at the side of the alley near the window, through the soldiers, who were in charge of Republicans, and who, I had no doubt, intended to vote Republican tickets. I asked the same privilege of Mr. Taylor, and he refused me.

Question. I ask you who Mr. Taylor is, what his politics, and what the character which he bears in the Hundred and neighborhood where he lives?

Answer. He is William Henry Taylor, a man who was born and raised in that neighborhood. I have never heard his politics doubted as being a Republican. He is a man with whom I have never had dealings enough to know, of my own knowledge, his manner of doing business. His character, if rumor is to be believed, in my opinion, is not very enviable.

Question. I ask you, sir, if Mr. Taylor is such a man as the people of Mispillion Hundred would have selected for the position of Provost Marshal, if they had desired an officer to secure a fair and impartial election?

Answer. My impression is, that he is not such a man as the people would have selected.

Question. I ask you whether, in your judgment, Mr. Taylor would not use any official position he might occupy for the promotion of his own ends, or the success of his own political party?

Answer. My impression is, from what I saw of his acts on the day of the election, that he would.

Question. Mr. Taylor has stated in substance, in his evidence before this Committee, that the Democrats, on the morning of the election, took possession of the window where the votes were to be deposited, and refused to allow Union men or Republicans to go to the window to vote until the Democrats had finished voting. I ask you whether this statement is true?

Answer. If such was the case, I did not see it, nor did I ever hear of it before. I arrived at the place of election not until after the election was open. At that time Mr. Taylor and the soldiers had entire control of the window.

Question. Mr. Taylor has spoken of a difficulty which occurred between yourself and George Ralston. Will you please to state what that difficulty was, and what the occasion of it?

Answer. George Ralston and myself were standing near Mr. Taylor, but on the outside of the file of soldiers. Ralston called to Taylor, and warned him that should Mark Johnson, who is a nephew of mine, offer to vote, that it should be rejected, that he was not of age. I replied that I had heard no talk of his offering to vote, which reply caused the controversy that Mr. Taylor referred to. And I here say that I never said one word to him on the subject of voting, nor would I have allowed him, if in my power, to have voted, knowing full well that he was under age.

Question. Mr. Johnson, was it, or was it not the impression and feeling among the voters in that Hundred, that the soldiers were brought there for the benefit of one political party, and for the injury of the other?

Answer. It is the universal opinion of all the Democrats of the Hundred, that I have conversed with on the subject, that they were.

Question. Mr. Johnson, was there, in your judgment, the slightest necessity for the presence of the military at the polls in Mispillion Hundred, or any other voting place in this County, to preserve the public peace or insure a fair election?

Answer. I unhesitatingly answer, no.

Question. Did you ever hear the intimation of a purpose or desire, on the part of the Democrats, to interfere with the polls on that day to prevent a fair and impartial election?

Answer. I never did; and should I have heard it, I would have discountenanced it.

Question. What was the general estimate of the Democrats in your Hundred, in this County, and throughout the State, previous to the last election, as to the probable result of that election, if there was no military interference?

Answer. I never conversed with any intelligent politician of the Democratic party of our Hundred, but who agreed with me that the Democratic majority in said Hundred would be far greater than the result showed. So in the County, and especially in the State. It was the general impression that this County would be carried by a far larger majority. So in Sussex, and throughout the State.

Question. In view of these facts, was it not the interest of the Democratic party that there should be a fair, full, free, and peaceable election?

Answer. I think so.

ALEX. JOHNSON.

JOHN W. SMITH, sworn and examined.

By the Chairman:

Question. Mr. Smith, where do you reside, and where did you vote on the day of the last general election?

Answer. In Mispillion Hundred, Kent County.

Question. Were there soldiers present at the polls in that Hundred on that day?

Answer. Yes, sir; there were.

Question. How many?

Answer. I did not count them. I think there were forty. Some told me there were forty-five.

Question. When did they arrive, and by what conveyance were

they brought there?

Answer. They walked.

Question. When did you first learn that soldiers were expected at Prospect on that day?

Answer. I never learned positively. I heard some one say there were to be soldiers there.

Question. Whom did you hear say that soldiers were expected to be there?

Answer. I heard Mr. Taylor say so, for one. I do not know that he was the first.

Question. When did you hear Mr. Taylor say so?

Answer. Previous to the election.

The Chairman. State how long previous, as nearly as you can recollect.

The Witness. A week, I suppose.

Question. I ask you whether, according to your best recollection, Mr. Taylor was, or was not, the first person who told you that soldiers were to be there that day?

Answer. I do not know.

Question. If any person or persons ever told you that soldiers were expected to be there on that day, please to name who the person or persons were?

Answer. I cannot say positively, as to any particular one. I was in conversation with Dr. Melvin, Clement Simpson, and others. They asked my opinion in reference to the matter.

Question. What opinion did you give them in reference to it?

Answer. I told them, from what I had heard rumored in our neighborhood, I thought it was best to have some to keep the peace.

Question. I ask you, sir, whether your desire for soldiers to be present at that place on that day, was not more for the benefit of the Republican party than for the preservation of the public peace?

Answer. No, sir.

Question. Did you then believe, or do you believe now, that

soldiers were necessary to be present at the polls, for the preservation of the public peace?

Answer. I did before the election, and since am more convinced.

Question. I ask you, sir, why you believed previous to the election that soldiers were necessary in Mispillion Hundred, on the 4th day of November last, to preserve the public peace; and what circumstances have occurred since to strengthen that opinion?

Answer. In the first instance, one of my neighbors, Jacob F. Lewis, said to me, that I ought to be shot for expressing my opinions. And since the election, I have understood that a large portion of the Democratic party were armed in the Western part of our Hundred—in fact, some of them told me so. Since the election, the morning after, I met three men from Maryland—Eben Wright, a Mr. Frame, I don't remember his first name. They said that they had arms, and were not afraid of the soldiers; that they could shoot as fast as they could, or anybody else.

Question. From whom did you learn that the largest portion of the Democrats in the western part of your Hundred were armed, and who of them told you that this was the case?

Answer. I cannot say that I remember all their names. Dr. Melvin told me for one—he belongs to the Union party. Sydney Melvin, I think, who also belonged to the Union party. I cannot recollect any Democrats who told me they were armed.

Question. I ask you whether you do not know that Republicans in that Hundred also had arms?

Answer. I know some of them who were armed. I suppose all the Republicans had arms of some kind about their houses.

Question. Were you afraid that the Democrats in that Hundred would injure you, or any other person, with the arms they had in their possession?

Answer. I was afraid.

Question. Was there ever any attempt made to injure you?

Answer. I do not know that there was.

Question.   I ask you now, sir, if all this idea that the people of one political party in that Hundred had any design to do personal violence to the other is not mere suspicion, founded on party prejudice?

Answer.   They were prejudiced against each other; no doubt about that.

Question.   I ask you whether you believe that the people of Mispillion Hundred, among whom you were born and raised, are so depraved as to conspire to commit personal violence upon each other, in consideration of mere party differences?

Answer.   They will fight and quarrel, if you call that depraved. I think there are some men in that Hundred would.

Question.   I ask you, sir, whether you do not believe there are as many Republicans who would do it as there are Democrats?

Answer.   I think not. I have had more intimacy with the Union party than I have with the others. I have seen more animosity with them than I have with the others.

Question.   I ask you, sir, whether you do not know, that if there had been any design by the Democrats, amounting to over four hundred, to interfere with the polls with arms in their possession, as you say they had, they could not have been prevented from doing so by the presence of forty soldiers?

Answer.   I think they could in the position they were fixed in at the election.

Question.   I ask you, sir, whether it is not great cowardice in one political party to be afraid of another amounting to four hundred in number, who could have been deterred from carrying into effect the purposes of a settled conspiracy by the presence of forty soldiers?

Answer.   I think it would.

JOHN W. SMITH.

RICHARD. N. MERRIKEN, affirmed and examined.

By the Chairman:

Question. Mr. Merriken, where do you reside, and where did you vote on the day of the last general election?

Answer. I reside in Mispillion Hundred, Kent County, and voted at Prospect.

Question. Were there soldiers present at the polls at Prospect on that day; if so, state the position they occupied in reference to the voting place?

Answer. There were soldiers. They were formed in lines immediately before the window, thereby forming an alley for the Democratic voters to walk through; while at the same time they had a private entrance at one side of the window for Republicans to take in doubtful voters.

Question. Who had charge of the soldiers there that day?

Answer. William H. Taylor, who told me that he was Provost Marshal.

Question. Who is William H. Taylor, and what is the character which he bears in that neighborhood?

Answer. He is a son of David Taylor, Esq. His general reputation, so far as I know, has no parallel in our section of the country for rascality.

Question. Is Mr. Taylor such a man as the people of Mispillion Hundred would have selected for the position of Provost Marshal, if they had desired an officer to insure a fair and impartial election?

Answer. He most assuredly would have been the last man that has the right to exercise the elective franchise.

Question. Is Mr. Taylor a man who, in your judgment, would use any official position he might occupy for the promotion of his own ends, or the success of his own political party?

Answer. He certainly is the very man.

Question. What time in the day did you arrive at the voting place in your Hundred on the day of the last general election?

Answer. The polls were opened when I arrived there, and the soldiers and Mr. Taylor, the Provost Marshal, had possession of the window.

Question. I ask you whether members of all political parties were permitted alike, and with equal privileges, to go to the window with their friends, or with doubtful voters to see that their ballots were deposited in the box?

Answer. All members were not. There was a manifest difference show, and the Republican party had the benefit of that difference.

Question. I ask you whether you ever heard of any conspiracy, on the part of the Democrats, to interfere with the polls on that day, so as to prevent a fair and impartial election?

Answer. I never did, not do I believe there ever was any.

Question. I ask you whether, from your knowledge of the people of that Hundred, any unusual number of arms of any kind were purchased and owned by Democrats just previous to the election?

Answer. I do not know of a single one of any description, nor did I see one in the possession of any Democrat on the day of the election. I had none myself.

Question. Was it not generally understood, previous to the last election, that all the volunteer companies in this County and this State, who were commanded by Democrats, and who had been furnished with arms by order of the Governor of the State from the State Arsenal, had been deprived of their arms previous to the 4th of November last, by persons understood to be acting by authority of the General Government; and that companies, commanded by Republicans, were permitted to retain possession of their arms up to and since that time?

Answer. I have been so informed and believe.

Question. Do you believe that there was any necessity for the presence of the military at the voting place in your Hundred, or at any other voting place in the two lower Counties of this State to preserve the public peace or insure a fair and impartial election?

Answer. None whatever.

Question. What was the general estimate, previous to the last election, as to its probable result, if there was no military interference?

Answer. The Democratic majority in Mispillion Hundred would have been much larger in my opinion, and, so far as I can learn, throughout the entire Counties of Kent and Sussex.

Question. I ask you whether, in view of these facts, it was not the interest as well as the desire of the Democratic party, that the election should be a fair, full, free, and peaceable one?

Answer. It unquestionably was.

R. N. MERRIKEN.

MARK A. JOHNSON, sworn and examined.

By the Chairman:

Question. Were you at the election in Mispillion Hundred on the 4th of November last?

Answer. I was.

Question. At what time in the day did you arrive there?

Answer. I do not know exactly. It was after the polls were opened.

Question. Were there soldiers stationed at the window when you arrived?

Answer. Yes, sir.

Question. Did you vote, or offer to vote there that day?

Answer. No, sir; I did not.

Question. Had you ever any intention or purpose to offer a vote there that day?

Answer. No, sir.

Question. Did your uncle, Alexander Johnson, ever advise or encourage you to offer a vote on that day?

Answer. He did not, sir.

MARK. A. JOHNSON.

W. N. W. Dorsey, sworn and examined.

By the Chairman:

Question. Where do you reside, and were did you vote on the 4th day of November last?

Answer. I reside in Kent County, town of Milford, in Milford Hundred, and voted at Milford.

Question. Did you see anything at or near the polls that day unusual, and different from what you had ever seen before at the polls? If so, state what it was.

Answer. I did. I saw soldiers having arms in their hands, said to be United States soldiers, placed around the window where the voters had to approach to vote, being and unusual and different from anything I had ever seen at the polls before. They were placed in an oblong square; persons wishing to go up to vote had to request the soldiers to raise their guns, which were locked, and also when they came out.

Question. I ask you whether the people had to pass between the files of soldiers stationed at the window, as you have represented, and whether it was not impossible to go to that window without the consent of the soldiers, or those having them in charge?

Answer. I believe that no Democrat was suffered to vote, unless they went through the file of soldiers. I saw some others, who were said to vote the Republican ticket, vote over the shoulders of the soldiers without going through. That was done by the direction of the Provost Marshal.

Question. Do you know why the persons, of whom you have spoken as having voted the Republican ticket over the shoulders of the soldiers, were permitted to do so by the Provost Marshal?

Answer. It was so reported to me that they declared that they would not pass through the file of soldiers to vote.

Question. Do you know any one of these persons? If so, state who he is.

Answer. I do. George S. Grier, an Englishman, was one. It was reported that he said he would not pass through the file of soldiers to vote. The Provost Marshal voted over the line at the same time. There were others I do not remember. The line on one side was several times pushed in for the purpose of giving Republicans a chance to vote. I protested against this, and told the Provost Marshal that he had declared that no person should vote unless he came up at one side of the oblong formed by the soldiers.

Question.   Who was the Provost Marshal on that day?

Answer.   James R. Lofland said he held the commission.

Question.   Who is James R. Lofland, and what are his politics?

Answer.   I should think that he is a sworn enemy of the Democrats. I think that is his politics.

Question.   I ask you, sir, if, in your judgment, James R. Lofland is a man who would use any official position he might occupy for the promotion of his own political purposes, and for the benefit of his own political party?

Answer.   I would say that he did do it on the 4th day of November last. He arrested a man, who was a soldier, while attempting to vote, as he alleged, a Democratic ticket, and declared that no soldier should vote there that day, unless he voted a Union ticket. He was arrested and carried to Mr. Shockley's hotel, and there detained until four or five o'clock—about a quarter of an hour before the polls were closed. He was then permitted to come to the polls, and voted the Republican ticket, I presume.

By Mr. Williams:

Question.   What reason have you to suppose he voted a Republican ticket?

Answer.   The parties who came with him said he voted the Republican ticket. I also saw the ticket—it had a flag on it, and the Democrats had no such tickets.

Question.   Do you know any other case in which Mr. Lofland interfered that day to prevent any citizen from voting in accordance with his political sentiments?

Answer. Only by hearsay. I heard that there was another case of a soldier whom Mr. Lofland tried to prevent from voting.

Question. Mr. Dorsey, what party had the majority in your Hundred?

Answer. The Republicans.

Question. With the Republican majority in that Hundred, would it have been possible for the Democrats to have prevented a fair election if they had been so disposed?

Answer. I should think not.

Question. Have you not always been an active Democrat, in the confidence of the party, understanding all its principal plans and purposes?

Answer. I have always been an active Democrat. How far I have had the confidence of the Democratic party, I cannot say. I believe I have generally known all the material workings of the Democratic party in Milford Hundred.

Question. Did you ever hear the intimation of a purpose or desire, on the part of the Democrats, to interfere with the polls on the 4th of November last to prevent a fair and impartial election?

Answer. No, sir; I never heard anybody intimate such a thing, and do not believe there was such an idea in the brain of a man in the Democratic party.

Question. Do you know where the soldiers, who were at Milford that day, were from?

Answer. About twelve o'clock at night on Monday night, being the night before the election, I heard the sound of the railroad whistle, and was awakened up. In about a quarter of an hour from that time, I heard a rapping at my front door. I went down to the door and opened it, and William D. Fowler and Dr. Mark Lofland came in, and told me that there were some one or two hundred troops over at the depot, and came down in the cars, and asked me what we should do—that they supposed we would all be arrested. I told them we could do nothing, only to wait until they did it; that they had better go home. They stated that they had in charge some Democrats that the Republicans were trying to get away from them. I told them not to jeopardize their own safety. They left, and I suppose went home. I then went to bed, and, in a few moments, the soldiers came parading by my house. I did not go out any more until next morning about eight o'clock. When I went to my front door, I looked down town and saw many of the soldiers standing before Shockley's hotel. While standing in my porch, several of the Democrats came to me, and asked me what we had better do. I told them I had made up my mind to go down and do all I could to get the Democrats to vote as early in the day as possible, more especially those who would be most likely to be arrested; as I had no doubt that many of us would be arrested. I went down to the polls, and, while going, I saw several soldiers acting as sentinels on the street and before Watson's hotel, the place of voting.

Question. Did the soldiers, by direction of the Provost Marshal, appear to be acting in concert with either of the political parties; and if so, with which party?

Answer. They were acting with the Republican party. I expostulated with them several times, and told them that they should give the Democrats the same chance that they did the Republicans; and they said they were soldiers, and were bound to obey orders, let it be right or wrong.

Question. Had the Democrats an equal chance with the Republicans, and had they the same privilege to go to the polls with their friends, and see that their ballots were deposited, that was accorded to the Republicans?

Answer. Not at all times.

Question. Was there, in your judgment, any necessity for the presence of the military at the polls in Milford, or at any other voting place in the two lower Counties of this State, to preserve the public peace, or insure a fair and impartial election?

Answer. I think not.

Question. What was the general estimate, previous to the last election, as to the probable result of that election, in relation to the County and State ticket, if there was no military interference?

Answer. My estimate, with those with whom I conversed, was from a thousand to fifteen hundred majority for the Democratic party in the State. The idea was that the Democrats would carry the Counties of Kent and Sussex by large majorities, and thereby secure a Democratic majority in the legislative branch of the State.

Question. Was it not the interest of the Democratic party, in consideration of these facts, that there should be a fair, full, free, and peaceable election?

Answer. I think it was. I will state, in addition to what I have said, that, on the evening of the little election, four weeks exactly before the general election, in an argument with Joseph S. Lofland, candidate upon the Republican ticket for Sheriff of Kent County, he stated that they could carry Milford Hundred by a majority of 225, or more, if they had a mind to make use of the means which were offered to them. I asked him what the means were. He said they were offered the purse and the bayonet, if they saw proper to accept them. There is another fact. Perry Rickards, a Democrat, told me that he did not vote because he would not go through the file of soldiers. Their presence produced great intimidation among the Democratic voters during the fore part of the day. The Democrats in our Hundred were all frightened—we did not know what to do. The soldiers were under the complete control of the Republicans, and we felt that we were in their power, and did not know what action they might take. I bade my family farewell when I left, not knowing whether I should be permitted to return.

W. N. W. Dorsey.

On motion,
The Committee adjourned until 7 ½ o'clock, P.M., on Monday the 9th instant.

MONDAY, March 9, 1863—7 ½ o'clock, P.M.

The Committee met pursuant to adjournment.
Present—Messrs. Saulsbury, Cahall, Hitch, Slay, and Waples.

WILLIAM HILL, sworn and examined.

By the Chairman:
Question. Where do you reside, and where did you vote on the day of the last general election?
Answer. I reside in Milford, and voted there.
Question. Did you observe anything unusual, and different from what you had ever seen before around the polls that day?
Answer. We had the soldiers around the polls, which was unusual and different from what I had ever seen before.
Question. What position did the soldiers occupy in reference to the polls?
Answer. They were standing on each side of the window, with their bayonets crossed. The voters had to pass between the files of soldiers. The soldiers would raise their bayonets for a voter to pass through, and cross them again on his entrance, also the same on his return. The soldiers blocked up the passage for voters on each side of the window of the house as far as they extended.
Question. Did all the voters there that day pass through the files of soldiers?
Answer. All that I saw. I understood that Mr. Grier refused to pass through the files of soldiers, and they took his vote on the outside of the soldiers. There might have been a few votes put into the box before the soldiers were placed around the window.
Question. By whose direction were soldiers placed on each side of the window as you have described?
Answer. James R. Lofland, who was said to be Provost Marshal, had charge of the soldiers, and seemed to have the management of things

around the window.

Question. Who is James R. Lofland, and to what political party does he belong?

Answer. He belongs to the Republican party, and votes that ticket.

Question. Is James R. Lofland a man who would take advantage of any official position he might occupy for the promotion of his own ends, or the success of his own political party?

Answer. From some circumstances which happened on that day, I should say he would.

Question. Did the soldiers, under his direction, appear to be acting in concert with and for the success of either of the political parties?

Answer. Yes, sir; I should say they acted in concert with the Republican party.

Question. Was the presence of the soldiers calculated to produce intimidation among any class of voters in Milford on that day?

Answer. I heard several persons say they would not vote in consequence of the soldiers being there; whether they did or not, I am not able to say.

Question. Do you know whether the Provost Marshal, or the soldiers under him, interfered that day to prevent any person from voting in accordance with his own political sentiments?

Answer. I will state a circumstance which happened that day. There was a soldier, by the name of Peter Minor, who lived immediately opposite our place of business. He came over to our side of the street. I, or some one present, asked him why he did not go and vote. His reply was, that he could not vote that day; that the Provost Marshal told him if he voted any other than a Republican ticket he would have him arrested. I remarked to Curtis S. Watson, who was standing by me, and a number of others, if he (Watson) would go with me to see the Provost Marshal, I would ask him whether he would permit Peter Minor to vote. We did ask him, and he said he had no objections to Peter Minor's voting. We then asked him why he objected to his voting. His reply was, that he would rather scare him out of his vote than buy it. I went back to Mr. Minor, and told him to take his ticket and vote. He took his ticket, and voted without objection, so far as I heard.

Question. How long have you lived in the town of Milford?

Answer. I have lived in the town thirteen years, and in the neighborhood all my life.

Question. Are you well acquainted with the voters at that place?

Answer. Yes, sir; I know the people very well.

Question. Was there, in your judgment, any necessity for the presence of military there to preserve the public peace, or insure a fair election?

Answer. I should think there was no necessity for them at all.

WILLIAM HILL.

WILLIAM D. FOWLER, sworn and examined.

By the Chairman:

Question. Where do you reside, and where did you vote on the 4th of November last?

Answer. In Milford, and voted in Milford Hundred.

Question. Did you see soldiers at or near the polls during the time of voting? If so, state what position they occupied in reference to the polls.

Answer. I saw them at the polls with the bayonets thrust in on each side of the window at the place of voting, out to the width of the porch. Two soldiers were standing, with bayonets locked, under which a greater portion of the voters had to pass as they went up to vote.

Question. Who had command of the soldiers?

Answer. My understanding was, that they were under the command of James R. Lofland, the Provost Marshal.

Question. Is James R. Lofland a man who would use any official position he might occupy for the promotion of his own ends, or the success of his own political party?

Answer. He did, sir, on that day, to an advantage.

Question. Did Mr. Lofland seem to be directing his efforts, through the agency of the soldiers under his command, for the preservation of the public peace and the insuring of a fair and impartial election, or did his efforts seem to be, through the agency of the soldiers, to promote the interests of his own party?

Answer. The interests of his own party, I would answer.

Question. Of what political party is Mr. Lofland a member?

Answer. He belongs to what is usually known as the Republican party.

Question. Do you remember any instance where Mr. Lofland interfered to influence unfairly the vote of any citizen of that Hundred?

Answer. I do. James R. Lofland, in company with two or more soldiers, came to the Democratic headquarters. I met him at the door. He said he wanted Joseph Sparks out of the room. Joseph Sparks, in the meantime, had voluntarily come into the room, and called me to one side, and asked me whether he would be arrested and placed in Fort McHenry if he voted a Democratic ticket. To use Sparks' own language, James R. Lofland told him so. He said he was a Democrat, and wanted to vote the Democratic ticket. I then started out of the room, in company with Sparks, to the polls to vote. We met James R. Lofland, with two or more soldiers, at the head of the staircase. James R. Lofland stopped Sparks himself, and told him that he should not vote with me, and asked him why he got out of the lines. Sparks answered that he had no right to hold him in the lines, as he was home on his parole. He was a paroled prisoner, having been taken by the Southern army. He told Lofland he was a Democrat, and was going to vote that ticket, that he had changed his views. Lofland told him he should not vote. I then made a proposition to Mr. Lofland to give him a ticket of each kind, and let him go by himself and deposit which one he saw proper. Lofland answered that he had no compromise to make. Sparks then went down the stairs, in company with myself, and went over into the store of William Hill &

Son. I there asked him if he had paid his tax, upon which he produced his tax receipt. I gave him a ticket, and told him to show his receipt, showing he had a right to a vote. He went, in company with Mr. Cannon, to the place of voting, or as near as he could get to the place of voting. The soldiers, who were standing with their bayonets locked, pushed him back, and told him he could not vote then. He produced his tax receipt, and told them he had a right to a vote, and was going to vote a Democratic ticket—holding it in his hand. I then demanded of the soldiers to know why they challenged his vote, to let him go to the window and the Judges would decide whether he was a qualified voter. The answer was, the Provost Marshal had told them not to allow Sparks to vote in his absence. In the meantime, James R. Lofland, the Provost Marshal, seized him by his coat, pulled him out of the porch, and ordered two soldiers to bear him away. To the best of my knowledge, I saw him no more until the next morning.

Question.   Do you know of any other instance of interference by the Provost Marshal with any voter there?

Answer.   He interfered with me. I was going, in company with Thomas Lollis, who had been living in Murderkill Hundred, to make an explanation to the Judges in regard to his tax. The soldiers, who were standing at the edge of his porch, would not let me come upon the porch. When he got to the window, the Provost Marshal was standing there, and had a private conversation with him. I do not know how he voted.

Question.   Did the Provost Marshal assume to have control of the voting, and allow such persons as he pleased to go to the window and vote, and refuse to allow others to go either by themselves or with their friends to vote until such times as suited him?

Answer.   He, through the soldiers, refused to allow me to go to the window with anybody. I never went to the window during the day, except at the time I voted. I made effort to go with several friends, but the soldiers would point their bayonets at me as soon as I approached.

Question.   Did the Provost Marshal, and the soldiers under him, act in concert with and for the benefit of either of the political parties?

Answer.   They did—for the benefit of the Republican party.

Question.   Did you ever hear of the intimation of a purpose or desire, on the part of the Democrats, to interfere with the polls on the 4th of November last, to prevent a fair and impartial election?

Answer.   We wanted to get all the votes we could, but we intended to use no violence.

Question.   What party is in the majority in Milford Hundred?

Answer.   The Abolition party holds the balance of power in our Hundred.

Question.   Was there, in your judgment, any necessity for the presence of the military in Milford, to preserve the public peace or insure a fair and impartial election?

Answer.   There was not.

Question.   About the time Mr. Sparks was arrested and taken off by the soldiers, was there any charge made by the soldiers upon the voters there?

Answer.   There was a disturbance. I do not know whether there was any regular charge.

WILLIAM D. FOWLER.

HENRY B. FIDDEMAN, sworn and examined.

By Mr. Cahall:

Question.   Where do you reside, and where did you vote on the day of the last general election?

Answer.   I reside and voted in Milford.

Question.   Was there free and uninterrupted access to the polls on that day?

Answer.   I do not consider that there was.

The Chairman.   State your reasons for there not being a free and uninterrupted access, as on former occasions.

Answer. There was a file of armed soldiers on either side of the window, which obstructed free access to the window.

Question. Did the presence of the soldiers produce much intimidation among any class of voters; and if so, what class?

Answer. I am inclined to think they did. Certain members of the Democratic party were intimidated. They may have voted, notwithstanding.

Question. Did you consider that intimidation sufficient to produce any marked difference in the political features of the votes that were cast on that day?

Answer. If there was any difference, it was in favor of the Republican party, and I consider there was a difference.

Question. To what extent do you think that difference was, so far as you have any means of judging?

Answer. I say I thought there was a difference, to what extent I am unable to say.

Question. Did you consider, from your knowledge of the citizens of Milford Hundred, that there was any need of the presence of soldiers at the polls on that day, in order to preserve the public peace, or insure a fair election?

Answer. Not the slightest.

Question. Did you consider that the presence of the military contributed to the preservation of the public peace on that day?

Answer. I do not think it did in any manner.

Question. Have you not been, and are you not now, an active member of the Democratic party, knowing all its principal plans and operations in conducting political campaigns?

Answer. I have been a member of the Democratic party ever since I was entitled to a vote. I think I understand its principles, and have endeavored to aid its success by all fair and honorable means.

Question. Did you ever hear of a purpose or desire, on the part of any Democrat, to interfere with the polls on the day of the election, so as to prevent a fair election?

Answer.   I never heard the intimation of any such design.

Question.   If there had been any intention or purpose of that kind, do you not believe that you would have known it?

Answer.   I believe I should.

Question.   Were the soldiers stationed at the polls acting under the direction of any one as Provost Marshal; if so, who was he?

Answer.   They seemed to be under the complete control of James R. Lofland, who was said to be Provost Marshal at the time, and was exercising authority as such.

Question.   Did the said James R. Lofland, together with the soldiers at his command, offer any opposition to any voter on that day, so as to prevent him from exercising the right of franchise according to his own will?

Answer.   I saw them prevent a man, by the name of Sparks, from approaching the window with the seeming intention of depositing his vote.

Question.   How did they prevent him from approaching the window? Was it by arrest or intimidation?

Answer.   By arrest, as I understood, by the order of the Provost Marshal.

Question.   Did that arrest produce any excitement?

Answer.   It did produce some.

Question.   Did the soldiers charge bayonets upon the citizens at the polls?

Answer.   Charges were made on one or two occasions, but I cannot say upon that one.

H. B. FIDDEMAN.

MARK G. LOFLAND, sworn and examined.

By the Chairman:

Question.   Did you vote in Milford on the 4th of November last?

Answer.   I did, sir.

Question.   Were there soldiers stationed near the polls during the time of voting?

Answer.   There were, sir; not at the beginning, but from a half hour to an hour after the polls were opened, until they closed they were there.

Question.   How many soldiers were there at Milford, according to your best recollection?

Answer.   I think, according to my best recollection, there were from twenty to twenty-four.

Question.   By what conveyance were they brought, and when did they arrive there?

Answer.   They came by cars, and, I think, they arrived in the night of the 3^{d} of November.

Question.   Were they in a regular or a special train of cars?

Answer.   I suppose it was a special train. There were no cars running there at night.

Question.   Do you know whether they were a part of the Maryland Home Guards, or were they a part of General Wool's command?

Answer.   I do not know to what regiment they belonged. I suppose they were under General Wool's command. He was in the State the next day.

Question.   How long did they remain in Milford?

Answer.   They remained there all the day of the 4th, and went away, I think, the next morning.

Question.   Under whose command were they while they remained in Milford?

Answer.   They seemed to be under the command of the Provost Marshal, Mr. Lofland.

Question.   Did they appear to be acting in concert with and for the benefit of either of the political parties?

Answer.   They seemed to give the preference to the Abolition or Republican party.

Question. Was it, or was it not, generally understood that they were brought there to aid the Republicans, and injure the Democrats?

Answer. That was my own impression, and seemed to be the impression of persons generally.

Question. Had their presence the effect to intimidate the Democrats, and to embolden the Republicans?

Answer. It did, sir; and we had a good deal of trouble to get some Democrats to vote.

Question. Did you hear any conversation between the Provost Marshal and Mr. Curtis Watson, or anybody else, in relation to Mr. Sparks' voting?

Answer. Yes, sir; I did so after his arrest was made. I was in Mr. Watson's office, with several prominent Democrats. The Provost Marshal came in—it was just a little while before the polls closed, between four and five, as well as I recollect. He said to Mr. Watson: "Come now, Curtis, let us go up and see what way Joe wants to vote. You may offer him a ticket, and I will, also, and which ever ticket he chooses to vote, let him go and do so." I remarked that he was very much frightened, and as long as they had arrested him, keep him in durance, and not let him vote at all, because he would be sure to vote the Republican ticket. The Provost Marshal said that he should vote now, anyhow.

Question. What was your reason for saying that he would vote a Republican ticket?

Answer. Because they had threatened him with incarceration in Fort McHenry, according to his own words—he told me so.

Question. Had he, or had he not, been for several hours a prisoner in the possession of the Provost Marshal?

Answer. He had been, three or four hours, I think.

Question. Were you present at the time he made an effort to vote in the morning, and was prevented by the soldiers?

Answer. I was. He went to the foot of the pavement, and one of the soldiers said to him that he had been there once before, and told him to go off. Sparks held up his tax receipt in one hand, and a Democratic ticket in the other, and said: "I have a right to vote, and am going to do it." Whereupon the soldier said: "Go away, God damn you, you shall not vote until we see the Provost Marshal." This aroused Mr. Fowler, and he asked the soldier what right he had to say that a man should not vote who had paid his tax, and had a right to a vote. He told him to let Sparks go to the window, and let the Judges decide the matter. They did not permit him to go to the window.

Question. Do you know how he did vote?

Answer. I do not. He went to the window with a Republican and voted. The Provost Marshal himself said that he voted the Republican ticket.

Question. Do you know whether, at any time previous to the election, a company of cavalry, headed by George P. Fisher, who was then the candidate on the Republican ticket for Congress, and Nathaniel B. Smithers, visited Milford, to attend a political meeting, or for any other purpose?

Answer. I do, sir. I cannot tell you what time; it was before the election. The company of cavalry, headed by Knight, came to Milford. Mr. Fisher and Mr. Smithers came along with them, and spoke at a political meeting at Milford that night.

Question. Were they understood to be cavalry in the service, or at least in the pay of the United States?

Answer. That was the understanding.

Question. Do you recollect about what number there were?

Answer. I do not know; there were a good many.

Question. What impression did the parading of a company of cavalry through this State, at a period so near the election, to attend political meetings, make upon the mind of the people generally?

Answer. I cannot say what impression it had on others. It led me to think they designed to intimidate voters. They did make an attack upon a Democrat, and drew their revolvers, and had it not been for one or two citizens, I believe the fellow would have been murdered for no cause. They attacked none but Democrats, and none but Democrats seemed to be alarmed.

Question. Was it not the general feeling among the Democrats, that that cavalry company was paraded through the State, and exhibited at political meetings, for the purpose of advertising that the Republican party had control of the military, and thereby to intimidate and alarm timid voters?

Answer. I have no doubt it was so myself; but I cannot speak in regard to others.

Question. Do you know whether, on the day of the election, the soldiers made an attack on any prominent Republican who was in the town of Milford on that day?

Answer. I do, sir. There was a little disturbance at the polls over a voter, whereupon the Captain ordered a charge. The soldiers, who were rushing towards Winlock H. Tomlinson, with their bayonets pointed at him, had got near Tomlinson, when Hiram W. McCauley, a brother-in-law of Mr. Fisher, then candidate for Congress, hallooed: "Stop! stop! he is a good Union man," and they immediately halted.

MARK. G. LOFLAND.

The examination of HENRY B. FIDDEMAN was resumed, he being recalled,

By the Chairman:

Question. Do you recollect whether a company of cavalry visited Milford at any time previous to the election? If so, please to state what you know about it.

Answer. I recollect that a very short time, perhaps one or two weeks before the election, a company of cavalry came to Milford on Saturday, and remained until Monday.

Question. Were they there ostensibly to attend a political meeting?

Answer. That seemed to be the understanding, and a political meeting was held by the Republican party that night—Saturday night. I saw Mr. Fisher and Mr. Smithers in a carriage, and, I think, they were at the head of the procession.

Question. What impression did the parading a company of cavalry through this State to attend political meetings, within a few days of the general election, make upon the minds of persons generally?

Answer. It made the impression, on my mind, that it was intended to overawe and intimidate timid voters of the Democratic party.

Question. Do you know whether any portion of that cavalry company made an attack upon any citizen of Milford during their stay there?

Answer. I understood that an attack was made upon Benjamin Y. Collins, which took place nearly opposite my residence. I was attracted by the noise to the front door, and heard a man, who I afterwards learned was Mr. Collins, begging to be released by some of the armed cavalry who surrounded him, and who, I afterwards learned, was released by the interference in his behalf of one of our most respectable citizens.

Question. Do you know why the cavalry made the attack on Mr. Collins?

Answer. I understood that night, or next day, that he was charged with hissing at one of the speakers who was on the stand; which charge he denied.

H. B. FIDDEMAN.

On motion,

The Committee adjourned until half-past eight o'clock to-morrow morning.

TUESDAY, March 10, 1863—8 ½ o'clock, A.M.

The Committee met pursuant to adjournment.

Present—Messrs. Saulsbury, Cahall, Hitch, Slay, Stubbs, and Waples.

WILLIAM THARP, sworn and examined.

By the Chairman:

Question.   Did you vote in Milford on the day of the last general election?

Answer.   Yes, sir.

Question.   Did you see anything unusual, and different from what you had ever seen before at or near the polls that day?

Answer.   I did. There were some armed United States soldiers there, a portion of them stationed at the polls. There were two files extending from the window, the width of the porch, with arms in hand, between which the voters had to pass to get to the window.

Question.   At what time in the day did you vote?

Answer.   I should judge about 11 o'clock.

Question.   Had you to pass between the two files of armed soldiers to get to the window to vote?

Answer.   I did.

Question.   Was the space between the two files of soldiers closed with locked bayonets in the hands of soldiers at the time you approached the window to vote?

Answer.   Yes. When I made the attempt to go up to the window, and approached the outer end of the file of soldiers, the bayonets were locked. I mentioned that I would go and vote. They then opened the bayonets, and allowed me to pass in. My impression is, they then locked the bayonets. I know they did when others passed in.

Question.   Under whose charge were the soldiers there that day?

Answer.   My understanding was, that they were under the charge of the Provost Marshal, James R. Lofland.

Question.   What are the politics of James R. Lofland?

Answer.   He professes to act with a party called the Union party, which, in our State, is understood to be the same as is recognized as the Republican party of the country. In our State, the term Republican party is rather unpopular.

Question.   Is James R. Lofland a violent and prejudiced partizan, and would he, in your judgment, use any official position he might occupy for the promotion of his own ends, or the success of his own political party?

Answer.   I think he would for the sake of obtaining votes for his party. I also think he is as violent a politician probably as we have in our Hundred.

Question.   Did Mr. Lofland, on the 4th of November last, through the agency of the troops under his command, act in concert with and for the benefit of either of the political parties?

Answer.   I think he did, for the benefit of the so-called Republican party.

Question.   Was the presence of troops, stationed in the position you have described, and commanded by James R. Lofland, calculated to produce, and did their presence produce, great dissatisfaction and intimidation among any class of voters in Milford Hundred?

Answer.   I think it did. I am also of the opinion that it had the effect which those who sent them desired it should have, which was to intimidate the Democrats and embolden the Republicans.

Question.   Were you ever the Governor of this State?

Answer.   I was, for four years.

Question.   Are you not well acquainted with the people of the whole state?

Answer.   I suppose I am as well acquainted with the people of the State as most persons.

Question.   Was there, in your judgment, any necessity for the presence of the military at any voting place in this State on the 4th of November last, to preserve the public peace, or insure a fair and impartial election?

Answer.   None, whatever.

Question.   By what party were you elected Governor of this State?

Answer.   The Democratic party.

Question.   Have you not frequently been elected to official position by the Democratic party in this State, and have you not always enjoyed the confidence of the party, and been generally consulted in reference to its plans and purposes?

Answer. I have been elected to both branches of the Legislature, and I think I have enjoyed the confidence of the party, and been generally consulted.

Question. I ask you whether you ever heard the intimation of a purpose or desire, on the part of the Democrats, to interfere with the polls on the 4th of November last, to prevent a fair and impartial election?

Answer. No, I never did. I think the desire of the Democratic party was to have a quiet, fair election.

Question. What was the general estimate of Democrats throughout the State, previous to the last election, as to the probable result of that election, if there was no military interference?

Answer. That the Democratic party would carry their County ticket by large majorities in the two lower Counties, and thereby secure a majority in the Legislature; and that they would also elect their State ticket. I think that was the universal calculation.

Question. In view of these facts, was it not the interest, as well as the desire of the Democratic party, that the election should be a fair, full, free, and peaceable one?

Answer. It is my opinion that it was their interest.

Question. Do you know whether a cavalry company visited your town for the purpose of attending a political meeting, of either party, a few days previous to the last general election?

Answer. Yes. There was a cavalry company visited our town, I think a week or two before the election, and attended a political meeting held by the Republican party. I should think there were very nearly one hundred.

Question. Did you see them as they passed through the town? If so, please to state who headed the procession.

Answer. I saw them when they passed my door, headed by George P. Fisher and Nathaniel B. Smithers in a double carriage.

Question. What impression did the parading of a cavalry company, amounting to about one hundred, through this State for the purpose of attending the meetings of one of the political parties, within a week or two previous to the general election, make upon the minds of persons generally with whom you have conversed?

Answer. It was generally condemned. I think the intention was to try to influence voters through intimidation.

WILLIAM THARP.

CHARLES WILLIAMSON, affirmed and examined.

By the Chairman:

Question. Were you at the voting place in Mispillion Hundred on the 4th of November last, and did you vote at that place?

Answer. I was there, and I voted.

Question. It was stated by the Provost Marshal of that Hundred, William Henry Taylor, that the Democrats of the Hundred, among whom you were particularly named, took possession of the polls soon after they were opened, and refused to allow Union men or Republicans to go to the window to vote. That some of the Union men requested that half the window be given to them, and that you replied that the Republicans might vote when the Democrats were done voting, and refused to allow them any space at the window. I ask you, sir, if this statement, or any part of it, is true?

Answer. The Democrats did not take possession of the window, nor did they refuse to allow Republicans to vote. I was there at the opening of the polls, when the window was raised, and it was proclaimed that the polls were open. There were a few, some five or six, advanced towards the window and commenced voting, and turning off as soon as they had voted. William Shaw came up and said: "We intend to have half of the window." At that time there was plenty of room for any man to vote. I, myself, was not at the window, but was not far off. I said to Mr.

Shaw: "There is room enough for men to vote if they wish to vote." I took him by the arm and said: "There is room at the window if you wish to vote; do you wish to vote?" He said: "Yes." I then pushed him along. When he and I got up near enough to the window to vote, Mr. Shaw said: "I do not want to vote now." I then said to him: "If you do not want to vote, stand out of the way and I will vote," and did vote. Then I left the window as soon as I was done voting, and I was no more at the window until the afternoon.

Question.   I ask you whether, during the time you were at or near the window, Democrats and Republicans both had not equal privileges, and did not alike go to the window and vote?

Answer.   They did.

Question.   Did you say to Mr. Shaw, or Mr. Taylor, or any other person, that Republicans should not vote until Democrats were done voting?

Answer.   I positively did not then, before, or since.

Question.   Did you use language which any honest and intelligent man could have construed to have that meaning?

Answer.   I think not, sir.

Question.   Are you acquainted with William H. Taylor, who was Provost Marshal for Mispillion Hundred, on the day of the last general election?

Answer.   I am, sir, and have been from his boyhood.

Question.   What character does he bear through that section of the country?

Answer.   I would like to be excused from answering that question. I have made it a rule in my life, if I could not say good of a man, to say as little harm as possible.

The Chairman.   The Committee would excuse you if they thought it consistent with their duty, but they deem it important that the character of the men who were selected as Provost Marshals, and placed in charge of the polls, should be known. They must, therefore, insist on an answer to the question.

The Witness. Well, Mr. Taylor's character, from general report, is not very good.

Question. Is he such a man as the people of Mispillion Hundred would have selected for the office of Provost Marshal, if they had desired an officer who would act justly, and use the position to secure a fair and impartial election?

Answer. He is not. He would have been, I think, one of the last men that would have been selected for that purpose.

Question. Is Mr. Taylor, in your judgment, a man who would use any official position he might occupy for the promotion of his own ends, or the benefit of his own political party?

Answer. I think he is.

Question. Did he, on the day of the last general election, use his influence as Provost Marshal of that Hundred, through the agency of the troops under his command, for the benefit of one political party, and the injury of the other?

Answer. He did, for the benefit of the Republican party.

Question. Did, or did not, the whole conduct of Mr. Taylor, as Provost Marshal, and as commander of the troops who were present, justify and induce the belief that the troops were brought there to promote the interests of one of the political parties?

Answer. It did; for the Republican party.

Question. How long have you been a citizen and voter in Mispillion Hundred?

Answer. I have been a voter nearly forty years, and always in that Hundred.

Question. Have you not received the confidence of the people of your Hundred and County by election to the Legislature, and in other ways?

Answer. I think I have.

Question. I ask you whether, in your judgment, there was any necessity for the presence of the military at the polls in Mispillion Hundred, or any other voting place in this County, to preserve the public peace, or insure a fair and impartial election?

Answer. I think there was no necessity whatever.

Question. Did the presence of the military in Mispillion Hundred tend, in your judgment, materially to benefit one party, and injure the other?

Answer. I am sure, in my judgment, that it did tend to benefit the Republican party and injure the Democratic party.

CHARLES WILLIAMSON.

On motion of Mr. Waples,
The Committee adjourned until 1 ½ o'clock this afternoon.

SAME DAY, 1 ½ o'clock, P.M.

The Committee met pursuant to adjournment.

Present—Messrs. Saulsbury, Hitch, Slay, Stubbs, Williams, and Waples.

GEORGE DAVIS, sworn and examined.

By the Chairman:

Question. Where do you reside, and where did you vote on the day of the last general election?

Answer. At Smyrna, in Duck Creek Hundred, in Kent County.

Question. Will you please to state whether there were armed soldiers, understood to be in the service of the United States, at or near the polls on that day?

Answer. There was a company of soldiers, said to be in the service of the United States, stationed opposite our voting place on the election day.

Question. Do you know under whose charge they were, and by whose direction they were placed opposite the polls?

Answer. William C. Eliason, who was said to be the Deputy

Provost Marshal, left the polls, and said that he would bring the soldiers, that he had authority to do so. I asked him by what authority he acted. He told me, in the first instance, that he acted by the authority of General Wool, and then amended it by saying, Secretary Stanton. I remarked to Mr. Eliason that I thought it was entirely unnecessary to bring the troops there—that instead of their having a tendency to allay the excitement, I thought they might possibly increase it. I remarked also, if you would control your side, meaning the Republican, we will control the other side, and keep peace and quiet at the election. Mr. Temple, and myself, and other prominent Democrats, had counseled together in the morning, and it was understood that Mr. George W. Cummins, who had previously been fixed upon for that purpose, should stand at the window, and make such arrangements as he saw proper to see that all parties had opportunity to vote in peace and quiet. He remarked that he had the power, and should exercise it, or something to that amount, and went and brought the troops on the election ground.

Question. Is William C. Eliason such a man as the people of Duck Creek Hundred would have selected as Provost Marshal, if they had desired an officer to secure a fair and impartial election?

Answer. I think I can say without hesitancy that a majority of the people of that Hundred would never have selected him.

Question. Is he, in your judgment, a man who would use any official position he might occupy for the promotion of his own ends, or the advancement of the interests of his own political party?

Answer. I do not think he is a very conscientious man upon that subject. I think it is very probable that he would take any little advantage he could for that purpose.

Question. You have spoken of Mr. George W. Cummins as having been selected by the Democrats, as you understood, to stand at the window. Was the understanding that he was to stand on one side of the window, and some member of the other party on the opposite side of the window, as has always been done heretofore, for the purpose of seeing that the voting went on properly, and that no illegal votes were received on either side?

Answer. My understanding was that Mr. Cummins was appointed for that purpose, and it has been usual for some member of the other party to stand at the window for a similar purpose.

Question. How long have you resided in Duck Creek Hundred?

Answer. I was born and raised in Smyrna, and resided there all my life, except sixteen or seventeen years, during which time I was farming in an adjoining County in Maryland.

Question. Are you not, therefore, well acquainted with the people of Duck Creek Hundred?

Answer. I am well acquainted with most of the citizens of that Hundred, excepting a few young men who grew up in my absence.

Question. Was there, in your judgment, any necessity for the presence of United States soldiers in Smyrna on the last election day, to preserve the public peace, or insure a fair and impartial election?

Answer. None whatever, sir. I do not think there was the least necessity for it.

GEO. DAVIS.

On motion,
The Committee adjourned until half-past eight o'clock this evening.

SAME DAY, 8 ½ o'clock, P.M.

The Committee met pursuant to adjournment.

Present—Messrs. Cahall, Hitch, Slay, Stubbs, Williams, Waples, and Horsey.

No witnesses being present,

On motion of Mr. Williams,

The Committee adjourned until to-morrow morning, at nine o'clock.

WEDNESDAY, March 11, 1863—9 o'clock, A.M.

The Committee met pursuant to adjournment.
Present—Messrs. Saulsbury, Cahall, Hitch, Slay, Stubbs, Williams, Waples, and Horsey.
No business appearing,
On motion of Mr. Waples,
The Committee adjourned until to-morrow evening at half-past 8 o'clock.

THURSDAY, March 12, 1863—8 ½ o'clock, P.M.

The Committee met pursuant to adjournment.
Present—Messrs. Saulsbury, Cahall, Slay, Stubbs, and Waples.

JAMES C. BIRD, sworn and examined.

By the Chairman:
Question. Do you know anything about a visit of a cavalry company to this town any time in the month of October last?
Answer. I know that on the 17th day of October last, Company A, of the first battalion of Delaware Cavalry, came to Dover, and encamped upon the Agricultural Fair Grounds.
Question. Was that at the time of the Agricultural exhibition in this County?
Answer. Yes, sir; on the second day of the exhibition.
Question. Are you a member and officer of the Agricultural Society?
Answer. I am a member and Recording Secretary of the Kent County Agricultural Society.
Question. Were they invited by the Agricultural Society to be present at that time?

Answer.   They were not. Several days before the exhibition, the Quartermaster made his appearance upon the ground, and took possession of the grounds without saying a word to any member or officer of the Society. Mr. Manlove Hayes and I called upon George P. Fisher, who, we were informed, was to be the Colonel of the regiment. We asked him if the cavalry were to take possession of the grounds. He said yes, it was the only suitable lot that they could find.

Question.   How long did they remain in this County?

Answer.   I do not recollect exactly; but I think between two and three weeks.

Question.   How were they employed during their stay here?

Answer.   In going about the County, and attending political meetings.

Question.   What impression did their presence here, and their attending political meetings in different parts of the County, make upon the minds of those with whom you conversed on the subject?

Answer.   That they were here to intimidate timid Democrats, and to make political capital for the party. I believe that it had that effect.

JAMES C. BIRD.

JOHN C. PENNEWILL, sworn and examined.

By the Chairman:

Question.   Do you know anything in reference to the visit of a company of cavalry to this County in the month of October last?

Answer.   I know that in the month of October last, at Pierson's Cross-Roads, where there was a Republican meeting being held, on that day there was a company of cavalry in attendance at the meeting.

Question.   Do you know about what time they came into this County?

Answer.   On the second day of the exhibition in October last, I was out at the Fair Ground, and saw a company of cavalry, numbering, as I was told, a hundred and twenty men and horses.

Question. What were they doing at the political meeting at Pierson's Corner, of which you have spoken?

Answer. They were walking about, mingling with the few persons that were there, and some of them were drinking, as I think, to excess.

Question. How long did they remain in this County?

Answer. To the best of my knowledge, from two to three weeks.

Question. What was the general opinion, as to their object and purposes in visiting this town at that time, and attending political meetings through the county?

Answer. At the political meeting, to which I have referred, I conversed with several prominent citizens of the County, and the prevailing opinion seemed to be that it was for the purpose of intimidating timid Democrats from going to the polls upon the day of the general election.

Question. Who were the speakers at the meeting at Pierson's Corner, to which you have alluded?

Answer. When I arrived at the meeting, Jacob Moore, from Sussex County, was speaking. When he ceased, William Cannon, the present Governor, made a few remarks. Next, Colonel George P. Fisher, and afterwards, James R. Lofland.

Question. Did you attend many Democratic meetings after that time and before the election?

Answer. I did, sir, quite a number. Being the candidate for the office of Sheriff, I felt it to be my duty to be present on every occasion.

Question. I ask you whether the Democratic speakers, at the meetings held after the visit of that cavalry company to this County, did, or did not, take great pains to persuade Democratic voters not to be intimidated, but to go to the polls on the 4th of November, and vote?

Answer. They did, invariably, in all the speeches I heard them make.

Question. I ask you whether the Democratic speakers did not urge the people to avoid all excitement, to be calm, prudent, and peaceable, and assure them that all this military parade was only intended to intimidate; and also give it as their opinion that if that course was pursued, there would be nothing to fear?

Answer. They did, invariably.

JOHN C. PENNEWILL.

ROBERT HILL, sworn and examined.

By the Chairman:

Question. Do you recollect seeing a company of cavalry pass through the town of Smyrna any time during the month of October last?

Answer. I recollect seeing a company of cavalry pass through our town, but I do not recollect exactly whether it was in the month of October or not. I presume it was, from the fact that they were on their way to Dover.

Question. Did they pass quietly through the town?

Answer. They did not. In passing the houses of some of the Republicans they cheered. In passing the houses of the Democrats, they groaned. In passing the houses of George Davis, John H. Bewley, and William Temple, they groaned.

Question. Was William Temple the candidate for Congress on the Democratic ticket at that time?

Answer. He was, sir.

Question. Was John H. Bewley a candidate on the Democratic ticket for the Legislature?

Answer. He was, sir.

Question. Was Colonel Davis an active supporter of the Democratic party?

Answer. He was one of our most active men during our last campaign.

ROBERT HILL.

On motion of Mr. Waples,

The Committee adjourned until Monday evening next at eight o'clock.

MONDAY, March 16, 1863—8 o'clock, P.M.

The Committee met pursuant to adjournment.

Present—Messrs. Saulsbury, Slay, Hitch, Waples, Horsey.

EDWARD L. MARTIN, sworn and examined.

By the Chairman:

Question. Where do you reside?

Answer. I reside near Seaford, in Sussex County.

Question. Were there any volunteer companies at or in the neighborhood of Seaford within the last two years?

Answer. There were two.

Question. Did those companies retain possession of their arms up to the last little or general election?

Answer. One did; the other did not.

Question. Who was the commander of the company that retained possession of their arms?

Answer. Henry L. Hopkins, I think.

Question. Of what political party is Henry L. Hopkins a member?

Answer. Of the so-called Republican party.

Question. Were the other officers of his company members of the same party?

Answer. I think they are, as well as the members.

Question. Who was commander of the company which had been deprived of its arms previous to the last general election?

Answer. I was commissioned Captain of that company by Gov. Burton.

Question.   To what political party do you belong?

Answer.   I belong to the Democratic party.

Question.   Were the other officers of your company also Democrats?

Answer.   They were.

Question.   By whom were you furnished arms for your company?

Answer.   By the Commissary of Sussex County, upon an order from Governor Burton.

Question.   Were they the arms of this State?

Answer.   They were.

Question.   By whom, and under what authority, were you deprived of those arms?

Answer.   By Major Andrews, in command of a detachment of two companies of the Second Delaware Regiment, acting under orders from General Lockwood, and, as I was afterwards informed, he received his orders from Major-General Dix, commanding the Middle Department.

Question.   Do you know why you were deprived of your arms?

Answer.   I was told by General Lockwood that it was from information communicated to General McClellan, by a prominent citizen of Delaware, that I intended to transfer those arms to Virginia for the use of the Secessionists.

Question.   Was that statement true or false?

Answer.   It was false. And I would like to state here, in explanation of that statement, the origin of the company and the reasons which gave rise to it. Some time in December of the year 1860, several prominent and influential gentlemen, in company with myself, in my office, in discussing the affairs of the country, which, at that time, were in a very unsettled state, and really seemed as if we were drifting into a state of anarchy, being situated, as we were, very near three of the largest cities in the United States, each of those containing a large floating population, to protect ourselves from roving bands of such characters, we deemed it a wise precaution to be prepared for any emergency. We therefore determined to issue a call to the young men of the neighborhood, without distinction of party, to meet in Seaford on a stated day, for the purpose of forming a volunteer military company. The meeting was held, and the company was organized; officers were elected, without any distinction of party. The officers were commissioned, and received their arms through the State authorities. At our next meeting, those officers and privates who had been connected with other *political* organizations, through the persuasions of evil-disposed persons, withdrew from the company. The company continued to drill, and to perfect its organization and efficiency, until the public excitement reached almost a climax. Then, to secure harmony of action, and to preserve the peace, offered its services, through its Captain, to any six town commissioners, having an equal interest in the preservation of the peace and good order of society, to be under their orders; which offer was refused peremptorily by the so-called Republicans of the village. After that time, there was another military organization formed, composed, exclusively, of the members of the other political party. After which time, my company ceased to have more than a nominal existence.

Question. Does Captain Hopkins' company still retain possession of their arms?

Answer. I think they do.

Question. Do you know of any other volunteer companies in your County which were deprived of their arms?

Answer. I know of one, certainly—Captain Paynter's company, in Georgetown.

Question. Was Captain Paynter's company commanded by Democrats?

Answer. Captain Paynter himself was a Democrat; as to the other officers, I do not know their political predilections.

E. L. MARTIN.

BENJAMIN DONOHO, sworn and examined.

By the Chairman:

Question.   Do you know anything of a company of cavalry passing through Smyrna in the month of October last?

Answer.   Yes, sir.

Question.   How many were there, according to the best judgment you could form?

Answer.   I think there were about one hundred, as well as I recollect.

Question.   Did they pass quietly through the town, offering no insult to any person?

Answer.   No, sir; they did not pass quietly through the town. When they got opposite Governor Temple's, going down, they groaned. They then came opposite Dr. Cummins', where they cheered. They then passed on to Colonel Davis' house, and groaned again. They then came to Mr. Wilmer's, and there cheered. As they came back two or three weeks afterwards, I think they commenced to groan at Mr. Bewley's; they cheered at Mr. Eliason's; they cheered again at Mr. Wilmer's; they groaned at Colonel Davis'; they groaned again at Mr. Temple's.

Question.   To what political party did Dr. Cummins, Mr. Wilmer, and Mr. Eliason belong?

Answer.   To the Republican party.

Question.   To what political party did Governor Temple, Colonel Davis, and John H. Bewley, belong?

Answer.   To the Democratic party.

Question.   Was it understood that the cavalry company groaned in front of the residences of those gentlemen to insult them?

Answer.   That was the impression.

Question.   Was Governor Temple a candidate on the Democratic ticket for Congress at that time?

Answer.   He was, sir.

Question.   Was Mr. Bewley a candidate on the Democratic ticket for the Legislature?

Answer. Yes, sir.

Question. Was Dr. Cummins a candidate on the Republican ticket for the State Senate?

Answer. Yes, sir.

Question. Do you know any of the officers who were commanding the company that day?

Answer. I did not, except Lieutenant Ayers, who had formerly lived in Smyrna, and was a preacher.

B. Donoho.

John Taylor, sworn and examined.

By the Chairman:

Question. Did you see a company of cavalry pass through the town of Smyrna any time in the month of October last?

Answer. I did, sir, as they came back. I did not as they went down.

Question. How long was that before the election?

Answer. Within a few days of the election, I think. I do not exactly recollect.

Question. Did they pass quietly through the town, offering no insult to anybody?

Answer. They did not. I spoke to Mr. Townsend, who was a member of the company, and a man I was formerly acquainted with. Mr. Ayers came along, and was forming his men into line. After he had got them formed into line, he then came along, and told them when they got to George Davis' and William Temple's to give three groans as loud as they ever could halloo. I was not more than eight or ten feet from him at farthest, and distinctly heard him mention George Davis and William Temple. He then gave them order to march.

Question. Was Mr. Ayers an officer in the company?

Answer. They called him First Lieutenant, I understood. He had the command that day.

Question. Had he ever lived about Smyrna?

Answer. He had, sir.

Question. What did he follow when he lived there?

Answer. He preached occasionally.

Question. How long had it been since he left there?

Answer. He left in March, I think, and went to Conference, I think, and was appointed to Camden Circuit. He quit preaching, and joined the cavalry company.

Question. Did you think, from his manner in giving the order, that he wanted to insult Mr. Temple and Colonel Davis?

Answer. It seemed so, from his manner. They were not disturbing him. I should regard it as an insult.

JOHN TAYLOR.

JOHN B. PENINGTON, sworn and examined.

By the Chairman:

Question. Will you please to state whether you know of any volunteer company or companies in this State which were deprived of their arms by persons professing to act by authority of the United States Government at any time previous to the 4th day of November last?

Answer. Of my own knowledge, I know of but one, and that one was deprived of a portion of their arms. I believe, however, they were nearly all taken away from the company; but of that fact, I can only speak from the statement of the officers and privates belonging to it. I refer to the Hazlet Guard, a company organized in the town of Dover, some time during the month of January, 1861. Of other companies, I know nothing, except statements made by parties belonging to such companies, and the statement of an officer and privates belonging to the First Maryland Eastern Shore Home Guards.

Question. Who commanded the Hazlet Guards at the time they were deprived of their arms?

Answer. They were under my command, as Captain of the company.

Question. Who were the other officers of the company?

Answer. William A. Atkinson was First Lieutenant; Isaac Davis, Jr., was Second Lieutenant; John C. Craig was Third Lieutenant.

Question. Of what political party were yourself and other officers of the company members?

Answer. William A. Atkinson, John C. Craig, and myself, were members of the Democratic party. Isaac Davis, Jr., I think, belonged to the Constitutional Union, or Bell & Everett party.

Question. By whom was your company deprived of their arms?

Answer. By one James Wallace, acting as Colonel of the First Maryland Eastern Shore Home Guards.

Question. Was there any other volunteer company in the town of Dover at the time?

Answer. There was.

Question. Who was the Captain of that company?

Answer. William Walker.

Question. What ticket was William Walker understood to vote at the last election?

Answer. I do not know what ticket Mr. Walker voted, but during the campaign he was regarded as being identified and connected with the self-styled Union party, which was understood to mean the Republican party; and, I presume, voted that ticket.

Question. Were the officers and members of Mr. Walker's company understood generally to belong to the same party?

Answer. The officers and acting members were; but, I think, there were some persons who originally belonged to the company, and perhaps may have belonged at that time, who were not.

Question. Was Mr. Walker's company deprived of its arms at the same time that you were deprived of yours?

Answer. They were not.

Question. Was it not generally understood in the town that Dr. Jump, who was the original Captain of that company, had a large number of arms in his possession, which he distributed or was understood to have distributed, to companies who were composed of and commanded by members of the Republican party throughout this County?

Answer. Shortly after the organization of the company which Isaac Jump originally commanded, and which was the same company of which I have spoken of William Walker as being Captain at the time the Hazlet Guards were deprived of their arms, Captain Jump procured from the Commissary of Kent County, on the order of the Governor, 105 or 110 flintlock muskets. Subsequently there were quite a number of boxes containing arms delivered in the back-yard of Captain Jump's dwelling, and by his orders conveyed into a room in his house. These arms were the old flint-lock musket, changed or altered to a percussion musket. With a portion of these percussion muskets he furnished his own company. A large number of the balance, if not all of them, were distributed and given out to companies commanded by persons belonging to the same political party with himself, the Republican party. What became of those he obtained from the Commissary of Kent County, I do not know.

Question. How many arms, from the best judgment you can form, did the boxes of which you have spoken, as having been delivered in the back yard of Dr. Jump's residence, contain?

Answer. I am not able to speak with any certainty, although I saw most, if not all of the boxes that were delivered, it being done immediately in front of one of the windows of my office. But my impression is that there were something over twenty boxes which contained arms; each box containing, usually, twenty muskets.

Question. Do you know whether, just previous to the last election, there were arms of any kind delivered at, and stacked up, in the office of Nathaniel B. Smithers, Esq.?

Answer. Some time previous to the general election of 1862,

there was a man came into town with a wagon load of muskets, and inquired for George P. Fisher, saying that the person having charge of Camp Fisher, near Camden, which place the Third Delaware regiment had then recently left, had directed him to deliver those arms to Mr. Fisher. He met with Mr. Fisher on the street, and, after some consultation between Mr. Fisher and Mr. Nathaniel B. Smithers, the arms which he had in charge were delivered or placed in Mr. Smithers's office.

Question. Was Mr. Fisher or Mr. Smithers the Commissary of this County?

Answer. No, sir. Mr. William J. Clark was then, and for ought I know, still is the Commissary of Kent County, and as such, by the law of our State, the custodian or keeper of the arms of the State within this County.

Question. With what political party is Mr. Clarke connected?

Answer. The Democratic party.

Question. To what political party did Nathaniel B. Smithers, to whom the arms were delivered, belong?

Answer. Mr. Smithers was then acting with, and professed to belong to the Republican party.

Question. You have spoken of what you were told in reference to other companies in this State, by persons belonging to a regiment of the Maryland Home Guards. Please state what you were told?

Answer. I was informed by a Captain of one of the companies belonging to the 1st Maryland Eastern Shore Regiment, that Colonel Wallace had visited Smyrna for the purpose of disarming a company under command of Captain Carr; that he had either obtained the arms from that company, or made some arrangement by which he would obtain them, and that he (Wallace) together with the men under his command at that time, had passed up the Delaware Railroad to the town of New Castle, for the purpose of disarming what had been represented to them as a Secession company in that town; and that a portion of the troops had likewise been sent to Delaware City, for the purpose of procuring the arms of what was termed a Secession company in that town. Subsequently the same Captain informed me that Colonel Wallace, having received a portion of the arms of the company at New Castle, had left one of his own companies at New Castle for the purpose of procuring the balance, and had, himself, with the remaining companies passed over to Wilmington for the purpose of disarming some companies in that city. This information was likewise communicated to me by privates belonging to some one of the companies of Colonel Wallace's regiment; but I supposed then, and believe now, that their information was obtained from the subordinate officers, who had learned the facts from the Captain of whom I have spoken.

Question. Was it not the custom of members of the Republican party to speak of all the volunteer companies in the State which were commanded by Democrats as Secession companies?

Answer. As far as my knowledge extends it was.

Question. I ask you whether your own company did not march invariably under the American flag, when it marched under a flag at all?

Answer. The company which I commanded was presented, by several ladies of the town of Dover, with a very beautiful silk flag, which was the national flag of our country, and which had inscribed upon it thirty-four stars, representing the States of the Union; under that flag, and under that one alone, did the company march or parade; and upon all fitting and appropriate occasions it was carried as the emblem of the sentiments of the company.

Question. I ask you whether it was not generally understood, previous to the last election, that all the volunteer companies in the State which were commanded by Democrats had been deprived of their arms; and that all companies which were commanded by Republicans were permitted to retain possession of their arms?

Answer. I believe it was so generally understood; and so far as I know, no company that was commanded by a Democrat was permitted to retain its arms; and no one that was commanded by a Republican was deprived of them.

JOHN B. PENINGTON.

On motion,

The Committee adjourned until 8 ½ o'clock, to-morrow morning.

TUESDAY, March 16, 1863—8 ½ o'clock, A.M.

The Committee met pursuant to adjournment.

Present—Messrs. Saulsbury, Cahall, Hitch, Stubbs, and Horsey.

MILTON STEEL, sworn and examined.

By the Chairman:

Question.   Where do you reside, and where did you vote on the day of the last general election?

Answer.   I reside in Mill Creek Hundred, in New Castle County, and voted at the Mermaid, the place of holding the election in that Hundred.

Question.   Did you see anything unusual, and different from what you had ever seen before at or near the polls on that day?

Answer.   I saw a company of military, armed with muskets and bayonets, swords and revolvers.

Question.   Will you please to state how they came to the polls, what position they occupied in reference to the polls, and what was their general conduct on that day?

Answer.   They formed themselves into line some two or three hundred yards from the polls; they marched by the place of voting, singing a political song. All that I could understand was: "Hang Jim Bayard on a sour apple tree." After marching some distance past, they again turned and came back. Their Captain came on the porch to clear the porch for the men to march up, which created some disturbance with the citizens. He then put his hand against one Mr. Jesse B. Ball, one of the citizens, told him to stand back, and drew his sword. Mr. Ball drew a revolver, and told the Captain that he would blow his heart out if he struck him with a sword. The officer having command of the company, then ordered the men forward with their arms into the porch.

Question.   Was Mr. Ball, at the time the Captain put his hand on him and pushed him back, creating any disturbance, or trying to prevent anybody from voting?

Answer.   He was not.

Question.   When the Captain drew his sword over Mr. Ball, was Mr. Ball committing, or attempting to commit, any acts of violence towards any person?

Answer.   At the time Mr. Ball was standing quietly on the porch, not speaking to any one.

Question.   Was there any obstruction of the window or voting place at the time, such as to interfere with free voting by the citizens of that Hundred?

Answer.   There was no obstruction, and no disturbance; the window was completely open.

Question.   Did the Captain draw a revolver upon Mr. Ball?

Answer.   After Mr. Ball drew his revolver, the Captain then put up his sword, and drew a revolver. At the same time the Lieutenant ordered the men forward, with their muskets and bayonets fixed, on to the porch, and one of the officers at the time held his revolver right across the window or the polls, swearing at the same time that he could kill a man eighty yards.

Question.   Did the soldiers, in compliance with the order of the Lieutenant, charge upon the men in the porch in front of the window?

Answer.   I do not know whether it could be called a charge or not, but they rushed in among the men with their muskets with bayonets fixed.

Question.   I ask you whether the soldiers did not create all the difficulty that was created there that day?

Answer.   I believe they were the cause of all the difficulty.

Question.   From their conduct, was it not apparent that their object was to create, and not prevent, trouble and difficulty?

Answer.   That was my opinion.

Question.   I ask you whether, in your judgment, there was any necessity for the presence of soldiers at those polls, to preserve the public peace, or to insure a fair and impartial election?

Answer.   I do not think there was any necessity at all.

Question.   I ask you whether the soldiers acted in concert with and for the benefit of either of the political parties?

Answer.   They acted in concert with and for the benefit of the Republican party.

Question.   I ask you whether they arrested any of the citizens of that Hundred on that day?

Answer.   They did arrest five.

Question.   Who were the persons they arrested?

Answer.   Jesse B. Ball, Andrew Shultz, Joseph Abbot, Isaiah Ball, Samuel Little.

Question.   Were these gentlemen Democrats or Republicans?

Answer.   They were all members of the Democratic party.

Question.   What time in the day did they make those arrests?

Answer.   I think it was near about eleven o'clock.

Question.   Did the soldiers induce any person or persons who were voters in that Hundred, through fear or intimidation, to leave the election ground at an earlier hour than usual?

Answer.   I personally know of but one that left.

Question.   Was that one a Democrat or a Republican?

Answer.   That one was a Democrat.

Question.   Do you know whether the soldiers induced or caused any other soldiers who were citizens of that Hundred, and Democrats, and who had been permitted to come into the Hundred for the purpose of voting, to be carried back to camp without voting?

Answer.   I know of one who was arrested on the morning of the election, and carried back to the camp, which I afterwards understood was to prevent him from voting the Democratic ticket. That one was out on furlough.

Question. Did they declare that no soldier should vote or ought to vote on that day, who would not vote a Republican ticket?

Answer. I understood from officers and privates, that they either had to vote the Republican ticket or remain in camp.

Question. Do I understand you to say that both officers and privates of that company told you they were required either to vote the Republican ticket or remain in camp on the election day?

Answer. I do mean that both officers and privates of that company—I do not mean all of them—have told me that they had to vote the ticket given to them or remain in camp. I did hear one of the privates say that an officer came to their company on the morning of the election and asked whether there was any man there who voted at the Mermaid. This soldier told him that he voted at the Mermaid. The answer to him was, that he voted the rebel ticket, and might remain where he was.

Question. Do you know what officer that was?

Answer. I do, sir. He was David Buckner, Lieutenant of Captain Harper's company.

Question. Do you know whether any soldiers who were voters in your Hundred and Democrats, were kept in camp, and prevented from coming home to vote?

Answer. I only know from what I have heard other soldiers say. Other soldiers have told me that two or three that vote at our place would not come to the election on the account that they could not vote the ticket they wished to vote.

Question. Were these persons at home to vote?

Answer. They were not at the place of voting; they were in camp.

Question. Do you know whether the landlord requested the soldiers to keep out of his house, and not interfere with the citizens of that Hundred on that day?

Answer. I know that he went to Captain Harper and said something to him about making a disturbance in the house. The answer to him was, that he had authority to take all that house, with the exception of the room where the officers sat, and close it up.

MILTON STEELE.

AQUILA DERRICKSON, affirmed and examined.

By the Chairman:

Question. Where do you reside, and where did you vote on the day of the last general election?

Answer. In New Castle County, and Mill Creek Hundred.

Question. Were there armed soldiers at or near the place of voting on that day?

Answer. Yes, sir.

Question. Will you please to state the general conduct of the soldiers around the polls?

Answer. The first that I saw of them they were coming up the road by the polls singing a song in the tune of what is called the John Brown song; all that I could make out was, "Hang Jim Bayard on a sour apple tree." They marched past the polls about one hundred yards, as nearly as I could guess, wheeled about, and marched down opposite the polls, singing the same song. In the mean time Captain Harper was on the porch, apparently to try to clear the porch; the window was cleared, and a space on each side of the window. I saw nothing whatever to try to prevent one of the soldiers from voting; everything was peaceable and quiet. Two of these men marched up to the window to vote, and two others stood on the porch. There was at least room for four others to stand on the porch at the same time. Mr. Harper took hold of two or three from three to six feet from the window, and told them to stand back. The reply was, that they had business there; that he had men in his company that had no right to vote, and they wanted to see no illegal votes put in the box. He instantly raised his hand, pushed Jesse P. Ball off, and drew his sword at the same time, telling Jesse P. Ball to stand back, that he had authority there, and he would let them know it. Then Jesse B.

Ball drew his revolver, and told him that if he struck him with the sword he would shoot him, or something of the kind; saying at the same time that he had as much business there as the officer. At that time there was a rush made by the soldiers in front of the polls, with their muskets and bayonets fixed, and in position for a charge upon the people on the porch; at the same time I saw revolvers drawn in different directions by the soldiers. One in particular was levelled over the shoulders of men by a soldier swearing that he could shoot. I do not remember exactly what he said.

Question. From the manner and conduct of the soldiers as they first approached the voting place, was it not apparent that their purpose was to insult the Democratic voters, and create a difficulty at the polls?

Answer. It had that appearance to me.

Question. I ask you if the soldiers did not create all the difficulty that occurred there that day?

Answer. It is my opinion that they did. Everything seemed to pass off as harmoniously at the election as I ever saw until they made their appearance, and I believe it would have continued so if they had not made their appearance.

Question. Did they act in concert with and for the benefit of either of the political parties?

Answer. They did, sir. They acted in concert with and for the benefit of the Republican party.

Question. I ask you whether, in your judgment, there was any necessity for their presence at the polls, to preserve the public peace, or secure a fair and impartial election?

Answer. There was none, sir.

Question. I ask you whether their whole conduct did not show that they were there to prevent a fair election?

Answer. It did appear so to me.

Question. Do you know whether there were soldiers belonging to the same company as the soldiers who were present at the election, and who were citizens and voters in your Hundred, and who were absent from the polls that day?

Answer.   I do.

Question.   Were those persons who were absent Democrats or Republicans?

Answer.   They were Democrats.

Question.   What effect do you believe the presence of the soldiers had upon the vote of your Hundred?

Answer.   I believe that if the voters of our Hundred could have voted their choice, the Republicans would have had a very small majority, if any—not half the majority they did get.

Question.   Did the presence of the soldiers at the polls produce much intimidation among the Democratic voters of your Hundred?

Answer.   I cannot say, for a certainty. But there was a Democrat that left the polls through fear of the soldiers. On his way home, he met a Democrat going to the polls. He advised him to go home; that it was dangerous to go there. He considered the matter a short time and concluded, to use own expression: "He would try it, and if he saw any danger, he would then run." He said he got to the polls, and voted as quietly as he could, with the determination not to say anything to any one. But he found that was out of the question. He left as soon as he could, and went home.

Question.   Had there been any previous threats by any of the soldiers who were present at your polls on that day, that they would come, on the day of the general election, armed to the polls?

Answer.   I heard Captain Harper say, on the day of the little election, that he would come armed at the next election, meaning the general election. He said, on the same day, pulling out a Republican ticket: "We, every man of us, voted that ticket, and the man who does not vote that ticket is a traitor."

AQUILA DERRICKSON.

The examination of MILTON STEELE was resumed, he being recalled.

By the Chairman:

Question. Did any soldier who was present at the polls in Mill Creek Hundred tell you of any order which was given to them by Colonel Grimshaw previous to leaving the camp to come to the election?

Answer. Yes, sir. There were two soldiers told me that their orders that morning were to bring four rounds of cartridge, one in the gun and three out; and they likewise told me that that was their order from Colonel Grimshaw; one of these soldiers was an officer. I will state, in addition to what I have stated before, that after the arrest of the first two persons of that Hundred in the morning, I left the porch and went into the crowd. There I heard Republicans of our Hundred naming other persons who ought to be arrested, among whom were Isaiah Ball and Samuel Little, who were subsequently arrested. I also heard the name of Jonathan Catlin as a person to be arrested. I then went to Mr. Catlin and told him that if he remained on the ground he would be arrested, upon which he left and went home. Samuel Little took a heavy cold from the exposure incident to his arrest and confinement, which resulted in a spell of sickness, from which, it is the impression, he will not recover. All the persons who were arrested were discharged five days afterwards, without trial or the semblance of trial.

MILTON STEELE.

JAMES SPRINGER, sworn and examined.

By the Chairman:

Question. Where do you reside, and where did you vote on the day of the last general election?

Answer. I reside in Mill Creek Hundred, New Castle County, and voted at the Mermaid tavern.

Question. Will you please to state all that you know in reference to the presence of soldiers at the polls in that Hundred on the 4th of November last?

Answer. I know but little, having arrived at the polls after the arrests were all made. Upon arriving, however, I observed a number of soldiers mixing promiscuously with the citizens at the polls, some with their arms and some without. I observed no direct interference of the soldiery at the polls. But from what had previously occurred, the feeling of the Democratic party was, that their rights as freemen had been outraged; also feeling that the presence of the soldiers at the polls was to intimidate Democratic voters and to strengthen the Republican vote, and I do believe it had that effect. On Friday before the election on Tuesday, I talked with a soldier who was on furlough, in consequence of having had his arm broken some weeks before. He told me that though his friends were very much opposed to his voting a Democratic ticket, but that he intended to do it notwithstanding, and that he intended to stay out on furlough. On the Monday after the election I met him, and he informed me that he was arrested and taken to his camp on the day of the election, and did not get to vote. His regiment, which had been ordered to Washington, was brought into Wilmington on Sunday following the election, and his furlough was extended, as his arm was not well enough to enable him to do duty.

JAS. SPRINGER.

On motion of Mr. Hitch,
The Committee adjourned until 8 ½ o'clock this evening.

SAME DAY, 8 ½ o'clock, P.M.

The Committee met pursuant to adjournment.
Present—Messrs. Saulsbury, Cahall, Hitch, Waples, Williams, and Horsey.
No business appearing.
The Committee adjourned to meet at the call of the Chairman.

MONDAY, March 23, 1863—8 o'clock, P.M.

The Committee met at the call of the Chairman.

Present—Messrs. Saulsbury, Cahall, Hitch, Slay, Williams, and Waples.

The examination of JOHN B. PENINGTON was resumed, he being recalled.

By the Chairman:

Question. Mr. Penington, will you please state about what time in the year 1862 Colonel James Wallace visited this town with a portion of the Maryland Home Guard under his command; about what time in the day he arrived in Dover; where he quartered his soldiers; what place he made his own headquarters; how long he remained in the town; whether he made any arrests while in the town, and if so, what persons were arrested; where he went when he left; what disposition he made of the persons he arrested here, if any, and how long he kept them in confinement; whether he informed them of any charges against them, and if so, what were the nature and character of the charges; when he discharged them, and upon what terms?

Answer. Colonel Wallace arrived in Dover on the 7th day of March, 1862, I think, about noon of that day. In the evening of the same day, some two or three companies, or portions of companies, belonging to the First Maryland Eastern Shore Home Guards, which were commanded by Colonel Wallace, arrived in town, I think, about eight o'clock, coming here in a special train of cars. They were immediately upon their arrival, marched up to the State House, and, after having made some preparations, the soldiers were quartered in the Court Room in said House. In about an hour after their arrival, a person dressed in the uniform of a Captain, and calling himself Keene, waited upon me, and inquired if I was Captain Penington, to which I replied in the affirmative. He then delivered me a note, which, upon reading, purported to come from one James Wallace, Colonel of the regiment of which I have spoken, and requested a conference with me immediately in the office of Mr. Charles H. B. Day, "on important business." In a few minutes I went in, in company with Captain Keene, to Mr. Day's office, where I met with Mr. Nathaniel B. Smithers, Hiram W. McCauley, and a stranger, who was introduced to me by Mr. Smithers as Colonel Wallace. He (Colonel Wallace) inquired of me if I was the Captain of a volunteer company in this town. Upon being told that I was, he desired to know whether we had any arms, and if any, what kind they were. I stated to him that we had, and that they were long-range Minie rifles. He stated that he was directed by orders from the General Government to request of me an order upon the members of my company for the delivery of all arms in their possession to him. I replied, in substance, that I had obtained those arms from the Commissary of Kent County, upon the order of the Governor of the State, that, by the laws of our State, I would be required in certain events to return them to the officer from whom I had obtained them; and that, if I were unable to do so, I might be held liable in double the value thereof. He then said that he had authority to discharge me from all liability or damage which I might sustain by reason of delivering them to him. I answered him that it might be true that he might have the authority to *indemnify* me for any loss or damage which I might sustain by reason of my complying with his request, but that it could not be possible that he had the power to *discharge* me from any *liability* which I might owe to the State Government. Something was then said by him about our both being lawyers, and that it was unnecessary to discuss the question; that he should hold me a hostage for the delivery of the arms in possession of the company, and ordered me under arrest, putting me in charge of Captain Keene and a squad of soldiers, who accompanied me to my dwelling, and from thence to the Court Room, where I was kept for about half an hour, and then moved to the Senate Chamber, where I remained about one hour under guard. At the expiration of that time, I was taken to my own office, in the southwest corner of the State House, and kept under guard the balance of the night. Shortly after being taken to my own office, Mr. James W. Wise, who was a member of my company, was brought into my office under guard, and kept confined with me the remainder of the night. Some time during the same night, Mr. John K. Jarvis, who was not, nor had he ever been, a member of the volunteer company which I had commanded, was arrested and confined in the Senate Chamber; of this fact I knew nothing until the next morning; at which time Mr. Wise and myself were taken from my office to the Senate Chamber, where we met with Mr. Jarvis, and where we were all three detained in custody. During that day, the 8th of March, Mr. William J. Clarke, the Commissary of the County, as I was informed, was placed under arrest, and detained for some time. Edward Ridgely, Esq., Secretary of State, came up into the Senate Chamber, by permission, to see me, and after having spent some time in conversation with myself and those who were in the room, started to go out, when he was informed by the guard at the door that he had no authority to pass him out, and he, too, was detained in custody for some two hours and until a permit could be obtained from Colonel Wallace for him to leave the room. Mr. William A. Atkinson, whom I have spoken of in my former testimony as the First Lieutenant of the company, was arrested about noon, and kept under guard in the Court Room for some time, and then brought to the Senate Chamber and there detained with the others. During the same day, Mr. Outen L. Hill, Mr. John O. Slay, John L. Pratt, Charles H. McWhorter, and Mr. Martin B. Hillyard, members of the same company, were likewise arrested, and confined in the same room, and also a Mr. George Gillespie, whom I did not know, and had never seen, that I am aware of, until that day. All of the persons of whom I have spoken as having been arrested were released during the afternoon and evening of the day of the 8th of March, except Mr. John L. Pratt, Mr. Charles H. McWhorter, Mr. George Gillespie, Lieutenant Atkinson, and myself, who were detained and taken from Dover by Colonel Wallace and the soldiers, accompanying him to Smyrna. During Colonel Wallace's stay in Dover, he made his headquarters in the office of Mr. Charles H. B. Day, who was at that time law-partner of Mr. George P. Fisher, and occupied the same office with him. Upon our arrival at the Smyrna depot, we were taken into Smyrna and kept there until after breakfast on Sunday morning, the 9th of March, when we were taken out to the Smyrna depot and kept confined in the ticket office, from which place, on that night, we were taken in a freight car to Salisbury, in the State of Maryland. Arriving in Salisbury about midnight, we were marched over to the encampment near that town, and placed in a room about eight by fourteen feet, without any window, without beds, blankets, or anything to sleep on, save the bare boards, and such things as we had taken with us. The rations, which were served out to us whilst there, were those of the common soldiers, and even they, in my opinion, inferior in quality to the kind contracted and paid for by the General Government. My reasons for saying this arise from the statements of all the privates with whom I conversed, that they were very inferior to those they had previous to that time received. On Monday morning, after breakfast, I obtained an interview with Colonel Wallace, and stated to him that whilst we were kept confined in that encampment, with his permission we would have our meals sent to us, and that we would pay for them; to which he replied that he could not grant any such permission, and that we would have to put up with soldier's fare. On the afternoon of Monday, Colonel Wallace, with three companies, left the encampment and proceeded up the Railroad, as I have been informed and believe, to Dover, for the purpose of procuring the remainder of the arms in possession of the members of my company. I should have stated in a former part of my testimony, that upon the visit on which the arrests of which I have spoken were made, he (Colonel Wallace) sent squads of soldiers around the town, escorted by one David Clayton, a citizen of our town, and others, who pointed out to the soldiers the houses in which lived the members of my company, which were searched by the soldiers and officers in command indiscriminately, having neither respect for the persons who occupied the houses nor principles which should characterize the position of a soldier. After Colonel Wallace left the encampment, as I have just said, we were, by order of the acting Lieutenant-Colonel, taken from the room in which we were first placed and put into another, which, whilst it afforded no accommodations, was somewhat less uncomfortable than the one from which we were removed. On Saturday, the 15th of March, Captain Graham, acting Lieutenant Colonel, came to our room and informed me that he had just received a despatch from Colonel Wallace, instructing him to release Lieutenant Atkinson and myself, which was done.—This was about five o'clock on Saturday evening. On Monday afternoon following, after Lieutenant Atkinson and myself had purchased our tickets to come home, and had put on board the train what baggage we had with us, Captain Graham, who was at the depot, received another despatch from Colonel Wallace, directing him to re-arrest Lieutenant Atkinson, which he did, and Mr. Atkinson returned to the encampment with him. I came on home. Lieutenant Atkinson, Mr. Pratt, and Mr. Gillespie were detained for some time afterwards, but I am not able to state the precise time. My impression is that Mr. Pratt and Mr. Gillespie were released about the 20th of March, unconditionally, without any charge being brought against them, and without knowing for what they were arrested. That Lieutenant Atkinson was released about the 25th or 26th of March, on giving what was termed his parole, to report himself when called for, but without any charge being made against him, or, if any, any intimation of its nature and character. Mr. McWhorter was released a few days subsequently to Lieutenant Atkinson, upon giving a similar parole, and also without any charge being made against him, or, if any, any intimation of the nature and character of it. My own release, as was also the first release of Lieutenant Atkinson, was unconditional, without any requirements, stipulations, or anything of the kind. It may not be improper here to say, that while held as a prisoner at Salisbury, and while Colonel Wallace was in Dover, on his second visit, it was stated to all of us then in custody, by the officer in command of the encampment, and some of the subordinate officers, that we ought not to think hard of them, that they were only performing their duty under the orders which they had received; and if we blamed any person at all, it should be some of our own citizens, who were continually writing letters, representing our company as being disloyal, and as having what was termed a Secession flag, which we marched and paraded under; that the interests and welfare of the General Government required that we should be disarmed and taken care of. I replied to the person communicating such information to me, that all such statements were false, and known to be so by the persons who made them at the time, and gave authority to Captain Graham to telegraph to Colonel Wallace, then, as I believed, in Dover, requesting him (Colonel Wallace) to call upon Mr. John W. Smith, ensign or standard-bearer of our company, in order that he might see the only flag which had ever belonged to the company, or under which it ever marched or paraded.

JOHN B. PENINGTON.

On motion,
The Committee adjourned to meet at the call of the Chairman.
    ATTEST,   J. O. SLAY,
                                          Clerk of the Committee.

CERTIFICATE

I hereby certify that by the authority contained in the following joint resolution of the General Assembly of the State of Delaware, adopted February 19, 1863, viz.: "Resolved, By the Senate and House of Representatives of the State of Delaware in General Assembly met, that the Joint Committee of the two Houses on so much of the Governor's Message as refers to military interference with the election on the 4th of November last be authorized to have printed for the use of the two Houses 3000 copies of their Journal and Report, under the supervision of their Clerk, John O. Slay, Esq.," I appointed James Kirk to print the foregoing Journal and Report of the Committee; that the printed copy has been carefully compared with the original manuscript, and that it contains all the testimony taken before the Committee, except a few sentences of the testimony of John L. Bacon, the sheet containing which mysteriously disappeared from my papers.

J. O. SLAY,
Clerk of the Committee.

Index to Testimony

Name	Page
Aaron, Caleb	342
Allen, Major W.	12
Bacon, John S.	147
Bacon, John L.	161
Bayman, James M.	122
Betts, Wm. H.	186
Bird, James C.	408
Boyce, James H. of S.	154
Bradford, Thomas B.	347
Brown, Charles	308
Brown, John	290
Brown, John A.	355
Burton, William	5
Calhoun, Peter	135
Calley, Andrew J.	339
Cannon, William	72
Carsons, John C.	303
Carlisle, Paris T.	322
Carrow, Jonathan	324
Clements, Jas. R.	267
Clements, John F.	328
Clifton, Jas. A.	255
Comegys, Jos. P.	271
Connoway, Jesse P.	230, 239
Connoway, Minos	233, 241
Connoway, Noble	231
Coulbourn, John L.	6, 30
Coulter, Wm. V.	125
Coverdale, Nunus H.	320
Dale, John	44
Davis, George	405
Denning, John M.	270
Derrickson, Aquila	426
Donoho, Benjamin	415
Dorsey, Wm. N. W.	381
Eliason, Wm. C.	258
Ellegood, William	85
Ewell, Daniel F.	261
Fiddeman, Henry B.	391, 397
Fisher, Saml. C.	238
Flowers, Henry	286
Fowler, Wm. D.	388
Giles, Isaac	211, 226
Gilpin, Vincent C.	349
Godwin, Daniel C.	274
Green, Stephen	150
Harmon, Geo. G.	334
Harrington, David	293
Hart, C. C.	168
Hawkins, Thomas F.	37
Hazzard, James S.	278
Hazzard, John C.	114
Hazzard, Rhodes	21
Hearn, Louder N.	181, 197
Heverin, James L.	319
Hill, Jacob M.	247
Hill, Robert	411
Hill, William	386
Houston, Shepard P.	136
Jacobs, Curtis W.	250
Jacobs, Thomas	31
James, John W.	203, 210
Jester, Wm. M.	227
Johnson, Alexander	371

Name	Page	Name	Page
Johnson, Mark A.	380	Robinson, Alfred P.	94
Jones, Wm. F.	89	Rodney, John D.	68
Kay, George T.	9, 30	Ross, William H.	111
Lacey, Robert L.	123	Rust, Catesby F.	33
Lacey, Samuel W.	205	Saulsbury, Eli	280
Lambden, Robt.	170, 178, 193	Scott, James	179
Layton, Garrett S.	21	Scotten, Philemon	306
Layton, Daniel J.	105	Scribner, William A.	221
Lofland, David	132	Shipley, Joseph P. H.	47, 88
Lofland, Mark G.	393	Smith, John W.	374
Long, Henry W.	199, 209	Sorden, John	55
Lord, Edward	337	Springer, James	429
Lyons, Laban L.	138	Steele, Milton	422, 429
Mahle, William	291	Stockly, Ayres	265
Martin, John E.	26	Stokley, John	133
Martin, Peter	60	Stuart, James	17
Martin, Edward L.	412	Taylor, Wm. H.	361
Marvel, Josiah P.	235	Taylor, John	416
Marvel, Aaron B.	242	Tharp, William	399
Marvel, Joseph	245	Turner, Lazarus	313
Marvel, Thomas J.	299	Walker, John W.	277
McFerran, Jos. A.	143	Warrington, Stephen H.	157
Merriken, R. N.	377	Watson, Jas. M.	359
Moore, Edward W.	159	Wharton, Benj.	119
Pennewill, John C.	409	White, George W.	218
Penington, J. B.	287, 417, 431	Whitaker, Henry	345
Pepper, Thomas	65	Williamson, Charles	402
Ponder, James	128	Wingate, John B.	58
Register, Elijah B.	326	Wootten, Edward	99, 103, 110
Ricords, William D.	173, 177	Wootten, George M.	166
Riddle, George R.	357	Wright, Charles	22, 29
Ridgely, Henry M.	222	Wright, Andrew J.	343

www.ingramcontent.com/pod-product-compliance
Lightning Source LLC
Chambersburg PA
CBHW040422100526
44589CB00022B/2800